Śrāddha-Sāgara

of

Kullūkabhaṭṭa

Śrāddha-Sāgara
of
Kullūkabhaṭṭa

With a Critical Exposition and Introduction

by

Prof. S.G. Moghe

D.K. Printworld (P) Ltd.
NEW DELHI-110015

Cataloging in Publishing Data -- DK

Kullūka Bhaṭṭa.
Śrāddha-sāgara of Kullūkabhaṭṭa.
Includes bibliographical references (p.).
Includes indexes.

1. Śrāddha (Hindu rite). 2. Hinduism -- Rituals.
I. Moghe, S. G. II. Title.

ISBN 81-246-0016-3

First Published in India in 1994

Published in India by :
D.K. Printworld (P) Ltd.
Regd. Office : H-12, Bali Nagar
NEW DELHI - 110015
Phone : (011) 546-6019 *Fax* : (011) 546-5927

Typeset at : Easy Computer Systems, New **Delhi-15, Phone : 5461078**

Printed at : D.K. Fine Art Press (P) Ltd, Delhi - 110052

Dedicated

to
the beloved memory
of
My Mother
Mrs. Manoramabai Ganesh Moghe

Preface

IT gives me great pleasure in presenting a critical edition of the *Śrāddha-Sāgara* of Kullūkabhaṭṭa to the world of scholarship.

The *Śrāddha-Sāgara* is a rare manuscript on the *Śrāddha* aspect of *Dharma-Śāstra* particularly written by Kullūkabhṭṭa, the illustrious commentator of the *Manusmṛti*. So far this manuscript is not published by any research scholar or any research Institute in India and abroad.

The present author has edited this rare manuscript with the help of the vast material available in the *Dharma-Śāstra* literature, in the forms of the *Smṛtis, Sūtra* works, commentaries on them and also the digest works.

The importance of this manuscript lies in the fact that it is a matured product of a deep-rooted scholar in the *Dharma-Śāstra.* The date of Kullūkabhaṭṭa is shrouded in mystery. The study of this manuscript has helped the present author to fix the date of Kullūkabhaṭṭa as 1520 A.D. to 1620 A.D. By this new research, the date of Kullūkabhaṭṭa fixed by MM. Dr. P.V. Kane, as 1150 to 1300 A.D. is brought home with more cogent arguments and reliable evidences.

In the Introduction to this work, the present author has discussed the problems such as 'Relation of *Śrāddha-Sāgara* to Lakṣmīdhara's *Kṛtyakalpataru-Śrāddha-Kāṇḍa*, Kullūka and other writers of Bengal, Kullūka and other writers on *Śrāddha* aspect of *Dharma-Śāstra,* and the place of the *Śrāddha-Sāgara* in the *Dharma-Śāstra* — the problems which are generally and prominently not discussed by other scholars of *Dhrma-Śāstra.*

The importance of this rare manuscript is really supreme from the point of view of interpretation otherwise known as *Pūrva-Mīmāṁsā*. The present author is constrained to remark only casually that in the employment of the *Mīmāṁsā* doctrines to the *Śrāddha* aspect of *Dharma-Śāstra*, Kullūka appears to have surpassed all his predecessors and even successors. Hence, for the *Mīmāṁsā* interpretation, the present author is tempted to bring out another study, which will be published in due course of time.

I take this opportunity to express my heart-felt thanks to my publishers Messers D.K. Printworld (P) Ltd., for agreeing to publish this brilliant study, with personal zeal and accurate printing and most enviable get-up.

Govt. Arts & Science College
Aurangabad-431001 (Maha.)
23-5-1994

S.G. Moghe

Contents

Part II
Critically edited text of Ś ddha-Sāgara

Appendices

Abbreviations

बौधायन	बौधायनस्मृति
भविष्य	भविष्यपुराण
बृहस्पति	बृहस्पतिस्मृति
दक्ष	बौधायनस्मृति
देवल	देवलस्मृति
गोविन्दाराज	Commntator of मनुस्मृति
गौतम	गौतम धर्मसूत्र
हारीत	हारीतस्मृति
H.D. or *H.D.S.*	*History of Dharma-Śāstra*
जाबालि	जाबालिस्मृति
जातुकर्ण्य	जातुकर्ण्यस्मृति
कार्ष्णाजीनि	कार्ष्णाजीनिस्मृति
KK-SK	कृत्यकल्पतरु-श्राद्धकाण्ड
लघुहारीत	लघुहारीतस्मृति
मनु	मनुस्मृति
मरीचि	मरीचिस्मृति
पराशरमाधव	Glossary of माधवाचार्य on पराशरस्मृति
पारस्कर	पारस्कर-गृह्यसूत्र

पैठीनसि	पैठीनसि-स्मृति
राघवानन्द	Commentator of मनुस्मृति
ऋष्यशृंग	ऋष्यशृंगस्मृति
सत्यव्रत	सत्यव्रतस्मृति
सुमन्तु	सुमन्तु-स्मृति
शातातप	शातातप-स्मृति
शंख	शंखस्मृति
SS	*श्राद्धसागर*
वसिष्ठ or वाशिष्ठ	वसिष्ठ-धर्मसूत्र
वायु	वायुपुराण
विष्णु	विष्णुस्मृति/विष्णुधर्मसूत्र
विष्णुधर्मोत्तर	विष्णुधर्मोत्तर पुराण
यम	यमस्मृति
याज्ञवल्क्य	याज्ञवल्क्यस्मृति

1

Śrāddha — An Introduction

Derivation and Meaning of *Śrāddha*

ŚRĀDDHA, or the funeral ceremony of the dead, is derived from the word *śraddhā*. In the definition given in the *Brahma Purāṇa* and that given by Marīci and Bṛhaspati emphasise the connection of *śrāddha* with *śraddhā*. In *śrāddha* one entertains the firm faith or conviction that what is given up to the *brāhmaṇas* for the benifit of the departed man or the fathers will reach him or them in some way. The *Skanda-purāṇa*, VI. 218.3 says that *śrāddha* is so-called because *śraddhā* is at the root of that rite. This means there is not only the conviction but these is also a firm belief that a person is under an obligation to offer it. *Śraddhā* is deified and addressed as a deity in *Ṛg*.[1]

Śrāddha, is an obsequial or funeral sacrifice, but it also implies offerings to the progenitors of an individual and of mankind, and always forms part of a religious ceremony on an occasion of rejoicing or an occasion of prosperity.

The *Brahma Purāṇa* defines *śrāddha* as follows: 'Whatever is given with faith to *brāhmaṇas* intending it to be for the benefit of *pitṛs* at a proper time, in a proper place, to deserving persons and in accordance with the prescribed procedure is called *śrāddha*'. The *Mitākṣarā* on *Yājñavalkyasmṛti,* I.217. defines *śrāddha* as 'abandonment with faith of an article of food or some substitute thereof, intending it for the departed'. The *Kalpataru* on *Śrāddha* defined it as 'the giving up of sacrificial material intending it for *pitṛs* and its acceptance by

1. श्रद्धयाग्निः समिध्यते श्रद्धया हूयते हविः । श्रद्धां भगस्य मूर्धनि वचसो वेदयामसि ॥ ऋ. X.151.1.

brāhmaṇaś. *Yājñavalkyasmṛti*, I.268 (=*Agni Purāṇa*, 163.440-41) states that the *piṭrs* viz. Vasus, Rudras and Ādityas that are the deities of *śrāddha,* being gratified by *śrāddha,* give gratification to the ancestors of human beings. This verse and *Manusmṛti,* III.284 make it clear that the three ancestors of a man, viz. the father, paternal grand-father and the paternal great grand-father are respectively to be identified with the three orders of superintending *pitṛ* deities when performing *śrāddha*. According to some,[1] *śrāddha* denotes three things, viz. *homa,* the offering of *piṇda* (ball of cooked food) and gratification of *brāhmaṇas* invited to a dinner, the application to this word to anyone of these three can only be in a secondary sense.

The Institution of *Śrāddha*

It appears very probable that the worship of ancestors by means of *śrāddha* was a very ancient institution and that the doctrines of *punarjanma* and *karmavipāka* were comparatively later ones and that Hinduism being all-embracing retained the institution of *śrāddhas* while adopting also the doctrine of metempsychosis. The institution of *śrāddha* is from one point of view an excellent one. It provides an occasion for remembrance of one's ancestors and relatives that were dear and near when living. The Āryasamāja objects to the institution of *śrāddha* and interprets *pitṛs* in the *Ṛgveda* as meaning living men in the *Vānaprastha* stage. It may be noted that the texts, support both the views. The *Śatapatha Brāhmaṇa* says that the food is offered to the father of the sacrificer in the words 'this is for thee'. *Viṣṇudharmasūtra,* 75.4. 'He whose father is dead may put down a *piṇḍa* for his father &c.' On the other hand *Manusmṛti*, III.284 states that fathers are spoken of as Vasus, grand-fathers as Rudras &c. and *Yājñavalkyasmṛti*, I. 269 provides that Vasus, Rudras and Ādityas are the *pitṛs* and the *devatāṣ* of *śrāddha.* These latter are to be explained as containing an injunction to contemplate upon the *pitṛs* as Vasus, Rudras, &c. It was on account of the supposed power of *pitṛs* to benefit or harm the living that the cult of the dead became a prominent father in primitive societies. Offerings and ceremonies which may have in

---

1. होमश्च पिण्डदानं च तथा ब्राह्मणतर्पगम् । श्राद्धशब्दाभिषेयं स्यादेकस्मिन्नौपचारिकः ॥ q. by श्राद्धसागर, p. 30. हरदत्त on आप. ध. सू., II.7.16.2 says the same thing. श्रीदत्त in पितृभक्ति (folio. 23a) says 'पिण्डदानं तु न श्राद्धं किं तु श्राद्धाङ्ग पिण्डत्रिरहेपि नित्यश्राद्धदर्शनात् ।'

most ancient times been prompted in part at least by the desire to placate the ancestors are continued as tokens of pure affection and remembrance. Various beliefs about *pitṛs* are mentioned in post-*Vedic* literature. The word *pitṛ* means 'father', but the word *pitaraḥ*, is used in two senses viz. (1) a man's three immediate deceased ancestors, (2) the early or ancient ancestors of the human race that were supposed to inhabit a separate world (*loka*) by themselves. It was supposed that the departed spirit, after the cremation of the body, was endowed with an ethereal body and became associated with Yama, the gatherer of departed men (*Ṛg*., X.14.1 and 8, X.15.14, X 16.5) and with *pitṛs.* The departed spirit went to the world of the *pitṛs* and Agni was implored to take the spirit of the world of the departed whose deeds were good and to the stride of Viṣṇu (*Ṛg*., X.14.9, X.15.3, X.16.4).

Classification of *Śrāddhas*

Śrāddhas are divided into three classes, *nitya*, *naimittika,* and *kāmya.* An observance is called *nitya* when it is laid down that it must be performed on a certain or fixed occasion (such as everyday, on an *amāvāsya,* or on *aṣṭakā* day). What is laid down for being done on an occasion which is uncertain is called *naimittika* (such as the birth of a son). What is ordained to be done in case one desires a certain reward or fruit is called *kāmya* (e.g. the performance of a *śrāddha* on Krttikā or Rohiṇi by one who desires heaven or progeny.

Some of the other types of *śrāddha* are: the *vṛddhi,* performed on occasions of rejoicing or prosperity; the *Sapiṇḍana,* offerings to all individual and to general ancestors; the *pārvaṇa śrāddha*. Offerings to the manes, on certain lunar days called *pārvaṇa;* the *goṣthī*, for the advantage of a number of learned persons, or of an assembly of *brāhmaṇas* invited for the purpose; the *śuddhi*, one performed to purify a person from some defilement; the *karmānga,* one forming part of the initiatory ceremonies, or *saṁskāras* observed at conception, bath, tonsure; the *daivia*, to which the gods are invited; the *yātrā śrāddha*, held by a person going a journey; and the *puṣṭi śrāddha*, one performed to promote health and wealth.

The *śrāddha*, or feast of the dead, in its earliest form was a pleasing expression of natural religion, which long preceded the advent of a priestly caste, or the introduction of a systematic ritual. But, like every other popular ceremonial which has been handed down amongst the Hindus from the *Vedic* period, it has been recast in a Brahmanical mould; and it is in this latter form that the institution appears in the epics as well as in the laws of Manu. It consists of three distinct rites:

(1) The daily *śrāddha,* to be performed in propitiation of the *piṭrs.*

(2) The monthly *śrāddha,* to be performed in propititation of the more immediate paternal ancestors. The ceremonies at the monthly *śrāddha* as described in the institutes of Manu are of a very intelligible character; and seem to have been laid down for the purpose of converting the old *Vedic* offering of food and water into a great feast to the *Brāhmaṇas*. Manu has given detailed lists of those who should be entertained, who should be excluded from the ceremony and the relative merits of the different kinds of rituals which may be offered at a monthly *śraddha.*

(3) The funeral *śrāddha*, to be performed within a certain period after death, or the hearing of the death of a near kinsman.

Śrāddhas are likwise performed on other occasions also and notably at the celebration of any marriage ceremony.

The *Dharmaśāstra* writers have given various views about the place of performing the *śrāddha*, countries not fit for *śrāddha,* the time for performing it, who should be and who should not be invited, number of invitees, materials to be employed, vessels to be used, rules for the performer, the *mantras*, rules for serving food and every detail of the ceremony. For example, the monthly *śrāddha* was performed on the dark day of the moon when the sun and moon are in conjunction. A sequestered spot was selected, (such as pleasing) and then the invited *brāhmaṇas* were conducted to their alloted seals, which had been purified with *kuśa* grass, and were presented with garlands of flowers and sweet perfumes. The officiating *brāhmaṇas* then satisfied the three *Vedic* deities — Agni, Soma and Yama — by pouring an oblation of *ghee* upon the sacred fire. He then proceeded to satisfy the ancestors of the giver of the *śrāddha.* He first sprinkled water on the ground with his right hand and then formed three balls or cakes of boiled riçe, which are called *piṇḍas.* One of these cakes is presented to each of the three immediate paternal ancestors. The offering of the *piṇḍas*, however, is said to be extended to the fourth, fifth and sixth degrees of paternal ancestors in the ascending line, by the simple process of wiping the hand with *kuśa* grass after offering the *piṇḍas* to the ancestors of the first, second and third degree. This ceremony was followed by a great feast to the *brāhmaṇas*, consisting of vessels filled with rice, together with broths, pot-herbs, milk, curd, *ghee*, spiced puddings, milky messes of various sorts, roots of herbs, ripe fruits and savoury meats; and during the feast, passages were read from the *śāstras*. The remains of the cakes were to be eaten by a cow, a *brāhmaṇa* or a kid; or to be cast into water or fire, but the wife of the householder was to eat the middle of the three cakes, in order that she might become the mother of a son. When the *brāhmaṇas* had duly feasted the householder gave a feast to the kinsmen of his father, and afterwards to the kinsmen of his mother. In cases of poverty, however, the offering of water seems to be considered a sufficient satisfaction of the spirits of the six paternal ancestors. As regards the persons to be invited to the monthly *śrāddha*, great stress is laid by the code upon the entertainment of learned *brāhmaṇas*, and the exclusion of ignorant ones. Manu's catalogue of the persons who were to be excluded from a monthly *śrāddha* is of a very detailed character and may be re-distributed under four general heads, according to the four different grounds upon which the individuals specified have been respectively excluded, namely, moral, religious, physical and professional.

Modern Men and *Śrāddha*

The most ancient literary monument, viz. the *Ṛgveda*, shows that the funeral rites performed immediately after death were prompted by affectionate concern for the departed spirit mingled with some element of fear, that the object of those rites was to provide sustenance to the departed spirit and to endow it with an intermediate body before it became one of the *pitṛs*. Also it has been found that in most ancient times of which we have literary evidence that there were rites for the worship of ancestors, being the *piṇḍapitṛyajña* performed every month on *amāvāsyā*, the *mahāpitṛyajña* performed in the *śākamedha* and the *aṣṭakā śrāddhas*. Gradually the rites for deceased ancestors became more and more frequent, all-inclusive and elaborate, so that ultimately an exaggerated importance came to be attached to the cult of *śrāddhas* over which there was an enormous expenditure time, effort and wealth. In the twentieth century in India when many *brāhmaṇas* even do not engage in any of the five daily obligatory *yajñas* (the *pañca-yajñas*, they are solicitous to offer *śrāddha* at least once a year to their ancestors. Those who have faith in the duty of performing *śrāddha* and their efficacy for the benefit of the dead may perform them on a small scale, bearing in mind the emphatic admonition of Manu (III.125-26), the *Kūrma Purāṇa*, II.22.27, *Padma Purāṇa*, V.9.98[1] that one should desist from extravagance in the matter, of *śrāddhas*, particularly in the number of *brāhmaṇas* to be invited. The main underlying conception; of *śrāddha* is cartainly admirable; viz. a tender and affectionate regard for one's near and dear ralatives. It is a good practice to set apart at least one day in a year for the remembrance of one's near and dear relatives who are no more, to invite freinds, relatives and learned people to a dinner in memory of the dead and to bestow monetary gifts on poor but learned persons of character and devoted to the practice of plain living and high thinking. This keeps up with the past traditions and gives a new orientation to and infuse new life into practices and usage that are becoming lifeless and meaningless to many these days. From very ancient times one of the fundamental conceptions of faith has been the idea of three debts owed to sages, gods and *pitṛs*. The debt owed to the ancestors is paid off by the procreation of a son who would offer *piṇḍas* to his and therefore also to his father's ancestors. This is an unique conception. Nothing can be more sublime than the formula which one has to repeat at the time of offering *piṇḍas* and water (with sesame) at Gayā 'may those of my ancestors that are in the form of *pretas* be all satiated by means of the (balls made) of barley flour mixed with sesame and may everything, whether moving or immovable from Brahmā up to blades of grass derive satisfaction from the water offered by me.' If the implication of this formula be thoroughly understood and implemented by actual practice, it will make the whole world kin.

---

1. द्वौ दैवे पितृकृत्ये त्रीनेकैकमुभयत्र वा । भोजयेदीश्वरोपीह न कुर्याद्विस्तरं बुधः । पद्म, V.9.98. जायमानो ह वै ब्राह्मणस्त्रिभिर्ऋणवा जायते ब्रह्मचर्येण ऋषिभ्यो यज्ञेन देवेभ्यः प्रजया पितृभ्य एष वा अनृणो यः पुत्री यज्वा ब्रह्मचारिवासी । तै. सं., VI. 3.10.5; ऋणमस्मिन् संनयत्यमृतत्वं च गच्छति । पिता पुत्रस्य जातस्य पश्येच्चेज्जीवतो मुखम् ॥ ऐ. ब्रा., 33.1. This subject has been also dealt in *History of Dharma-Śāstras*, Vol. III., pp. 414-16 and may be further dilated upon under Gayāśrāddha of Vol. IV. ये केचित्प्रेतरूपेण वर्तन्ते पितरो मम । ते सर्वे तृप्तिमायान्तु सक्तुभिस्तिलमिश्रितैः ॥ आब्रह्मस्तम्बपर्यन्तं यत्किंचित्सचराचरम् । मया दत्तेन तोयेन तृप्तिमायान्तु सर्वशः ॥ वायुपुराण, 110.63-64. Compare also a similar invocation in वायु., 110. 21-22 and the *Mettasutta* in the Suttanipāta.

2

The Present Edition of *Śrāddha-Sāgara*

THE present critical edition of the *Śrāddha-Sāgara* of Kullūkabhaṭṭa is based on the only one manuscript of this work that exists in the Calcutta Sanskrit College, (Cat. Vol. II, p. 405, No. 446) as pointed out by MM. Dr. P.V. Kane in his *History of Dharma-Śāstra*, Vol. I, Part II, p. 758.

Through the kindness of the Principal, Sanskrit College, Calcutta, I first secured a microfilm of the said manuscript. Later on I also procured the Devanāgarī transcript of the said manuscript entitled: *Śrāddha-Sāgara* of Kullūkabhaṭṭa.

It must be emphasised in this very context that the University Grants Commission, New Delhi sanctioned financial assistance for this project.

In his *Śrāddha-Sāgara* Kullūka has profusely quoted several *smṛti* works, digest works, *paurāṇic* texts, astronomical works and even grammatical authorities. In the foot-notes, the important variations from the printed editions of these works have been pointed out by me.

I have tried to trace out all the quotations in the present work entitled *Śrāddha-Sagara* of Kullūkabhaṭṭa to their original sources. As far as possible, I have made the best use of the critical editions of the authorities cited by Kullūkabhaṭṭa. When, however, such standard critical editions of the works are not available, I have utilised standard editions of the texts relied upon by Kullūkabhaṭṭa in his work.

In spite of the great labour put in by me, there are some places which have completely defied all attempts to identify the quotations.

Such places are clearly noted in the foot-notes.

An attempt is also made to point out the places where Kullūka's readings are corrupt, deficient and grammatically wrong. In the foot-notes, I have recorded the variant readings of the quoted passages available elsewhere and passed incidental observations. I have not discussed at any length the different readings noted in the foot-notes.

The special feature of the introduction is that in the foot-notes, I have shown the places whether the particular passages cited are available in the editions critically brought out or not and also the works to which the particular passages are ascribed.

Another noteworthy feature of this work is that I have improved the present work by referring in season and out of season to all the works on the *Śrāddha* so far published by the different research institutes and other agencies. To enhance the value of this work, I have also consulted the Ph.D. thesis of Miss. J.H. Shroff on the *Śrāddha Prakāśa of Mitramiśra* which is available only in the library of the University of Bombay.

In order to enhance the utility of this work, several appendices have been added. Appendix 'A' gives the index of the *smṛti* works quoted by Kullūkabhaṭṭa in this work. Appendix 'B' brings together the *Purāṇas* quoted by the author of this work. Appendix 'C' enlists the commentators and digest works cited in this work. Appendix 'D' makes the list of the *Śruti* passages and *sūtra* works quoted in this work. Appendix 'E' sums up the astronomical and astrological works referred to in the work entitled *Śrāddha-Sāgara.* Appendix 'F', however, gives the list of the authorities quoted in the foot-notes to identify the citations given by Kullūkabhaṭṭa. Appendix 'G' gives the places where the *Pūrva-Mīmāṁsā* doctrines are relied upon by Kullūkabhaṭṭa in the course of his discussion.

3

Nature of the Manuscript

THIS manuscript is in Bengali script. Through the kindness of the Principal, Sanskrit College, Calcutta, I could get the Devanagari transcript of the said manuscript.

The transcript of the manuscript shows that it is written in a legible way, without at the same time indicating the full stop after a sentence. At times, we come across brackets, which if removed, convey a very good sense. If, however, the brackets are retained, then the passage becomes unintelligible. I have clearly indicated the places where the brackets are introduced and also remarked in the foot-notes where possible, that if the bracket is removed, the sentence would yield a good sense.

At some places, however, the manuscript is highly corrupt and it defies all attempts to identify the passage or to emend the same in the light of the works available to us.

The manuscript, at some places, records some new readings which are not at all available in the printed critical editions of the works that are available to us. At times, these readings help us a lot to improve the sense of the passage.

It is observed, at other places, that some words in the manuscript are missing or additional or indicative of the after-thought either of the author or of the scribe.

I have attempted to classify the causes of corruption in a manuscript in the light of Chapter V of *Introduction to Indian Textual Criticism* brought out by Dr. S.M. Katre.

It may be mentioned here that in the examples given below the first figure refers to the page number and the latter figure refers to the number of the foot-notes on the particular pages.

Confusion of Proper Names

This is possible on account of the ignorance of the scribe. We get the example of this sort as *karyoṭhabhaṭṭaḥ* 3.5. This should be read as *Kayaṭabhaṭṭaḥ* in view of several references to this name in the said manuscript on pages 160, 222 and 282. Another example of this kind of *Kamaṇḍanabhaṭṭaḥ* on page 163. According to MM. Dr. P.V. Kane, this may be read as *Kamaṇḍalubhaṭṭaḥ* (Vide *History of Dharma-Śāstra* Vol. I, Part II, p. 1165). One may make a reference to the name *Lollabhaṭṭa* on page 163. Dr. Kane suggests that this should be read as *Lollaṭabhaṭṭaḥ*.

Corrupt

At some places, the mauscript is hopelessly corrupt and it defies all our attempts either to identify the passage from some other works or to substitute a better reading for such passages. One could refer to several such cases as 4.1, 4.4, 6.1, 11.1-2, 12.5, 44.1, etc. As all such places are clearly noted in the foot-notes, I avoid making any further references to this aspect.

Duplication

It is surprising that in this manuscript chapter XXXII is found copied twice. It must be emphasised here that whatever portion was common from the point of view of repetition is treated as one chapter and whatever portion is uncommon is naturally treated as two separate sections. Hence for chapter XXXII, there are two separate sections A and B in addition to the regular chapter XXXII which deals with the *Ekoddiṣṭa Śrāddha*. (ii) In addition to this, at some places, however, we have the unnecessary repetition of some words in a reverse manner. e.g. 74.6.

Redundant

The manuscript betrays, at some places, that some words are redundant. e.g. 94.3; 231.2 etc.

Two Readings at Two Different Places

At times, it is evident that manuscript presents two different readings of one and the same word at two different places. This point can be best clarified by inviting the attention of the readers to the chapter VII dealing with *Maghātrayodaśī-Śrāddha*. Here in the stanza No. 32, we have the reading *tathā* on page 53.3. While in the stanza No. 49 of the same chapter VII, we have the reading *tadā*. This point can be further clarified by referring to other examples of this sort. e.g. 48.2.; 183.3; 216.2 and 6 and 216.6 and 217.1.

Misleading Readings

At some places, however, we get the misleading readings in the manuscript. To clarify this point, one could refer to the case of *ojanam* 6.2. In the bracket, however, we get the reading *yajanam*. The context favours the reading in the bracket. In the absence of a bracket, however, the reading is certaily misleading.

Introduction of Brackets

The manuscript displays the tendency of introducting brackets at some places. One could refer to the cases of this type. e.g. 4.2. and 5.2. If, however, these brackets are removed, then it helps to get a good meaning of the passage under discussion.

Order of the Sentences

In chapter VIII, we have the discussion on the *Aṣṭakā Śrāddha*. After stanza No.7, however, we have a quotation from the *Viṣṇu-Dharmottara Purāṇa*, I.142.3b. This appears as 68.5. Actually this should have appeared immediately after *ataḥ eva Viṣṇudharmottare*. But it appears that through the ignorance of the scribe possibly, the order of the sentences appears to have undergone a change. (ii) If, however the text presented in this manuscript is compared with the other printed texts that are available to us, one will easily detect that at times, the order of the words also is changed. To substantiate this point, one could refer to chapter VII in which in the stanza No. 36, we have the quotation from the *Bhaviṣya Purāṇa*. If this 2nd line of the stanza No. 36 is compared with the line from the *Parāśara-Mādhava*, Vol. I, p.667, then it is possible to see that the order of the words in our text is changed, though there is no possibility of any change in the meaning of the sentence.

Omission of the Group of Letters or Words or Lines

To illustrate this point, one could refer to the case available on 10.8. Here instead of *darvi* we have the reading *davi*, which clearly shows the omission of one रेफ्.We also get another example of this type in the reading *dhrute* which appears in place of *ṛte* which is found recorded in the *Kṛtyakalpataru-Śrāddhakāṇḍa*, p.5. Also see 61.6 and 14.3 for the examples of this sort.

Wrong Junctions or Division of Words

This kind of arrangement of the words or letters in words also baffles the careful reader of the manuscript. We have three such examples e.g. 148.3; 187.2; 202.1. In chapter XXI, we have in the stanza No. 8 the example of *ekoddiṣṭe na tarpayet.* If, however, this is compared with the text of *Jābāla* quoted in the *Pṛthīcandra*'s *Śrāddha-Prakāśa,* XVIII.17 p. 432 we find that the two words *ekoddiṣṭe* and *na* are joined together. This certainly helps us to improve the sense of a sentence.

Omission or Insertion of Seemingly Unimportant Words or Letters

At times, however, in the manuscript, some unnecessary letters appear in a word and this certainly baffles the reader's mind. We have several cases of this type e.g. 6.3; 6.4; 7.7; 119.1; 123.3; 4.4 and 159.1. I may point out only one case here. On page 159, in chapter XXIV, we have the quotation from the *Mādhyandinī Śruti* in which we have the reading *āhuyati* in place of *āhuti.* Also in chapter I, we have the reading *vedameya* instead of *vedyam*. Such places are clearly discernible in the manuscript and are pointed out at proper places.

Interchange of Letters

If, however, the letters in the words are interchanged, one is likely to be confused. In chapter I on page 9, however, we have the reading *anuditiśati* in place of *atidiśati.* But we have another case on 24.13 in which the word *ca* appears before *pūjayet*. But if this is compared with the *Śrāddha Prakāśa of Mitramiśra,* p. 333, then one comes to know that in the *Śrāddha-Prakāśa,* Mitramiśra has put *ca* after *pūjayet.*

Missing Words

If, however, the text preserved in the manuscript *Śrāddha-Sāgara* is compared with the other texts which are printed or edited, then one notices that in our manuscript some words are additional, which are not found elsewhere. To expount this point, one may refer to the case 22.7. In chapter II dealing with *Śrāddha-bheda,* we find that the word *yen* which is found on page 22 is, however, not found in the *Kṛtyakalpataru-Śrāddha-Kāṇḍa,* p. 7. Hence the utility of our manuscript to edit the other works on *Dharma-Śāstra* can hardly be denied. Also see 80.6; 86.2.

New Readings

The special feature of this manuscript preserved for the posterity is that at some places, it records some new readings which are not at all found in the critical editions which are brought out by well-known scholars like Dr. George Bühler. In chapter XVII dealing with the *brāhmins* to be avoided for the *Śrāddha* ceremony, however, our manuscript quotes the text of *Vasiṣṭha-Dharma-Sūtra,* III.12 on page 123. It further records the reading *icchanti* in place of or in addition to *ṛcchanti.* This has escaped the notice of the great scholar Dr. Bühler. Hence the utility of this manuscript for critically editing other texts can hardly be denied.

Quotation Without Location

At several places, in the manuscript, we find some citations without disclosing the exact source from which the same are given. On a careful comparison of the quoted passages, it appears that in other printed editions the passage is either ascribed to some author or to some *Purāṇa* e.g. 205.3. and 224.1 etc. In chapter XXXII, on page 205, there is a quotation in stanza No. 32 without any mention of the work from which the same is quoted. If this quotation, however, is traced in the other texts and particularly in the *Kṛtyakalpataru-Śrāddha-Kāṇḍa,* p. 6 one locates that this stanza is quoted from the *Bhaviṣya Purāṇa.* There are several places of this type which are clearly located in the foot-notes by me and hence one example of the above kind is sufficient to bring out my case.

Emendations on Several Grounds

At some places, it is observed that the readings recorded in the manuscript are corrupt. However, it is possible to emend the same on the strength of the context, occurrence of the same word elsewhere in the said manuscript or on the ground of grammatical authority or on the strength of the textual authority to change the wrong reading.

(i) Emendation on the basis of the context: 10.8; 34.6; 200.8 etc.

(ii) Emendation to avoid metrical irregularity: 166.1.

(iii) Emendation on the basis of textual authority:181.7; 266.3. etc.

(iv) Emendation on the basis of grammar: 76.3 75.6; 193.5 etc.

Ascription of One Quotation to Different Texts or Authors

It is surprising that the manuscript betrays the tendency of ascribing one quotation to one author or work and also ascribing the same quotation to some other work or author. In chapter XXIX dealing with *Śrāddham,* we find that the stanza No. 6 is ascribed to *Laghuhārīta;* while in the same chapter, the same stanza is quoted as stanza No. 36 and is ascribed to *Hārīta*. Also see: 26.9; 75.3. This tendency is also noticed in the *Śrāddha-Tattva* of Raghunandana and is pointed out in the foot-notes. (ii) It is also observed here that when our author Kullūkabhaṭṭa quotes verses 2 and 3 from the *Vāyu-Purāṇa*, 78.21-23, it is observed that Nīlakaṇṭha in his *Śrāddha-Mayūkha*, p. 31 ascribes the stanza No. 3 to the *Brahmāṇḍa-Purāṇa*. This feature is noticed in chapter IV when we find the description of the places where the performance of the *Śrāddha* ceremony is particularly condemned. We also further get the illustrations of this type at several places. Such places are properly pointed out in the foot-notes.

Wrong Readings

The manuscript presents at several places the readings that are wrong.

These readings are said to be wrong either grammatically or contextually or even metrically. I indicate such places below by way of few examples:

(i) Grammatically wrong readings: 27.4.

(ii) Contextually wrong readings: 27.6; 45.5.

(iii) Metrically wrong readings: 192.2

This chapter may be concluded by remarking that the manuscript entitled *Śrāddha-Śāgara*, though hopelessly corrupt at some places, displays the above characteristics and it will not be wrong if it is legitimately held that at times this manuscript will serve our purposes even in editing other texts or even making the proper improvement upon the other critically edited texts.

4

Kullūkabhaṭṭa and his Works

THE introductory verses in the commentary of Kullūka on the *Manu-Smṛti*[1] gives us a little information about himself. He came of a Varendra *Brāhmaṇa* family of Bengal (Gauḍa) residing in Nandana and was the son of Bhaṭṭa Divākara. He wrote his commentary in Kāśī in the company of *Puṇḍits.*

The introductory portion[2] further reveals that Kullūka mastered the branches of learning like *Pūrva-Mīmāṁsā, Vedānta* and *Vyākaraṇa.* The study of the manuscript[3] further reveals that he studied *Nyāya-Śāstra* also.

The very fact that Kullūka refers to some Gauḍa, i.e., Bengal writers in the course of his discussion in the *Śrāddha-Sāgara* reveals that he must have either spent some part of his life in Bengal or has made a close study of the works of the writers from Bengal on *Dharma-Śāstra*. In this respect, one could refer to the mention of Gauḍabhaṭṭa (p. 149). Gauḍa Vācaspati (p. 219) in the manuscript *Śrāddha-Sāgara.* A close study of the manuscript further reveals that Kullūka seems to have read the works of Raghunandana, i.e., *Smṛti-Tattvas* as is evident from the Appendix 'F' which contains the list of the authorities consulted for the preparation of the critical edition of the manuscript *Śrāddha-Sāgara* and the sources to which the passages quoted by Kullūkabhaṭṭa can be traced.

1. गौडे नन्दनवासिनाम्नि सुजनैर्नन्धै वरेन्धां कुले ।
श्रीमद्भट्टार्दवाकरस्य तनयः कुल्लूकभट्टोऽभवन् ॥ *मनुस्मृति,* I. 1.
2. मीमांसे बहु सेवतासि सुहृदस्तर्काः समस्ताः स्थ मे ।
वेदान्ताः परमात्मबोधगुरवो भूयं मयोपासिताः । *Ibid.*, I. 1.
3. References to न्यायशास्त्र terms in श्राद्धसागर — अव्याप्ति, अतिव्याप्ति etc. support this view, p. 76.

MM. Dr. P.V. Kane has already pointed out in his *History of Dharma-Śāstra*, Vol. I, Part II, p. 759 that Raghunandana in his *Smṛti-Tattvas* has quoted Kullūka's commentary on the *Manu-Smṛti* and has shown his disagreement with him at some places. This fact further helps us to infer that Kullūka must have passed some part of his life in Bengal. In this very context, it must be emphasised that Raghunandana in his *Smṛti-Tattvas* never quotes a passage from the *Śrāddha-Sāgara* of Kullūkabhaṭṭa or the *Āśauca-Sāgara* or the *Vivāda-Sāgara.*

It may be further added that MM. Dr. P.V. Kane in his *History of Dharma-Śāstra*, Vol. I, Part II, p. 883 points out that Kullūka is also quoted by Govindānanda who is placed between 1500-40, in the *Śrāddha-Kriyā-Kaumudī.* On verification, it is found that Govindānanda has quoted Kullūka's comments on the *Manu-Smṛti*, III.258 on the *Śrāddha-Kriyā-Kaumudī*, p. 207. It must also be noted here that there is no quotation from the *Śrāddha-Sāgara* of Kullūkabhaṭṭa even in the *Śrāddha-Kriyā-Kaumudī* of Govindānanda.

As regards the works of Kullūka, it may be pointed out that he has written an illustrious commentary known as *Manvarthamukāvalī* on the *Manu-Smṛti, Śrāddha-Sāgara, Āśauca-Sāgara* and *Vivāda-Sāgara.* Unfortunately the other works of Kullūka have not, so far, come to light. The present author is happy to mention here that he has now edited the *Śrāddha-Sāgara* of Kullūkabhaṭṭa which will throw more light on some of the problems connected with the date of Kullūkabhaṭṭa.

The introductory verses of the *Śrāddha-Sāgara* further exhibits that it was the intention of Kullūka to write a vast digest entitled *Smṛti-Sāgara.* Here he specifically states that as per the order of his revered father, the works — *Vivāda-Sāgara, Śrāddha-Sāgara* and *Āśauca-Sāgara* are composed by him. We do not find anywhere in any descriptive catalogue of the Sanskrit manuscripts, so far, published, mention of the other works of Kullūka such as *Vivāda-Sāgara* and *Āśauca-Sāgara.*

Now the question arises whether there are two Kullūkas or there is only one Kullūkabhaṭṭa the author of the commentary on the *Manu-Smṛti* and the *Śrāddha-Sāgara.*

Actually this cannot be a debatable point. MM. Dr. P.V. Kane in his *History of Dharma-Śāstra*, Vol. I, Part II, p. 758 admits that Kullūka is the author of both these works.

However, as a critical student of *Dharma-Śāstra* and *Pūrva-Mīmāṁsā*, it is necessary to establish once for all that the author of both these works is one and the same. As this is not, so far, proved by anyone, the present author thinks it fit to discuss this problem at full length here.

At the very outset, it may be pointed out that Kullūka in his introductory verses to the commentary on the *Manu-Smṛti* never makes a mention of his other works and particularly his *Śrāddha-Sāgara*. Besides, in his work entitled *Śrāddha-Sāgara* also, Kullūka does not make any specific mention of his commentary on the *Manu-Smṛti*.

Before entering into the discussion proper, it is necessary on the part of the present author to remark that Kullūka's commentary on the *Manu-Smṛti* is not of the nature of a digest like the commentary entitled *Mitākṣarā* of Vijñāneśvara on the *Yājñvalkya-Smṛti*. In addition to this, in the *Śrāddha-Sāgara*, however, Kullūka is not commenting on any *Smṛti* work as such. The work *Śrāddha-Sāgara* is of the nature of a digest. Hence Kullūka has full scope to quote the *smṛti* dicta available to him and also to refer to the other commentators and digest works in the course of his discussion. The full scope of Kullūka's presenting the matter, however, seems to be curtailed particularly in his commentary on the *Manu-Smṛti*.

It will not be out of place, if it is casually shown or remarked here that it is the firm opinion of the present author that Kullūka seems to have written a commentary on the *Manu-Smṛti* in the former part of his life. It is particularly in the latter part of his life or particularly in his old age, he seems to have composed his good work *Śrāddha-Sāgara*. If, however, this surmise is not accepted, then it will be very difficult to explain the silence of the authors on *Dharma-Śāstra* particularly about the *Śrāddha-Sāgara* of Kullūkabhaṭṭa. MM. Dr. P.V. Kane in his *History of Dharma-Śāstra*, Vol. I, Part II, p. 758 refers to the views of Dr. Bühler, MM. Chakravarti and Sir Asutosh Mukerji who have placed Kullūka in the fifteenth century A.D. Dr. Kane rejects the viewpoints of the above scholars and places Kullūkabhaṭṭa between

1150 and 1300 A.D.[1] The present author finds it very hard to agree with the learned authority on the *Dharma-Śāstra* particularly on this aspect of the date of Kullūkabhaṭṭa. I propose to discuss this topic of the date of Kullūkabhaṭṭa in the next section at full length. Here, however, incidentally it may be remarked that Kullūka seems to have written his commentary on the *Manu-Smṛti* in the former part of his life and has written his digest work *Śrāddha-Sāgara* in the latter part of his life and particularly in his old age. Besides, the silence on the part of the author writers on *Dharma-Śāstra* about the work *Śrāddha-Sāgara* of Kullūkabhaṭṭa cannot be adequately explained. It is rather surprising that this work of Kullūkabhaṭṭa is not quoted by the writers for four centuries. Even Kamalākara the author of the *Nirṇayasindhu,* does not make any reference to the work *Śrāddha-Sāgara.* Nīlakaṇṭha, the author of the twelve *Mayūkhas,* also passes over this work in silence. This silence can be adequately explained if we surmise that Kullūka seems to have written this work particularly in his old age. This is the main reason why other writers on *Dharma-śāstra* have not quoted this work.

In passing, it may also be remarked that Kullūka seems to have revised his views on the *Manu-Smṛti* in his *Śrāddha-Sāgara.* At some places, however, it is noticed that he has made improvement upon the *Manvarthamuktāvalī.* He has, at other places, copied verbatim his own views in the *Manvarthamuktāvalī* in his *Śrāddha-Sāgara.* It is also seen that at some places in the *Śrāddha-Sāgara,* his treatment to the topic under discussion is very detailed as compared to the meagre treatment given to the topic in his *Manvarthamuktāvalī.*

I hope that in the light of this background, the discussion that will follow now will prove to be very useful even in admitting the profound scholarship of Kullūkabhaṭṭa as the interpreter of the *Manu-Smṛti* and also as the digest author. This discussion will further reveal that the author of the *Manvarthamuktāvalī* and the *Śrāddha-Sāgara* is one and the same.

(I) It is noticed that the comments of Kullūka on the *Manu-Smṛti* and the *Śrāddha-Sāgara* are identical. For the clarification of this point, one may refer to the comments of Kullūkabhaṭṭa on the *Manu-Smṛti,*

1. P.V. Kane, *History of Dharma-Śāstra,* Vol. I, Part II, pp. 758-59.

III.281 with the *Śrāddha-Sāgara*, chapter XV, p. 113. In his *Manvarthamuktāvalī*, however, Kullūka has not quoted a passage from the *Matsya-Purāṇa* (XVI.57) in support. One may also refer to the comments of Kullūkabhaṭṭa on the *Manu-Smṛti*, III.144 with the *Śrāddha-Sāgara*, chapter XVII dealing with the *brāhmaṇas* to be avoided for the *Śrāddha* ceremony and particularly page 122. At both these, Kullūka has employed the *Mīmāṁsā* technical term *Pratiprasava*. The identical comments of Kullūka further help us to infer that the author of the two works is one and the same.

(II) It is possible to strengthen my contention by pointing out that Kullūka has raised the same *Mīmāṁsā* technical points in his discussion on the *Manvarthamuktāvalī* and also in the *Śrāddha-Sāgara*. For the clarification of this point, one can very well refer to the comments of Kullūkabhaṭṭa on the *Manu-Smṛti*, III.129 which points out that the feeding of the *brāhmaṇas* is a *pradhāna kriyā* and *piṇḍadāna* is a subsidiary act. Even though the fruit is laid down for the subsidiary act, yet it is to be treated as a *guṇaphalavidhi*. If these comments are read with the chapter XXVII, p. 170, one will detect that the import of the comments of Kullūka is one and the same. He holds the same view at both the places. Again the attention of the readers may be drawn to the comments of Kullūka on the *Manu-Smṛti*, III.280. Here he has employed the *Mīmāṁsā* technical term *Paryudāsa*. If this view is compared with the *Śrāddha-Sāgara*, p. 83, one will detect that the *Mīmāṁsā* comments are the same, though a careful reader has to admit that Kullūka is more elaborate in his comments on the *Manu-Smṛti*, III. 280. Possibly Kullūka has cut short the lengthy discussion here.

(III) Kullūka's criticism of Medhātithi's view is also the same at both the places. Here one may invite the attention of the readers to the comments of Kullūka on the *Manu-Smṛti*, III.125. By the side of this, a careful student of *Dharma-Śāstra* may read the portion from the *Śrāddha-Sāgara* on page 135. This identical criticism of Medhātithi's views at both the places mentioned above is also an indication of the fact that the author of both the works is one and the same.

(IV) It is further interesting to note that Kullūka, at times, records some readings in the commentary on the *Manu-Smṛti* and these are also found in the *Śrāddha-Sāgara*. To expound this point, one may draw the attention of the readers to the commentary of Kullūka on the

Manu-Smṛti, III.207, p. 128. Here in the foot-note we have the reading *jalatīreṣu* for *nadītīreṣu* in the text of the *Manu-Smṛti.* If this is compared with the *Śrāddha-Sāgara*, chapter III, stanza No. 8, p. 28, one finds the reading *jalatīreṣu.* This aspect of the same reading at both the places is also an indication of the common authorship of both the works. Another case of this type is the *Manu-Smṛti*, III.133. Here in the foot-note on page 113, we have the reading *Preto* for *Pretya.* It may be noted here that the same reading *preto* is also found in the *Śrāddha-Sāgara*, chapter XVII, stanza No. 5 on page 122. It may be incidentally noted here that the readings noted in the foot-notes in the Nirṇaya Sāgara Press, Bombay edition can be supported by quoting the text of *Śrāddha-Sāgara* in favour.

(V) At some places, Kullūka has recorded the different readings in the *Śrāddha-Sāgara* as compared with the readings already noted in his commentary on the *Manu-Smṛti.* This point can be expounded by drawing the attention of the readers to the readings in the *Manvarthamuktāvalī,* III.125 with *Śrāddha-Sāgara,* p.12, *Manvarthamuktāvalī,* III.284 with *Śrāddha-Sāgara*, p. 17, *Manvarthamuktāvalī,* III.220 with *Śrāddha-Sāgara*, p.18, *Manvarthamuktāvalī,* III.274 with the *Śrāddha-Sāgara,* p.46. All these readings clearly indicate that in the latter part of his life, Kullūka seems to have adopted different readings or perhaps changed the meanings of the words also.

(VI) It is further evident that whatever meanings are assigned by Kullūka to the words in the *Manu-Smṛti* particularly in his *Manu-Smṛti-ṭikā,* are changed by him in his *Śrāddha-Sāgara.* To explain this point, one can draw the attention to the *Manvarthamuktāvalī*, III.207. Here the expression *ukṣeṣu* is explained by Kullūkabhaṭṭa as 'the regions such as forest etc.' which are naturally pure. But in the *Śrāddha-Sāgara*, chapter III, stanza No. 8 on page 29 he explains the same *manohareṣu*, i.e., charming or delightful. One may note here that the meaning assigned here in the *Śrāddha-Sāgara*, p. 29 completely agrees with the sense that is given by Rāghavānanda on the *Manu-Smṛti* (*Cf. Manu-Smṛti*, Vol II, p. 212 by J.H. Dave.) This agreement is very striking and it may be noted here that Rāghavānanda is placed after 1350 A.D. This agreement on the part of Kullūka with Rāghavānanda helps one to infer that possibly Kullūka has revised his views particularly at the end of his life. Also see Kullūka on *Manu*, III.185-86 with the *Śrāddha-Sāgara*, p. 116 for the change of meaning of *pravaktā*.

(VII) It may also be noted that sometimes in giving treatment to the text of *Manu-Smṛti*, Kullūka quotes the same *smṛti* texts. It may be pointed out here that while explaining the idea in the *Manu-Smṛti*, II.44, Kullūka quotes only one line from the text of *Devala.* While in the *Śrāddha-Śāgara*, chapter XXII, stanza No. 4 on page 151, Kullūka quotes the complete stanza from the text of *Devala.* This resemblance in the treatment also is a further proof of the two works being written by one and the same author.

(VIII) In the matter of utilising the *Mīmāṁsā* doctrines for interpreting the *Dharma-Śāstra* texts, Kullūka has made considerable progress over his *Manvarthamuktāvalī* in the *Srāddha-Sāgara.*

5

Date of Kullūkabhaṭṭa

THE date of Kullūkabhaṭṭa is shrouded in mystery or obscurity. MM. Dr. P.V. Kane remarks that the date of Kullūka cannot be settled with certainty.

In this respect, Dr. George Bühler, MM. Chakravarti, Asutosh Mukerjee, J.C. Ghose and MM. Dr. P. V. Kane have propounded their own theories.

Before the fixation of the proper date of Kullūka, however, it will be proper on the part of the present author to state clearly the viewpoints expressed by the above-mentioned scholars and subject their views to scrutiny or critical examination.

The Theory of Dr. George Bühler

Dr. George Bühler has placed Kullūkabhaṭṭa, the commentator of the *Manu-Smṛti* in the fifteenth century A.D., particularly in his discussion in the *Sacred Books of the East Series*, Vol. XXV, p. CXXXI, mainly relying upon the fact that Kullūkabhaṭṭa is quoted by Raghunandana in the beginning of the sixteenth century A.D.

Examination of this Argument

(i) It must be pointed out here that Dr. Bühler has not given an elaborate treatment to this problem as such. He has, in fact, given the meagre treatment to this topic.

(ii) Dr. Bühler has not considered the other works on *Dharma-Śāstra* indicating the influence on the writing of Kullūka.

(iii) The learned doctor also has not consulted the other work of Kullūkabhaṭṭa, i.e., *Śrāddha-Sāgara* possibly because it was not, so far, published by any scholar or considered for any research Institute.

(iv) The learned scholar also has not consulted the vast *Dharma-Śāstra* utilised by Kullūka, *Purāṇic* texts quoted by him and the grammatical authorities employed by him for the exhibition of his deep scholarship in the *Manvarthamuktāvalī* and the *Śrāddha-Sāgara.*

In the light of the above arguments, it is better not to agree with the above-mentioned learned authority on the *Dharma-Śāstra.*

The Theory of J.C. Ghose and Asutosh Mukerjee

J.C. Ghose in his *Principles of Hindu Law,*[1] has placed Kullūkabhaṭṭa in the fifteenth century A.D., without quoting any authorities in support.

Asutosh Mukerjee remarks that Kullūka is to be placed in the fifteenth century A.D. He has introduced discussion in the *Indian Law Report,* 48 Calcutta p. 688.

Examination of the views of Ghose and Mukerjee

(i) It may be pointed out here that both the scholars have not made any thorough discussion in their works and have not based their theories on firm foundation.

(ii) Besides, both these scholars also have not consulted several sources for properly discussing this problem — The present author does not think it proper to subject their views to further criticism. He categorically states that the theory of these scholars stands rejected.

The Theory of MM. Chakravarti

MM. Chakravarti has devoted one printed paragraph for the date of Kullūkabhaṭṭa in the *Journal of the Asiatic Society Bengal,* Vol. XI,1915, p. 345.

MM. Chakravarti states that there is a mention of Kullūka's views on the *Manu-Smṛti* in the commentary of Śrīnātha Ācārya-Cūḍāmaṇi on the *Dāyabhāga* of *Jīmutavāhana.* He further adds that in the works

1. Also *see*: J.C. Ghose, *Principles of Hindu Law.*

of Śūlapāṇi, there is no mention of Kullūkabhaṭṭa and his works. It may be observed here that Śūlapāṇi is also the accredited master of *Dharma-Śāstra* particularly from Bengal. He further draws our attention to Vardhamāna Upādhyāya's *Daṇḍaviveka.* This author has quoted Kullūka's commentary on the *Manu-Smṛti* about 50 times. In the light of these arguments, MM. Chakravarti concludes that Kullūka is to be placed in the fifteenth century A.D.

Examination of the theory of MM. Chakravarti

(i) As regards the point of the commentary of Śrīnātha Ācārya Cūḍāmaṇi on the *Jīmutavāhana's Dāyabhāga*, it may be casually pointed out that the above author has also written a commentary on the *Śrāddha-Viveka* of Śūlapāṇi. Jīmutavāhana, the author of *Dāyabhāga*[1] is placed by MM. Dr. P.V. Kane in his *History of Dharma-Śāstra* between 1090 and 1130 A.D. Śūlapaṇi,[2] the celebrated author from Bengal, is placed between 1375 and 1460 A.D. by MM. Dr. P.V. Kane. And Śrīnātha Ācārya Cūḍāmaṇi[3] is placed by MM. Dr. P.V. Kane between 1470 and 1540 A.D. If all these dates are accepted, then Kullūka who is quoted by Śrīnātha Ācārya Cūḍāmaṇi, will have to be placed in the first or second quarter o the sixteenth century A.D. If this surmise is accepted, then the date of Kullūkabhaṭṭa cannot be fixed in the fifteenth century A.D.

(ii) As regards the silence of Śūlapāṇi about the work of Kullūka, it can be remarked that this argument is of a negative character. Besides, Kullūka also is silent about the works of Śūlapāṇi. Hence it will not be proper on our part to attach more weight to this negative argument of MM. Chakravarti.

(iii) As regards the fifty quotations from Kullūka's commentary on the *Manu-Smṛti* in the *Daṇḍaviveka* of Vardhammāna Upādhyāya, it can be respectfully submitted as below: (a) Vardhamāna Upādhyāya is the pupil of Vācaspatimiśra, the famous author *Dharma-Śāstra* from Mithila. Vācaspatimiśra is placed by MM. Dr. P.V. Kane in his *History of Dharma-Śāstra*[4] between 1425 and 1480 A.D. It, therefore, follows

1. *History of Dharma-Śāstra*, Vol. I, Part II, pp. 708-13.
2. *Ibid.*, p. 839.
3. *Ibid.*, p. 711.
4. *Ibid.*, p. 853.

that the literary activity of Vardhamāna Upādhyāya, the author of *Daṇḍaviveka,* might have started either in the last quarter of the fifteenth century A.D. or in the first or second quarter of the sixteenth century A.D. (b) MM. Dr. P.V. Kane in his *History of Dharma-Śāstra*[1] remarks that Śūlapāṇi, Rudradhara and Vācaspatimiśra are more or less contemporaries of one another. The very fact that they have not quoted Kullūka indicates that Kullūka has flourished after them. (c) Kullūkabhaṭṭa in his *Śrāddha-Sāgara,* p. 252 has quoted Vācaspatimiśra. He also refers to Gauḍa Vācaspati in his *Śrāddha-Sāgara* on page 219. These two references clearly distinguish Vācaspatimiŕa, the writer on *Dharma-Śāstra* from Mithilā, from Vācaspati who comes from Bengal. It is worthy of note here that about Gauḍa Vācaspati, we know nothing except perhaps a bare reference to his name. Even in the *History of Dharma-Śāstra,* we do not get any reference to him. If this internal authority is accepted, then naturally Kullūkabhaṭṭa will have to be placed in the sixteenth century A.D. and possibly as the contemporary of Vardhamāna Upādhyāya. (d) Incidentally, however, it must be emphasised here that the learned MM. Chakravarti has not consulted the internal evidence tendered by the *Manvarthamuktāvalī,* and *Śrāddha-Sāgara* quoting several *Dharma-Śāstra* authorities, *Purāṇic* authorities and grammatical authorities. His arguments, however, are purely based on the external evidence. Hence, the present author is constrained to observe that the arguments of MM. Chakravarti are one sided, purely based on the external evidence and completely displaying the studied silence about the *Śrāddha-Sāgara.* It is, therefore, proper on the part of the present author to reject the view of MM. Chakravarti with due deference to the profound scholarship of the learned Mahāmahopādhyāya.

Theory of MM. Dr. P.V. Kane

MM. Dr. P. V. Kane in his *History of Dharma-Śāstra*, Vol. I, Part II, p. 759 has placed Kullūkabhaṭṭa between 1150 A.D. and 1300 A.D. on the basis of following arguments:

(1) MM. Dr. Kane points out in his *History of Dharma-Śāstra*[2] that as Kullūka has quoted Bhojadeva, Govindarāja Lakṣmīdhara's

1. *History of Dharma-Śāstra*, Vol. I, Part II, p. 840.
2. *Ibid.*, p. 759.

Kṛtyakalpataru and *Halāyudha,* he is certainly later than 1200 A.D.

2. He further shows that Raghunandana in his *Smṛti-Tattvas,* several times mentions Kullūka and sometimes criticizes him also. He draws our attention to the following places:

Smṛti-Tattva, Vol. I —

(a) *Śrāddha Tattva*, pp. 225-26 quotes Kullūka.

(b) *Āhnika Tattva,* pp. 353, 454.

(c) *Prāyaścitta Tattva,* pp. 472, 530.

(d) *Saṁskāra Tattva*, pp. 893-94, 903.

Smṛti Tattva. Vol. II —

(a) *Udvāha Tattva,* p. 144.

(3) Govindānanda in his *Śrāddha-Kriyā-Kaumudī* refers to Kullūka's explanation on the *Manu-Smṛti*, III.258.

(4) Caṇḍeśvara in his *Rājanītiratnākara* quotes Kullūka's explanation of the word *rāja* on the *Manu-Smṛti*, VII.1.

(5) MM. Dr. Kane in his *History of Dharma-Śāstra*[1] points out that in Kullūka's *Śrāddha-Sāgara* we have a reference to Prabhākara and Kamalākarabhaṭṭa (on *Kāla* and *Kāma* being *devatas*) and in another place to Gauḍa-maithila-mayūkhabhaṭṭāḥ (which are probably marginal notes creeping into the manuscript or refer to authors other than the well-known ones).

(6) Dr. Kane also advances a negative argument that our author Kullūka is silent about *Jīmutavāhana*'s *Dāyabhāga.*[2] This is explicable in two ways (i) Kullūka wrote in Kashi and (ii) he was not in Bengal.

Examination of the Arguments of Dr. Kane

(i) As regards the first argument of Dr. Kane, there is no scope for any difference of opinion.

(ii) As regards the second argument of Dr. Kane, it can be

1. *History of Dharma-Śāstra*, Vol. I, Part II, p. 758
2. *Ibid.*, p. 759.

respectfully submitted that Raghunandana who is placed by MM. Dr. P.V. Kane — between 1510 and 1580 in his *History of Dharma-Śāstra,* Vol. I, Part II, p. 897 has quoted passages from Kullūka's commentary on the *Manu-Smṛti.* The present author has great pleasure in pointing out here that he has examined all the places pointed out by Dr. Kane and also other places where Kullūka's views are referred to by Raghunandana in his *Smṛti-Tattvas* and has come to the pointed conclusion that there is no reference to the *Śrāddha-Sāgara* of Kullūkabhaṭṭa. This silence on the part of Raghunandana is very important. It further exhibits that he has not before him the *Śrāddha-Sāgara* of Kullūka, possibly because it seems to have been written at a very later stage of life. In addition to this, it will not be out of place, if it is remarked here that Kullūka must have spent some part of his life in Bengal even after writing his *Manvarthamuktāvalī, or Kullūka must have become so famous by his commentary that Raghunandana is very much impressed by the same.*

(iii) As regards the third argument of Dr. Kane, it should be noted that Govindānanda in his *Śrāddha-Kriyā-Kaumudī* or *Varṣakriyā-Kaumudī* or *Dāna-Kriyā-Kaumudī* has quoted only from the *Manvarthamuktāvalī* and not from the *Śrāddha-Sāgara* of Kullūkabhaṭṭa. His silence about the other work, i.e., *Śrāddha-Sāgara* of Kullūkabhaṭṭa is also very important. Possibly by the time, he wrote his *Śrāddha-Kriyā-Kaumudī,* Kullūka might not have dreamt of writing *Śrāddha-Sāgara.* Besides, Govindānanda also appears to be a writer from Bengal as proved by Dr. Kane himself. If this is accepted, then it is evident that Kullūka who is quoted by him also must have spent some part of his life in Bengal and some part in Benares or he might have migrated from one place to another quite often.

(iv) As regards the fourth argument of Dr. Kane, it may be respectfully submitted that Kullūka also has quoted *Maithila-Ratnākara* in his *Śrāddha-Sāgara*, p. 220. (a) This *Maithila-Ratnākara* is certainly a reference to Caṇḍeśvara who is the celebrated author of the works of *Dāna-Ratnākara, Vivāda-Ratnākara* etc. and is placed by Dr. Kane in his *History of Dharma-Śāstra* between 1314-70. If this is accepted, then it is difficult to place Kullūka before 1300 A.D. (b) Now the question arises as to how a reference to the commentary of Kullūka on the *Manu-Smṛti*, VII.1 occurs in the *Rājanīti-Ratnākara.* It is very likely that this might have crept into the manuscript from the marginal note or somebody else might have been responsible for this interpolation. The other internal evidence of the *Śrāddha-Sāgara* makes it highly improbable to place Kullūka before 1300 A.D. (c) In addition to this, the way in which the passage from the commentary of Kullūka on the *Manu-Smṛti*, VII.1 in the *Rājanīti-Ratnākara* of Caṇḍeśvara is quoted helps us to infer that there is some difference in the passage found in the edition of the *Manvarthamuktāvalī* brought out by Nirnaya Sagara Press, Bombay and the passage quoted in the *Rājanīti-Ratnākara.* (d) It must, however, be emphasised that the internal evidence must agree with the external evidence. The complete text of the *Śrāddha-Sāgara* furnishes us with the information and evidence which clearly goes against the evidence tendered by Dr. Kane who wants to place him in the thirteenth century A.D. Hence one will have to admit that more importance will have to be attached to the internal evidence than to the external evidence.

(v) As regards the fifth argument of Dr. Kane, one will make bold to say that this is the imagination or perhaps the bold imagination on the part of Dr. Kane to treat the references to Prabhākara and Kamalākarabhaṭṭa as marginal notes creeping into the manuscript. (a) He should have taken pretty care to see whether the passage quoted is really available in the *Nirṇaya-Sindhu* of Kamalākarabhaṭṭa. (b) In addition to this Dr. Kane states that there is a reference to Kamalākarabhaṭṭa only once in the manuscript entitled *Śrāddha-Sāgara.* Here with due deference to the profound scholarship of MM. Dr. Kane, it may be pointed out that Kamalākarabhaṭṭa is quoted by Kullūkabhaṭṭa in his *Śrāddha-Sāgara* at six places (*Cf.* pp. 147, 191, 240, 247, 279 and 282). Is it possible to treat all these six places as marginal notes? The present author makes bold to say that if such places are examined from the *Nirṇaya-Sindhu*, then one is convinced that Kullūkabhaṭṭa has before him the text of *Nirṇaya-Sindhu.* Besides at one place, Kullūka goes to the extent of contradicting the view of Kamalākarabhaṭṭa. This happens particularly in respect of *Kāla* and *Kāma* as the deities for the *Śrāddha*-ceremony. This is the chapter XXI of the *Śrāddha-Sāgara* edited by the present author. If, however, this internal evidence is accepted, then it is difficult to agree with Dr. Kane who places our author Kullūkabhaṭṭa in the thirteenth century A.D. It may be pointed out here that Dr. Kane himself has stated in his *History of Dharma-Śāstra,* Vol. I, Part II, p 932 that Kamalākarabhaṭṭa has comepleted his *Nirṇaya-Sindhu* in 1612 A.D. If this date proposed by Dr. Kane is accepted, naturally one will have to admit that Kullūka seems to have completed his work after the completion of the work entitled *Nirṇaya-Sindhu.* Hence the present author categorically states that the argument of Dr. Kane does not hold water. (c) Dr. Kane also draws our attention to the important reference 'Gauḍa-Maithila-Mayūkha-bhaṭṭāḥ' in the *Śrāddha-Sāgara* of Kullūkabhaṭṭa. This reference occurs in the text of *Śrāddha-Sāgara* on page 149. Dr. Kane holds that this reference to Mayūkhabhaṭṭa is also a marginal note or refers to the author other than well-known. It is hard to agree with Dr. Kane on this point. Dr. Kane should have taken care to see whether the passage quoted by Kullūka is found in the *Śrāddha-Mayūkha* of Nīlakaṇṭha or not. But it seems that the learned doctor had no time to verify this reference. This discussion takes place in the *Śrāddha-Sāgara* chapter XXI, pp. 148 and 149. Here Kullūka asserts that Gauḍa-Maithila and Mayūkha-Bhaṭṭas have quoted stanza Nos. 10 and 11 (of my critical edition) from the *Brahma-Purāna*. But this is baseless. Actually if these references are verified, one finds that the second line of the stanza No. 11 is found quoted in the *Śrāddha-Mayūkha* from the *Āditya-Purāṇa.* In this very context, it may be further pointed that in the *Śrāddha-Candrikā*, p. 28 these two stanzas Nos. 11 and 11 are quoted from the *Śrāddha-Kāṇḍa* of Hemādri. Hemādri also quotes these stanzas from the *Āditya-Purāṇa.* Possibly Kullūka may have befors him some other manuscript of the *Śrāddha-Mayūkha* of Nīlakaṇṭha, which, however, is not now available to us. As the quoted text is found in the *Śrāddha-Mayūkha,* one cannot make bold to say that this is also a marginal note. (d) In this very context, it must also be shown that in the *Dharma-Śāstra*, Nīlakaṇṭha is the only author who is known as Mayūkhabhaṭṭa. Dr. Kane's *History of Dharma-Śāstra* also does not show that there is some other Mayūkhabhaṭṭa who is other than Nīlakaṇṭha. Hence there is no point in the argument of Dr. Kane. In fact, the above argument will smoothen the warmth of the argument of Dr. Kane. It may be incidentally remarked that all the works of Nīlakaṇṭha bear the wording Mayūkha e.g. *Vyavahāra-Mayūkha, Ācāra-Mayūkha, Nīti-Mayūkha* etc. (e) Dr. Kane in his *History of Dharma-Śāstra*, Vol. I, Part II, p. 941 has placed Nīlakaṇṭha's literary activity between 1610 and 1645. In this very context, it will be proper to refer to the chronological order of the works of Nīlakaṇṭha. Dr. Kane in his Introduction to the *Vyavahāra-*

Mayūkha, p. xx has shown that the order is as follows: (1) *Saṁskāra*; (2) *Ācāra*; (3) *Samaya*; (4) *Śrāddha*; (5) *Nīti*; (6) *Vyavahāra*; (7) *Dāna*; (8) *Utsarga*; (9) *Pratiṣṭhā*; (10) *Prāyaścitta*; (11) *Śuddhi* and (12) *Śānti*. If this very order established by Dr. Kane is accepted, and the literary activity of Nīlakaṇṭha is placed between 1610 and 1645 A.D., then one will have no other alternative but to admit that Nīlakaṇṭha seems to have composed this *Śrāddha-Mayūkha* in or about 1617 or 1618 A.D. If this internal evidence is accepted, then it supports the date of Kamalākara's *Nirṇaya-Sindhu* and also the other external evidence led above.

(vi) As regards the sixth argument of Dr. Kane is concerned, it is evident that it is of a negative character. (a) There is no hard and fast rule that Kullūka should have referred to all his predecessors and particularly *Jīmutavāhana* in his work. (b) It is further clear that the scope of *Manvarthamuktāvalī* is limited as it is a commentary on the *Manu-Smṛti*. Unless the other works of Kullūkabhaṭṭa such as *Āśauca-Sāgara* and *Vivāda-Sāgara* are brought to light, one cannot say conclusively that Kullūka has not referred to *Jīmutavāhana*. We reserve this discussion pertaining to *Āśauca-Sāgara* and *Vivāda-Sāgara* for the future workers in the field of Indology. (iii) The reasons for the absence of any reference to *Jīmutavāhana* in the work of Kullūkabhaṭṭa, given by the learned Dr. Kane are either based on his study of the *Manvarthamuktāvalī* only or funny and hence not acceptable. It may be respectfully pointed out that in the *Śrāddha-Sāgara*, Kullūka refers to Vācaspati Gauḍa at one place p. 219, and Gauḍa-Maithila-Mayūkhabhaṭṭāḥ at another place p. 149. This shows that Kullūka has spent valuable time of his life in Benares and was aware of the progress in the field of *Dharma-Śāstra* and particularly in Bengal. A good student of *Dharma-Śāstra* will certainly appreciate that in the Appendix 'F', the present author has brought together the places where the quotations from Kullūka's *Śrāddha-Sāgara* could be traced or located. There the present author has traced some of the quotations from the *Smṛti-Tattvas* of Raghunandana and particularly his *Śrāddha-Tattva* and *Malamāsa-Tattva*. At times, however, it is seen that in some chapters some quotations are bodily taken from the chapters of the *Śrāddha-Tattva* of Raghunandana and at one place, the explanation of one word given by Kullūka completely agrees with that of Raghunandana. Whenever any quotation given by Kullūka from the

Brahma-Purāṇa is not traced in the extant *Brahma-Purāṇa*, the same is found quoted in the particular chapters of Raghunandana and no where else. A close study of such quotations from the works of Raghunandana will unmistakably lead one to the conclusion that Kullūka has read very minutely the works of Raghunandana. The above discussion further helps one to conclude more reasonably that no importance can be attached to the negative argument advanced by Dr.Kane. Here incidentally it may be remarked that the theory advanced by Dr. Kane in respect of the date of Kullūka in his *History of Dharma-Śāstra* is unreasonable, unconvincing and hence deserves to be rejected.

Independent Arguments Advanced by the Present Author

(1) If as proposed by Dr. Kane, Kullūkabhaṭṭa is placed in the thirteenth century A.D., then how is it possible to explain the silence of the other writers on *Dharma-Śāstra* as regards Kullūka's other work *Śrāddha-Sāgara* for four centuries and more?

(2) The present author has consulted all the works on *Śrāddha* so far published. The *Smṛticandrikā-Śrāddha-Kāṇḍa* of Devaṇṇabhaṭṭa (between 1150 and 1225 A.D.), *Caturvargacintāmaṇi* and particularly *Śrāddha-Kāṇḍa* and Hemādri (1270 A.D.) *Śrāddha-Mayūkha* of Nīlakaṇṭha (1600-60 A.D.), Kamalākarabhaṭṭa the author of *Nirṇayasindhu* (between 1610-40 A.D.), *Śrāddha-Kalpa* of Śrī Dattopādhyāya (1200 and 1300 A.D.), *Śrāddha-Kalpalatā* of Nandapaṇdita (1580-1630 A.D.), *Śrāddha-Candrikā* of Divākarabhaṭṭa (the grand-son of Nīlakanṭhabhaṭṭa), Bālaṁbhaṭṭi on *Ācāra* portion of the *Mitākṣarā* of Bālaṁbhaṭṭa Payagunde (1730-1820 A.D.), *Smṛtimuktāphalam* of Vaidyanātha Dīkṣit (1600 A.D.) *Smṛti-Tattvas* of Raghunandana (1510-80) have ignored this important work of Kullūka particularly coming from the pen of the illustrious commentator of the *Manu-Smṛti* for a period of four centuries. This silence cannot be adequately explained if Dr. Kane's theory is accepted by the scholars.

(3) It is Kāśināth Upādhyāya (1790-91) who in his *Dharma-Sindhu*, p. 568 has referred to our author's work *Śrāddha-Sāgara*, in the plural number. Incidentally it may be remarked here that the viewpoint of the author of *Śrāddha-Sāgara* quoted in the *Dharma-Sindhu*, however, cannot be traced in the manuscript *Śrāddha-Sāgara* edited by the

present author. But a reference to this work in the eighteenth century A.D. can be adequately understood, if, however, we place Kullūkabhaṭṭa between (1530-1620 A.D.).

(4) It is further interesting to note that Nīlakaṇṭha in his *Saṁskāra Mayūkha* and *Vyavahāra-Mayūkha* quotes Kullūka as an authority; but he does not care to refer to the important work *Śrāddha-Sāgara* particularly in his monograph on the *Śrāddha* section of the *Dharma-Śāstra.*

(5) Śaṅkarabhaṭṭa (1540-1600 A.D.) has not at all referred to Kullūkabhaṭṭa particularly in his *Dharma-Dvaita-Nirṇaya.*

(6) All the above-mentioned scholars who have advanced different theories have not consulted the *Śrāddha-Sāgara* of Kullūkabhaṭṭa and particularly references to Gauḍa Vācaspati, Vācaspatimiśra, Nārāyaṇabhaṭṭa, Maithila Ratnākara, Ratnākarabhaṭṭa in the work *Śrāddha-Sāgara.*

(7) The present author feels certain that Kullūka also must have before him the works of Śūlapāṇi, though in fact, he has not quoted him in the body of his work. One quotation from the *Viṣṇudharmottara-Purāṇa* could not be identified by the present author in the extant *Viṣṇudharmottara-Purāṇa.* In the *Śrāddha-Sāgara*, chapter XV, we have the stanza Nos. 22, 23 and 24 quoted from the *Viṣṇudharmottara-Purāṇa.* The same, however, could not be identified by the present author. It is only after the completion of the editing work that the present author came across the *Journal of the Poona Orientalist*, Vol. VI, Nos. 3 and 4. In this issue, Dr. S.C. Bannerji from Calcutta has edited the *Tithi-Viveka* of Śūlapāṇi. Here on page 233, the present author could get the above citations from the *Viṣṇudharmottara-Purāṇa* bearing numbers 22, 23 and 24. Moreover the text of *Śātātapa* quoted in Kullūka's *Śrāddha-Sāgara*, p 88 is also found in the *Tithi-Viveka* of Śūlapāṇi. If this evidence is considered, then one will not be far from the truth if one simply holds that Kullūka seems to have made adequate use of the works on *Dharma-Śāstra* on the part of the writers from Bengal.

Conclusion

In conclusion, the present author thinks it proper, in the light of the long discussion that Kullūkabhaṭṭa seems to have written his commentary on the *Manu-Smṛti* in the former part of his life (i.e., between 1525 to 1550) and he seems to have composed his *Śrāddha-Sāgara* at the end of his life and particularly after 1618 A.D. Hence the present author is placing Kullūkabhaṭṭa between 1520-1620. He appears to have led a long life like Dr. Kane and hence the above conclusion seems more reasonable, convincing and satisfactory.

6

Relation of Kullūka's *Śrāddha-Sāgara* to Lakṣmīdhara's *Kṛtyakalpataru-Śrāddha-Kāṇḍa*

MM. Dr. P.V. Kane in his *History of Dharma-Śāstra*, Vol. I, Part II, p. 759 points out that Kullūka has profusely quoted Lakṣmīdhara's *Kṛtyakalpataru.* Here it may be stated that in his *Manvarthamuktāvalī,* Kullūka has not quoted *Kṛtyakalpataru-Śrāddha-Kāṇḍa* (*KK-SK*) but it is only in his *Śrāddha-Sāgara* that he has made the best use of the work of Lakṣmīdhara. In this chapter, therefore, an attempt is made to discuss the relation of the two woks.

From the Appendix 'C' it is evident that Kullūka has quoted Lakṣmīdhara's *Kṛtyakalpataru-Śrāddha-Kāṇḍa* in his *ŚS* about thirteen times. From Appendix 'F', however, it is clear that the quotations in the *ŚS*, can be traced in the *KK-SK* several times. In the light of this background, the discussion is introduced in this chapter.

(I) It is clear that at some places, the quotations from the *KK-SK* as given in the *ŚS* cannot be traced or found in the critical edition of the *KK-SK* brought out by the Oriental Institute, Baroda in 1950. (i) To clarify this point further, one could draw the attention of the readers to the *ŚS*, chapter V, p. 33 referring to the explanation of the word *Vyatipāta*[1] occurring in the text of the *Yājñavalkya-Smṛti*, I. 218 from the pen of Lakṣmīdhara. This explanation, however, is not found in the critical edition of the *KK-SK*, p. 9. (ii) Another example of this type

1. कृत्यकल्पतरु-श्राद्धकाण्ड, p. 9, *see* also p. 33.

is available in the *ŚS*, chapter VII, p. 45. Here Kullūka quotes a line from the *Brahma-Purāṇa* and refers to the view of *KK-SK* that like *gajacchayāyoga,* for the *Śrāddha* on the *Maghātrayodaśī* also, there is a special fruit. This view of *KK-SK*, however, is not found in the critical edition of the *KK-SK,* pp. 9-10.

(II) It is also observed at some places that the viewpoints of *KK-SK* quoted in the *ŚS* are found with slight variations in the critical edition of the *KK-SK*. For the clarification of this point, one could refer to the *ŚS* chapter XXIII[1] referring to the viewpoint of Hemakarabhaṭṭa and Kalpataru that the *nyubjīkaraṇa* is to be done to the north of the other *brāhmaṇas*. This view of *KK-SK* is found in the critical edition of the *KK-SK*[2]. Here in *KK-SK* we have the reading *Brāhmaṇāt* for *Brāhmaṇasya*. For another example of this sort refer to the *ŚS,* chapter XV, p. 109 and compare it with the *KK-SK,* p. 12 already noted in the above chapter XV.

(III) At times, however, it is noticed that Kullūka in his *ŚS* has copied some portion from the *KK-SK* without acknowledging his indebtedness to the author of the *KK-SK*. For the elucidation of this point, one could refer to the *ŚS*, chapter I, p. 2, foot-note 4; chapter II, p. 22, foot-note 10[3]. There are ample illustrations of this type; but the two cited above are sufficient to prove my finding in the above matter.

(IV) At some places, however, it is located that Kullūka in his *ŚS* quotes some texts which are also found quoted in the *KK-SK* but with different readings. Hence the utility of the text of the *ŚS* for the critical edition of the *KK-SK* can hardly be denied. To explain this point, one can very well refer to the *ŚS,* chapter I.27 (p. 17). Here the text of *Devala* is quoted. The same text is also found quoted in the *KK-SK*[4] which, however, records the readings which are different from the readings which are found recorded in the *ŚS*. The present author avoids further unnecessary discussion in this chapter particularly of the above variety.

---

1. *श्राद्धसागर,* p. 157.
2. *कृत्यकल्पतरु-श्राद्धकाण्ड,* p. 146.
3. *श्राद्धसागर,* pp. 2 and 22.
4. *कृत्यकल्पतरु-श्राद्धकाण्ड,* p. 230.

(V) It is further evident that at other places, Kullūka's *Śrāddha-Sāgara* records some readings or words which are totally absent in the critical edition of the *KK-SK*. To expound this point, one could refer to the *ŚS*, chapter XI, p. 80 on which the viewpoint of *Kalpataru* is quoted from the *KK-SK*.[1] On a closer comparison of both the texts, it is clear that the expression *dvitīyāṁ* recorded by Kullūka is missing in the *KK-SK*.

(VI) Kullūka in his *Śrāddha-Sāgara*, refers to the viewpoints of some writers on *Dharma-Śāstra* by the expression *itikecit* and *iti anye*. On a complete study of the *KK-SK*, it is noticed that the same views are also found quoted in the *KK-SK*. *ŚS*, chapter XV, p. 111 illustrates this point. Here the viewpoint of some writers on *Dharma-Śāstra* is referred to by the expression *iti kecit* and *iti apare*[2]. The same views are found quoted in the *KK-SK*, p. 11. From this, it is evident that Kullūka has before him the text of *KK-SK* and has not even cared to verify the authors whose viewpoints are referred to here.

(VII) At some places, however, it is observed that in the text quoted by Kullūka in his *Śrāddha-Sāgara,* some words are missing. Such words, however, are supplied from the *KK-SK,* if one traces the quotations in the *KK-SK*. One can explain this point by inviting the attention of the readers to the *ŚS*, chapter XXXV. Here Kullūka quotes the text of *Laghuhārīta* in the stanza No. 33, p. 265. If, however, this stanza is traced in the *KK-SK*[3], one notes the reading *tad* after the reading *tasmāt* which is found recorded in the *ŚS* of Kullūka. *Mitākṣarā*, p. 90, however, reads other readings which are also noted in the foot-notes on the respective pages.

(VIII) On a closer study of both the works, it is further clear that Kullūka in his *ŚS* rejects the viewpoint of the *KK-SK* purely on the ground of *Mīmāṁsā* technicality. In the *ŚS* chapter XV after stanza No. 16[4], Kullūka rejects the viewpoint of the *KK-SK* on the strength of the *Virodhādhikaraṇa* of the *Pūrva-Mīmāṁsā*. At another place, however, Kullūka rejects the viewpoint of *KK-SK* by posing some

1. कृत्यकल्पतरु-श्राद्धकाण्ड, p. 21.
2. *Ibid.*, p. 11.
3. *Ibid.*, p. 258.
4. श्राद्धसागर, p. 109.

difficulty and also relying upon some principles introduced by other. This discussion takes places in the *ŚS*, chapter XXXII[1].

(IX) At times, however, Kullūka rejects the interpretation of the *KK-SK* on the particular word occurring in the quoted text. This point can be made succinctly clear by pointing out that *Kullūka* in his *ŚS*, chapter XXIX, p. 177 discusses the *Śrāddha* and points out that *Āmaśrāddha* is to be performed by a *Śūdra*. Here *Kullūka* refers to the viewpoint of *KK-SK* quoting *Matsya-Purāṇa* to show that as *Śrāddha* fulfils all desires, it may be performed by others. This view of *KK* is found in the *KK-SK*[2] with slight variations. *KK-SK* interprets the expression *anagnau* as 'in the absence of fire'. Kullūka thinks[3] it is wrong one and maintains that even a *niragni* person should perform a *Śrāddha* which is a part of the cooked food.

(X) At one place, however, it is observed that on a debatable point Kullūka quotes the two divergent viewpoints and favours one view and rejects the viewpoint of *KK-SK*. To illustrate the truth of this remark, one may refer to the *ŚS*, chapter XXXIII[4]. Here the position of the *brāhmaṇas* invited for the *Śrāddha* ceremony is discussed. Here he quotes the viewpoint of Hemakarabhaṭṭa and Kalpataru who hold that this has a reference to the *brāhmaṇa* who has sat to the northern side of the *brāhmaṇas*. Kullūka here quotes[5] the viewpoint of Halāyudha and holds that this refers to the *brāhmaṇas* who have sat near and particularly to the left hand side. It is surprising that *Kullūka* gives his decided opinion in the matter.

(XI) Kullūka, in his *Śrāddha-Sāgara,* at times quotes some texts without disclosing the source. If, however, such sources are properly examined in the light of the *KK-SK*, one easily detects that *KK-SK* appears to be a strong source or the main source of our author Kullūkabhaṭṭa. For the elucidation of this point, one may refer the readers to the *ŚS*, chapter XXXII, stanza No. 23 on page 205. This stanza No. 23 however, is found quoted in the *KK-SK*, p.6 by quoting

1. श्राद्धसागर, p. 208.
2. कृत्यकल्पतरु-श्राद्धकाण्ड, p. 235.
3. श्राद्धसागर, p. 109.
4. *Ibid.*, p. 157 quotes कृत्यकल्पतरु-श्राद्धकाण्ड, p. 145.
5. *Ibid.*, p. 157.

the same from the *Bhaviṣya-Purāṇa*. We get ample illustrations of this type and such stanzas or the texts when quoted by Kullūka can be better identified with the help of the other texts which are printed and which are particularly written by other well-known writers on *Dharma-Śāstra* like Devaṇṇabhaṭṭa, Nīlakaṇṭha, Kamalākarabhaṭṭa, Raghunandana and others.

(XII) It is further noticed at some places that the reading recorded in the manuscript is hopelessly corrupt and if the same is traced in the *KK-SK*, one gets a grammatically pure reading which may be substituted for the corrupt reading. One gets the example of this sort in the *ŚS*, chapter XX, stanza No.6[1] quoted particularly from the *Vāyu-Purāṇa.* Here in the quoted text, the word *saṁskṛtaḥ* occurs. Kullūka in his gloss on the same explains it is *sakradaṁṣṭāḥ* which is hopelessly corrupt. If, however, by the side of this place, one reads *KK-SK*[2] then one gets the reading *saṁsṛṣṭāḥ*, which appears to be a pure reading and which deserves to be substituted for the corrupt reading.

(XIII) A careful study of both the works further reveals that at some places, in the *ŚS,* we find that some words are either doubly written or unnecessary and this point becomes clear to us only if we compare the same with the passage already quoted in the *KK-SK.* For the clarification of this point, one may refer to the discussion in the *ŚS* chapter XXXV[3]. Here the passage is quoted from the *Āśvalāyana-Pariśiṣṭa.* In this quotation, the expression *samānīva* occurs twice. If, however, this quotation is traced in the *KK-SK*, p. 253 then one detects that the word *samānīva* which is repeated here, is unnecessary. Hence the Utility of the *KK-SK* for removing such defects in the manuscript *ŚS* which is edited by the present author can hardly be denied by any careful student of *Dharma-Śāstra.*

(XIV) It is further evident that in the *ŚS* at some places some words are missing and the sense of the sentence thus becomes incomplete. This irregularity in the critical edition of the *ŚŚ* can be removed provided one traces the same passage in the *KK-SK* and supplies the

---

1. श्राद्धसागर, p. 143.
2. कृत्यकल्पतरु-श्राद्धकाण्ड, p. 114.
3. श्राद्धसागर, p. 256.

necessary words for the completion of the sense. To bring this point home to the readers, one may refer to the *ŚS*, chapter XXIV, p. 160 on which the text of *Paiṭhīnasi* is quoted. After the expression *anujñāpya* however, it is noticed that in the *KK-SK*[1] there is the addition of the expression *saumyaḥ santu iti ukta*, which if supplied to our present text, the sense would become more complete. Hence the Utility of *KK-SK* can hardly be denied.

(XV) It is also explicit at some places that Kullūka rejects the viewpoint of *KK-SK* along with Prabhākara and Kamalākarabhaṭṭa who treat *Kāla* and *Kāma* as the deities for the *Śrāddha*-ceremony. This discussion takes place in the the *ŚS*, chapter XXI, pp. 147-48 and Kullūka rejects this view by quoting *Āśvalāyana-Gṛhya-Pariśiṣṭa* in support and here these two stanzas quoted from the *Āśvalāyana-Gṛhya-Pariśiṣṭa* bear the numbers 6 and 7. From this, it is evident that Kullūka is inclined to reject the viewpoint of *KK-SK* only on the strength of the textual authority available to him.

To sum up, one will have to admit that Kullūka has treated Lakṣmīdhara's *KK-SK* as a model for his work and mainly depended upon the same for several quotations. This discussion also finds support from the Appendix 'F', in which the present author has taken pains to point out the places from the *KK-SK* where the quotations from the *ŚS* could be traced. In conclusion, the influence of the *KK-SK* on the *ŚS* is noticed on almost every page of the *ŚS* and is almost undeniable.

1. कृत्यकल्पतरु-श्राद्धकाण्ड, p. 167.

7

Kullūkabhaṭṭa and the Writers from Bengal

MM. Dr. P.V. Kane in his *History of Dharma-Śāstra*, Vol. I, Part II, p. 759 remarked that Kullūka is silent about the *Dāyabhāga* of *Jīmutavāhana*. This silence is explicable in two ways. (1) Kullūka wrote in Kashi and (2) He was not in Bengal.

He also draws our attention to the *Smṛti-Tattvas* of Raghunandana who quotes Kullūka several times. e.g.

Smṛti-Tattva, Vol.I —

(i) *Śrāddha-Tattva*, pp. 225-26.

(ii) *Āhnika-Tattva*, pp. 472, 530.

(iii) *Prāyaścitta-Tattva,* pp. 472, 530.

(iv) *Saṁskāra-Tattva,* pp. 893-94, 903

Smṛti-Tattva, Vol. I —

(i) *Udvāha-Tattva*, p. 144.

On a careful examination of these places, the present author has come to the conclusion that Raghunandana has not quoted any passage from the *Śrāddha-Sāgara* of Kullūkabhaṭṭa. The very fact that Kullūka is quoted by Raghunandana indicates that either Kullūka seems to have spent some part of his life in Bengal or he might have become so famous by his *Manvarthamuktāvalī* that even Raghunandana has quoted him.

Here it may be pointed out that Kullūka in his *Śrāddha-Sāgara* seems to have read the *Smṛti-Tattvas* of Raghunandana. This is evident from the following considerations:

(i) There are some quotations in Kullūka's *Śrāddha-Sāgara* which are traced only in the works of Raghunandana and nowhere else. At times, in a chapter, the series of quotations can be traced to the *Smṛti-Tattvas* and particularly *Śrāddha-Tattva* and *Malamāsa-Tattva*. This is evident from the Appendix 'F'.

(ii) In the *Smṛti-Tattvas* of Raghunandana, we sometimes, come across some references to the astrological works without the proper mention of the astrological author. Here such references are vague. It appears that Kullūka has copied verbatim such references. One can draw the attention of the readers to the *Śrāddha-Sāgara*, chapter XIV, page 96, foot-note 1 and page 97, foot-note 1 where we have the references to the astrology. These can be traced in the *Śrāddha-Tattva*, p. 252.

(iii) At times, Raghunandana quotes passages from some *Purāṇas* like *Brahma-Purāṇa* and *Devī-Purāṇa* and even *Varāha-Purāṇa*. These references cannot be traced in the printed editions of such texts. They are also not available in the other printed works on *Śrāddha*. To clarify this point, one could draw attention to the *Brahma-Purāṇa* quoted in the *Śrāddha-Sāgara*, chapter XII, p. 82, foot-note 5 where it is shown that this is traced only in the *Śrāddha-Tattva*, p. 265. For *Varāha-Purāṇa* quoted in the *Śrāddha-Sagara*, chapter VI, p. 38, refer to the foot-notes 1 and 2 where it is shown that this is quoted in the *Śrāddha-Tattva* p. 260. For the *Devī-Purāṇa* quoted in the *Śrāddha-Sāgara*, chapter VII, pp. 50 and 51, one may refer to the *Śrāddha-Tattva*, p. 257. All these references clearly indicate that Kullūka has before him the works of Raghunandana.

(iv) At some places, it is seen that the explanation given by Kullūka of the quoted passage completely agrees with that of Raghunandana. For this point, one could draw attention of the readers to the *Śrāddha-Sāgara*, chapter VI, p. 38 stanza No. 13. In this stanza, the expression *navodake* occurs. The explanation of this word as given by Kullūka shows that he has copied from the *Śrāddha-Tattva*, p. 260.

(v) A reference to the expression *Rambhātṛtīya Vrate Śivarahasye* in the *Śrāddha-Sāgara*, chapter XIV, p. 98 and the quotation given from this work are the cases in the point. These two can be completely traced in the *Malamāsa-Tattva*, p. 841 and nowhere. One can conclude this point by drawing the attention of the readers to the texts of *Satyavrata* (*ŚS*, pp. 100, 101), *Kāśyapa Smṛti* (*ŚS*, p. 97), *Brahma-siddhānta* (*ŚS*, p. 93) etc.

(vi) It may be noted here that in the *Śrāddha-Sāgara* chapter XIV dealing with *Ādhimāsa*, we find some quotations only from the *Malamāsa-Tattva* of Raghunandana and nowhere else. These are also pointed out in the foot-notes.

(vii) It may be pointed out that Kullūka also differs from Raghunandana in understanding the *Muhūrta* known as *Rauhiṇa*. In the *Śrāddha-Sāgara*, chapter XII, p. 81, Kullūka connects the *Muhūrta Rauhina* with the constellation Rohiṇī. Raghunandana however, in his *Śrāddha-Tattva*, p. 265 connects this *muhūrta Rauhiṇa* with the deity Rohiṇī on the strength of the authority from the astrological works. This is a minute point of difference between the two authors.

The above discussion further reveals that Kullūka seems to have before him the *Smṛti-Tattvas* of Raghunandana, who, however, does not quote from the *Śrāddha-Sāgara* of Kullūkabhaṭṭa possibly for the simple reason that Kullūka has written this work only at the end of his life.

Again references to the Gauḍa-Vācaspati in the *Śrāddha-Sāgara*, p. 149 and a general reference to the expression Gauḍa-Maithila-Mayūkhabhaṭṭāḥ point in the direction that Kullūka has read some works from Bengal particularly on the *Dharma-Śāstra*.

One can also form the opinion that Kullūka has before him the works of Śūlapāṇi who is placed by MM. Dr. P.V Kane in his *History of Dharma-Śāstra*, Vol. I, Part II between 1375 A.D. to 1460 A.D. The stanza Nos. 22, 23 and 24 from the *Śrāddha-Sāgara*, chapter XV could be traced in the *Tithi-Viveka*, p. 283 edited by Dr. S.C. Bannerji in the *Poona Orientalist*, Vol. VI, Nos. 3 and 4. These are the stanzas from the *Viṣṇudharmottara-Purāṇa* which could not be identified in the extant *Viṣṇudharmottara-Purāṇa*.

In the light of the above discussion, it would be fair on the part of the present author to conclude that Kullūka had before him the works of Raghunandana and Śūlapāṇi and has also referred to the authors like Gauḍa-Vācaspati and made a general reference to the author from the Bengal. If all these references are taken into consideration, then one will be inclined to hold that though Kullūka had spent most of his life in Benares, yet he was aware of the further development of Hindu law particularly in Bengal. He also possibly might have migrated from Benares to Bengal and from Bengal to Benares; otherwise so many quotations in Kullūka's *Śrāddha-Sāgara* could not have been traced in the works from the authors of Bengal.

8

Kullūka and other Writers on *Śrāddha*

APART from Kullūka's *Śrāddha-Sāgara,* there are many works on *Śrāddha* which may be enumerated here:

(1) Lakṣmīdhara's *Kṛtyakalpataru-Śrāddha-Kāṇḍa.*

(2) Mitramiśra's *Śrāddha-Prakāśa.*

(3) Devaṇṇabhaṭṭa's *Smṛticandrikā-Śrāddha-Kāṇḍa.*

(4) Pṛthvīcandra's *Śrāddha-Prakāśa.*

(5) Divākarabhaṭṭa's *Śrāddha-Candrikā.*

(6) Nandapaṇḍita's *Śrāddha-Kalpalatā.*

(7) Nīlakaṇṭha's *Śrāddha-Mayūkha.*

(8) Vaidyanātha Dīkṣita's *Smṛtimuktāphalam-Śrāddha-Kāṇḍam.*

(9) Vācaspatimiśra's *Śrāddha-Cintāmaṇi.*

In addition to these regular works on the *Śrāddha*, there are some exhaustive commentaries on the *Śrāddha*-section of the *Dharma-Śāstra* which deserve special mention here.

(1) Vijñāneśvara's commentary *Mitākṣarā* on the *Yājñavalkya-Smṛti.*

(2) Viśvarūpa's commentary on the *Yājñavalkya-Smṛti.*

(3) Aparārka's commentary on the *Yājñavalkya-Smṛti.*

(4) Eight commentaries of Medhātithi, Nandana, Rāmchandra, etc. on the IIIrd chapter of the *Manu-Smṛti.*

(5) Exhaustive commentary of Bālaṁbhaṭṭa Payagunde on the *Mitākṣarā* on the *Yājñavalkya-Smṛti.* This is known as *Bālaṁbhaṭṭī-Ācāra* Section covering about 626 pages.

(6) The exhaustive commentary of Mādhavācārya on the *Parāśara-Smṛti* otherwise known as *Parāśaramādhava.*

(7) Kamalākarabhaṭṭa's *Nirṇayasindhu.*

(8) Kāśīnātha Upādhyāya's *Dharma-Sindhu.*

Out of these works mentioned above, it is surprising that Kullūka quotes only few like Lakṣmīdhara's *Kṛtyakalpataru-Śrāddha-Kāṇḍa*, and Vācaspatimiśra without mentioning their works. Kullūka's indebtedness to *KK-SK* is already brought out by me in the chapter 6 which is discussed above.

Kullūka's indebtedness to Kamalākara's *Nirṇayasindhu* is also evident since he quotes the latter at six places as already noted.

Raghunandana's *Smṛti-Tattvas* and particularly his *Śrāddha-Tattva* is also an important work on *Śrāddha.* He does not quote him by name. But a close study of the works of the *Smṛti-Tattvas* and particularly his *Śrāddha-Tattva* in comparison with the *Śrāddha-Sāgara* of Kullūkabhaṭṭa further reveals that Kullūka has properly read the works of Raghunandana or has made the best use of the quotations available in his work whenever the opportunity so has arisen. This remark also finds support from the discussion in chapter 7 which is specifically devoted to show the relation of the *Śrāddha-Sāgara* of Kullūka to the *Smṛti-Tattvas* of Raghunandana.

Though it is evident that Kullūka has not quoted *Smṛticandrikā-Śrāddha-Kāṇḍa,* Mitramiśra's *Śrāddha-Prakāśa* and Pṛthvīcandra's *Śrāddha-Prakāśa* (in a Ph. D. thesis form in the University of Bombay), it must be stated without any fear of contradiction that some of the most important quotations could be traced only in these works.

Kullūka also refers to Gauḍa-Vācaspati and Nārāyaṇabhaṭṭa without making any specific mention of their works. As regards, Gauḍa-Vācaspati, however, it can be said that in the present state of our knowledge, however, nothing is known about him. As regards the works of Nārāyanabhaṭṭi who is placed by MM. Dr. P.V. Kane in his *History of Dharma-Śāstra,* Vol. I, Part II, p. 906 between 1513-70 A.D., it can be said that all his works are not so far brought to light except perhaps his *Nārāyaṇabhaṭṭī* and *Tristhalīsetu.* In these two works, however, references to Nārāyanabhaṭṭa in the *Śrāddha-Sāgara* (pp. 169-208) could not be located. Any way, Kullūka's indebtedness to this work is an admitted work, since he not only criticized Nārāyaṇabhaṭṭa at one place but at another places shown his agreement with him by quoting the principle of interpretation utilised by Nārāyaṇabhaṭṭa, in some of his works.

It must be mentioned here that Kullūka's work on *Śrāddha* is not at all mentioned by any recognised writers on *Dharma-Śāstra* possibly because this seems to have been written by Kullūka at the end of his life and particularly after leading a very long life.

The silence on the part of Nīlakaṇṭha, Kamalākarabhaṭṭa Nandapaṇḍita as regards *Śrāddha-Sāgara* cannot, however, be adequately explained if the above hypothesis is not accepted.

A reference to the *Śrāddha-Sāgara* of Kullūka, however, can be noticed only in the *Dharma-Sindhu*, p. 656 of Kāśīnātha Upādhyāya who is placed at the end of the eighteenth century A.D. by MM. Dr. P.V. Kane.

9

The Importance of Kullūka's *Śrāddha-Sāgara* in the *Dharma-Śāstra* Literature

THIS work will have to be regarded as the product of Kullūka's mature thought. Kullūka in his *Manvarthamuktāvalī* simply wrote a commentary on the *Manu-Smṛti.* His first work is in the nature of a commentary.

As compared with the *Manvarthamuktāvalī,* it is observed that Kullūka has made the abundant use of the doctrines of *Pūrva-Mīmāṁsā.* In fact, in the matter of the employment of the doctrine of *Pūrva-Mīmāṁsā,* on *śrāddha* aspect Kullūka has, in the opinion of the present author, surpassed all the writers on *Śrāddha* even including Nīlakaṇṭha and Mitramiśra.

It must be emphasised here that the use of the *Mīmāṁsā* doctrines in the *Manvarthamuktāvalī* on the part of Kullūka appears to be very meagre as compared with his digest work *Śrāddha-Sāgara.* The present author has already contributed a paper on 'The position of Kullūkabhaṭṭa as a *Mīmāṁsaka* to the *Journal of the Bhāratīya Vidyā, Bhavan*, Bombay, Vol. XXVIII, Nos. 1-4, pp. 93-102. He has also discussed some of the passages from the commentary of Kullūka on the *Manu-Smṛti* in the *Journal of Oriental Research Institute and Manuscripts Library,* University of Kerala, Vol. XVIII, Nos. 2 and 3. Besides, in the *Śrāddha-Sāgara*, however, Kullūka has quoted several *smṛti* authorities, digest authors, *Purāṇic* works and even grammatical authorities and has entered into the acute discussion of *Pūrva-Mīmāṁsā.* One will have to admit that Kullūka has drunk deep in the fountain of *Purva-Mīmāṁsā.*

As the *Śrāddha-Sāgara* is in the nature of a digest, the scope of Kullūka is very wide and he has satisfied the readers by his maturity of thought.

The importance of this work lies in the fact that it at times, presents some readings which have escaped the notice of the great scholars like Dr. Bühler, A. Führer and the help rendered by Kullūka for interpreting some baffling passages of *Dharma-Śāstra* can hardly be gainsaid by any comparative student of *Dharma-Śāstra* and *Pūrva-Mīmāṁsā.*

Kullūka as the interpreter of some *Purāṇic* passages and the *Smṛti* works or the *Dharma-Sūtra* works will be a further topic for research and the present author notes here his willingness to discuss all such topics in the future research activities likely to be undertaken for the thorough justice to Kullūka.

This work further reveals that Kullūka has made changes in his *Manvarthamuktāvalī*, improvement and even welcome addition to some of the topics of *Śrāddha* particularly from the point of view of *Mīmāṁsā* interpretation and the senses attached to the words in the text of the *Manu-Smṛti.*

It is pity that this work is hardly quoted in the vast *Dharma-Śāstra* literature. It is Kāśīnātha Upādhyāya who in his *Dharma-Sindhu* has quoted Kullūka, the author of the *Śrāddha-Sāgara* in the plural number, thereby recording his respect for him.

If, however, the treatment given to the topics in the *Śrāddha-Sāgara* is compared with the topics that are generally discussed in other *Śrāddha*-works, one notices the following peculiarities.

Though Kullūka has looked upon Lakṣmīdhara's *Kṛtyakalpataru-Śrāddha-Kāṇḍa* as a model for his work, yet there are some topics in the latter which are not at all touched by him. One can here refer to the topics such as *Havīṁṣi, Vivarjyāni, ātithyam, pariveṣaṇavidhi, bhojana-vidhi* and *jīvat-śrāddha-vidhi* which are not at all discussed by Kullūka in his *Śrāddha-Sāgara.*

One may here incidentally add that his discussion on the *Pārvaṇa* and *Ekoddiṣṭa* modes of *Śrāddha* is not at all full of *Pūrva-Mīmāṁsā* discussion as is the case with the *Mitākṣarā* on the *Yājñvalkya-Smṛti.*

In addition to this, one may point out that Nīlakaṇṭha in his

Śrāddha-Mayūkha has also discussed some topics at good length. Kullūka, however, has omitted some such topics as *piṇḍadāna udakumbha-śrāddha, jaladhenu-vidhi, mṛtaśayyādāna vidhi, sanyāsāṅga-śrāddha,* the rules to be observed by the *brāhmaṇa* who are fed at the *Srāddha*-ceremony, and the smaller topics such the *Śrāddha* to be performed if the day of death of a person is not known or the month unknow. etc.

Raghunandana in his *Śrāddha-Tattva* has also discussed the *Śrāddha* section in details. The Appendix 'F' to this work will show how some of the *Smṛti-Tattvas* are particularly before the mind of the author of *Śrāddha-Sāgara.* From the *Śrāddha-Tattva* of Raghunandana, however, Kullūka has dropped the chapters on the vessels to be used in the *Śrāddha* (*pātrāṇi*), the use of the sacred thread (*yajñopavitāni*) and the details in respect of the *Śrāddha* to be performed at the sacred places otherwise known as *Tīrthakṣetrāṇi.*

One may also refer to the topics which are discussed at length in the *Smṛticandrikā-Śrāddha-Kāṇḍa* of Devaṇṇabhaṭṭa but there are some topics in this work which are not at all discussed by Kullūkabhaṭṭa. Here a mention can be made of the topics of the disposal of the *piṇḍas* at the end of the *Śrāddha, anna-vikiraṇādi* — the activities to be undertaken by the *yajamāna* on the preceding day of the *Śrāddha* ceremony, and also the activities to be undertaken on the succeeding day of the *Śrāddha.* He has also not discussed the topic of the *Śrāddha* which is of a subsidiary nature and the time for the same.

From the contents of the *Śrāddha-Sāgara*, it is further evident that the topic Nos. 1, 2, 3, 4, 5, 6, 8, 9, 10, 11, 12, 13 etc. are given by Kullūkabhaṭṭa very meagre treatment. It is further evident that he has given very elaborate treatment to some of the topics like *Maghātrayodaśī Śrāddha*, and the *Ekoddiṣṭa Śrāddha* in comparison with the treatment given to these topics by other writers on *Dharma-Śāstra.*

In conclusion, one will have to admit that though some of the important topics on *Śrāddha* do not find any discussion in the *Śrāddha-Sāgara* of Kullūkabhaṭṭa, yet some topics are elaborately treated by him. The supreme importance of the work *Śrāddha-Sāgara* lies from the point of view of the *Mīmāṁsā* doctrines appealed to by him and particularly in comparison with the works of his predecessors. Kullūka's original contribution to the proper sense of the words in the quoted texts will form another topic for further research. The readings recorded by him and the authorities quoted by him indeed betray some limitations and wide scope of the knowledge of the author, though in fact he has not made the specific mention of the several works on *Śrāddha.* His work also bears testimony to his mind which displays his eagerness to revise, improve and add to the matter which is presented by him many many years ago. Hence Kullūka impresses the readers by his ardent desire for truth, thought on *Mīmāṁsā* technical points he has not exhibited his acuteness and minuteness of intellect by contradicting or challenging the accepted authorities like Vijñāneśvara, Kamalākarabhaṭṭa, Nīlakaṇṭha, Mitramiśra and others. In fine, one will have to appreciate that the position of the work *Śrāddha-Sāgara* coming from the pen of the author of the illustrious commentator of the *Manu-Smṛti* and particularly as the product of his mature genius can hardly be gainsaid by any critical student of *Dharma-Śāstra* and *Pūrva-Mīmāṁsā.*

10

Chronological Dates of the Authorities quoted by Kullūkabhaṭṭa in his *Śrāddha-Sāgara*

IT may be noted here that these dates are taken from MM. Dr. P.V. Kane's *History of Dharma-Śāstra*.

800 B.C.-400 B.C.	*Śrauta Sūtra* works like *Āśvalāyana, Baudhāyana, Kātyāyana* etc.
600 B.C.-300 B.C.	*Gautama, Āpastaṁba, Vasiṣṭha* and *Baudhāyana Dharma-Sūtras.*
500 B.C.-300 B.C.	Jaimini's *Pūrva-Mīmāṁsā Sūtras.*
150 B.C.	The *Mahābhāṣya* of Pātañjali.
200 B.C.-100 A.D.	The *Manu-Smṛti.*
100 A.D.-300 A.D.	*Yājñavalkya-Smṛti.*
100 A.D.-300 A.D.	*Viṣṇu Smṛti* or *Viṣṇu Dharma-Sūtra.*
300 A.D.-600 A.D.	Some of the extant *Purāṇas* such as *Vāyu, Viṣṇu, Mārkaṇḍeya, Matsya, Kūrma.*
900 A.D.	*Medhātithi.*
1080-1140 A.D.	Govindarāja, the commentator of the *Manu-Smṛti.*

1100-50 A.D.	Lakṣmīdhara, the author of the *Kṛtyakalpataru-Śrādddha-Kāṇḍa, Vrata Khaṇḍa* etc.
1290-1370 A.D.	Caṇḍeśvara, the author of the *Rājanītiratnākara, Vivādaratnākara* etc.
1500-59 A.D.	Vācaspatimiśra, the author of the *Vivādacintāmaṇi* and several other works.
1520-75 A.D.	Raghunandana, the author of the *Smṛti-Tattvas.*
1610-40 A.D.	Kamalākarabhaṭṭa, the author of the *Nirṇayasindhu* etc.
1615-45 A.D.	Nīlakaṇṭha, the author of the *Śrāddha Mayūkha, Ācāra Mayūkha, Vyavahāra-Mayūkha* etc.
7th century A.D. (latter half of the 7th century A.D.)	*Devī-Purāṇa.*
9th century A.D.	*Narasiṁha-Purāṇa.*
Later than 900 A.D. and earlier than 1500 A.D.	*Padma-Purāṇa.*
Between 10th century and 12th century A.D.	*Brahma-Purāṇa.*
Not later than 1000 A.D.	*Bhaviṣya-Purāṇa.*
Between 4th and 6th century A.D.	*Matsya-Purāṇa.*
Between 4th and 6th century A.D.	*Mārkaṇḍeya-Purāṇa.*
Earlier than 10th century A.D.	*Varāha-Purāṇa.*
600 A.D. and 900 A.D.	*Vāmana-Purāṇa.*

350 A.D. to 550 A.D.	*Vāyu-Purāṇa.*
300 A.D. to 500 A.D.	*Viṣṇu-Purāṇa.*
Between 200 A.D. and 300 A.D.	*Viṣṇudharmottara-Purāṇa.* (According to Prof. R.C. Hazra).
Between 600 A.D. and 1000 A.D.	*Viṣṇudharmottara-Purāṇa* (According to Dr. P.V. Kane)
1250 A.D.-1325 A.D.	*Viṣṇudharmottara-Purāṇa* (According to Dr. Ashok Chatterji Shastri)
Earlier than 1250 A.D.	Jikana.
Between 900 A.D. and 1100 A.D.	Lollaṭa.
1513 A.D. to 1570 A.D.	Nārāyaṇabhaṭṭa.
1790 A.D.	Kāśīnātha Upādhyāya, the author of *Dharma-Sindhu.*
Not later than 1100 A.D.	Kāmadhenu.

The Dates of the Authors Quoted in This Work

1590-1630 A.D.	Nandapaṇḍita, the author of *Dattaka, Mīmāṁsā* and *Keśava Vaijayantī.*
1500-40 A.D.	Govindānanda, author of *Śrāddha-Krīyā-Kaumudī.*
1560-20 A.D.	Śaṅkarabhaṭṭa, the author of *Dharma-Dvaita-Nirṇaya.*
1500-50 A.D.	Vardhamāna Upādhyāya, author of *Daṇḍaviveka.*

PART II

कुल्लूकभट्टविरचित

श्राद्धसागर

Śrāddha-Sāgara

of

Kullūkabhaṭṭa

(critically edited text)

१

श्राद्धमाहात्म्यम्

ओँ नमो महामायायै ।

विलोक्य धर्मशास्त्राणि वेदार्थानि च तत्त्वतः ।
क्रियते स्मृतितन्त्राणां सागरस्य मयाधुना ॥१॥
समीक्ष्य तन्त्राणि मया मुनीनां
यदत्र भट्टादिमिरुक्तमेतत् ।
न तन्मनोहारि सतां कदाचित्
सम्भाव्यते मे वचनप्रमाणम् ॥२॥
कुल्लूकेन मया ज्ञातं स्मृतिकारणम् ।
तदर्थं क्रियते धीराद्बोध्यं ज्ञानसमाधिना ॥३॥
क्विदसागरो[1] ज्ञेयस्तथा श्राद्धपदस्य च ।
अशौचसागर[2]श्चापि क्रियते पितुराज्ञया ॥४॥

तथा च मनु[3]:

श्राद्धशब्दं कर्म प्रोवाच प्रजनिःश्रेयसार्थम् । तत्र पितरो देवता ब्राह्मणाश्चा[4]हवनीयार्थे । मासि मास्य[5]परपक्षस्य परत्वे:[6] श्रेयानित्यापस्तम्ब स्वरसात । पितॄनुद्दिश्य द्रव्यत्यागो ब्राह्मणस्वीकारपर्यन्त[7]श्च श्राद्धम् । देवे श्राद्ध[8] तु[9] श्राद्धशब्दो गौणस्तद्धर्म प्राप्त्यर्थः । कौण्डपायिनामयन[10] इवाग्निहोत्रशब्दः ।

---

1. P.V. Kane — *History of Dharma-Śāstra,* Vol. I, Part II, p. 758 suggests that this work is *विवादसागर* and not *क्विदसागर* which is corrupt.
2. *Ibid.*, p. 758 reads आशौचसागर for अशौचसागर.
3. This view of मनु is quoted in the *आपस्तम्ब धर्मसूत्र,* II. 7.16.1-5, pp. 76-77.
4. *Ibid.*, p. 76 reads ० तु ० for ० च ०.
5. *Ibid.*, p. 76 reads कार्यं after मासि which is dropped here.
6. *Ibid.*, p. 77 reads अपराह्णः for परत्वे:
7. The expression पितॄनुद्दिश्य up to पर्यन्त is found in *कृत्यकल्पतरु-श्राद्धकाण्ड*, p. 4.
8. *कृत्यकल्पतरु-श्राद्धकाण्ड,* p. 5 reads देवश्राद्धादौ for देवश्राद्ध and explanation of कुल्लुक agrees with that of *कृत्यकल्पतरु-श्राद्धकाण्ड.*
9. *Ibid.*, p. 5 reads अन्यत्र before तु of our ms.
10. *Ibid.*, p. 5 reads होम after oo of our ms. The word होम is dropped in our ms.

श्राद्धमिति शब्दो वाचको यस्य तत्तथा । त्यक्तद्रव्यप्रतिपत्तिस्थानत्वेन[1]। ब्राह्मणस्याहवनीय तुल्यतेति । तन्न । देवश्राद्धस्य श्राद्धशब्दानभिधेयत्वे दैविकं दशमं स्मृतमिति श्राद्धभेदत्वानुपपत्तेः । किं च

प्रास्येदग्नौ तदन्नन्तु[2] दद्याद्वा ब्रह्मचारिणः[3] ।५।

इति वशिष्ठवचनाद्ब्राह्मणासम्पत्तावग्निप्रतिपत्ति पक्षेष्व व्याप्तेः । किं च पिण्डपितृयज्ञस्य ब्राह्मणा प्रतिपत्तिपर्यन्तत्वाभावात् श्राद्धरूपता न स्यत् । न स्यादेवश्चेन्न । पिण्डपितृयज्ञमभिधाय तत् श्राद्धमितरामावास्यायामिति गोभिलविरोधात् ।

पिण्डांस्तु गोऽजविप्रेभ्यो दद्यादग्नौ जलेऽपि वा ।६।

इति याज्ञवल्क्य (१.२५७अ) वचनस्तस्यापि ब्राह्मणपर्यन्तेति चेत् । न । पित्रबलिदान-स्यापिश्राद्धत्वापत्तेः । पिण्डवच्च पश्चिमा प्रतिपत्तिरिति छन्दोगपरिशिष्टे कृता । तस्यापि ब्राह्मणप्रतिपत्ति-देशात् । किं च पितृगतफलाभिसन्धाने हिरण्यदानादावतिव्याप्तेः । किं च वक्ष्यमाणैकरूपेशा[4] देवश्राद्धादौ मुख्यत्वसंभवे गौणत्वमन्याय्यं उच्यते । सम्बोधनपदोपनीतान् पित्रादीन् चतुर्थन्त[5]पदेनोद्दिश्य हविस्त्यागं श्राद्धम् । अतो न हिरण्यदानादावतिव्याप्तिः । नापि देवश्राद्ध पिण्डपितृयज्ञादावव्याप्तिः । एवमृषिमनुजादि श्राद्धे श्राद्धशब्दो मुख्यः स्यात् ।

यथा सन्यासं प्रकृत्य नरसिंहपुरारो[6]

दिव्यपितृभ्यो देवेभ्यः इव पितृभ्यश्च यत्नतः[7]।
दत्वा श्राद्धमृषिभ्यश्च मनुजेभ्यस्तथात्मने ॥७॥

ननु श्राद्धं यागदानहोमानां किं रूपं त्यागस्य चैतत् प्रकारत्रितयान्यरूपं तेषामधिकरणे दर्शितम् ।

अत्र कर्योठभट्टः[8]

यागोऽयं देवतोद्देशेन द्रव्यत्यागो याग इति यागलक्षणाव्यापनात् । तन्न् । यागोद्देश्या देवता । देवतोद्देशेन द्रव्यत्यागो याग इत्यन्योन्याश्रयणापत्तेः । न च हविः प्रत्युद्देश्यत्वं देवतात्वम् । घृतादिदाने ब्राह्मणस्य तथात्वापत्तेः । न च हूयत इति हविरिति व्युत्पत्त्याग्निप्रक्षणोपहित त्यागकर्मत्वं हविस्त्वं घृतादीनां दानविषये नास्तीति वाच्यम् । पदे जुहोति, वर्त्मनि जुहोति इत्यादावव्याप्तेः । अपितो[9] (अत्र पितृ)[10] द्देश्यत्वं यदि प्रयोजनत्वं यागोत्पत्तेः । प्रागबुद्धिदत्वम्वा[11] उभयथा पूर्वेति व्याप्तिः । न च त्यागं प्रति

1. The expression from श्राद्धमिति up to स्थानत्वेन is found in *कृत्यकल्पतरु-श्राद्धकाण्ड*, p. 4.
2. *वसिष्ठ धर्मसूत्र*, XI.31 reads तदन्नं वा for तदन्नन्तु.
3. *Ibid.*, p. 31 reads ब्रह्मचारिणे for ब्रह्मचारिणा.
4. The expression ०एकरूपेशा appears to be corrupt. Is it possible to take it as ०एकरूपैषा?
5. This may be emended as चतुर्थ्यन्त for चतुर्थन्त which is corrupt.
6. This may be emended as *नरसिंहपुराणे* for नरसिंहपुरारो on the strength of *श्राद्धप्रकाश*, p. 4.
7. *Ibid*, p. 4 reads स्वपितृभ्यस्तथैव च for इव पितृभ्यश्च यत्नतः.
8. This may be emended as कैयटभट्टः in view of its references at three other places in the *श्राद्धसागर*.
9. The word अपितो is corrupt and conveys no good sense.
10. The words अत्र पितृ in the bracket, if taken out of bracket, would yield a good sense.
11. Is it possible to emend this as ००दत्तं वा for ००दत्वम्वा ?

चतुर्थ्यन्तपदनिर्देशत्वम् । देवता स्वस्वगतोद्देशेन द्रव्यत्यागेकृते तस्य देवतापत्तेः । न च वेदमेय[1] चतुर्थ्यन्तपदनिर्देशत्वं देवतात्वम् । धृतिहोमे धृती । त्यागी नाम देवतात्वप्रसङ्गात् । तत्र चतुर्थीनिषेधात्।

यथा छन्दोगपरिशिष्टम् –

धृतिहोमेन प्रयुञ्जाद् गोनामसु तथाष्टसु ।
चतुर्थीमघ्न इत्येतद् गोनामसु हि हूयते ॥८॥

किं च दाने चतुर्थान्तर पदनिर्देश्यत्वस्य वेदमेयत्वादिति व्याप्तेः ।

यथा तेनैव अहमस्मै ददानी एवमाभाष्य दीयते । तस्माद्देवतोक्तम् । उदगाह पशुदक्षिणादिभिर्नीयते यागः ।

गोभिलेनापि पशुक्षीराज्यादिभिर्होमकरणादिभिर्नियतैरुपकरणैः काम्यनैमित्तिकान्तं दक्षिणादिभिः समापनं यजनम् । एतेन याजनं व्याख्यातम् । अतो न यागरूपता होमरूपता च यागावान्तर प्रकारत्वात्तस्य याग एव — विशिष्टादशपक्षोपाहत[2] (पक्षेपोपहित[3]) होमं इत्युक्तत्वात् । न च दानरूपता पित्रादित्रादि[4]गत स्वामित्वाजनकत्वात् । अस्वामित्वं च पित्रादीनां ममेदमिति स्वीकारभावात् । आदित्यादि संप्रदानकदाने दानशब्दो गौणः । तद्धर्म दक्षिणादानाद्यतिदेशार्थः । देशग्रामो हस्तिग्राम प्रयोगस्तु गौण एवेत्युक्तं तिर्यगधिकरणे[5]। उच्यते । एवं विद्वान् पितॄन् यजते, पितृभ्यो दद्यात्, हूयते च इति त्रितयपदन[6]-प्रयोगदर्शनात्रितयलक्षणव्यापनाच्च यागदानरूपत्वमस्य पितरो देवता ब्राह्मणाश्चहवनीया[7] इत्यापस्तम्बेनैव पूर्वैरप्युक्तं लक्षणम् । देवतापूजापि याग एव । मातृयागः शचीयागः इति पूजायां देवतात्वं च । देवमेयत्यागोद्देश्यत्वं उद्देश्यत्वं तस्येदमित्यारोपज्ञानविषयत्वम् । ब्राह्मणश्चाहवनीय इत्यनेन स्वामित्वजनकस्त्यागो दानमिति दानलक्षणं उक्तम् । तद्गतस्वामित्वजनकत्वात् न तु उद्देश्यगतत्वमिति तत्र विशेषणमव्यावर्तकत्वात् । द्वितीयायाः क्रियाफलं विरोधकत्वे इप्सि[8]तत्त्वमिव अस्ति चोद्देश्यनापि ब्राह्मणस्य तद्गतस्वामित्वाभिसन्धानेन द्रव्यत्यागात् । पित्र्यपेक्षया यागत्वं, ब्राह्मणापेक्षया दानत्वं च प्रतियोगिभेदान्न विरुद्धम् । भ्रान्तिज्ञानस्यैव परमते प्रमाणाप्रमाणता अनुमानस्यैव । स्वमते आत्मत्वार्थांशे प्रत्यक्षरूपता अविरूद्धशंकरोत्तरस्यैव । मिथ्योत्तरस्यापि कारणोत्तरतांशभेदात् ब्राह्मणस्य संप्रदानकत्वे कथं पितृभ्यो दद्यादिति चतुर्थी चेत् ? न हीयं मुख्यसंप्रदाने चतुर्थी । किन्तु वनिराकर्तृके[9] तच्च गौणमेवेति न विरोधः। देवलवचनं तु प्रत्येकसमुदायाभ्यां दर्शपौर्णमासादव्यापकत्वान्न लक्षणपरम् । किन्तु वोजनं (याजनं)[10] योनिसंबन्धं स्वाध्यायं सहभोजनं कृत्वा सद्यः पतन्त्येते पतितेन न संशयः । स्वयमुक्त सद्यः

1. The expression वेदमेय is corrupt and is it possible to read it as वेद्यमेव for वेदमेय?
2. This expression is corrupt.
3. This appears to be a marginal note.
4. The word ०त्रादि० appears to be redundant.
5. This has a reference to *जैमिनि's पूर्वमीमांसा,* VI.1.2.
6. This may be emended as त्रितयपद for त्रितयपदन. 'न' is redundant here.
7. The line पितरो देवता etc. is a quotation from the *आपस्तम्ब-धर्मसूत्र,* II.7.16 (p. 76).
8. This may be emended as ईप्सितत्त्वमिव for इप्सितत्त्वमिव.
9. The expression वनिराकर्तृके appears to be corrupt.
10. The word याजनं in bracket appears to be the reading in view of the context and the reading वोजनं appears to be misleading and corrupt.

पतनहेतुयाजनपदस्य गुरुतरयाजनविशेषोपसंहारार्थं न तद् यजनमेव भवतीति तस्यार्थः । इतरथा प्राग् यज्ञपदार्थापरिज्ञाने आत्मश्रयापत्तेः । अत एकाचार्यकृत नियमशुश्रूषादिभिः त्रयीविद्योपादानमध्ययनमेव भवतीति । यत्तु जिकेनोक्तं[1] साक्षात् परस्मरोदासीन-उद्देश्यगत भोगजनकस्त्यागो दानमिति दानलक्षणम् । भोगं च परंपरया पित्रादीनां श्रयते[2]।

यथा विष्णुपुराणम् —

श्रद्धासम्मनितैर्दत्तं पितॄणां नाम गोत्रतः।
यदा हारास्तु ते जातास्तदाहारत्वमेति तत् ॥९॥

यथा मत्स्यपुराणम् — (२०.७अ-९अ)

देवो यदि पिता जातः शुभकर्मानुयोगतः ।
तस्यान्नममृतं भूत्वा देवत्वे[3]ऽप्यनुगच्छति ॥१०॥
देवत्वे[4] भोगरूपेण पशुत्वे च तृणं भवेत् ।
श्राद्धं तु[5] वायुरूपेण नागत्वे[6]ऽप्यनुतिष्ठति[7] ॥११॥
दनुजत्वे तथा मद्यं[8] प्रेतत्वे रूधिरोदकम् ।
मनुष्यत्वेऽन्नापान्नादि नानाभोगरसं भवेत् ॥१२॥

तच्चिन्त्यम् । प्रतिग्रहीता भुक्तनष्टधने लक्षणाव्याप्तेः । किं चैवमादीनामपि बहुशो भोगः ।

श्रुतेर्यागोऽपि दानं स्यात् । स्तुतिमात्रं तदिति चेत् । प्रकृतेऽपि तुल्यत्वात् बाधकाभावात् । नेह स्तुतिलक्षणेति चेत् । न । यागोऽपि तुल्यत्वत्वाविग्रहवत्वं चेन्द्रादीनामपि तिर्यगाधिकरणे[9] दर्शितम् । देवतात्वं च तथा विधानानेष्टमिति[10] ।

ननु इन्द्रादीनां विग्रहवत्वे किं प्रमाणम्? अर्थवाद इति चेत् । न । तस्य सिद्धेऽर्थे प्रामाण्यात् । कथं वा विग्रहवतामदेवतात्वम्? ऐन्द्रं हविरित्यादौ तद्धिताभिः प्रकृत्यर्थस्य देवतात्वबोधनात् । इन्द्रादिपदानि च सहस्त्रचरादिमतीषु व्यक्तिषु मुख्यानि । मुख्यपरत्वे लक्षणाप्रसङ्गात् ।

उच्यते । ऐन्द्रादिपदकामाधिकारिक विधिवाक्यानि श्रुतिपरं च प्रमाणम् । स्वर्गे शरीरेऽप्यनाश्वासः स्यात् । यत्राप्यनुवादात् ऐन्द्रादिपदप्राप्ति-अवगतिः । तत्रापि तत् फलत्वे रात्रिसत्र[11] एव प्रमाणम् ।

---

1. It is better to emend this as जिकनेन for जिकेन, in view of references to this word in other places in the manuscript *श्राद्धसागर*.
2. Is it possible to emend श्रूयते for श्रयते?
3. *मत्स्यपुराण*, 20.7a (p. 33) reads दिव्यत्वे for देवत्वे.
4. *Ibid*., 20.7b. reads दैत्यत्वे for देवत्वे.
5. *Ibid*., 20.8a. reads श्राद्धान्नं for श्राद्धं तु.
6. *Ibid*., 0.8a. reads सर्पत्वे for नागत्वे.
7. *Ibid*., 20.8a. reads ०उपतिष्ठति for ०अनुतिष्ठति.
8. *Ibid*., 20.9a. reads माया for मद्यम्.
9. This may be emended as तिर्यगधिकरणे for तिर्यगाधिकरणे.
10. The expression विधानानेष्टमिति appears to be corrupt.
11. This refers to the रात्रिसत्रन्याय in *जैमिनि, पूर्वमीमांसा*, IV.I3.17.

विग्रहवतामिन्द्रादीनां सन्निधानस्य प्रत्यक्षबाधितत्वेन तथा विधानात् । द्रव्यत्वासंभवात् अगत्या तदाकारतया आध्मातस्य मन्त्रस्य लक्षितस्य देवतात्वमिति । लक्षितं रहस्यं इन्द्राकारतया आधमानात् इन्द्रप्रीतिरपि उपपन्ना ।

तथा च योगियाज्ञवल्क्यः[1]

यस्य यस्य तु मन्त्रस्य उद्दिष्टा या च देवता ।
तदाकारं भवेत्तस्य देवत्वं देवतोच्यते ॥१३॥

ननु देवानां विग्रहवत्वे तेषामेवाराधितानां फलदातृत्वं कुतो न भवेदलमपूर्वकल्पनया ।

तथा भविष्यपुराणे —

यद् यद् द्रव्यं नरो तूष्णमादित्याय प्रयच्छति ।
तत्तस्य शतसाहस्रमुत्पादयति भास्करः ॥१४॥

याज्ञवल्क्यः (१.२७०)

आयुः प्रजां धनं विद्यां स्वर्गं मोक्षं सुखानि च ।
प्रयच्छन्ति तथा राज्यं प्रीता नृणां पितामहाः ॥१५॥

तदा च देवताधिकरणसिद्धान्तविरोधः स्यात् । उच्यते । देवानामिन्द्रादीनां पितॄणां वरस्वादीनां युगमन्वन्तरादि भेदेन नानाद्वारगम्यं फलोदयकाले पूर्वस्यच्युताधिकारत्वेन फलदातृत्वाशक्तेरन्यस्य चानावधिसत्वेन फलदातृत्वायोगात् । तत्रापूर्वे शब्दशक्तौ वाचकशब्दसद्भावात् सर्वत्र तदभिधानम् । अत एव काम्ये क्लृप्तशक्तिर्लिङ्गादिनित्ये निषेधे चापूर्वमाहइत्युक्तम् । एवं च अपूर्वानुप्रवेशात् सहकारि तथा यदि वेतापि फलदात्री क्वचित् को विरोधः? किन्तु ब्राह्मणसम्प्रदानक हिरण्यदानादौ ब्राह्मणस्य कालान्तरे फलदातृत्वमसंभवात् अवश्यमदृष्टं वाच्यम् । तथा च पूर्वोक्तरीत्या सर्वत्रैव तत्सिद्धिः । देवतां प्रति सहकृतजनितापूर्वस्य फलदातृत्वाद्धेतावपि फलदात्रीत्युच्यते ।

ननु पित्रादीनां न निरपेक्षाणां देवतात्वम् ।

अथ श्राद्धममावास्यायां पितृभ्यो दद्यादिति गौतम (१५.१) वचने, पितृभ्यो दद्यात् पूर्वेद्युर्ब्राह्मणान् सन्निपात्येति[1] वसिष्ठ (११.१७) वचने च बहुवचनात् साहित्यप्रतीतेः । साहित्यो हि द्विवचन बहुवचने द्वंद्वसमासो वा इति दर्शितत्वात् । परस्परसापेक्षाणां 'पितरो देवता' इत्यापस्तम्ब (२.७. १६.३)[3] वचने देवता इति बहुवचनात् प्रत्येकं देवतात्वावगमात् प्राङ्निवेशितत्वात् । बहुत्वस्य तथार्ध्यो दानान्नोत्सर्ग पिण्डदानेषु श्रुतौ स्मृतौ च बहुशः प्रत्येकं एव देवतात्वमवगम्यते ।

यथा श्रुतिः[4] —

---

1. This stanza is not found in the *योगयाज्ञवल्क्य*, edited by P.C. Divanji.
2. Here कुल्लूक connects some portion of the *वसिष्ठधर्मसूत्र,* XI.16 and XI.17 together.
3. Here कुल्लूक has not given the complete citation from the *आपस्तम्ब,* He omits the expression ब्राह्मणस्त्वाहनीयार्थे.
4. This श्रुति passage is found quoted in *श्राद्धप्रकाश,* p. 8.

असावेतत्ते इति यजमानस्य पित्रे असावेतत्त इति पितामहाय इति बैजवापः ।
पितरे तत्तेऽर्घ्यं पितामहैतत्तेऽर्घं प्रपितामहै तत्तेऽर्घं इत्यनुदितिशति[1]।

तथा विष्णुः[2]—

नमो विश्वेभ्यो देवेभ्यो इत्यनुमानादौ[3] प्राङ्मुखयोर्ब्राह्मणयोर्निवेद्य[4] पित्रे पितामहाय प्रपितामहाय च नामगोत्राभ्यामुदन्मुखेषु ।

ब्रह्मपुराणे[5] —

पितृभ्यश्च ततो दद्यात् अनुमामन्त्रशो न[6] तु ।
अमुकामुकगौत्रैस्त[7]तुभ्यमन्नं स्वधा नमः ॥१६॥

विष्णुः — (७३.१७-१९)

उच्छिष्टसन्निधौ दक्षिणाग्रेषु[8] पृथिवी दवि[9]रक्षितामित्येकं पिण्डं पित्रे निदध्यात् । अन्तरिक्षं दर्वि रक्षितामिति द्वितीयं पिण्डं पितामहाय[10]दर्वि रक्षितामिति तृतीयं पिण्डं प्रपितामहायेत्यादि ।

कात्यायनः —

पितृभ्यः पितामहेभ्यः प्रपितामहेभ्यः स्वधोच्यतामित्यादि ।

अत्रोभयोरेव प्रामाणिकत्वात् विकल्प इति केचित् । वस्तुतस्तु सहितानां देवतात्वे प्रमाणं नास्ति । न हि पितृभ्यो दद्यादिति चतुर्थी देवतात्वं कथयन्ति, तत्रानुशासनात् । किन्तु यदग्नये च प्रजापतये च सायंप्रातर्जुहोति इति वत् चतुर्थ्यवगता निराकर्तृकसंप्रदानानुपपत्त्या कल्पनीयम् । न च तत् सहितानां कल्पयितुं शक्यते । पूर्वोप[11]दर्शितवचनैर्निरपेक्षदेवतात्वावगमात् । साहित्यं तु अभिधानक्रियापेक्षया लोके दृष्टम् । गर्गा भोज्यन्तामित्यादौ श्रुतौ च क्षैमेवसाना[12]रग्निमादधीयताम् । अत्र भोजनावसानयोः प्रत्येक परिसमाप्तत्वे न तदपेक्षया साहित्यासम्भवात् ।

---

1. Is it possible to emend this as इत्यतिदिशति for as इत्यनुदितिशति ?
2. This citation from *विष्णु,* can be traced in the extant *विष्णुस्मृति,* 73.13-14 and *कृत्यकल्पतरु-श्राद्धकाण्ड,* p. 183.
3. *कृत्यकल्पतरु-श्राद्धकाण्ड,* p. 183 reads ०अन्नमादौ for ०अनुमानादौ.
4. *Ibid.*, p. 183 reads निवेदयेत् for निवेद्य.
5. The text of *ब्रह्मपुराण* is quoted in *कृत्यकल्पतरु-श्राद्धकाण्ड,* p. 184.
6. *Ibid.*, p. 184 reads अन्नमामन्त्रणेन for अनुमामन्त्रशो न.
7. *Ibid.*, p. 184 reads ००गोत्रैतत् for ००गोत्रैस्तत्.
8. *विष्णुस्मृति,* 73.17 reads कुशेषु before पृथिवी; our manuscript omits कुशेषु.
9. It is better to emend दवि as दर्वि in view of its use immediately in the text and also in *विष्णुस्मृति,* 73.17, p. 765.
10. *विष्णुस्मृति,* p. 765 reads द्यौः before दर्वि.
11. The expression पूर्वोप appears to be corrupt and defective.
12. The expression क्षैमेवसान appears to be corrupt.

अत एव परिषदधि[1]करणे सप्तदशशाखात् ऋद्धिकामा सत्र अपासीवन्निति प्रत्येकपरिसमाप्तत्वात् फलस्य न परिषदोऽधिकार इत्युक्तम् । अतः साहित्यमन्यथाप्युपपठ्यमानं प्रमाणसिद्धं देवतानैरपेक्ष्यं वारितुमीष्टे । ननु विधिवाक्यस्थत्वाच्च साहित्यमेव बलवत् अर्घ्यानोत्सर्ग पिण्डदानादि मन्त्रावगतं नैरपेक्ष्यं, बाधतां मन्त्रस्य । विधि सापेक्षत्वात् । दृष्टा च अग्निषोमीयं पशुमालभतेत्यत्र उत्पत्तिविशिष्ट देवतासाहित्यविरोधात् केवलाग्निपदवतिमनोहामन्त्रे सोमसाहित्यलक्षणा । तन्न । पितरो देवता इति तद्धित समानार्थ देवतापदात्, प्रत्येकं देवता द्वारगमात्, तद्विरोधात्र चतुर्थीतः साहित्यकल्पना दुर्बलत्वात् । यदाहुः—

तद्धितेन चतुर्थ्या वा मन्त्रलिङ्गेन बोध्यते ।
देवतासङ्गतिस्तत्र दुर्बलं तु परं परम् ॥१७॥

अन्ये तु एकब्राह्मणपक्षे समुदितमनेक ब्राह्मणपक्षे चासमुदितन्धत्वं वर्णयन्ति । न तु शब्दानुपात्ताभिधानक्रियापेक्षया साहित्यमुक्तम् । अगत्या हि गर्गा भोज्यन्तामित्यादौ तथेति । तन्न उक्तम् । उक्तेर्देवता साहित्यानवगमाद्द्वयवयस्थाया निर्वासनत्वाच्च ।

किं च 'पितृभ्यो दद्यात् पूर्वेद्युः ब्राह्मणान् सन्निपात्येति वशिष्ठ (११.१७) वचने ब्राह्मणानिति बहुवचनात् अनेकब्राह्मणपक्षे एव साहित्यश्रुतेः । शब्दानुपपत्तित्वं च उद्देश्य क्रियाया अपि अविशिष्टं धातोस्त्यागमात्रपरत्वात् । एतेनेदं निरस्तम् । समुदितदैवतं श्राद्धं असमुदितदैवतत्वं समुच्चये वैकस्मिन्नेव प्रयोगे कर्तव्यमिति एव समुदितासमुदितपक्षाभ्यां ब्राह्मणद्वये चतुष्टये वा —

द्वौ दैवे पितृकृत्ये[2] त्रीणि[3] एकैकमुभयत्र वा ।१८।

इति मनुवचन (३.१२५) विरोधात् । तत्र पितरो देवताः पितृभ्यो दद्यादिति विधिवाक्य अर्घ्यदानान्नोतसर्ग पिण्डदानादिमन्त्रेषु च पानी निरपेक्षामेव । पित्रादीनि कीर्तनान्न सपत्नीकानि देवतात्वम्[4]।

तथा [5]

न योषिद्भ्यः पृथक् दद्यात् अवसानदिनाद्धते[6] ।
सभर्तृ[7]पिण्डमात्राभ्यस्तृप्तिरासां यतः स्मृता ॥१९॥ इति ।

छन्दोगपरिशिष्टवचने अवसानदिनव्यतिरेकेन[8] योषितं दाननिषेधान्न पत्नीविशिष्टस्य देवतात्वम् । पत्नी विशिष्टस्या हि देवतात्वे तद्दानं पत्न्या अपि स्यात् ।

---

1. This has a reference to *जैमिनि's पूर्वमीमांसा.*
2. *मनुस्मृति,* III.125 reads पितृकार्ये for पितृकृत्ये.
3. *Ibid.*, reads त्रीन् for त्रीणि.
4. The comments of कुल्लूक on *मनुस्मृति,* III.125 are different from those in his *मन्वर्थमुक्तावली.*
5. By the word तथा, the stanza that is quoted below is from the text *शातातप* quoted in *कृत्यकल्पतरु-श्राद्धकाण्ड*, p. 5.
6. *Ibid.*, p. 5 reads ००क्रते for ००धृते which is corrupt.
7. *Ibid.*, p. 5 and *श्राद्धप्रकाश*, p. 9 read स्वभर्तृ०० for सभर्तृ००.
8. This may be emended as ००व्यतिरेकेण for ००व्यतिरेकेन.

अत्र हेतुमाह । स्वभर्तृपिण्डभागादेव तत्तृप्तेः । विशिष्टदेवतापक्षे स्वभर्तृपिण्डेति न स्यात् । तत् पिण्डदानादपि तस्य । अत हेतुमन्निग[1]धविरोधादपि न सपत्नीकस्य देवतात्वम् ।

यथा शातातपः[2] —

> सपिण्डीकरणाद्वदर्ध्व[3] यत् पितृभ्यः प्रदीयते ।
> सर्वेस्वंशहरा[4] माता इति धर्मेषु निश्चयः ॥२०॥

पितृमात्रस्यैव दाने मातुरंशहरत्वाभिधानात् । अन्यथोभयोरेवांशहरत्वाभिधानमसंगतं स्यात् । न च अंशहरत्वानुपपत्त्यैव तदुद्देशेन दानमवगम्यते । हिरण्यदाने पत्नीविशिष्टस्य ब्राह्मणानुदेशेऽपि पत्न्यास्तदंशहरत्वात् । अत एव दम्पत्योर्मध्यगं धनमित्युक्तम् ।

ननु न योषिद्भ्यः पृथग् दद्यादित्यत्र[5] पृथक् पदोपादानादेव पित्रादिविशेषणतया योषितां दानमवगम्यते । अन्यथा दानमात्रनिषेधे न पृथक् वैयर्थ्यापत्तेः । किं च पृथङ्न दद्यादिति नायं निषेधविधिः । पृथग् दानस्य शास्त्रतो रागतो वाऽप्राप्तेः । किन्तु अपृथग् दद्यादिति पर्युदासविधिस्तदा व्यक्तमेव । सहभावेन योषितां दानं हेतुमन्निगदस्त्वन्यथा व्याख्येयः । स्वपिण्डं च भर्तृपिण्डश्चेति स्वभर्तृपिण्डस्तस्य मात्राभ्यो यतस्तृप्तिरासाम् । अतोऽपृथक् पिण्डो देयः । उभयोद्देशेन देय इत्यर्थः ।

उच्यते । एवं पित्रादीनां अप्यवसान दिवादन्यतामिति चेत् । न । हेतुमन्निगधविरोधात्तदुत्तरम् । पृथग् दानाद् योषिद्भ्यः इत्यनर्थकं स्यात् । सर्वेषां पृथग् दानं विधीयते । योषित्पदमनुवादमात्रमिति चेत् । न । हेतुमन्निगदविरोधात् । तदुत्तरं पृथक्पदमनुवादोऽस्तु । योषितां दानमात्रं निषेध्यताम् । अवसानदिनादन्यत्र सामान्यतो योषितां दानप्राप्तौ कथं निषेधः पर्युदासो व इति चेत् । न । वृद्धिश्राद्धान्वष्टकादौ शाखिमात्रकर्तृकतया योषितां दानप्राप्तौ छन्दोगानां निषेधः पर्युदासो वा भविष्यति ।

यथा मत्स्यपुराणे (१७.६५ब-६६अ) —

> उत्सवानन्दसन्ताने[6] यज्ञोद्वाहादिमङ्गले ।
> मातरः प्रथमं पूज्याः पितरस्तदनन्तरम् ॥२१।

विष्णुः (७४.१) —

अन्वष्टकास्वष्टकावत्[7] हुत्वा[8] मात्रे पितामह्यै प्रपितामह्यै पूर्ववत् ब्राह्मणान् भोजयित्वेत्यादिवत् ।

यत्तु बृहपति[9]वचनम् — (श्राद्ध ८५.२९)

---

1. This has a reference to *जैमिनि, पूर्वमीमांसा.*
2. The text of शातातप is quoted in *कृत्यकल्पतरु-श्राद्धकाण्ड,* p. 258.
3. *Ibid.*, p. 258 reads ००ऊर्ध्वं for वदर्धं.
4. *Ibid.*, p. 258 reads सर्वेषु०० and *श्राद्धप्रकाश,* p. 9, reads सर्वत्रांशहरा for सर्वेसु००.
5. This refers to the text of शातातप quoted in stanza No. 19.
6. *मत्स्यपुराण,* reads ००संभारे for ००सन्ताने.
7. *विष्णुस्मृति,* p. 769 reads वह्नौ before हुत्वा and after ०अष्टकावत्.
8. *Ibid.*, p. 769 reads दैवपूर्वमेव before मात्रे and after हुत्वा.
9. The text of बृहस्पति is quoted in *कृत्यकल्पतरु-श्राद्धकाण्ड,* p. 259.

स्वेन भर्त्रा सह[1] श्राद्धं माता भुङ्क्ते स्वधामयम् ।
पितामही च स्वेनैव स्वेनैव[2] प्रपितामही ॥२२॥

इति । तद्भोजन एव सहभावं बोधयति । न दाने भोजने सहभावानुपपत्त्या दानेऽपि सहत्वं कल्पनीयमिति चेत् । न । हिरण्यदानादौ व्यभिचारात् । किं च भर्तृरिव सहभावोऽत्रावगम्यते। न पत्न्यास्तदा स्वभर्तृकार्यै मात्रे इति वाक्यं स्यात् ।

यत्तु पठन्ति —

अन्वष्टकायां वृद्धौ च गयायां मृतवासरे ।
अत्र मातुः पृथक् श्राद्धमन्यत्र पतिना सह ॥२३॥

इति । तदनाकरम् । साकरत्वेऽपि विधौ मन्त्रे च निरपेक्ष्य देवतात्वं त्ववगम्यते । भोग्यपदमध्याहार्यम्। बृहस्पतिसमानार्थम् । किञ्चैवं पत्युरेव सहभावः स्यात् न पत्न्या इति प्रागेवोक्तम् ।

ननु चित्रादीनां प्रत्येकं देवतात्वे कुशासनगन्धादिदानात् न उत्सर्गेषु तन्त्रता न स्यात् । न हि देवताभेदे तन्त्रमनुष्ठानं दृष्टं संभवति वा । देवतैक्या हि दधिपयसोन्तन्त्रमनुष्ठानं दृष्टं संभवति वा देवतैक्या हि दधिपयसोस्तन्त्रमनुष्ठानं दृष्टम् । ऐन्द्रंदध्यमावास्यायामैन्द्रं पदः अमावास्यायामित्यत्र । द्रव्यता भेदे हि द्रव्यैक्यात् कुतो न तन्त्रानुष्ठानम् । पित्रे पितामहाय प्रपितामहाय इदमन्नं स्वधेति तन्त्रे सैकोत्सर्गवाक्यमस्त्विवति चेत् । न । प्रत्येकं स्वधेति अनुषङ्गः । अनुषङ्[3]गाधिकरणन्यायाद्वाक्यभेदे कथं तन्त्रतेति ? अनुषङ्गे च सन्निधानात् प्रपितामहसम्बन्धे पित्रादीनामुत्सर्गक्रियान्वयो न स्यात् । सहितदेवतापक्षे पितृ-पितामह-प्रपितामहेभ्य एतदन्नं स्वधेति घटत एव तन्त्रता । अत एव जैमिनिराचार्यो देवताभेदे द्रव्यैक्येऽपि न तन्त्रतां क्वचिदुक्तवान् । न हि आज्यद्रव्यकानां पञ्चानां प्रयाजानामाधारयोः आज्यभागयोः अनुयाजां च तन्त्रता दृश्यते । यदि च स्यात् त्रयोदशाहेति संख्यान्वय्येत । अत्र कश्चिदाह कुशासन-गन्धादिदानोत्सर्गादिषु तन्त्रता नास्त्येव । तदसत् ।

अर्घ्येक्षय्योदके चैव पिण्डदानेऽवनेजने ।
तन्त्रस्य विनिवृत्तिः स्यात् स्वधा वाचन एव च ॥२४॥

इति छन्दोगपरिशिष्टवचने अर्घ्यादिविशेषोपादानादन्यत्र तन्त्रताप्रतीतेः ।

उच्यते । एवं मा भवतु नैयायिकी तन्त्रता । वाचनिकैव सा भविष्यति । किञ्च यदि न्यायतोऽप्राप्ता तन्त्रता कथं वचनेन निषिध्यते । किं च सेति बाधके लाघवमेव । तन्त्रता न्याये युक्तिः। सा चेहाप्यास्ति, तुभ्यमिति पदेन प्रकृतवाचिनां निरपेक्षायामेव पित्रादीनां संबोधनपदोपनीतानां तन्त्रेणोद्देश संभवात् । तन्त्रेणैव स्वधासम्बन्धाऽप्रयाजादौ तु नेतादृशी वाक्यरचना । वचनाभावात् । अत्र तु अनभिरेव सा कृता ।

यथा ब्रह्मपुराणम्[4]—

---

1. *Ibid.*, p. 259 reads समं for सह.
2. *Ibid.*, p. 259 and *श्राद्धप्रकाश*, p. 9, read तथैव for स्वेनैव.
3. This has a reference to *जैमिनि, पूर्वमीमांसा,* IX.1.46.
4. The text of *ब्रह्मपुराण* is quoted in *कृत्यकल्पतरु-श्राद्धकाण्ड,* p. 184.

पितृभ्यश्च ततो दद्यादन्नमामन्त्रणेन च[1]।
अमुकामुकगोत्रैतत्तुभ्यमन्नं स्वधा नमः ॥२५॥

इत्यादि वक्ष्यते । ननु जनकादीनां श्राद्धेन देवता नु किन्तु वसुरुद्रादित्यानां पितृ-पितामह-प्रपितामह पदोपनीतानाम् ।

यथा मनुः (३.२८४) —

वसून् वदन्ति हिं[2] पितृन् रूद्रांश्चैव पितामहान् ।
प्रपितामहांस्तथादित्यान् श्रुतिरेषा पुरातनी[3]॥२६॥

देवलः —

वसवः पितरो ज्ञेया रूद्रा ज्ञेया[4] पितामहाः ।
प्रपितामहस्तथादित्या[5] श्रुतिरेव[6] पुरातनी[7]॥२७॥

याज्ञवल्क्यः — (१.२६९)

वसुरुद्रादितिसुताः पितरः श्राद्धदेवताः ।
प्रीणयन्ति मनुष्याणां पितॄन् श्राद्धेन तर्पिताः ॥२८॥

पैठीनसिः —

क एते पितरो नाम येभ्यो दत्तमया[8]क्षयम् ।
वसवः पितरो रूद्राः प्रख्याताः स्युः पितामहाः[9] ॥२९॥

अनादित्याः प्रपितामहास्तेभ्यो दत्तमथाक्षयं भवति । उच्यते । असावेतत्ते इति यजमानस्य पित्रे असावेतत्ते इति पितामहाय, असावेतत्त इति प्रपितामहाय इत्यादि श्रुतौ जनकादीनां देवत्वादवगमविरोधान्मन्त्रादि स्मृतीनामन्यथावर्णनं कार्यम् । उक्तं हि विरोधाधिकरणे[10] श्रुत्या स्मृतिर्बाधिते।

तथा जाबालः[11]—

1. *कृत्यकल्पतरु-श्राद्धकाण्ड*, p. 184 reads तु for च.
2. *मनुस्मृति*, III.284 reads तु for हि.
3. कुल्लूक on *मनुस्मृति*, III.284 reads सनातनी for पुरातनी.
4. *कृत्यकल्पतरु-श्राद्धकाण्ड*, p. 230 reads ज्ञेयाः for ज्ञेया.
5. *Ibid.*, p. 230 reads ००आदित्याः for ००आदित्या.
6. *Ibid.*, p. 230 reads ०एषा for ०एव.
7. *Ibid.*, p. 230 reads सनातनी for पुरातनी.
8. *Ibid.*, p. 231 reads ०इह० for ०अय०. This reading is corrupt.
9. *Ibid.*, p. 231 reads पितामहा आदित्याः प्रपितामहाः for प्रख्याताः स्युः पितामहाः ।
10. This refers to *जैमिनि कृत पूर्वमीमांसा*, I.3.3.
11. The text of *जाबाल* is quoted in *पृथ्वीचन्द्र — श्राद्धप्रकाश*, II.34, p. 18.

श्रुतिस्मृतिविरोधे तु श्रुतिरेव गरीयसी ।
अविरोधे सदा कार्यं स्मार्तं वैदिकवत् सता[1]॥३०॥

तथा समृतिभ्यो बहुशो गोत्रनामसम्बन्धकीर्तनबलात् स्वजनकादीनां देवतात्वमवगम्यते ।

ब्रह्मपुराणम्[2] —

अमुकामुकगौत्रेतत्तुभ्यमन्नं[3] स्वधा नमः ३१।

छन्दोगपरिशिष्टम्

गोत्रनामाभिरामन्त्र्य पितॄनर्घ्यं प्रदापयेत् ।३२।

मनुः — (३.२२०)

क्रियमाणे[4] तु पितरि पूर्वेषामेव निर्वपेत् ।३३।

विष्णुः — (७५.४)

यस्य पिता प्रेतः स्यात् स पित्रे पिण्डं निधाय प्रपितामहा[5]ऽपरत्[6] द्वाभ्यां पिण्डं दद्यात् ।

देवलः[7] —

प्रेतानुद्दिश्य यत् कर्म क्रियते मानुषैरिह ।
तुष्यन्ति पितरस्तेन न प्रेताः पितरः स्मृताः ॥३४॥

पितृपराधीनाः प्रेता इत्यर्थः । तदेवमादि श्रुतिस्मृतिविरोधात् वस्वादीनां पदानां मुख्यार्थत्वे पित्रादिपदैस्तुल्याधिकरणत्वानुपपत्तेः । गौणं पित्रादिषु वस्वादिपदम् । वस्वादिरूपतया पितॄणां ध्यानातिदेशार्थम् । वस्वादिरूपतया ध्यानप्रीता वस्वादयः पितॄन् प्रीणयन्तीत्युक्तम् ।

अत एव पैठीनसिः[8] —

यः एवं विद्वान् पितॄन् यजते इति वस्वाद्याकारतया धानेन जनकादीनां देवतात्वात् श्राद्धदेवतात्वव्यपदेशः । इन्द्राकाराद्यतया ध्यानेन मन्त्र इव इन्द्रादिव्यपदेश इति सर्गम[9]नाकुलम् ।

---

1. *Ibid.*, p. 18 reads सदा for सता.
2. The text of *ब्रह्मपुराण* is quoted in *कृत्यकल्पतरु-श्राद्धकाण्ड*, p. 4 and *पृथ्वीचन्द्र-श्राद्धप्रकाश*, X.14, p. 232.
3. *Ibid.*, p. 232 reads अस्तु for अन्नम्, and reads 2nd line as__ 'अवनेनिक्त इत्यन्ते जपेच्च सुसमाहितः'.
4. *मनुस्मृति*, III. 220 reads म्रियमाणे for क्रियमाणे.
5. *विष्णुस्मृति*, p. 75 reads पितामहात् for प्रपितामहा.
6. *Ibid.*, p. 775 reads परं for अपरत् which is corrupt.
7. The text of *देवल* is quoted in *कृत्यकल्पतरु-श्राद्धकाण्ड*, p. 230.
8. The text of *पैठीनसि* is quoted in *श्राद्धप्रकाश*, p. 13.
9. Is it possible to emend सर्वं० for सर्गं० ?

२

अत्र[1] श्राद्धभेदाः

अत्र विश्वामित्रः ।

> नित्यं नैमित्तिकं काम्यं वृद्धिश्राद्धं प्रपिण्डनम्[2] ।
> पार्वर्णश्चेति[3] विज्ञेयं गोष्ठ्यां शुद्ध्यर्थमष्टकम्[4] ॥१॥
> कर्माङ्गं नवमं प्रोक्तं दैविकं दशमं स्मृतम् ।
> यात्राष्वेकादशं[5] प्रोक्तं पुष्टार्थं[6] द्वादशं स्मृतम् ॥२॥

एतच्च भविष्यपुराणे विवृतम् ।

यथा भविष्ये

> अहन्यहनि यच्छ्राद्धं तन्नित्य[7]मभिधीयते[8] ।
> वैश्वदेवविहीनं तदंशतुगवुदकेन[9] तु ॥३॥
> एकोद्दिष्टं तु[10] यच्छ्राद्धं तन्नैमित्तिकमुच्यते ।
> तदप्यदैवं कर्तव्यमयुग्मानाशयेद्द्विजान्[11] ॥४॥
> कामाय तहितं[12] काम्यमभिप्रेतन्निषिद्धये[13] ।
> पार्वणेन विधानेन तदप्युक्तं खगाधिपः[14] ॥५॥

---

1. It may be emended as अथ for अत्र.
2. *श्राद्धचंद्रिका*, p. 3 and *कृत्यकल्पतरु-श्राद्धकाण्ड*, p. 6 read सपिण्डनं for प्रपिण्डनम्.
3. *Ibid.*, p. 3 reads पार्वणं चेति for पार्वणश्चेति.
4. *कृत्यकल्पतरु-श्राद्धकाण्ड*, p. 6 reads ००अष्टमम् for ००अष्टकम् । *श्राद्धचंद्रिका*, p. 3 reads ००अष्टम्.
5. *श्राद्धचंद्रिका*,. p. 3 reads यात्रासु० for यात्राषु०.
6. *Ibid.*, p. 3 and *केशववैजयन्ती*, p. 76 read पुष्ट्यर्थं for पुष्टार्थं which is corrupt.
7. *Ibid.*, p. 4 reads इति after नित्यम्.
8. *Ibid.*, p. 4 reads कीर्तितं for अभिधीयते.
9. *Ibid.*, p. 4 reads तदशक्तावुदकेन for तदशतुगवुदकेन which is corrupt.
10. *Ibid.*, p. 4 reads च for तु.
11. *Ibid.*, p. 4 reads ००भोजयेत्० for ००आशयेत्०.
12. *श्राद्धचंद्रिका*, p. 4 reads निहितं for त्तहितं which is corrupt.
13. *Ibid.*, p. 4 reads ०अभिप्रेतार्थ सिद्धये for ०अभिप्रेतात् निषिद्धये.
14. *Ibid.*, p. 4 reads खगाधिप for खगाधिपः.

वृद्धौ यत् क्रियते श्राद्धं वृद्धिश्राद्धं तदुच्यते ।
सर्वं प्रदक्षिणं कार्यं पूर्वाह्णे तूपवीतिना ॥६॥
गन्धोदकलिलैर्युक्तं कुर्यात् पात्रचतुष्टयम् ।
अर्घ्यार्थं पितृपात्रेण प्रेतपात्रं प्रसेचयेत् ॥७॥
ये समाना इति द्वाभ्यां एतज्ज्ञेयं[1] सपिण्डनम्।
नित्येन तुल्यं शेषं स्यात् एकोद्दिष्टं[2] स्त्रिया अपि ॥८॥
अमावास्यां यत्क्रियते तत्पार्वणमुदाहृतम् ।
क्रियते[3] पर्वणि यत्तत् पार्वणमिति स्थितिः ॥९॥
गोष्ठ्यां यत्क्रियते श्राद्धं गोष्ठीश्राद्धं तदुच्यते ।
वहनी[4] विदुषां सम्पत्सुखान्नं[5] पितृतृप्तये ॥१०॥
क्रियते शुद्धये यतु ब्राह्मणानां च[6] भोजनम्।
शुद्ध्यर्थमिति तत्प्रोक्तं वैनतेय[7] मनीषिभिः ॥११॥
निषेककाले सोमे च सीमन्तोन्नयने तथा ।
ज्ञेयं पुंसवने चैव श्राद्धं[8] कर्मापिमेव च[9]॥१२॥

तेनायमर्थः । सपिण्डीकरणस्योभयार्थत्वात् । पार्वणांशे पार्वणेन तुल्यम् । एकोद्दिष्टांशे एकोद्दिष्टेन तुल्यम् । शेषमङ्गजातं बोधव्यम् । एकोद्दिष्टमितित[10] ? भोगात् सपिण्डीकरणं लक्ष्यति तेन सपिण्डीकरणं स्त्रिया अपि कर्तव्यमिति प्रसङ्गादुक्तमिति कल्पतरूः[11] । तन्न[12] । 'एतत् सपिण्डीकरणं एकोद्दिष्टं स्त्रिया अपि' इति याज्ञवल्क्येन (१.२५४) सपिण्डनैकोद्दिष्टयोः पृथगुपादानात् । तस्माद्ब्राह्मणेषु मध्ये एतदेव श्राद्धद्वयं स्त्रियै कर्तव्यं स्त्रिया वा इति नियमार्थमिदमुक्तम् । अमावास्यायामिति पर्वशब्दोऽत्र संक्रान्त्यादिपरः ।

तथा विष्णुपुराणम् (३.११.११४) —

चतुर्दशी अष्टमी चैव[13] अमावस्या च पूर्णिमा[14] ।
पर्वाण्येतानि राजेन्द्र रविसंक्रान्तिरेव च ॥१३॥

---

1. *श्राद्धचंद्रिका*, p. 6 reads द्वाभ्यामेतज्ज्ञेयं for द्वाभ्यां एतज्ज्ञेयम्.
2. *Ibid.*, p. 6 reads स्यादेकोद्दिष्टं for स्यात् एकोद्दिष्टम्.
3. *Ibid.*, p. 6 reads वा after क्रियते.
4. *Ibid.*, p. 6 reads बहूनां for वहनी.
5. *Ibid.*, p. 6 reads सुखार्थं for सुखान्नम्.
6. *Ibid.*, p. 6 reads तु for च.
7. *Ibid.*, p. 6 reads ' after वैनतेय.
8. *Ibid.*, p. 6 reads कर्माङ्गं for श्राद्धम्.
9. *Ibid.*, p. 6 reads श्राद्धमुच्यते for कर्मापिमेव च.
10. This portion of the sentence is corrupt and defies all attempts.
11. This view of *कल्पतरु* is found in the *कृत्यकल्पतरु-श्राद्धकाण्ड*, p. 7.
12. It seems that the view of *कल्पतरु* is rejected by कुल्लूक on the strength of the text of *याज्ञवल्क्यस्मृति*, I.254.
13. *विष्णुपुराण*, reads अथ for च.
14. *Ibid.*, reads पौर्णिमा for पूर्णिमा.

एतेन युगाद्यादिषु पार्वणशब्दो गौण: । तद्धर्मातिदेशार्थ: । गोष्ठ्यामिति गोष्ठी चात्र श्राद्धकर्तृसमुदाय:[1] सम्पादनेन श्राद्धम् । 'श्राद्धं सम्पादयेत् सुखम् । तदर्थं बहूनां विदुषां येन[2] केनचिन्निमित्तेन युगपच्छ्राद्धे कर्तव्ये समुपस्थिते[3] पृथक् पाकादय: सम्पत्तौ[4] संभूय श्राद्धसामग्री संपादनेन श्राद्धं यत्[5] क्रियते तद् गोष्ठीश्राद्धमिति'शंखधर: । क्रियते शुद्धये ।

देवानुद्दिश्य यच्छ्राद्धं तद्दैनिकमिहोच्यते[6] ।
हविष्येण विशिष्टेन[7] सप्तम्यादि[8] प्रयत्नत: ॥१४॥
गच्छन्देशान्तरं यत्तु[9]श्राद्धं कुर्याच्च[10] सर्पिषा ।
यात्रार्थमिति तत् प्रोक्तं प्रवेशे च न संशय: ॥१५॥
शरीरोपचये श्राद्धमर्थोपचय एव च ।
पुष्ट्यर्थमेताज्विज्ञेयं[11] औपचायिकमुच्यते[12] ॥१६॥

कामायत्तं हितमिति अन्वयप्रदर्शनमुखेन काम्यशब्दार्थो निरुक्त: । सर्वेषां श्राद्धकर्मणां पितृप्रीति-कलत्वात् काम्यता स्यात् इत्याह अभिप्रेतार्थ सिद्धय इति । अभिप्रेतं स्वगतत्वेन धनपुत्रादिलक्षणम् । तत् सिद्धयेत त्तत् तिथिश्राद्धादि एतेनानुवादिक पितृप्रीतिफलत्वाद्धिषुवादि श्राद्धानामपि काम्यत्वे तत्र धूरिलोचनो स्यातामिति निरुक्तम् । अत एव 'कामायत्तं हितं काम्य'मिति शातातपवचनं[13] तिथिश्राद्धोपक्रमे कामधेनुकृता[14] लिखितम् । वृद्धि:[15] पुत्रजन्मादि । यत् भूतं सन्निमित्तं नित्येनेति पूर्वपरिभाषितमित्यस्या-संभवात् । आवश्यकं नित्यं पार्वणमेकोद्दिष्टं चाभितम् ।

प्रायश्चित्तवचनान्तरं कर्तव्यं पापक्षयार्थं यद्विहितं श्राद्धम् ।

यथा जाबाल:[16] —

---

1. This explanation is similar to the explanation in *कृत्यकल्पतरु-श्राद्धकाण्ड*, p. 7.
2. The word येन is dropped in the *कृत्यकल्पतरु-श्राद्धकाण्ड*, p. 7.
3. *कृत्यकल्पतरु-श्राद्धकाण्ड*, p. 8 reads उपस्थिते for समुपस्थिते.
4. *Ibid.*, p. 8 reads ०पाकाद्यसंपत्तौ for ०पाकादय:०.
5. *Ibid.*, p. 8 reads यत् before श्राद्धं and this is more reasonable.
6. *श्राद्धचंद्रिका,* p. 6 reads ०दैविकं०० for ०दैनिकं००.
7. *Ibid.*, p. 6 reads विशेषेण after विशिष्टेन.
8. *Ibid.*, p. 6 reads सप्तम्यादिषु for सप्तम्यादि.
9. *Ibid.*, p. 7 reads यस्तु for यत्तु.
10. *Ibid.*, p. 7 reads ०तु for ०च.
11. *Ibid.*, p. 7 reads ०एतत्० for ०एताज्०. The reading एताज् is corrupt.
12. *कृत्यकल्पतरु-श्राद्धकाण्ड*, p. 7 reads औपचारिकमेव वा for औपचायिकमुच्यते.
13. This line is not found in extant *शातातपस्मृति.*
14. This work is not available to us.
15. It must be pointed out that from वृद्धि: पुत्रजन्मादि: up to शेषमङ्गजातं बोधव्यम्. The portion seems to have been copied by कुल्लूक from *कृत्यकल्पतरु-श्राद्धकाण्ड*, p. 7.
16. The text of *जाबालि* is quoted in the *स्मृतिमुक्ताफलम्,* p. 941.

आरम्भे सर्वकृच्छ्राणां समाप्तौ च विशेषतः।
आत्मनैव[1] हि शालाग्नौ जुहुयादाहुतीः[2] पृथक् ॥१७॥

श्राद्धं कुर्याद्व्रतस्यान्ते गोहिरण्यानुदक्षिणम् । निषेककाल[3] इति सकलश्रौतस्मार्तकर्मोपलक्षणम्[4] । 'यानिष्ट्वा तु पितॄन् श्राद्धे कर्मवैदिकमारभेदिति शातातपवचनात् गच्छन् देशान्तरमिति तीर्थयात्राविषयम् । प्रवेशी तीर्थयात्रां कृत्वा इत्याह ब्रह्मपुराणे —

यो यः कश्चित्तीर्थयात्रां तु गच्छेत् सुसंयतः सुमनाः समाहितः[5]।
सः पूर्वं स्वेगृहे[6] कृतोपवासः (शुचिरप्रमतः)[7] संपूजयेद्विधिव[8]द्भक्तिनम्रो गणेशम् ॥१८॥

देवान् पितॄन् ब्राह्मणांश्चैव साधून्
धीमान् प्रीणयन्[9] वित्तशक्त्या[10] प्रपन्नान्[11] ।
प्रत्यागतश्चाथ पुनस्तथैव देवान्
पितॄन् ब्राह्मणांश्च पूजयेत[12]॥१९॥

शरीरोपचय इति शरीरोपचये हेतौ रसायशादिके[13] कर्तव्ये । कथं तर्हि पञ्चविधत्वमाह बृहस्पतिः[14]—

नित्यं नैमित्तिकं काम्यं वृद्धिश्राद्धं तथैव च ।
पार्वणं चेति मनुना श्राद्धं पञ्चविधं स्मृतम् ॥२०॥

कूर्मपुराणे (२.२०.२५-२६ अ)

अहन्यहनि नित्यं स्यात् काम्यं नैमित्तिकं पुनः ।
एकोद्दिष्टं च विज्ञेयं[15] वृद्धिश्राद्धं तु पार्वणम् ॥२१॥

---

1. *स्मृतिमुक्ताफलम्,* p. 941 reads आज्येन० for आत्मना०.
2. *Ibid.*, p. 941 reads ०व्याहृती: for ०आहुतीः.
3. *कृत्यकल्पतरु-श्राद्धकाण्ड,* p. 8 reads निषेककाले सोमे च for निषेककाले.
4. This is found copied from *कृत्यकल्पतरु-श्राद्धकाण्ड,* p. 8.
5. *श्राद्धप्रकाश,*. p. 333 reads सुसमाहितः for समाहितः.
6. *Ibid.*, p. 333 reads स्वगृहे for स्वेगृहे.
7. *Ibid.*, p. 333 drops शुचिरप्रमतः.
8. *Ibid.*, p. 333 omits विधिवत्.
9. *Ibid.*, p. 333 reads प्रीणन् for प्रीणयन्.
10. *Ibid.*, p. 333 reads वितनोति शक्त्या for वित्तशक्त्या.
11. *Ibid.*, p. 333 reads प्रयत्नात् for प्रपन्नान्.
12. *Ibid.*, p. 333 reads च after पूजयेत् and not after ब्राह्मणान्.
13. *कृत्यकल्पतरु-श्राद्धकाण्ड,* p. 8 reads रसायनादौ for रसायशादिके.
14. This stanza from the text of *बृहस्पति,* is not found in the *स्मृतिसंदर्भ,* Vol. III.
15. *कूर्मपुराण,* p. 501 reads एकोद्दिष्टादि विज्ञेयं for एकोद्दिष्टं च विज्ञेयं. In the foot-note on p. 501 we have other readings such as तु for च and विक्षेपं for विज्ञेयम्.

एतत् पञ्चविधं श्राद्धं मनुना परिकीर्तितम् ।२२।

सत्यं स्वरूपतो द्वादशविधत्वेऽपि पञ्चविधानोपाधिभेदात् पञ्चविधत्वम् । नित्यपार्वणात् गोष्ठीश्राद्धादीनां पार्वणकाम्य वृद्धिश्राद्धेष्वेव पृथक् विधानादेष्वेवान्तर्भाव इत्यभिप्रायः । सपिण्डीकरणस्याप्यंशतः । पार्वणविधानादंशतः । एकोद्दिष्टविधेरुभयात्मकत्वात् न पृथक्त्वम् । नित्यं पार्वणात् । काम्यस्य देवता भेदात् । पृथग्विधानं वस्तुतः प्रपञ्चार्थमेव । द्वादशविधत्वं युगाद्यादि श्राद्धानामपि सत्वात् ।

यत्तु मत्स्यपुराणम् (१६.५)

नित्यं नैमित्तिकं काम्यं त्रिविधं श्राद्धमुच्यते[1] ।२३।

इति तत्र नित्यपदमुक्तार्थमेव । नैमित्तिकपदमागन्तुकनिमित्त उत्पन्नत्वेन पार्वणैकोद्दिष्टयोरपि परिग्रहार्थम् । काम्यपदं दृष्टफलत्वेन तिथिश्राद्धादीनामभ्युदयस्य च ग्रहणार्थमित्यविरोधः ।

विष्णुना[2] नित्यकाम्यरूपत द्वैविध्यं वक्ष्यते । तत्र नित्यपदमावश्यकतया पार्वणैकोद्दिष्टयोः परिग्रहार्थं काम्यपदमनावश्यकार्थम् । सर्वमिदमुपाधिभेदादविरुद्धम् ।

---

1. This line completely agrees with the extant *मत्स्यपुराण*.
2. The passage from the text of *विष्णु* relied upon by कुल्लूक cannot be traced.

३

अथ श्राद्धदेशः

तत्र विष्णुः (८५.१-३)

पुष्करेष्वक्षयं श्राद्धम् ॥१॥ जप[1]होमतपांसि च ॥२॥
पुष्करे स्नानमात्रं तु[2] सर्वपापेभ्यः पूतो भवति ॥३॥

इत्यभिधाय एवमन्येषु तीर्थेषु सरिद्वरासु । संगमेषु प्रभवेषु । पुलिनेषु। निकुञ्जेषु । प्रस्रवनेषु[3] । वनेषु । उपवनेषु च गोमयेनोपलिप्तेषु गृहेषु । मनोद्देशेषु । प्रभवोऽत्र[4] नदीनामुत्पत्तिदेशः[5]। सरिद्वरासु । संगमेषु चेति प्रस्तुत्य प्रभवेष्वित्यभिधानात् । पुलिनं नदीतोयान्वितः[6] प्रदेशः । निकुञ्जं[7] लतादिवेष्टितः प्रदेशः । प्रस्रवणं निर्भरः । उपवनं गृहवाटिका । मनोज्ञं रमणीयम् ।

देवलः

श्राद्धेषु[8] पूजितो देशो गया गंगा सरस्वती ।
कुरुक्षेत्रं प्रयागश्च[9] नैमिषं पुष्कराणि च ॥१॥
नदीतटेषु तीर्थेषु शैलेषु पुलिनेषु च ।
विविक्तेषु च[10] तृप्यन्ति[11] दत्तेनेह पितामहाः ॥२॥

विविक्तं विजनम् ।

---

1. *विष्णुस्मृति,* p. 811 reads जप्य for जप.
2. *Ibid.*, p. 811 reads स्नानमात्रात् for स्नानमात्रं तु.
3. *कृत्यकल्पतरु-श्राद्धकाण्ड,* p. 31 reads प्रस्रवणेषु for प्रस्रवनेषु.
4. *Ibid.*, p. 31 reads प्रभवेषु for प्रभवोऽत्र.
5. *Ibid.*, p. 31 reads उत्पत्तिदेशेषु for उत्पत्तिदेशः.
6. *Ibid.*, p. 31 reads नदीतोयोत्थितः for नदीतोयान्वितः.
7. *Ibid.*, p. 31 reads निकुञ्जो for निकुञ्जं.
8. *श्राद्धप्रकाश,* p. 140, *श्राद्धमयूख,* p. 30, *बालंभट्टी,* p. 489, *पराशरमाधव,* Vol. I, p. 656 read श्राद्धस्य for श्राद्धेषु.
9. *श्राद्धमयूख,* p. 30 reads प्रयागं च for प्रयागश्च and ascribes this stanza to *आदित्यपुराण.*
10. *श्राद्धप्रकाश,* p. 140, and *बालंभट्टी,* p. 489 read विविक्तेष्वेव for विविक्तेषु च.
11. *श्राद्धतत्त्व,* p. 199 reads तुष्यन्ति for तृप्यन्ति.

बृहस्पतिः —

कांक्षन्ति पितरः पुत्रान् नरकपात[1]भीरवः ।
गयां यास्यन्ति[2] यः कश्चित् सोऽस्मान् संस्तारयिष्यति[3] ॥३॥
करिष्यति वृषोत्सर्गमिष्टापूर्तं तथैव च ।
फलयिष्यति[4] वार्द्धको[5] श्राद्धं दास्यति चान्वहम् ॥४॥
गयायां धर्मपृष्ठे च सदसि ब्राह्मणस्तथा ।
गयाशीर्षऽक्षयवटे[6] च[7] पितॄणां दत्तमक्षयम् ॥५॥
धर्मारण्यं धर्मपृष्ठं धेनुकारस्य[8]मेव च ।
दृष्ट्वैतानि पितृंश्चार्घ्य[9] वंशान् विशंतिमुद्धरेत् ॥६॥

तत्र गयायामुपादाय गयास्थानविशेषोपन्यासोऽधिक फलार्थः । इह श्राद्धत्वेन कथित नानादेशतीर्थ-विशेषस्वरूपास्तद्देशनिवासिभ्योऽवगन्तव्याः । अत्र पुष्करे क्षयमित्यादि विष्णवादिवाक्यैः सामान्यतस्तीर्थप्राप्तिनिमित्तेऽमावास्यादि श्राद्धे च प्राप्तेः पुष्करादिदेशाख्यं तु गुणविधिः । गोदोहेनापः प्रणयेत् पशुकामस्येतिवत् । न तु विशिष्टश्राद्धान्तरविधानं विधिगौरवापत्तेः । अगत्या हि सोमेन यजेतेत्यादौ ।

तथा मनुः (३.२०६-२०७)

शुचिं देशं विविक्तं च गोमयेनोपलेपयेत् ।
दक्षिणाप्रवरान्[10] चैव प्रयत्नेनोपपादयेत् ॥७॥
अवकाशेषु चोक्षेषु जल[11]तीरेषु चैव हि ।
विविक्तेषु च तुष्यन्ति दत्तेन पितरः सदा ॥८॥

---

1. *स्मृतिमुक्ताफलम्,* p. 646 reads नरके पात, *कृत्यकल्पतरु-श्राद्धकाण्ड,* p. 32 and *श्राद्धप्रकाश,* p. 141 read नरकापात for नरकपात.
2. *श्राद्धप्रकाश,* p. 141 reads यास्यति for यास्यन्ति. Here the reading of Kullūka noted above is grammatically wrong.
3. *स्मृतिमुक्ताफलम्,* p. 646 and *कृत्यकल्पतरु,* p. 32 and *श्राद्धप्रकाश,* p. 141 read संतारयिष्यति for संस्तारयिष्यंति. The above reading is evidently wrong.
4. *श्राद्धप्रकाश,* p. 141 reads पालयिष्यति for फलयिष्यति. Here the context will not favour फलयिष्यति.
5. *Ibid.*, p. 141 reads वृद्धत्त्वे for वार्द्धको.
6. *कृत्यकल्पतरु श्राद्धकाण्ड,* p. 32 and, *पराशरमाधव,* Vol. I, p. 654 read गयाशीर्षेवटे for गयाशीर्षऽक्षयवटे.
7. *पराशरमाधव,* Vol. I, p. 654 reads चैव for च.
8. *Ibid.*, Vol. I, p. 654 reads कारण्य for कारस्य.
9. *Ibid., p. 654 reads* पितृंस्तर्प्य; *कृत्यकल्पतरु-श्राद्धकाण्ड,* p. 32 reads पितृंश्चार्च्य.
10. कुल्लूक on *मनुस्मृति,* III, 206 reads प्रवणं. And this is accepted by all the commentators.
11. कुल्लूक on *मनुस्मृति,* III, 207 reads नदी० for जल०.

अशुचिमविविक्तमदक्षिणाप्रवरणं[1] यत्नतः[2] शुचित्वादिना उपपादयेत्[3]। विविक्तं विजनम् । चोक्षेषु मनोहरेषु[4] । विविक्तेषु वनादिषु ।

यमः

दक्षिणाप्रवणं स्निग्धं विविक्तं शुभलक्षणम् ।
शुचिदेशं परीक्ष्याशु गोमयेनोपलेपयेत् ॥९॥
अगारेषु विविक्तेषु तीर्थेषु च नदीषु च ।
विविक्तेषु च देशेषु तुष्यन्ति पितरः सदा ॥१०॥
पारक्ये भूमिभागे[5] च पितॄणां निर्वपेत्तु यः ।
तद्भूमिस्वामिपितृभिः श्राद्धकर्म विहन्यते ॥११॥
तस्मात् श्राद्धानि देयानि पुण्येष्वायतनेषु च ।
नदीतीरेषु तीर्थेषु स्वभूमौ च विशेषतः[6] ॥१२॥
उपकुर[7] नितम्बेषु[8] तथा पर्वतसानुषु ।
गोमयेनोपलिप्तेषु विविक्तेषु गृहेषु च ॥१३॥

स्निग्धं स्तिमितम् । विविक्तेषु स्वभावतो वनादिषु । उपकुरमत्र पर्वतान्तिकम् ।

---

1. कुल्लूक, on *मनुस्मृति*, III, 206 reads प्रवणं.
2. *Ibid.*, explains as प्रयत्नतः.
3. *Ibid.*, explains as संपादयेत्.
4. *Ibid.*, explains as स्वभावशुचयोऽरण्यादिप्रदेशाः and follows मेधातिथि; रामचंद्र explains उक्षेषु as उच्चस्थानेषु; सर्वज्ञनारायण explains उक्षेषु as शुद्धेषु; नन्दन and राघवानन्द explain this as मनोहरेषु.
5. *स्मृतिमुक्ताफलम्*, p. 758 reads भूमिदेशे and ascribes this stanza to भारत—अनुशासन पर्व 65.32.
6. *अपरार्क*, p. 471 reads प्रयत्नतः for विशेषतः.
7. *Ibid.*, reads उपह्वर for उपकुर.
8. *Ibid.*, reads निकुञ्जेषु for नितम्बेषु.

४

अथ निन्दितदेशाः

विष्णुः (८४.१-२; ४अ)

न म्लेच्छविषये[1] श्राद्धं कुर्यान्न गच्छे[2]त्तथा ।
चातुर्वर्ण्य व्यवस्थानं यस्मिन् देशे न विद्यते ॥१॥

वायुपुराणे (७८.२१-२३)

त्रिशङ्को[3]र्वर्जयेद्देशं सर्वं द्वादशयोजनम्।
उत्तरेण महानद्या दक्षिणेन तु[4] कीकटम्[5] ॥२॥
देशस्त्रैशङ्करो[6] नाम श्राद्धकर्मणि गर्हितः[7] ।
कारस्कराः[8] कलिङ्गाश्च सिन्धोरुत्तरमेव च ॥३॥
प्रणष्टा[9]श्रमधर्माश्च[10] देशा वर्या[11]प्रयत्नतः ।
कारस्करो देशाविशेषः । कीकटो मगधः । सिन्धुर्नदीविशेषः ।

ब्रह्मपुराणे

परकीयगृहे यस्तु अस्मान्[12] पितृन् तर्पयेज्जडः ।

---

1. *विष्णुस्मृति,* p. 809 reads म्लेच्छविषयं for म्लेच्छविषये.
2. *विष्णुस्मृति,* p. 809 quoted in श्राद्धतत्व; p. 197 reads नेच्छेत्तु तं तथा.
3. *वायुपुराण,* त्रिशङ्कु for त्रिशङ्कोः; *H.D.S.*, IV, p. 378 also reads त्रिशङ्कुं
4. *Ibid.*, reads च for तु; *श्राद्धमयूख,* p. 31 ascribes this st. to *ब्रह्माण्डपुराण.*
5. *Ibid.*, and *H.D.S.*, IV, p. 378 reads कीकटम्; *श्राद्धकल्पलता,* p. 35 reads कैकटम्.
6. *वायुपुराण,* reads त्रैशङ्कवो.
7. *H.D.S.*, IV, p. 376 reads वर्जितः for गर्हितः; *श्राद्धमयूख,* p. 31 reads वर्ज्यो वै श्राद्धकर्मणि for श्राद्धकर्मणिगर्हितः and ascribes this st. to *ब्रह्माण्डपुराण.*
8. अपरार्क on *याज्ञवल्क्यस्मृति,* p. 472 reads पारस्कराः for कारस्कराः.
9. अपरार्क on *याज्ञवल्क्यस्मृति,* p. 472 reads प्रनष्ट for प्रणष्ट.
10. *H.D.S.*, Vol. IV, p. 378 reads वर्णाश्च for धर्माश्च.
11. अपरार्क on *याज्ञवल्क्यस्मृति,* p. 472 reads वर्ज्या for वर्या; Also *वायुपुराण* reads वर्ज्या देशा प्रयत्नतः. Here the order is changed.
12. *श्राद्धकल्प,* p. 35, *श्राद्धतत्त्व,* p. 198 and *श्राद्धप्रकाश,* p. 147 read स्वान् for अस्मान्.

तद्भूमिस्वामिनस्तस्य हरन्ति पितरो बलात् ॥४॥
अग्रभागं ततस्तेभ्यो दद्यान्मूल्यं च जीवताम् ॥५॥

ग्रह इति भूभागोपलक्षणमात्रम् । पारको भूमिभाग इति यमवचनात्[1]। स्वभूम्यभावे श्राद्धं कथं स्यादित्याह । अग्रभागमिति श्राद्धीय द्रव्यस्य तेभ्यस्तद्भूमिस्वामी पितृभ्यः उत्सृज्य देयं जीवतां जीवतां मूल्यं देयम् ।

यमः

अटव्यः पर्वताः पुण्या नद्यस्तीर्थानि[2] यानि च ।
सर्वाण्यस्वाम्यकान्याहुर्नहि तेषु परिग्रहः ॥६॥

स्वाम्यभावे हेतुमाह । न हि तेष्वेति परिग्रहो दानविक्रयणादि यथेष्टविनियोगलक्षशः ।

तथा

रूक्षं कृमियुतं[3] क्लिन्नं संकीर्णानिष्ठगंधकम्[4]।
देशं त्वनिष्टशब्दं च वर्जयेत् श्राद्धकर्मणि ॥७॥

रूक्षं धूलियुतम् । क्लिन्नं पङ्किलम् । अनिष्टशब्दं प्रतिकूलशब्दम् ।

---

1. Also see पारक्ये भूमिभागे च quoted in *श्राद्धसागर-श्राद्धदेश* section.
2. For *स्मृतिचंद्रिका*, p. 143 ascribes this stanza to *पुराण*, and *श्राद्धतत्त्व*, p. 199 and *श्राद्धप्रकाश*, p. 148 read नदीतीराणि for नद्यस्तीर्थानि.
3. *श्राद्धकल्पलता*, p. 35 and *श्राद्धतत्त्व*, p. 197 read कृमिहतं for कृमियुतं; *पराशरमाधव*, Vol. I, p. 652 reads क्रिमिहतं for कृमियुतं.
4. *मार्कण्डेयपुराण*, 29.19 quoted by *श्राद्धप्रकाश*, p. 139 and *H.D.S.*, IV, p. 379 and *श्राद्धकल्पलता*, p. 35 and *श्राद्धतत्त्व*, p. 197 and *श्राद्धचंद्रिका*, p. 144 read संकीर्णानिष्टगन्धिकं for संकीर्णानिष्ठगन्धकम्.

५

अथ श्राद्धकाल:

याज्ञवल्क्य: (१.२१७-२१८)

अमावास्याऽष्टका वृद्धि: कृष्णपक्षोऽयनद्वयम् ।
द्रव्यं ब्राह्मणसंपत्तिर्विषुवत् सूर्यसंक्रम: ॥१॥
व्यतीपातो गजच्छाया ग्रहणं चंद्रसूर्ययो: ।
श्राद्धं प्रति रुचिश्चैते श्राद्धकाला: प्रकीर्तिता: ॥२॥

अष्टकायोदर्ध्वमाग्रहायण्यास्तामिति गोभिलेनोक्ता: । वृद्धि:[1] पुत्रजन्मादि: । कृष्णपक्ष: सर्व एव अमावास्याग्रहणं प्रशस्तार्थम् । द्रव्यं[2] खड्गमांसादि: । ब्राह्मणसंपत्ति: पङ्क्तिपावनादिसम्पत्ति: । सूर्यसंक्रम इति विषुवद्वायतनेपरम् । गोवृषन्यायात्[3]। अयनिर्विषुवयो: पृथगुपादानं फलातिशयार्थम्[4] । व्यतीपात: सूर्यचन्द्रमसो: संक्रान्ति: । ज्योतिरागमनमिति । गम्यमिति कल्पतरु:[5]। योगविशेष: इति केचित् । गजच्छाया ब्रह्मपुराणोक्ता ।

योगमघात्रयोदश्यां[6] कुञ्जरच्छायसत्थित:[7]।
भवेन्मघायां संस्थे च शशिन्यर्के करे[8]स्थिते ॥३॥

मुख्यत्वार्थं देशपरतैवमुक्तकालपरतत्वे लक्षणाप्रसङ्गात् इति चेन्न । श्राद्धकाला: प्रकीर्तितो[9] इति

---

1. *मिताक्षरा* on *याज्ञवल्क्य,* I. 217 also explains as पुत्रजन्मादि:.
2. *मिताक्षरा,* explains this कृसरमाषादिकम्.
3. Both विज्ञानेश्वर and नीलकण्ठ do not use any maxim to interpret the expression सूर्यसंक्रम:.
4. The purpose of repetition noted above is accepted by others also. Also see *मिताक्षरा,* p. 74.
5. This explanation of *कल्पतरु* is not found in the critical edition of *कृत्यकल्पतरु-श्राद्धकाण्ड*. *कृत्यकल्पतरु-श्राद्धकाण्ड,* p. 9 which explains व्यतीपात as सूर्याचन्द्रमसो: कान्तिसाम्यसमय:.
6. This stanza cannot be traced in the *ब्रह्मपुराण.* This is, however, quoted in *कृत्यकल्पतरु-श्राद्धकाण्ड,* p. 9. This *श्राद्धकाण्ड* reads योगोमघात्रयोदश्यो: for योगमघात्रयोदश्यां.
7. *कृत्यकल्पतरु-श्राद्धकाण्ड,* p. 9 reads संज्ञक: for सत्थित:.
8. *Ibid.,* p. 9 reads कर for करे.
9. *याज्ञवल्क्यस्मृति,* reads प्रकीर्तिता: for प्रकीर्तितो. प्रकीर्तितो is obviously wrong as this is a part of the quotation.

वाक्यावधृत कालपरत्वानुपपत्त्या लक्षणाया एव युक्तत्वात्। दृष्ट्वा च वाक्यावधूत[1] तण्डुलपरत्वानुपपत्त्या धान्यमसीतिमनो तण्डुललक्षणा द्रव्यशब्दे द्रव्यप्राप्तिकालवत् गजच्छायाप्राप्तिकाललक्षणैव वम्घतो[2]न भविष्यतीति चेन्न । निरूढलक्षणावसायत्वात् । अन्यथा शंकेत वैयर्थ्यापत्तेः । किं च देवदत्तादिशब्दवत् शंकेति तस्यापि मुख्यतैव श्राद्धं प्रति रुचिरिति । यदैव यजमानस्य श्राद्धेच्छा भवति तदैव श्राद्धकाल इति शुक्लपक्षेऽपि यस्यामपि तिथावित्यर्थः ।

1. This is corrupt. From the context the correct reading appears to be ०**अवधृत.**
2. It is better to read **वदतो** for **वम्घतो** which is corrupt. The context also would favour this reading **वदतो.**

अथ नित्यश्राद्धकाल:

तत्र विष्णु: (७६.१.२)

अमावास्यास्तिस्रोऽष्टकास्तिस्रोऽन्वष्टका माघी प्रौष्ठपद्यूर्ध्वं कृष्णात्रयोदशी[1] व्रीहियवपाकौ चेति ।

एतांस्तु श्राद्धकालान्[2] वै नित्यानाह प्रजापति: ।
श्राद्धमेतेष्वनुकुर्वाणो[3] नरकं प्रतिपद्यते ॥१॥

तिस्रोऽष्टका इति अष्टकान्तरस्य नित्यत्वव्यवच्छेदार्थम् ।

'याप्यन्या[4] चतुर्थी स्यात्तांच कुर्याद्विशेषत:' इति वायुपुराण (८१.५अ) दर्शनात् । तिस्रोऽन्वष्टका इति — अन्वष्टकान्तरव्यवच्छेदार्थमेव । माघी पौर्णमासीति कल्पतरु:[5]। तथा विष्णुधर्मोत्तरे (१४२.२६ ब-२७ अ)

व्रीहिपाके च कर्तव्यं यवपाके च पार्थिव[6]।
न तावाद्यौ[7] महाराज विना श्राद्धं कथंचन ॥२॥
(१४२.१ब-२अ)

पौर्णमासी तथा माघी श्रावणी च नरोत्तमा[8]।
प्रौष्ठपद्यामतीतायां तथा कृष्णत्रयोदशी ॥३॥
(विष्णुधर्मोत्तर १.१४२.१ब-२अ)

---

1. *विष्णुस्मृति,* p. 777 reads कृष्णत्रयोदशी for कृष्णात्रयोदशी.
2. *Ibid*., p. 777 records another reading एतानि श्राद्धकालानि in the foot-note for एतांस्तु श्राद्धकालान्.
3. *Ibid*., p. 777 reads ००ष्वकुर्वाणो for ००ष्वनुकुर्वाणो.
4. *वायुपुराण,* p. 300 reads यदन्या for याप्यन्या.
5. *कृत्यकल्पतरु-श्राद्धकाण्ड,* p. 10 reads 'माघी' पौर्णमासी, तथैव समुदायप्रसिद्धे:।
6. *विष्णुधर्मोत्तर-पुराण,* reads तथैव च for च पार्थिव.
7. *Ibid*., reads तानद्यु: for तावाद्यौ.
8. *Ibid*., p. 92b reads नरोत्तम for नरोत्तमा.

एतांस्तु श्राद्धकालान्वै नित्यानाह प्रजापति: । त्रयोदशी विशेषणमित्यन्ये । ननु मघायुक्ता त्रयोदशी प्रौष्ठपद्यूर्ध्वमेव संभवति । अतस्तदनर्थकं स्यात् । न श्रावणी ऊर्ध्वमपि सिंहस्थ चंद्रेणोत्तर फल्गुनीनक्षत्रेण अमावास्यायां तत: प्राक् त्रयोदशीं मघानक्षत्र संभवात् । व्रीहि: शरत् पक्वे धान्यम् । तत्रैव व्रीहिशब्दस्य मुख्यत्वात् । अन्यथा व्रीह्युपचारे शालिं प्रति निधानदर्शनं पृथगुपादानं च नोपपद्यते ।

तथा छन्दोगपरिशिष्टम् ।

कात्यायन:

यथोक्त वस्त्वसम्पत्तौ ग्राह्यं तदनुकारि यत् ।
यवानामिव गोधूमा व्रीहीणामेव शालय: ।।४।।
व्रीहय: शालयो मुद्रा गोधूमा: सर्षपास्तिला: ।
यवाश्चौषधय: सप्त विपदो[1] घ्नन्ति[2] वारिता:[3] ।।[4]५।।

वायुपुराणे (६८.२१)

हविषा संस्कृता ये तु यवगोधूमशालय: ।
तिलमुद्गादयो माषा व्रीहयश्च प्रिया हरे: ।।६।।

अत एव कामधेनुकृता आश्विनमासीय तिथिकृत्यं नवान्नश्राद्धविषयं ब्रह्मपुराणवचनलिखितम् । यथा

शुक्लपक्षे नवं धान्यं पक्वं ज्ञात्वा सुशोभनम् ।
गच्छेत् क्षेत्री विधानेन गीतवादस्य पुर:सर: ।।[4] ७।।

इति अभिसन्धीयते ।

'न देवान्[5] पितृंश्चैव तर्पयेदर्चयेत्तथा ।८।

इत्यस्मादेव वचनात्[6] शुक्लपक्ष एवैतद् ग्राह्यम् ।

वृश्चिके व्रीहिपाके निमित्तं श्राद्धं न स्यादिति चेत् । न । स्यादेव नवान्नोगमनिमित्तमिति ब्रूम: । अत एव 'नवोदके नवान्ने च'[7] इति वक्ष्यते । आवा व्रीह्यप्राप्तौ व्रीहिपाकनिमित्त एव धान्यान्तरविधानात्

1. *कात्यायनस्मृति,* p. 1376 reads विपदं for विपदो.
2. *Ibid*., p. 1376 reads धारिता: for वारिता:.
3. *Ibid*., 26.13 (*स्मृतिसंदर्भ,* Vol. III, p. 1376).
4. This stanza is found quoted in the *श्राद्धतत्त्व* p. 261 and reads गीतवाद्य for गीतवादस्य. This stanza cannot be traced in the extant *ब्रह्मपुराण.*
5. *Ibid*., p. 261 reads तेन देवान् for न देवान् and quotes from the *ब्रह्मपुराण.*
6. This line though quoted from the *ब्रह्मपुराण* in the *श्राद्धतत्त्व,* p. 261, is not found in the extant text of the *ब्रह्मपुराण.*
7. This line is quoted from the *शातातपस्मृति* in the *श्राद्धतत्त्व,* p. 260.

वृश्चिके व्रीहिपाकनिमित्तमेवं श्राद्धम् ।

तथा छन्दोगपरिशिष्टम्[1]

शरद्वसन्तयोः केचिन्नवयज्ञं प्रचक्ष्यते[2] ।
धान्यपाकवशादन्ये श्यामाको वनिनः स्मृतः ॥९॥

वनी वानप्रस्थः । यज्ञतुल्यन्यायत्वाच्छ्राद्धमपि धान्यपाकवशादेव । अत एव नित्यत्वं शुक्लपक्षनियतत्वं च नवान्नागमनिमित्तमपि नित्यमिति वक्ष्यति । धनुष्वपि कुतो न क्रियते इति चेत् । न । ज्योतिःशास्त्रविरोधात् ।

यथा वराहः[3]

वृश्चिके शुक्लपक्षे तु नवान्नं शस्यते बुधैः ।
अपरे क्रियमाणं हि धनुष्येव कृतं भवेत् ॥१०॥
धनुषि कृतं श्राद्धं मृगनेत्रासु राशिषु ।
पितरस्तन्न गृह्णन्ति नवान्नमिषगर्द्धिनः[4] ॥११॥

एवं च धनुषा पर्युदासात् वृश्चिके तदकरणे माघे अपि तत् कर्तव्यमेव । नित्यानिति नित्यकर्मसम्बन्धान्नित्यान् । नित्यत्वमत्रावश्यकमभिप्रेतम् । अकरणे प्रत्यवायश्रुतेः ।

तथा शातातपः[5]

सर्वस्वेनापि कर्तव्यं श्राद्धं वै राहुदर्शने ।
अकुर्वाण एतच्छ्राद्धं पङ्के गौरिव सीदति ॥१२॥
नवोदके नवान्ने च गृहप्रच्छदने[6] तथा ।
पितरः स्पृहयन्त्यन्नमष्टकासु मघासु च ॥[7] १३॥

सर्वस्वेनापि इति यथाल्पवित्तस्य श्राद्धसामग्रीव्ययेन सर्वस्वोपक्षयो भवति । तेनापि कर्तव्यमित्यर्थः । एतेनावश्यकत्वं दर्शितम् । नवोदके वर्षोपक्रमे[8] । गृहप्रच्छादने नवगृहसम्पत्तौ। मघासु त्रयोदशीयोगे विद्वत्सु ब्राह्मणेषु च प्राप्तेष्विति शेषः । युक्तो यत्नवान्। – सदाग्रहणान्नित्यत्वम् ।

हारीततीर्थे[9] द्रव्योपपत्तौ च न कालमवधारयेत् । पात्रं च ब्राह्मणं प्राप्य सद्यः श्राद्धं विधीयते ।

---

1. The text of *छन्दोगपरिशिष्ट*, is quoted in the *श्राद्धतत्त्व*, p. 260.
2. *श्राद्धतत्त्व*, p. 260 reads प्रचक्षते for प्रचक्ष्यते.
3. *Ibid*., p. 260 quotes this stanza. This however is not found in the extant *वराहपुराण*.
4. *Ibid*., p. 260 reads ००काङ्क्षिणः for ००गर्द्धिनः.
5. This stanza "सर्वस्वेनापि etc." is not found in the *शातातप स्मृति-स्मृतिसमुच्चय*, pp. 396-410.
6. *श्राद्धतत्त्व*, p. 260 reads प्रच्छादने for प्रच्छदने. It may be added here that in his gloss कुल्लूक reads प्रच्छादने as noted above.
7. *Ibid*., p. 260 quotes this stanza from the *शातातप स्मृति*.
8. The same explanation of नवोदके is also given by *रघुनन्दन* in his *श्राद्धतत्त्व*, p. 260.
9. This is an eminent place for the श्राद्ध ceremony and is mentioned in the *मत्स्यपुराण*, 22.68 as beyond वसिष्ठतीर्थ. Also see *History of Dharmaśāstra*, Vol. IV, p. 756.

तीर्थं वाराणस्यादि । द्रव्यं खड्गमांसादि । न कालमवधारयेत् । नामावास्यामपराह्णं प्रतीक्षते निषिद्धं तु रात्र्यादिकं वर्जयेत् ।

अत एव देवीपुराणे[1]

अकालेऽप्यथवा काले तीर्थे श्राद्धं तथा नरै: ।
प्राप्तैरेव सदा कार्यं कर्तव्यं पितृतर्पणम् ॥१४॥
पिण्डदानं तु तच्छस्तं पितॄणां चातिदुर्लभम् ।
विलम्बो नैव कर्तव्यो नैव विघ्नं समाचरेत् ॥१५॥

न कालमवधारयेदित्यनेन नित्यत्वं दर्शितम् ।[2]

व्यक्तमाह स एव

अष्टकामाघ्यभ्युदयास्तीर्थे पात्रोपपत्तय: ।
पितृणामतिरेकोऽयं मासिकार्थो ध्रुव: स्मृत: ।[3] १६॥

मासिकार्थादमावास्याश्राद्धादयमतिरेकोऽधिकोऽष्टकादि श्राद्धगण: । ध्रुव आवश्यक इत्यर्थ: ।

कृष्णपक्षमात्रं नित्यमित्याह कात्यायन: —

श्राद्धान्वित:[4] श्राद्धं कुर्वीत शाकेनापि । अपरपक्षं नातिक्रमेत् ।[5] मासि मासि वोऽशनमिति श्रुते: ।[6]

बैजवाप: —

कृष्णपक्षे श्राद्धं कुर्वीतान्नं सुसंस्कृत: ।[7]१७।

ब्रह्मपुराणे[8]

पयोमूलफलै: शाकै: कृष्णपक्षे च सर्वदा ।
पराधीन: प्रवासी वा निर्धनो वापि मानव: ॥१८॥
मनसा भावशुद्धेन श्राद्धं[9] दद्यात्तिलोदकम् ।
नाश्नन्ति पितरश्चेति कृत्वा मनसि यो नर:[10] ॥१९॥

---

1. This text is not found quoted in the *Dharma Śāstra* literature.
2. This explanation seems to be an after-thought of कुल्लूक. Actually this should have appeared much before the citation from *देवीपुराण*.
3. This appears to be a citation from the text of *शातातप*.
4. *कृत्यकल्पतरु-श्राद्धकाण्ड*, p. 14 quotes कात्यायन and reads श्रद्धायुतं for श्राद्धान्वित:.
5. *Ibid.*, p. 14 changes the order of the words and reads न before अपरपक्षम्.
6. *Ibid.*, p. 14 reads श्रुति: for श्रुते:.
7. *Ibid.*, p. 14 reads संस्कृत्य for सुसंस्कृत: and also explains it as पक्त्वा.
8. *ब्रह्मपुराण* is quoted in the *कृयकल्पतरु-श्राद्धकाण्ड*, p. 15.
9. *कृत्यकल्पतरु-श्राद्धकाण्ड*, p. 15 reads श्राद्धे for श्राद्धम्.
10. *Ibid.*, p. 15 reads हव्यमले तु य: for मनसि यो नर:.

न तर्पयति तान् भक्तया देहात्तद्रुधिरं च ते[1] ।
पिबन्ति सर्वनाशं च कुर्वन्त्याप[2] पदे पदे ॥२०॥

एतेन कृष्णपक्षे यस्यां कस्याञ्चित्तिथौ श्राद्धं कर्तव्यम् ।

दशम्यादौ प्राशस्त्यमाह मनुः (३.२७६) —

कृष्णपक्षे दशम्यादौ वर्जयित्वा चतुर्दशी[3]।
श्राद्धे प्रशस्तास्तिथयो यथैतान् तथेतराः ॥२१॥

आपस्तम्बः — (२.७.१६. ४-७ अ)

मासिमास्यपपक्षस्यापराह्नः[4] । श्रेयान् । तथापरपक्षस्य जघन्यान्यहानि । सर्वेष्वेषा[5]परपक्षस्याहः[6] स्वक्रियमाणे[7] पितॄन् प्रीणाति ।

तथा श्रेयांसीत्यर्थः । जघन्यानि दशम्यादीनि । यथैतान् तथेतराः प्रशस्ताः । श्रेयांसीत्यभिधानादन्यास्वपि तिथिषु श्राद्धं कर्तव्यम् ।

अमावास्यायामतिप्राशस्त्यमाहं निगमः[8]। अपरपक्षे यदहः सम्पद्यते । अमावास्यायां तु विशेषेण । एतत् कृष्णपक्षविहितश्राद्धं साग्निना अमावास्यायामेव कर्तव्यमित्याह मनुः । (३.२८२ब)

न दर्शेन विना श्राद्धमाहिताग्नेर्द्विजन्मनः ।२२।

दर्शेष्वाङ्गभूताग्न्युद्धरणस्य विद्यमानत्वादिति भावः[9]।

अष्टकादिकं तु अङ्गबाधेनापि अगत्या यथा कथञ्चित् प्रपञ्चादौ कर्तव्यमिति वक्ष्यते । शक्तिसंभवासंभव तारतम्येन बहून् कल्पानाह गौतमः । (१५.१-५)

अथ श्राद्धममावास्यायां पितृभ्यो दद्यात् । पञ्चमीप्रभृति वापरपक्षस्य यथाश्राद्धम् । सर्वस्मिन्वा । द्रव्यदेशब्राह्मणसन्निधाने वा । कालनियमः शक्तितः[10]।

---

1. *कृत्यकल्पतरु-श्राद्धकाण्ड*, p. 15 reads बत for च ते.
2. *Ibid*., p. 15 reads ०अनु for ०आप.
3. The *मनुस्मृति*, III.276 reads चतुर्दशीं for चतुर्दशी. Possibly one अनुस्वार is missed in our Ms.
4. *आपस्तम्ब धर्मसूत्र*, p. 77 reads ०अहण: for ०अह्नः.
5. *Ibid*., p. 77 reads ०ष्वेवा for ०ष्वेषा.
6. *Ibid*., p. 77 reads ००अहस्सु for ००आहः.
7. *Ibid*., p. 77 reads क्रियमाणे for स्वक्रियमाणे.
8. This viewpoint of निगम can be supported by quoting *कृत्यकल्पतरु-श्राद्धकाण्ड*, p. 16.
9. For this view also cf: *मनुस्मृति*, III.211 and also the comments of *कुल्लूक* on the same.
10. *गौतमधर्मसूत्र*, 15.5 (p. 249) reads ०श्शक्तितः for ०शक्तितः.

योऽमावास्यादि काल उक्त: स शक्तस्य द्रव्यादि संपन्नया रोगिणो: बोद्धव्य:[1]।

तथा पार्वणश्राद्धमभिधायाह देवल: —

> अनेन[2] विधिना श्राद्धं कुर्थ्यात्संवत्सरं सकृत्[3]।
> त्रिचतुरी[4] यथा श्राद्धं मासे मासे दिने दिने ॥२३॥

अत्र 'दिने' इति वीप्सा श्रुता । अपरपक्षश्राद्धमवगम्यते ।

---

1. This explanation of कुल्लूक agrees well with that of *मस्करि* on *गौतमधर्मसूत्र,* XV.5 (p. 249), though there is the absence of the expression रोगिणो: बौद्धव्य: . It must be noted here that the splitting up of the सूत्र of *गौतमधर्मसूत्र* by both हरदत्त and मस्करि is different. हरदत्त connects the word शक्तित: in the *गौतमधर्मसूत्र,* XV.5 with the succeeding सूत्र. It seems that कुल्लूक follows the order of the सूत्र preferred by मस्करि, though he does not quote him.
2. *कृत्यकल्पतरु-श्राद्धकाण्ड,* p. 22 quotes *देवल* and reads एतेन for अनेन.
3. *श्राद्धप्रकाश,* p. 322 reads द्विज: for सकृत्.
4. *कृत्यकल्पतरु-श्राद्धकाण्ड,* p. 22 and *श्राद्धप्रकाश,* p. 322 read द्विश्चतुर्वा for त्रिचतुरी.

७

अथ मघात्रयोदशी

ब्रह्मपुराणे[1]

योगी[2]मघात्रयोदश्यां[3] कुञ्जरछायासङ्गित:[4] ।
भवेन्मघायां संस्थ च शशिन्यर्के करेस्थिते[5]॥१॥
आश्वयुज्याश्च[6] कृष्णायां त्रयोदश्यां मघासु च ।
प्रावृद्धतौ[7] यमः प्रेतान् पितॄंश्चाथ यमालयात् ॥२॥
विसर्जयति मानुष्ये कृत्वा शून्यं स्वकं पुरम् ।
क्षुधार्त्ता:[8] कीर्तयन्तश्च दुष्कृतंश्च[9] स्वयं कृतम् ॥३॥
काङ्क्षन्तः पुत्रपौत्रेभ्यः पायसं मधुसंयुतम् ।
तस्मात् तान्[10] पुत्र[11] विधानात्[12] तर्पयेत् पायसेन तु ॥४॥
मध्याह्न[13] तिलमिश्रेण तथा सीतेन[14] चाम्भसा ।
ग्रासमात्रं परगृहान्नक्तं[15] यः प्राप्नुयान्नरः ॥५॥

1. These stanzas cannot be traced in the extant *ब्रह्मपुराण*.
2. *कृत्यकल्पतरु-श्राद्धकाण्ड*, p. 9 reads योगो for योगी.
3. *Ibid*., p. 9 reads ०त्रयोदश्यो: for ०त्रयोदश्यां.
4. *Ibid*., p. 9 reads ०च्छायसंज्ञक: for ०छायासङ्गित:.
5. *Ibid*., p. 9 reads करस्थिते for करेस्थिते.
6. *Ibid*., p. 21 reads ०च for ०ज्व.
7. *Ibid*., p. 21 reads प्रावृड्तौ for प्रावृद्धतौ which is corrupt.
8. *Ibid*., p. 21 reads क्षुधार्ता: for क्षुधार्त्ता: which is grammatically wrong.
9. *Ibid*., p. 21 reads ०च for ०श्च.
10. *Ibid*., p. 21 reads तां for तान्.
11. *Ibid*., p. 21 reads तत्र for पुत्र.
12. *Ibid*., p. 21 reads विधिना for विधानात्.
13. *Ibid*., p. 21 reads मध्वाज्य for मध्याह्न which is corrupt contextually.
14. *Ibid*., p. 21 reads शीतेन for सीतेन which is evidently corrupt.
15. *Ibid*., p. 21 reads ०व्यक्तं for ०नक्तम्.

भिक्षामात्रेण यः प्राणान् संधारयति वा नरः[1]।
यो वा समुद्धरे[2]द्देहं प्रत्यहं स्वात्मविक्रयात् ॥६॥
श्राद्धं तेनापि कर्तव्यं तैस्तैर्द्रव्यैरसञ्चितैः[3]।
त्रयोदश्यां प्रयत्नेन वर्षासु च मघासु च ॥७॥
नास्मात् परतरः कालः श्राद्धेष्वन्यत्र विद्यते ।
यत्र साक्षात्तु पितरो गृह्ण[4]न्त्यमृतमुत्तमम्[5]॥८॥

करे हस्ता[6] नक्षत्रे । सार्द्धनवदिवसोपरि सपादत्रयोविंशतिदिवसपर्यन्तं हस्तावस्थानमर्कस्य । आश्वयुजी त्रयोदशी । पौर्णमास्यन्तमासेन 'प्रौष्ठपद्यामतीतायाम्' इति शंखवचनात्[7]। मघासु तृप्यते इति शेषः । प्रावृडूत्तरमासचतुष्टयं त्यत्त समुत्सवमतेन[8]।

यथा मनुः[9] —

ग्रैस्य हैमन्तिकान् मासानष्टौ भिक्षुर्विचक्रमेत् ।
चत्वारि भद्रान्याप्नोति कीर्तिमायुर्यशोबलम् ॥९॥

प्रेतानविकरणभागिनः कीर्तयन्तो मानुष्यमायान्तीति शेषः । सूत्रविधिना गृह्योक्तविधानेन तन्त्रविधिनेति वा पाठः । 'भिक्षामात्रेण यः प्राणान् यो वा समुद्धरेद्देहं' इत्यर्थवादै[10]रेवाश्वयुज्यां मघात्रयोदश्यां श्राद्धस्यावश्यकत्वं दर्शितम् । कुञ्जरच्छायायोगे तु फलातिशेषः । तत्र कल्पतरुः[11] कुञ्जरच्छायावन्मघायोगोऽपि फलातिशयार्थमेव ।

विष्णुना मनुष्यानां[12] केवल मघात्रयोदशी विधानात् ।

विष्णुः — (७८.५२-५३)

अपि जायते सोऽस्माकं कुले कश्चिन्नरोत्तमः ।
प्रावृट् कालेऽसितेपक्षे त्रयोदश्यां समाहितः ॥१०॥

---

1. *कृत्यकल्पतरु-श्राद्धकाण्ड*, p. 21 reads स्वयं for नरः.
2. *Ibid*., p. 21 reads संवर्धयेत्० for समुद्धरेत्०.
3. *Ibid*., p. 21 and *श्राद्धसागर*, p. 107 read ०००सुसंचितैः for ०००असञ्चितैः.
4. *Ibid*., p. 21 reads गृह्णन्ति० for गृह्णन्ति० which is grammatically incorrect.
5. *Ibid*., p. 21 reads ००अक्षयम् for ००उत्तमम्.
6. Grammatically it should be हस्त. This is a scribal mistake.
7. The text of *शंख* is also quoted in *कृत्यकल्पतरु-श्राद्धकाण्ड*, p. 20.
8. The portion from त्यत्त समुत्सवमतेन defies all attempts at identification.
9. This stanza cannot be traced in the extant *मनुस्मृति*.
10. These lines are quoted here from *ब्रह्मपुराण*.
11. This view of *कल्पतरु*, however, has no place in the critical edition of *कृत्यकल्पतरु*. Posibly कुल्लूक has before him some other mannuscript.
12. Grammatically it should be emended as मनुष्याणाम्.

मधुप्लुतेन[1] यः श्राद्धं पायसेन समाचरेत् ।
कार्तिकं सकलं वापि[2]प्राक्च्छाये कुञ्जरस्य च ॥११॥

कार्तिकविधिरयं कन्यागतश्राद्ध एव। कन्यायामकरणे सतीति वक्ष्यते। कार्तिकं सकलं कृष्णपक्षमित्यर्थः। अन्यथा कन्याश्राद्धप्राप्तकृष्णपक्षस्य बाधा[3] स्यात्। प्राक् छाये[4] प्राच्यां दिशि गतायां हस्तिछायायामित्यर्थः।

मनुः — (३.२७४)

अपि नः स कुले जायाद्यो[5] नो दद्यात् त्रयोदशीम् ।
पायसं मधुसर्पिर्भ्यां प्राक्च्छाये कुञ्जरस्य च ॥१२॥

न च वाच्यं माघीप्रौष्ठपद्यूर्ध्वं कृष्णत्रयोदशीत्येतद्विहितं श्राद्धं मनुष्यस्य यद्यनेन केवलत्रयोदशी विधीयते। तदा कालद्रव्योभयलक्षण गुणद्वयविधाने वाक्यभेदः स्यात्। अत एव उपसद्भिश्चरित्वा मासमग्निहोत्रं जुहोतीति विशिष्टकर्मान्तर विधिरुक्तः। अत[6] त्रयोदशीमनूद्य तत्कालीन-श्राद्धद्रव्यमात्रविधिरिति। एवमपि द्रव्यकुञ्जरछायदेशलक्षणद्वयविधिर्दुष्परिहरः। किं चैवमुपसद्भिश्चरित्वेतिवत् कालद्रव्योभय गुणविशिष्टं श्राद्धविधौ तत्राप्तं श्राद्धमनूद्य माघी प्रौष्ठपद्यूर्ध्वमित्यनेन त्रयोदशी विशेषणत्वेन नक्षत्रमात्र गुणविधिः फलातिशयार्थं भविष्यति। विधिपदं चोभयत्रैव[7] कल्पनीयम्। अरुणैकहायनीवाक्ये[8] आरुण्यैकहायनीत्व लक्षणगुणद्वयविशिष्टक्रयविधौ तत्राप्तक्रयोद्देशेन वाससा क्रीणाति इति वासो लक्षणगुणविधिवत्। तन्न। एतयोर्मनुविष्णुवचनयोः पितृगाथात्वेन अनुवादरूपत्वात्। सर्वशब्दानां च कार्यबोधकत्व व्युत्पत्तेरर्थवादानां विध्यैकवाक्यतया कार्यबोधकमित्युक्तमर्थवादाधिकरणे[9]। तत्र क्लृप्तविधिशेषत्वे सम्भवति कल्पविधिशेषत्वमन्याय्यम्। अतः क्लृप्तविध्यनुरूपैव स्तुतिरनेन कार्या। विधौ च मघाप्रयोगः श्रूयते।

तत्र मनुः — (३.२७३)

यत् किञ्चिन्मधुना मिश्रं प्रपद्यात्तु त्रयोदशीम् ।
तदप्यक्षयमेव स्याद्वर्षासु च मघासु च ॥१३॥

---

1. *विष्णुस्मृति*, p. 787 reads मधूत्कटेन for मधुप्लुतेन.
2. *Ibid.*, p. 787 reads मासं for वापि.
3. The word बाधा may be emended as बाधः grammatically.
4. The explanation of प्राक्-छाये offered by कुल्लूक agrees with the explanation of *नन्दपण्डित कृत केशववैजयन्ती*, p. 788.
5. This stanza No. 12 is found in the *महाभारत*, XIII.88.12, *मनुस्मृति*, III.274 and *वर्षक्रियाकौमुदि*, p. 357. *मनुस्मृति* reads भूयात्० for जायात्०.
6. The word अत may be emended as अतः and it seems that the विसर्ग (:) is dropped by a scribe.
7. This may indicate the use of 'देहलीदीपकन्याय' or काकाक्षिगोलकन्याय.
8. This has a reference to अरुणन्याय discussed in *जैमिनि कृत पूर्वमीमांसा*, III.1.12.
9. This अर्थवादाधिकरण has a reference to *जैमिनि कृत पूर्वमीमांसा* 'विधीनां तु एकवाक्यत्वात् स्तुत्यर्थेन विधीनां स्युः'. II.1.7.

शंखः — (१४.३२)

प्रौष्ठपद्यामतीतायां मघायुक्तां[1] त्रयोदशीम् ।
प्राप्य श्राद्धं हि[2] कर्तव्यं मधुना पायसेन तु[3]।।१४।।

ब्रह्मपुराणे[4]

श्राद्धं तेनापि कर्तव्यं तैस्तैर्द्रव्यैः सुसञ्चितैः[5]।
त्रयोदश्यां प्रयत्नेन वर्षासु च मघासु च ।।१५।।

याज्ञवल्क्यः — (१.२६१)

यद् ददाति गयस्थश्च सर्वमानन्त्यमश्नुते ।
तथा वर्षा त्रयोदश्यां मघासु च न संशयः[6]।।१६।।

कुञ्जरछायायोगश्चैकेन मुनिना पृथगुपादानात् फलातिशयार्थ उक्तः ।

किं च

मनुना (३.२७३) त्रयोदशीमात्रश्रवणात् प्रावृट् कालोऽपि फलातिशयार्थः स्यात् । तथा विष्णुवचने (७८.५२) प्रावृण्मात्रश्रुतेः प्रौष्ठपद्यनन्तरितमपि फलातिशयार्थं भवेत् ।

अपि च[7]

पिता पितामहश्चैव तथैव प्रपितामहः ।
उपासते सुतं जातं शकुन्ता इव पिप्पलम् ।।१७।।
मधुमांसैश्च शाकैश्च पयसा पायसेन तु[8]।
एष दो[9]दास्यति श्राद्धं वर्षासु च मघासु च ।।१८।।

इति वसिष्ठधर्मसूत्र (११.३९.४०) वचनात् वर्षासु मघामात्र एव श्राद्धं स्यात् । तस्मान्नाना मुनिवचनैकवाक्यतया प्रौष्ठपद्यनन्तरित त्रयोदश्यां मघायुक्तायां श्राद्धम् । तथा महाभारतादिवचने[10]ष्वर्थवादरूपेषु

---

1. *पराशरमाधव*, I. 669 reads माघायुक्तां for मघायुक्ताम्.
2. *Ibid.*, read तु for हि; *श्राद्धप्रकाश*, p. 318 reads हि as above *A.B.O.R.I.*, Vol. VIII, p. 96 reads न for हि.
3. *श्राद्धतत्त्व*, p. 257 and कुल्लूक on *मनुस्मृति*, III. 274 read च for तु.
4. This stanza from *ब्रह्मपुराण* is quoted in *कृत्यकल्पतरु-श्राद्धकाण्ड*, p. 21.
5. It is surprising that कुल्लूक gives two different readings असञ्चितैः (p. 105) and सुसञ्चितैः p. 107. Is it possible to take the first reading असञ्चितैः as a scribal mistake ?
6. *याज्ञवल्क्यस्मृति*, I. 261 reads विशेषतः for न संशयः .
7. These stanzas Nos. 17 and 18 are quoted from *वसिष्ठ धर्मसूत्र*, XI.39.40.
8. Führer, p. 31 reads च for तु.
9. *Ibid.*, p. 31 reads नो for दो which is wrong.
10. This refers to the *महाभारत*, XIII.88.12 which is quoted below in stanzas 19 and 20.

मघायोगः श्रूयते । तद्वचनाच्च विधिः कल्प्यमानो मघायुक्तायां त्रयोदश्यां श्राद्धमित्येकत्र सर्वानुगतः कल्पनीयः । इतरथा त्रयोदश्यां श्राद्धमित्येको विधिः परश्च मघायोगे फलातिशयार्थ इति कल्पनागौरवं स्यात् ।

यथा महाभारते[1] (१३.८८.१२अ-१३)

अपि नः स कुले जायाद्यो[2] न दद्यात् त्रयोदशीम् ।
मघासु सर्पिषा युक्तं पायसं दक्षिणायने ॥१९॥
अजे[3] सर्वलोहेन[4] मघासु[5] च[6] यतव्रतः[7]–
हस्तिछायासु विधिवत् कर्णव्यजनवीजितम् ॥२०॥

दक्षिणायने वृत्तेर्वर्षास्वित्यर्थः । सर्वलोहेन सर्वतो लोहितवर्णेन । सर्वलोहितछागेनानत्यमिति — वचनात् ।

तथा देवलः[8] —

आनन्त्याय भवेद्दत्तं खड्गमांसं दिनक्षये ।
महाशल्कलिको मत्स्यान् छागो वा सर्वलोहितः ॥२१॥

पुनर्मघाग्रहणं स्तुत्यर्थम् । हस्तिच्छायास्विति देशपरम् ।

परमानन्नेन यो दद्यात् पितॄणामौर्ध्वदेहिकम् ।
गजछायां तु पूर्वस्यां कुरुते दक्षिणामुखः ॥२२॥

इतिमहाभारत[9] (XIII. App.14.221B) वचनात् ।

प्राक्छाये कुञ्जरस्य चेति मनु[10]विष्णु[11]वचनात् कर्णव्यजनवीजितमित्यवधानाच्च । कालप्रकरणात् स्नानात् कुञ्जरछायाख्यकालपरमिदम् । कर्णव्यजनेन वीजितमित्यर्थवाद इति हलायुधवचनं दुर्वचनमेव । प्रकरणात् वाक्यस्य बलवत्वात् ।

---

1. The first line of stanza 19 can be traced in the *मनुस्मृति*, III.274.
2. *Ibid.*, III.274 reads भूयात्० for जायात्०.
3. *स्मृतिचंद्रिका-श्राद्धकाण्ड*, p. 24 reads आजेन for अजे.
4. *महाभारत*, XIII.88.13 reads वापि लोहेन for सर्वलोहेन.
5. *स्मृतिचंद्रिका-श्राद्धकाण्ड*, p. 24 reads वर्षासु for मघासु.
6. *महाभारत*, XIII.88.13 reads ०एव for ०च.
7. *Ibid.* and *स्मृतिचंद्रिका-श्राद्धकाण्ड*, p. 24 read नियत० for यत०.
8. The text of *देवल* cannot be traced in *स्मृतिसंदर्भ*, Vol. III.
9. This stanza is also found quoted in गोविन्दानन्द कृत *श्राद्धक्रियाकौमुदी*, p. 13.
10. This refers to *मनुस्मृति*, III.274.
11. This refers to *विष्णुस्मृति*, 78.53.

उपकुरनितम्बेषु छायायां कुञ्जरस्य चेति विष्णुधर्मोत्तरवचने देशप्रकरणात् स्थानाच्च पिण्डदानं चान्ते ज्येष्ठपुत्रिणा न कार्यम् ।

यथा कन्यागतापरपक्षाधिकारे देवीपुराणे —

कन्यास्थे तु रवावीशे पूजनीया यथाविधिः ।
भौजङ्गीं तिथिमासाद्य यावच्चंद्रार्कसंगमम्[1] ॥२३॥
तत्रापि महती पूजा कर्तव्या पितृदैवते ।
पक्षे[2] पिण्डप्रदानं तु ज्येष्ठपुत्री[3] विवर्जयेत् ॥२४॥

भौजङ्गीं पञ्चमी । चन्द्रार्कसङ्गमोऽमावास्या ।

अथ कन्यागतापर पक्षः ब्रह्मपुराणे[4] —

अश्वयुक् कृष्णपक्षे तु श्राद्धं कुर्या[5]द्दिने दिने ।
त्रिभागहीनं पक्षं वा त्रिभागं तु ऊर्ध्वमेव[6] वा ॥२५॥
न सन्ति पितरश्चेति कृत्वा मनसि यो नरः ।
श्राद्धं न कुरुते तत्र तस्य रक्तं पिबन्ति ते ॥२६॥
यावच्च कन्यातुलयोः क्रमादास्ते दिवाकरः ।
तावत् श्राद्धस्य कालः स्याच्छून्यं प्रेतपुरं तदा ॥[7]२७॥

दिने दिने इति वीप्सा पक्षश्राद्धार्था । तेन पञ्चदशश्राद्धानि दर्शितानि । ननु तिथिहासादौ कस्मिन् पक्षे चतुर्दश द्वादश चतुर्दश श्राद्धानि प्राप्नुवन्ति । एवं तिथिवृद्धावह वृद्धौ षोडशः स्युः । न पञ्चदशतिथ्यात्मकत्वाच्चान्द्रपक्षस्य दिने दिने पञ्चदशतिथिष्वित्यर्थः ।

यथा विष्णुधर्मोत्तरे प्रथमकाण्डम् —

तिथिनैकेन दिवसश्चान्द्रमाने प्रकीर्त्तितः ।
अहोरात्रेण चैकेन सावनो दिवसः स्मृतः ॥२८॥

त्रिभागहीनं पक्षं वेति षष्ठ्यादिकल्पः उक्तः । त्रिभागामित्येकादश्याद्विकल्पः । अर्धमेव वेति त्रयोदश्यादि कल्पः । न त्वर्द्धमिति पक्षार्द्धं व्याख्यानं कल्पतरुक्तमुक्तम् । उत्तरत्र लघुकालोपदेशात् सन्निधानाच्च । त्रिभगार्द्धात्प्रतीतेः त्रिभागहीन त्रिभागपदयोरपि पञ्चम्यादि दशम्यादि विवेचनं कल्पतरु[8]क्तमयुक्तमेव । पक्षापेक्षया पञ्चम्यादेः त्रिभागहीनादि पदार्थत्वानुपपत्तेरयुग्यत्वाद्गौतमोक्त पञ्चम्यादि

---

1. *श्राद्धतत्त्व*, p. 257 reads ००संगमः for ००संगमम्.
2. *Ibid.*, p. 257 and अपरार्क on *याज्ञवल्क्यस्मृति*, p. 557 read ऋक्षे for पक्षे.
3. *Ibid.*, p. 257 reads ०पुत्रो for ०पुत्री.
4. The text of *ब्रह्मपुराण* is quoted in *कृत्यकल्पतरु-श्राद्धकाण्ड*, p. 16.
5. *Ibid.*, p. 16 reads कार्यं० for कुर्वात्०.
6. *Ibid.*, p. 16 reads त्वर्धमेव० for तु उर्ध्वमेव०.
7. The stanza No. 27 is quoted in *अपरार्क on याज्ञवल्क्यस्मृति*, p. 424 and *कृत्यकल्पतरु-श्राद्धकाण्ड*, p. 16 and *श्राद्धसागर*, p. 110.
8. *कल्पतरु-श्राद्धकाण्ड*, p. 16 records this view of *कल्पतरु*.

कल्पस्य सामान्योपक्रमान्नाश्वयुक् परत्वम् ।

अत एव विष्णुधर्मोत्तर (१.१४२.१९-२०-२१अ) प्रथमकाण्डम् ।

उत्तरादयनाच्छ्राद्धे[1] श्रेष्ठं स्याद्दक्षिणायनम्[2] ।
चातुर्मास्यञ्च तत्रापि प्रसुप्ते केशवे हितम् ॥२९॥
प्रौष्ठपद्यापर:[3] पक्ष[4]स्तत्रापि[5] च विशेषत:[6]।
पञ्चम्यूर्द्धं च तत्रापि दशम्यूर्द्धवमतोप्यति[7]॥३०॥
मघायुक्ता[8] च तत्रापि शस्ता राजस्त्रयोदशी ।३१।

पञ्चम्यूर्द्धंच दशम्यूद्धर्वमित्यनेन षष्ठ्याद्येकादिकल्पा युक्तौ । न सन्तीत्यकरणे प्रत्यवायदर्शनं नित्यत्वज्ञापनार्थम् । तत्र च पक्षश्राद्धादिकल्पानां विषमशिष्ठत्वेन इच्छाविकल्पासंभवात् । एका देया तिस्रो देया: षड् देया इतिवत् फलभूमा कल्पनीय: । एतेषामेव कल्पानां दर्शितत्वात् ।

आश्विने एकस्मिन् दिने श्राद्धं कर्तव्यमिति पक्षश्चिन्तनीय: । सामान्यमासविहितं तु स्यादेवात्र संशय:। प्रोष्ठपद्यूद्धर्वय: कृष्णपक्ष: स पौर्णमास्यन्तमासव्यवस्थीयाऽश्वयुक् कृष्णपक्षो भवति । स यदा कन्योपक्रम: कन्या समाप्यश्च तदा तत्र पक्षश्राद्धमविवादमेव । यदा सिंहोपक्रम: कन्यासमाप्यश्च समस्त एव वा सिंहसमाप्य: । तदा कीदृश: शास्त्रार्थ: ।

अत्र जिकनप्रभृतय: ब्रह्मपुराणादि वचनेनैव व्यवस्था द्रष्टव्या ।

यथाब्रह्मपुराणे[9]—

यावच्च कन्यातुलयो: क्रमादास्ते दिवाकर: ।
तावच्छ्राद्धस्य काल: स्यात् शून्यं प्रेतपुरं तथा[10]॥३२॥

यथा भविष्यपुराणे[11]

कन्यां[12] गते सवितरि पितृराजानुशासनात्[13]।

---

1. *विष्णुधर्मोत्तर पुराण*, reads ००श्राद्धं for ००श्राद्धे.
2. *Ibid.*, reads ०दक्षिणायने for ०दक्षिणायनम्.
3. *Ibid.*, reads प्रौष्ठपद्यपरं for प्रौष्ठपद्यापर: .
4. *Ibid.*, reads पक्षं for पक्ष: .
5. *Ibid.*, reads तथापि for तत्रापि.
6. *Ibid.*, reads विशेषवत् ० for विशेषत: .
7. *Ibid.*, reads ००ततोप्यति for ००अतोप्यति.
8. *विष्णुधर्मोत्तर पुराण*, reads ०युता० for ०युक्ता०.
9. The text of *ब्रह्मपुराण* is quoted in *कृत्यकल्पतरु-श्राद्धकाण्ड*, p. 16.
10. *Ibid.*, p. 16 reads तदा for तथा.
11. These verses are quoted from *पुराणेऽपि* in *पराशरमाधव*, Vol. I. p. 667.
12. *Ibid.*, p. 667 reads कन्यागते for कन्यांगते.
13. *Ibid.*, p. 667 reads पितरो यान्ति वै सुतान् for पितृराजानुशासनात्.

तावत् प्रेतपुरी शून्या[1] यावत्[2] वृश्चिकदर्शनम् ॥३३॥
ततो वृश्चिक आयाते[3] निराशाः पितरो नृपः[4]।
पुनः स्वभवनं यान्ति शापं दत्वा सुदारुणम् ॥३४॥
हंसे[5] वर्षासु कन्यास्थे शाकेनापि गृहे वसन् ।
पञ्चम्या उतरे[6] दद्यादुभयोर्वंशवर्द्धनम्[7] ॥३५॥
सूर्ये कन्यास्थिते[8] श्राद्धं यो न कुर्याद् गृहाश्रमी ।
कुतस्तस्य धनं पुत्राः[9] पितृनिश्वासपीडनात् ॥३६॥
हंसे सूर्ये तृणमिव तृणं पितृमातृकुलश्च ।३७।

इदमवश्यं परिशोध्यमित्यर्थः । एवमादिवचनैः कन्यासम्बन्धेनैव श्राद्धप्रतिपादनादेतस्यापि वचनस्य तदेकवाक्यतया सौराश्विनपरत्वम् । सौरपरत्वे लक्षणा स्यादिति चेन्न । पौर्णमास्यन्तेऽतथात्वात् । अतः सिंहोपक्रमे कृष्णपक्षे कन्यासम्बन्धिन्येव भागे श्राद्धं न सिंहसम्बन्धिनि । अतः पक्षश्राद्धं तत्र निवर्त्तत एव । त्रिभागहीनमित्यादयः पक्षास्तत्र यथासंभवं बोद्धव्याः । कन्यासम्बन्धिन्यपरपक्षे श्राद्धविधानात् । उपक्रमे सिंहसम्बन्धेऽपि पक्षस्य कन्यासम्बन्धोऽस्त्येवेति चेन्न । एकस्य पक्षावयविनः पञ्चदशतिथ्यात्मकस्य अभावात् । अत एव पञ्चदशब्राह्मणसमुदायमध्ये एकस्य पुरुषोत्तमस्पर्शेन सर्वेषां फलभागिता । एतन्मूलमेवेदं वचनम् ।

कृत्तिकादि भरण्यन्तं वारावारविसप्तकाः ।
नैते संयोगमात्रेण पुनन्ति सकलां तिथिम् ॥३८॥

एकस्य तिथ्यवयविनोऽभावादित्यर्थः । इतरथा पूर्वदिने रात्रौ चतुर्थीं भौमवारयोगे बुधवारेऽपि भौमवारयुक्ता चतुर्थीविहितस्नानाद्यापत्तेः । यदा समस्त एवापरपक्षः सिंहार्के निपतति तदा तं पक्षं विहाय कन्यागतपरपक्ष एव श्राद्धम् । न त्वेवं पञ्चमपक्षवचन विरोधः ।

यथा कार्ष्णाजिनिः[10]

शक्रध्वजनिपातोऽङ्को यः स्यात् पक्षस्तु पञ्चमः ।
स विज्ञेयो परः पक्षः श्राद्धं तत्र विधीयते ॥३९॥

---

1. *पराशरमाधव,* Vol. I, p. 667 reads शून्या प्रेतपुरी सर्वा for तावत् प्रेतपुरी शून्या.
2. *Ibid.*, p. 667 reads यावद्०० for यावत्००.
3. *Ibid.*, p. 667 reads संप्राप्तौ for आयाते.
4. *Ibid.*, p. 667 reads गताः for नृपः .
5. *Ibid.*, p. 667 quotes this stanza from यम.
6. *Ibid.*, p. 667 reads पञ्चम्योरन्तरे for पञ्चम्या उत्तरे.
7. *Ibid.*, p. 667 reads उभयोरपि पक्षयोः for उभयोर्वंशवर्द्धनम्.
8. *Ibid.*, p. 667 reads ०गते for ०स्थिते.
9. *Ibid.*, p. 667 reads धनं पुत्राः कुतस्तस्य for कुतस्तस्य धनं पुत्राः . The order of the words is changed here.
10. The text of *कार्ष्णाजिनि* is quoted in *स्मृतिचंद्रिका श्राद्धकाण्ड,* p. 365.

पुत्रमायुर्धनं धनमारोग्यं भूतिमेव च ।[1]
प्राप्नोति पञ्चमे दत्वा श्राद्धं कामां[2]स्तथा परान्[3]।।४०।।
एतानेवाहं[4] हिंसन्ति पञ्चमं[5] यो[6] व्यतिक्रमेत्[7]।
तस्मान्नातिक्रमेद्विद्वान् पञ्चमे[8] पैतृकं विधिम् ।।४१।।

जातुकर्ण्यः[9] —

आषाढीमवधिं कृत्वा यः स्यात् पक्षस्तु पञ्चमः ।
तत्र श्राद्धं प्रकुर्वीत कन्यां गच्छतु वा न वा[10] ।।४२।।

जाबालः[11]—

आगतेऽपि[12]रवौ कन्यां श्राद्धं कुर्वीत यत्नतः[13]।
आषाढ्याः पञ्चमः पक्षः प्रशस्त[14] पितृकर्मणि ।।४३।।

उच्यते । एषां पुत्रादिफलसम्बन्धावगमात् काम्यम् । एषां वचनानां भोजदेवप्रभृतिभिरलिखितत्त्वाद-मूलत्वम् । समूलत्वेऽपि नित्यत्वे प्रमाणाभावात् । प्रत्युत पुत्रादिफलसम्बन्धावगमात् । काम्यं तद्भविष्यति। कन्यागतस्य च नित्यत्वं प्रागेवदर्शितम् । न च काम्याधिकारनित्याधिकारयोरेकशास्त्रार्थत्वम् । यावज्जीवाधिकरणविरोधात् । तद्यदि फलान्वित कन्यासमन्धिरहित एव श्राद्धं कृतम् । तथापि कन्यायामवश्यं कर्तव्यम् । वस्तुतस्तु श्राद्धभेदकल्पनागौरवापत्तेः । कन्याश्राद्ध एव फलान्वितया पञ्चमपक्षाख्य गुणफलविधिः । तदा केवलपञ्चमपक्षे श्राद्धमसङ्गतमेव ।

'कन्यां गच्छतु वा न वा' इति पञ्चमपक्षस्तुत्यर्थम् । न तु कन्यासम्बन्धाभावेऽपिश्राद्धविधानपरम् । प्राप्ते कन्यागतश्राद्धे गुणफलविधित्वात् तदसङ्गतम् ।

---

1. *स्मृतिचंद्रिका-श्राद्धकाण्ड*, p. 365 reads first line of stanza No. 40 as —
   पुत्रमायुस्तथाऽरोग्यमैश्वर्यमतुलं तथा ।
2. *Ibid.*, p. 365 reads श्राद्धकालान् for श्राद्धकामान्.
3. *Ibid.*, p. 365 reads च दुष्कलान् for तथा परान्.
4. *Ibid.*, p. 365 reads प्रेतांस्ते चैव for एतानेवाहं.
5. *Ibid.*, p. 365 reads पञ्चमे for पञ्चमम्.
6. *Ibid.*, p. 365 reads च for यो.
7. *Ibid.*, p. 365 reads व्यतिक्रमात् for व्यतिक्रमेत्.
8. *Ibid.*, p. 365 reads पञ्चमो for पञ्चमे.
9. The text of *जातुकर्ण्य* is ascribed to *बृहन्मनु* in *श्राद्धमयूख*, p. 9.
10. The second line of stanza No. 42 is read as — तत्र श्राद्धं प्रकुर्वीत कन्याथाऽर्को भवेन्न वा ।
11. This may be emended either as जाबालः or जाबालिः and the text of *जाबाल* is quoted in *पराशरमाधव*, Vol. I. p. 665 and *स्मृतिमुक्ताफलम्*, p. 745.
12. *पराशरमाधव*, Vol. I, p. 665 reads अगतेऽपि for आगतेऽपि.
13. *स्मृतिमुक्ताफलम्*, p. 775 reads सर्वथा for यत्नतः .
14. *Ibid.*, p. 775 reads प्रशस्तः for प्रशस्त.

ब्रह्मपुराणे पौर्णमास्यन्तमासेन समस्ततिथि कृत्याभिधानात् । अश्वयुक् शब्दस्यापि पौर्णमास्यन्तपरत्वात् ।

आश्वयुज्याञ्च[1] कृष्णायां त्रयोदश्यामिति ब्रह्मपुराण एवाश्वयुश्वक्शब्दस्य पौर्णमास्यन्तपरत्वाच्च लक्षणा च सौरेणाप्यविशिष्टा । अत एव मुख्यद्वयेन दर्शान्तिपरता क्लृप्तताहपर्यानुपपत्त्या लक्षणाया प्राधान्यमस्याधिकरणे दर्शितत्वात् ।

इदं तु उच्यते । उक्तमुक्तेः पौर्णमास्यान्ताश्विनपरत्वे कन्यानिरपेक्ष्य पञ्चमपक्षे पक्षश्राद्धादिकल्पना नित्यतयाऽवगम्यन्ते । न कन्याविशिष्टे निरपेक्षश्रुतेः । अत एव गुणफल गुणविधिः । अत एव कन्यासम्बन्धानुद्धेदेनैव पञ्चमपक्षे पक्षश्राद्धादिकं दर्शयति विष्णुधर्मोत्तरे प्रथम काण्डम् । (१.१४२.१९-२०-२१अ)

उत्तरायणात् श्राद्धं[2] श्रेष्ठं स्याद्दक्षिणायनम्[3]।
चातुर्मास्यञ्च तत्रापि प्रसुप्ते केशवे हितम् ॥४४॥
प्रौष्ठपद्याः पर पक्षस्तत्रापि च विशेषतः ।
पञ्चमयूर्द्ध्वञ्च तत्रापि दशम्यूर्द्ध्वमतोऽप्यति[4]॥४५॥
मघायुक्ता च तत्रापि शस्ताराजंस्त्रयोदशी ।
तथाऽक्षयं भवेच्छ्राद्धं मधुना पायसेन च ॥४६॥
सर्वस्वेनापि कर्तव्यं श्राद्धमत्र नराधिप ।
परान्नभोजी त्वपचः श्राद्धमत्र तु कारयेत् ॥४७॥

यानि च कन्याविषयाणि वचनानि तानि पञ्चमपक्षानपेक्ष्य श्राद्धान्तरविधायकान्येव । कन्यापञ्चमपक्षे समुच्चये तु कन्यागतस्यापि श्राद्धस्य नित्यत्वेनावगम्यमानस्य तन्त्रादेरसिद्धेर्न पृथकरणम् ।

यदा कन्यागतसमुच्चयस्तदा कन्यायामपि नित्यत्त्वात् तत् कर्तव्यमेव । परं पक्षश्राद्धादिकल्पेषु प्रमाणाभावात् । सकृत्कृते कृतः शास्त्रार्थ इति न्यायात् । सकृदेव कर्तव्यं श्राद्धम् । अधिमासेन तत्र श्राद्धं न कर्तव्यम् ।

यथा लघुहारीतः[5]—

सपिण्डीकरणादूर्ध्वं यत् किञ्चिच्छ्राद्धादिकं भवेत् ।
इष्टम्वाप्यथवा पूर्तं तन्न कुर्यान्मलिम्लुचे ॥४८॥

एवमेवमधिमासदोषेण पाटवादिना च तत्र श्राद्धाधिकरणे तुलायां कर्तव्यमाह ब्रह्मपुराणे ।

---

1. This line from *ब्रह्मपुराण* is quoted in *कृत्यकल्पतरु-श्राद्धकाण्ड,* p. 21 and it reads आश्वयुज्यां च for आश्वयुज्याञ्च.
2. In the stanza No. 29, however, we have the reading श्राद्धे for श्राद्धम्.
3. *विष्णुधर्मोत्तर पुराण,* reads ०दक्षिणायने for ०दक्षिणायनम्.
4. *Ibid.*, reads ००ततोप्यति for ००अतोऽप्यति.
5. The text of *लघुहारीत* is quoted in *अपरार्क on याज्ञवल्क्यस्मृति,* p. 548.

यावच्च कन्यातुलयोः क्रमादास्ते दिवाकरः ।
तावच्छ्राद्धस्य कालः स्याच्छून्यं प्रेतपुरं तदा[1]॥४९॥

अत्र कन्यातुलयोर्दिवाकरस्थितेः क्रमादेव प्राप्तत्वात् । क्रमाच्छ्राद्धस्य कालः स्यादित्यन्वयः । मुख्यकल्पार्थ कल्पभावेनेत्यर्थः । यावच्चेति सकलकृष्णपक्षव्याप्त्यावगतेः तुलाकृष्णपक्षे यस्यां कस्याञ्चितिथौ श्राद्धं कार्यम् ।

अत एव 'कार्तिकं सकलं वेति' विष्णुवचनम्[2](७८.५३ब) ।

अमावास्यायामिति आशयमाह भविष्यपुराणे[3] —

येयं द्विपान्विता राजन् ख्याता पञ्चदशी भुवि ।
तस्यां दद्यान्नचेद्दतं पितॄणां वै महालये ॥५०॥

महालये कन्यागतापरपक्षे न च पञ्चदशी पौर्णमासी ग्राह्या । 'एकोऽथवा दीपवरश्च देय' इत्यादिना आदिपुराणे दीपदानविधानादिति युक्तम् । संशये पितृकर्मणि प्रशस्ततया प्रदोषेऽमावास्यायाभावेऽपि सम्पूर्णत्वेन ग्रहणस्य युक्तत्वात् । अङ्गभूत कृष्णपक्षबाधापतेश्च ख्यातेत्यनन्वयश्च स्यात् । नानास्थानेष्वनेकेन दीपदानेन एवमुल्कायास्तस्या अमावास्याया एवाख्यातत्वात् । यथा तामधिकृत्य ब्रह्मपुराणे—

दर्शे दीपज्वलौ देयौ पितृदेवहितौ शुभौ ॥५१।

इति वचनात् ।

दीपमालाश्च कर्तव्याः शक्त्या देवगृहेषु च ।
रथ्यापनश्मशानेषु नदी पर्वतसानुषु ॥५२॥
उज्ज्वलज्योतिषा देहं प्रपश्यन्तो व्रजन्तु ते ॥५३।

इत्यादि वचनैर्दीपज्वलौ प्रदोषे देयौ । अमावास्यापरत्वे प्रतिमासपार्वणस्य प्राप्तत्वाद्विधिर्नस्यादिति चेन्न । प्रतिमासपार्वणार्देयस्य प्रकरणभेदेन भेदात् । अनुष्ठानविशेषानाह बहुत्वान्न विधिरितिचेन्न । एवं कन्यायामपि विधिर्न स्यात् । अशक्तपक्षेऽवश्यानुष्ठानार्थं विधिः ।

अत एव

अनेन विधिना श्राद्धं त्रिरब्दस्येह निर्वपेत् ।
कन्याकुम्भवृषस्थेऽर्के कृष्णपक्षे च[4] सर्वदा ॥५४॥

इति मत्स्यपुराण (१६.५८) मिति चेन्न प्रकृतेऽपि तुल्यत्वात् । अथ प्राप्तं तदैकेन मुनिना

1. *कृत्यकल्पतरु-श्राद्धकाण्ड*, p. 16 and stanza No. 32 above note the readings तदा and तथा respectively. Our manuscript, pp. 109, 110 offers two different readings at two different places.
2. This is *विष्णुस्मृति*, p. 787.
3. The text of *भविष्यपुराण* is quoted in पृथ्वीचन्द्र कृत *श्राद्धप्रकाश*, XV.37.
4. *मत्स्यपुराण*, XVI.58 reads कृष्णपक्षेषु for कृष्णपक्षे च.

सामान्यप्राप्तस्य पितृप्रीत्यतिशयार्थं विधानं भविष्यति किं च कार्तिकपौर्णमास्यामपि प्राप्तत्वात् ।

यथा यमः[1]—

आषाढ्यामथा कार्त्तिक्यां माघ्यां[2] त्रीन् पञ्च[3] द्विजान् ।
तर्पयेत् पितृपूर्वन्तु तदन्यो[4]क्षयमुच्यते ॥५५॥

तस्मादमावास्यैव ग्राह्या।कन्यायाः षोडशेषु दिनेषु श्राद्धमुक्तं ब्रह्मपुराणे[5]।

कन्याङ्गते[6] सवितरि यान्यहानि तु षोडश ।
क्रतुभिस्तानि तुल्यानि तेषु दत्तमथाक्षयम् ॥५६॥

काम्यमिदम् । नित्यत्वे प्रमाणाभावात् । फलश्रुतेश्च ।

तथा ब्रह्मपुराणम्— (२२०.४६ब-४७अ)

दीव्यभौमान्तरिक्षाणि स्थावराणि चराणि च ।
पिण्डमिच्छन्ति पितरः कन्याराशिं गते रवौ ॥५७॥
कन्यां गते सवितरि यान्यहानि तु षोडश ।
क्रतुभिस्तानि तुल्यानि देवो नारायणोऽब्रवीत् ॥५८॥
राजसूयाश्वमेधाभ्यां यदीच्छेत् सदृशं फलम् ।[7]
अप्यमुषव्ये मूलाद्यैः पितॄन् कन्यां गतेऽर्चयेत् ॥५९॥

षोडशदिनानि दर्शितानि सूर्यसिद्धान्ते (१४.४-५)

तुलादि षडशीत्यंशे[8] षडशीति मुखं दिनम्[9]।
तच्चतुष्टयमेवं स्यात् द्विस्वभावेषु राशिषु ॥६०॥
षड्विंशे धनुषो भागे द्वाविंशेऽनिमिषस्य[10] च ।
मिथुनाष्टादशे भागे कन्यायाश्च[11] चतुर्दशे[12]॥६१॥

1. The text of यम is quoted in *कृत्यकल्पतरु-श्राद्धकाण्ड*, p. 15.
2. *Ibid*., p. 15 reads माघ्यां for माघ्याम्.
3. *Ibid*., p. 15 reads वा after पञ्च.
4. *Ibid*., p. 15 reads ०अस्य०० for ०अन्य००.
5. *Ibid*., p. 16 *अपरार्क on याज्ञवल्क्यस्मृति*, p. 424 ascribe this stanza to *ब्रह्मपुराण;* and *पृथ्वीचंद्र-श्राद्धप्रकाश*, XVI.18, p. 406.
6. *कृत्यकल्पतरु-श्राद्धकाण्ड*, p. 16 and *श्राद्धप्रकाश*, p. 406 read कन्यां गते for कन्याङ्गते which is corrupt, but *पृथ्वीचंद्र-श्राद्धप्रकाश*, XV.16, p. 371 records the reading कन्यागते for कन्याङ्गते.
7. This is *ब्रह्मपुराण*, 220.47b-48a.
8. *सूर्यसिद्धान्त*, p. 291 reads ०अह्नां for ०अंशे.
9. *Ibid*., p. 291 reads क्रमात् for दिनम्.
10. *Ibid*., p. 291 reads ०निमिषस्य for ०अनिमिषस्य.
11. *Ibid*., p. 291 reads कन्यायास्तु for कन्यायाश्च.
12. *Ibid*., p. 291 reads चतुर्दश for चतुर्दशे.

अत ऊर्ध्वं तु कन्याया यान्यहानि तु षोडश ।
क्रतुभिस्तानि तुल्यानि पितृभ्यो दत्तमक्षयम् ॥६२॥

एतेन कन्यांशेषु शुक्लकृष्णसाधारणानि षोडशदिनानि श्राद्धकालः । अनिमिषो मीनः । पौर्णमास्याद्यमावास्यापर्यन्तं षोडशेषु दिनेषु श्राद्धमिति प्राचामाचारो दुराचारो निष्प्रमाणक एव ।

अथ शस्त्रहतानां चतुर्दशी ।

तत्र विष्णुः — (७६.५०)

युद्ध[1] हतानां श्राद्धकर्मणि चतुर्दशी प्रशस्ता[2] युद्धहतानामेवेति न नियमार्थम् ।

ब्रह्मपुराणे[3]

प्रयोजनशस्त्राग्निविषोद्बन्ध निनान्तथा ।[4]
चतुर्दश्यां तु कर्तव्यं तृप्त्यर्थमिति[5] निश्चयः ॥६३॥

प्रायो महापथगमनं वायुपुराणे (८१.१८)

अबालास्तु गृहे यत्र मृतास्तेषां प्रदापयेत् ।[6]
शस्त्रेण तु हता ये वै तेषां दद्याच्चतुर्दशीम् ॥६४॥

युवा स एव पित्रादयो मृता इत्यर्थः ।

मरीचिः [7]—

विषशस्त्रश्वापदा हि[8] तिर्यग् ब्राह्मणघातिनाम् ।
चतुर्दश्यां क्रिया[9] कार्या[10] अन्यैषां तु विगर्हिता ॥६५॥

ब्राह्मणकृतो घातोऽस्यास्तीति ब्रह्मघाती । तेषां ये च वै ब्रह्मणैर्हता इति ब्रह्मपुराणदर्शनात् । न तु कृतब्राह्मणघातस्तस्य पतितत्वात् । अन्येषामशस्त्रहतानां एतच्च शस्त्रहतं श्राद्धं विष्टरादिभिः सामान्यप्रकरण-दर्शनात् । सकल कृष्णपक्षसाधारणमेव । पित्रादीनामेव पार्वणविधिप्रकरणात् पार्वणविधिना कर्तव्यम् ।

---

1. *विष्णुस्मृति,* p. 786 reads शस्त्र० for युद्ध०.
2. *Ibid.*, p. 786 reads शस्ता for प्रशस्ता.
3. The text of *ब्रह्मपुराण,* is quoted in *पृथ्वीचन्द्र-श्राद्धप्रकाश,* XV.147, p. 392.
4. The first line of stanza No. 63 is read as — प्रायो न शतशस्त्राणि विषोद्वन्धवतां तथा ।
5. *पृथ्वीचंद्र-श्राद्धप्रकाश,* XV.147, p. 392 reads तृप्तर्थ इति for तृप्त्यर्थं इति.
6. *वायुपुराण,* p. 300 reads first line of stanza No. 64 as — युवानश्च मृता यस्य गृहे प्रदापयेत् ।
7. *श्राद्धकल्प,* p. 48 quotes the text of मरीचि.
8. *Ibid.*, p. 48 reads ०००आदि for ०००हि.
9. *Ibid.*, p. 48 reads भवेत् for क्रिया.
10. *Ibid.*, p. 48 reads पूजा for कार्या.

सपिण्डीकरणादूर्ध्वं यत्र यत्र प्रदीयते ।
तत्र तत्र त्रयं कुर्याद्वर्जयित्वा मृताहनि ॥६६॥

इति शंखवचनात् ।

ननु अन्येषां विगर्हितेतिश्रवणात् कथं त्रैपौरुषिक पार्वणविधिः । यस्य पुरुषास्त्रय एव शस्त्रेण एव शस्त्रहतास्तस्य त्रैपौरुषिकविधिरूपपद्यते एव । यस्य द्वौ शस्त्रहतौ एको वा तेनापि द्वौ पौरुषिकमेव पार्वणं कर्तव्यम् ।

यथा मनुः —(३.२२१)

पिता यस्य तु वृत्तः स्यात् जीवेद्वापि[1] पितामहः ।
पितुः स नाम संकीर्त्य कीर्तयेत् प्रपितामहम् ॥६७॥

यथा हारीतः[2]

पितामहेऽपि[3] जीवे द्वौ[4] पितर्येव समापयेत् । नन्वेकोद्दिष्टं न कारयेत् ।

यमः —

सपिण्डीकरणादूर्ध्वं सपिण्डीकरणे कृते ।
एकोद्दिष्टविधानेन तत्कार्यं शस्त्रघातिने ॥६८॥

उच्यते । एषां वचनानां अमूलत्वात् । समूलत्वेऽपि पार्वणशक्तविषयान्येतानि । विष्टरादि वचनेषु पार्वणाय तेः[5]। भ्रात्रादीनां तु शस्त्रहतानामेकोद्दिष्टविधिना कार्यम् ।

अपुत्रा ये मृताः केचित् स्त्रियो वा पुरुषाश्च ये ।
तेषामपि च देयं स्यादेकोद्दिष्टं न पार्वणम् ॥६९॥

इत्यापस्तम्ब[6]वचनेन पार्वणनिषेधात् । तच्च सकलकृष्णपक्षसाधारणम् । विष्ण्वादिवचने श्राद्धशब्दस्य पार्वणपरत्वोक्तेः । किन्त्वाश्विनमासीय कृष्णपक्षविषयम् । ब्रह्मपुराणे 'प्राया[7]नशयने'त्यादिना सकलकृष्णपक्षसाधारणं श्राद्धमभिधाय आश्विने तर्पणीयाश्चतुर्दश्यां लुप्तपिंडोदकक्रिया इति यत् पुनरभिधानं तच्छस्त्रहतभ्रात्रादिविषयम् । अत एव तत्रैवामावास्यायां पितरः पूज्या नान्दीमुखाः । अपि तु वृद्धप्रपितामहादीनामपि श्राद्धं दर्शितम् । इयश्चतुर्दश्यामशस्त्रहतश्राद्धनिन्दा आश्विनमासीयपक्षश्राद्धादि-विकल्पव्यतिरिक्त सामान्यकृष्णपक्षविहित श्राद्धकाम्याश्राद्धविषया । प्रकरणभेदेन श्राद्धकर्मभेदात् ।

1. *मनुस्मृति,* reads ०च अपि for ०वापि.
2. The text of *हारीत,* is quoted in *कृत्यकल्पतरु-श्राद्धकाण्ड*, p. 237.
3. *Ibid.*, p. 237 reads ०च for ०अपि.
4. *Ibid.*, p. 237 reads वै for द्वौ.
5. This expression seems to be corrupt.
6. This stanza is not found in the आपस्तम्बस्मृति.
7. The text of *ब्रह्मपुराण* is quoted in *कृत्यकल्पतरु-श्राद्धकाण्ड,* p. 27 where it is written as प्रायानशनशस्त्राग्नि etc.

सामान्यविशेषन्यायात् । इतरथा चतुर्दश्यां संक्रान्तिश्राद्धे शस्त्रहतनिन्दा स्यात् ।

अत एव

कृष्णपक्षे दशम्यादौ वर्जयित्वा चतुर्दशीम् ॥७०॥

इति मनुवचने (३.२७६) चतुर्दशीवर्जनं पक्षश्राद्धादिव्यतिरिक्तविषयम् । ननु शस्त्रादिहतानां श्राद्धनिषेधः श्रूयते ।

यथा छागलेयः[1]—

शस्त्रविद्युद्धतानाञ्च शृंगिदंष्ट्रिसरिसृपैः ।
आत्मनस्त्यागिनाञ्चैव श्राद्धमेषां न कारयेत् ॥७१॥

सत्यं बुद्धिपूर्वमतानामेव । अबुद्धिपूर्वमतानां च श्राद्धमाह अंगिराः[2]।

अथ कश्चित् प्रमादेन म्रियतेऽग्नयुदकादिभिः ।
अशौचं तस्य कर्तव्यं कर्तव्या चोदकक्रिया ॥७२॥

अबुद्धिपूर्वमपि शृङ्ग्यादिभिः क्रीडां कुर्वतां मृतानां न कर्तव्यम् ।

यथा वायुपुराणे[3]—

शृंगि दंष्ट्री नखि व्याल विषवह्नि स्त्रिया जलैः ।
आदरात् परिहर्तव्यं कुर्वन् क्रीडां मृतस्तु यः ॥७३॥

परिहर्तव्यः श्राद्धादौ शास्त्रानुमत्या वृद्धिपूर्वमृतानामपि कर्तव्यम् ।

यथा वृद्धगार्ग्यः[4]—

वृद्धः शौचः स्मृतेर्लुप्तः प्रत्याख्यात भिषक् क्रियः ।
आत्मानं घातयेद्यस्तु भृग्वग्न्यशनाम्बुभिः ॥७४॥
तस्य त्रिरात्रमशौचं द्वितीये त्वस्थि सञ्चयः ।
तृतीये तूदकं कृत्वा चतुर्थे श्राद्धमिष्यते ॥७५॥

एवं क्रीडाव्यतिरेकेन अबुद्धिपूर्वकं मृताः शास्त्रानुमत्या च बुद्धिपूर्वमृता अपि श्राद्धार्हाः । कथं लुप्तपिंडोदकत्वमिति चेन्न । गौणत्वमिति ब्रूमः । बुद्धिपूर्वे पिण्डोदकक्रियालोपादिति ।

---

1. The text of *छागलेय* cannot be traced.
2. The text of *अंगिरस् स्मृति* cannot be traced in *स्मृतिसंदर्भ,* Vol. I, and Adyar edition, Madras.
3. This stanza cannot be traced in the extant *वायुपुराण.*
4. The text of *वृद्धगार्ग्य* cannot be traced.

८

अथ अष्टका:

वायुपुराणे (८१.२-५)

पित्र्यदानाय मूले स्यु[1]रष्टकास्तिस्रमेव[2] च ।
कृष्णपक्षे वरिष्ठा हि पूर्वा चैन्द्री विभाव्यते[3]॥१॥
प्राजापत्या द्वितीया स्यात् तृतीया वैश्वदेविकी[4]।
आद्याऽपूपै:[5] सदा कार्या मांसैरन्या भवेत्तथा[6]॥२॥
शाकै: कार्या तृतीया स्यादेष द्रव्यगतो विधि: ।
अन्वष्टका पितॄणां तु[7] नित्यमेव विधीयते ॥३॥
या च्याप्यन्या[8] चतुर्थी स्यात् तां च कुर्याद्विशेषत: ।
आसु[9] श्राद्धं द्विज:[10] कुर्यात् सर्वस्वेनापि नित्यश:[11]॥४॥
क्षिप्रं प्राप्नोति श्रेयांसि परत्रेह च मोदते ।
पितर: पूर्वकालेषु[12] तिथिकालेषु देवता: ॥५॥
सर्वे गृहस्थमायान्ति निपानमिव धेनव: ।
यस्य ते प्रतिगच्छेयुरष्टकास्वप्य[13] पूजिता:[14]॥६॥

---

1. *कृत्यकल्पतरु-श्राद्धकाण्ड,* p. 17 reads स्यू: for स्यु: .
2. *Ibid.*, p. 17 reads तिस्र एव fr तिस्रमेव.
3. *Ibid.*, p. 17 reads इति भाष्यते for विभाव्यते.
4. *वायुपुराण,* 81.3 reads ०दैविकी for ०देविकी.
5. *कृत्यकल्पतरु-श्राद्धकाण्ड,* p. 17 reads ०यूपै: for ०अपूपै: .
6. *वायुपुराण,* 81.3 reads सदा for तथा.
7. *Ibid.*, 81.4 and *कृत्यकल्पतरु-श्राद्धकाण्ड,* p. 17 read वै for तु.
8. *कृत्यकल्पतरु-श्राद्धकाण्ड,* p. 17 reads चाप्यन्या for च्याप्यन्या, which is obviously wrong.
9. *वायुपुराण,* 81.5 reads तासु for आसु.
10. *Ibid.*, 81.5 reads बुध: for द्विज:. While *कृत्यकल्पतरु-श्राद्धकाण्ड,* p. 17 reads च य: for द्विज:
11. *Ibid.*, 81.5 reads शक्तित: for नित्यश: .
12. *कृत्यकल्पतरु-श्राद्धकाण्ड,* p. 17 reads पर्वकालेषु for पूर्वकालेषु.
13. *Ibid.*, p. 17 reads अष्टकासु for अष्ठकास्वप्य.
14. *Ibid.*, p. 17 reads ह्यपूजिता: for पूजिता: .

मोघास्तस्य भवन्त्याशाः परत्रेह च नित्यशः ॥७॥

मूलेआदौ प्रधानस्थाने[1] इत्यर्थः। अमावास्या हि प्रधानं श्राद्धकालः। तस्मिन् स्थाने तत्तुल्या इत्यर्थः। अत एव विष्णुधर्मोत्तरे — अमावास्या श्राद्धकाल इत्याभिधाय आग्रहायन्यामतीतायां[2] कृष्णास्तिस्त्रोष्टकास्तथा[3]।

तथा तद्रूपा इत्यर्थः। एतच्चाग्रहायण्याया उर्ध्वं तिस्त्रोऽष्टका इतिवचनात्।

यत्तु ब्रह्मपुराणवचनम्—

ब्रह्मलोके तपस्तप्त्वा पितरो लेभिरे वरम्।
पौषे कृष्णाष्टकायां तु शाकैः संतर्पयेत् पितॄन् ॥[4]८॥

तथा छन्दोगपरिशिष्टम्—

शाकं तु फाल्गुणाष्टम्यां[5] स्वयं पत्यपि वा पचेत्।
वास्तु शाकादि होमश्च कार्यः पूपाष्टकावृता ॥९॥

तत्तु पौर्णमास्यन्तमासेन। वरिष्ठा श्रेष्ठा। ऐन्द्री इन्द्रदेवता यागसम्बन्धेन। एवं प्राजापत्या वैश्वदेवी च मांसैः पशोरिति शेषः।

यद्युवाल्पसम्भावतमः स्यात्। अपि पशुनैव कुर्वीतेति अष्टकायां गोभिलदर्शनात्[6]। पशुरपि छाग एव। 'छागोऽनादेश पशु'रिति गृह्यान्तरवचनात्[7]। छागाभावे स्थालीपाकः। 'अपि वा स्थालीपाकं कुर्वीत' इति गोभिलवचनात्[8]।

तथा छन्दोगपरिशिष्टम्

स्थालीपाकं पशुस्थाने कुर्याद्यद्यनुकल्पितम्[9]।
श्रपयेत्तं सवत्सायास्तरुण्या गोः पयःसु[10]॥१०॥ इति।

अन्वष्टकेन आन्वष्टकं मध्यमायामिति गोभिलगौतमौ। वकिः शण्डिश्च सर्वासु कौतसामेनेष्टकासु च इति छन्दोगपरिशिष्टवचनात्[11]।

---

1. This explanation is the same as the one offered in *कृत्यकल्पतरु-श्राद्धकाण्ड*, p. 18.
2. *विष्णुधर्मोत्तरपुराण*, reads आग्रहायण्यतीतायां for आग्रहायन्यामतीतायाम्.
3. This line is from the *विष्णुधर्मोत्तर पुराण*, I.142.3b.
4. This stanza cannot be traced in the extant *ब्रह्मपुराण*.
5. It may be emended as फाल्गुनाष्टम्यां for फाल्गुणाष्टम्याम्.
6. *श्राद्धतत्त्व*, p. 259 reads यद्युवाल्पतरसम्भारः स्यादिति पशुनैव कुर्यात्.
7. *श्राद्धतत्त्व*, p. 259 reads छागोऽनादेशो पशुः इति गौतमात्.
8. Also see *श्राद्धतत्त्व*, p. 259.
9. *Ibid.*, p. 259 reads ००आनुकल्पिकम् for ००अनुकल्पितम्.
10. *Ibid.*, p. 259 reads परस्यनु for पयः सु.
11. The citation from *छन्दोगपरिशिष्ट* cannot be traced.

मध्यमायामेवान्वष्टकायागस्य गोभिलसंमतत्वात् तत् समानतन्त्रत्वात् । अन्वष्टका श्राद्धमपि गोभिलीया नान्तत्रैवेति[1] चतुर्थी स्यादिति वर्षासु ज्ञेया । 'वर्षासु मध्यशाकैस्तु चतुर्थ्यामेव सर्वदा' इति ब्रह्म[2]पुराण दर्शनात् । 'वर्षास्वपि प्रौष्ठपद्या उर्ध्व प्रौष्ठपद्यामतीतायामष्टकात्वं भविष्यति' इति वरदानश्रवणात् । यत्तु चतुरष्टको हेमन्तस्ता: समांसाश्चिकीर्षेदिति कौत्स इति गोभिलसूत्रात[3]। क्रतुसंवत्सर व्यवस्थाया: हेमन्तशिशिरयोश्चतस्रो अष्टका: प्रतीयन्ते । तत्तु शाखान्तरीयं त्र्यष्टकपक्षस्य गोभिलसंमतत्वात्[4]।

तथा गोभिल: —

'त्र्यष्टक इति औद्गातृमानि: ।'

तथा गौतमावार्कशण्डी ।

अत एव शौनकसूत्रम्[5]—

'हेमन्त शिशिरयोस्त्रयानामपरक्षणामष्टमीष्टका: ।'

नन्वेवं वर्षास्वष्टकाविधिविरोध: । न तस्य श्राद्धविषयत्वात् । त्र्यष्टकपक्षस्येष्टि विषयत्वादविरोध: ।

ब्रह्मपुराणे

ऐन्द्यान्तु प्रथमायान्तु शाकै: संतर्पयेत् पितृन् ।
प्राजापत्यं[6] द्वितीयायां मांसै: शुद्धैश्च तर्पयेत् ॥११॥
वैश्वदेव्या[7]स्तृतीया[8]पूपैश्च यथाक्रमम् ।
वर्षासु मेध्यशाकैस्तु चतुर्थ्यामेव सर्वदा ॥१२॥

अत्र शाकादिर्विकल्प: । शाखाभेदव्यवस्थित:। अत्र गोभिलपारस्करीययो:[9]। स्वगृह्यतुल्यत्वाद्वायु-पुराणोक्त एव क्रम: । अष्टकादि श्राद्धे शूद्रादीनामप्यधिकार: ।

यथा मत्स्यपुराणे (१७.२ब)

अमावास्याष्टका कृष्णपक्ष[10] पञ्चदशीसु च ॥१३॥

---

1. This reading seems to be corrupt.
2. *कृत्यकल्पतरु-श्राद्धकाण्ड,* p. 18 quotes *ब्रह्मपुराण* and reads मेध्यशाकैस्तु for मध्यशाकैस्तु. But on the next page 70 the ms. i.e, p. 121 records the reading मेध्यशाकैस्तु.
3. This view of कौत्स referred to by गोभिल is hardly quoted in the *Dharma Śāstra* literature.
4. This is not found in the Digest work.
5. *अपरार्क on याज्ञवल्क्यस्मृति,* p. 431 and *पराशरमाधव,* Vol. I., p. 654 read चतुर्णां for त्रयानाम्. *श्राद्धमयूख,* p. 3 quotes this from *आश्वलायन गृह्यसूत्र,* II.41. Even त्रयानाम् may be emended as त्रयाणाम्.
6. *कृत्यकल्पतरु-श्राद्धकाण्ड,* p. 18 quotes *ब्रह्मपुराण* and reads प्राजापत्यां for प्राजापत्यं.
7. *Ibid.*, p. 18 reads वैश्वदेव्यां for वैश्वदेव्या:.
8. *Ibid.*, p. 18 reads तृतीयायां for तृतीयाम्.
9. This view of पारस्कर cannot be traced in the *पारस्कर गृह्यसूत्र,* pp. 323 & 324.
10. *मत्स्यपुराण,* p. 29 read कृष्णपक्षे for कृष्णपक्ष.

इत्यष्टकादि श्राद्धमभिधायोक्तम् ।

'एतच्चानुपनीतोऽपि कुर्यात् सर्वेषु पर्वसु ।
श्राद्धं साधारणं नाम सर्वकामफलप्रदम् ॥१४॥[1]
भार्याविरहितोऽप्येतत् प्रवासस्थोऽपि नित्यशः[2]।
शूद्रोऽप्यमन्त्रवत् कुर्यादनेन विधिना बुधः ॥१५॥

तत्रैवशब्दात् प्रकृतसर्वश्राद्धप्रतीतेः । अन्वष्टका श्राद्धं च मातृपूर्वमेव कार्यम् ।

यथा ब्रह्मपुराणे (२२०.५१ब-५२अ)

अन्वष्टकासु च कर्तव्यं श्राद्धं हैमन्तिकीसु च[3]।
अन्वष्टकासु क्रमशो मातृपूर्वं तदिष्यते ॥१६॥

विष्णुः (७४.१)

अन्वष्टकास्वष्टकावत् मात्रे[4] पितामह्यै प्रपितामह्यै च पूर्ववत् ब्राह्मणान् भोजयित्वा इत्यादि । मातृश्राद्धं च छन्दोगैर्न कार्यम् । मातामहादि श्राद्धं च न योषिद्भ्यः पृथग् दद्यादवसानदिनादृते ।

तथा

'कर्षुसमन्वितं त्यक्ता[5] तथाद्यं श्राद्धषोडशम् ।
प्रत्याब्दिकं च शेषेषु पिण्डाः स्युः षडिति स्थितिः ॥१७॥[6]

इति छन्दोगपरिशिष्टवचनविरोधात् ।

तथवनावश्यक श्राद्धकालाः । तत्र मन्वन्तरादयः ।

वायुपुराणे

एतेषामभ्युपगमान्मनुर्मन्वन्तरेश्वरः ।
मन्वन्तरादौ श्राद्धानि प्रावर्तयत सर्वतः ॥१८॥[7]

एतेषां पितॄणामित्यर्थः ।

मत्स्यपुराणे (१७.५ब-८ब)

तथा मन्वन्तरादौ च श्राद्धं देयं विजानता ।
अश्वयुक् शुक्लनवमी द्वादशी कार्तिके तथा ॥१९॥

---

1. *कृत्यकल्पतरु-श्राद्धकाण्ड,* p. 235 quotes this stanza from the *मत्स्यपुराण.*
2. *Ibid.*, p. 235 reads भक्तिमान् for नित्यशः and quotes from the *मत्स्यपुराण.*
3. *ब्रह्मपुराण,* reads मन्वन्तरासु वै for हैमन्तिकीसु च.
4. *विष्णुस्मृति,* p. 769 reads वह्नौ हुता दैवपूर्वमेव before मात्रे.
5. *श्राद्धमयूख,* p. 9 reads मुक्त्वा for त्यक्ता.
6. This stanza is quoted in the *श्राद्धमयूख,* p. 9 and on p. 25, this is quoted from the text of *कात्यायन.*
7. This citation cannot be traced in the *वायुपुराण.*

तृतीया चैव माघस्य[1] तथा भाद्रपदस्य च ।
फाल्गुनस्याप्यमावास्या पौषस्येकादशी तथा [2]॥२०॥
आषाढस्यापि दशमी तथा माघस्य सप्तमी।
श्रावणस्याष्टमी कृष्णा तथाषाढी[4] च पूर्णिमा ॥२१॥
कार्तिकी फाल्गुनी चैत्री ज्येष्ठी पञ्चदशी सिता[5]।
मन्वन्तरादयस्त्वेता दत्तस्याक्षयकारिकाः ॥२२॥
अमावास्याष्टमी व्यतिरिक्ता द्वादशतिथयः ।

शुक्ला प्रतिपत्तुल्या । पुनः पुनस्तथा शब्दोपादानात् । उपक्रमउपसंहारयोः[6] शुक्लकीर्तनाच्च । एतच्च नित्यत्वे प्रमाणाभावात् काम्यम् । आनुवादिकी पितृप्रीतिः फलम् ।

---

1. *मत्स्यपुराण,* reads चैत्रमासस्य for चैवमाघस्य which is corrupt.
2. *श्राद्धमयूख,* p. 6 reads सिता for तथा.
3. *मत्स्यपुराण,* p. 6 reads माघमासस्य सप्तमी for माघस्य सप्तमी.
4. *श्राद्धमयूख,* p. 6 reads माघी च for आषाढी च.
5. *Ibid*., p. 6 reads ज्येष्ठ पञ्चदशी सिता and in the foot-note we have the reading ज्येष्ठे.
6. This has a reference to उपक्रम-उपसंहारन्याय cf: *भामती* on शा० भा० on *बादरायण कृत ब्रह्मसूत्र,* III. 3.17.

१

अथ युगाद्या:

ब्रह्मपुराणे—

युगाद्येषु युगान्तेषु श्राद्धमक्षयमुच्यते ।
तथा[1] वैशाख शुक्लपक्षे तु[2] तृतीयायां कृतं युगम् ॥१॥
कार्तिके शुक्लपक्षे तु[3] त्रेताथ[4] नवमेऽहनि ।
अथ भाद्रपदे कृष्णा[5] त्रयोदश्यां तु द्वापरम् ॥२॥
माघे[6] च[7] पौर्णमास्यां च[8] घोरं कलियुगं स्मृतम् ।
सूर्यस्य सिंहसंक्रान्त्यामन्त: कृतयुगस्य तु ॥३॥
ज्ञेयस्तु[9] वृषसंक्रान्त्यां[10] द्वापरान्तश्च संज्ञया[11]।
तथा च कुंभसंक्रान्त्यामन्त: कलियुगस्य तु[12]॥४॥

तत्र वैशाखादय: पौर्णमास्यान्ता: ग्राह्या:। ब्रह्मपुराणे तथैव तिथिकृत्यभिधानात् । किं च 'कार्तिके शुक्लपक्षे तु त्रेताऽथ नवमेऽहनि' इत्यत्र दर्शनान्ते कार्तिके नवमेऽहनि इत्यनेनैव शुक्लपक्षप्राप्तौ शुक्लपक्षपदानर्थक्यात् । युगान्तेषु सौरमासग्रहणं राश्यवच्छेदविधानात् ।

नन्वमावास्या युगादिरित्युक्तं विष्णुपुराणे (३.१४.१२-१३अ-१४)

वैशाखमासस्य तु या[13] तृतीया नवम्यसौ कार्तिकशुक्लपक्षे ।

1. *स्मृतिचंद्रिका-श्राद्धकाण्ड,* p. 28 quotes *ब्रह्मपुराण* and drops तथा.
2. *Ibid.*, p. 28 drops तु.
3. *Ibid.*, p. 28 reads च for तु.
4. *Ibid.*, p. 28 reads ०च for ०अथ.
5. *Ibid.*, p. 28 reads कृष्णे० for कृष्णा०.
6. *श्राद्धमयूख,* p. 6 quotes *ब्रह्मपुराण* and reads माघस्य for माघे.
7. *Ibid.*, p. 6 drops च.
8. *Ibid.*, p. 6 reads तु for च.
9. *स्मृतिचंद्रिका-श्राद्धकाण्ड,* p. 28 reads ज्ञेयो for ज्ञेयस्तु.
10. *Ibid.*, p. 28 reads वृषभ० for वृष०.
11. *Ibid.*, p. 28 reads संख्यया for संज्ञया.
12. *Ibid.*, p. 28 reads कलियुगे स्मृत: for कलियुगस्य तु.
13. *Ibid.*, p. 28 quotes *विष्णुपुराण* and reads सिता for तु या.

नभस्य मासस्य तमिस्रपक्षे[1]
त्रयोदशी पञ्चदशी च माघे ॥५॥
एताः युगाद्याः कथिताः पुराणेषु[2]
अनन्तपुण्यास्तिथयश्चतस्रः[3]।
पानीयमप्यत्र तिलैर्विमिश्रं
दद्यात् पितृभ्यः प्रयतो मनुष्यः ॥६॥
श्राद्धं कृतं तेन समाः सहस्रम्[4]।
रहस्यमेतत् पितरो वदन्ति ॥७॥

अत्र तमिस्रपक्षे पदानुषङ्गात् पञ्चदशम्यमावास्या प्रतीयते । न ब्रह्मपुराणविरोधेनानुषङ्गायोगात् ।

ननु—'द्वे शुक्ले शुक्ले द्वे[5] तथा कृष्णे युगाद्ये परिकीर्तिते ।
शुक्ले पूर्वाह्णिके ज्ञेयः कृष्णे चैवापराह्णिके ॥८॥ इति पठन्ति ।

तेन विरोधः । न एतस्य अनाकरत्वात् । साकरत्वेऽपि कल्पभेदेऽपि व्यवस्थितो विकल्पः ।

तथा[6]—

नवम्यां शुक्लपक्षस्य कार्तिके निरागात् कृतम् ।
त्रेतासित तृतीयायां वैशाखे समपद्यत ॥९॥
दर्शे च माघमासस्य प्रवृत्तं द्वापरं युगम् ।
कलिः कृष्णत्रयोदश्यां नभस्ये मासि निर्गतः ॥१०॥

इत्यपि वचनं समूलत्वे कल्पभेदेन बोद्धव्यम् । तथा श्राद्धं पौर्णमास्यामेव । ब्रह्मपुराणे तस्या[7] युगादित्वात् ।

अत्र

'कृष्णपक्षे त्रयोदश्यां श्राद्धं यः कुरूते नरः ।
पञ्चत्वं तस्य जानीयात् ज्येष्ठपुत्रस्य निश्चितम्[8]॥'११॥
'त्रयोदश्यां तु वै श्राद्धं न कुर्यात् पुत्रवान् गृही[9]।'१२।

---

1. *स्मृतिचंद्रिका-श्राद्धकाण्ड,* p. 28 and *स्मृतिमुक्ताफलम्,* p. 761 read च कृष्णपक्षे for तमिस्रपक्षे.
2. *विष्णुपुराण,* reads पुराणै: for पुराणेषु.
3. *स्मृतिचंद्रिका-श्राद्धकाण्ड,* p. 28 drops this complete line.
4. *Ibid*., p. 28 reads समास्सहस्रं for समाः सहस्रम्; *स्मृतिमुक्ताफलम्,* p. 761 reads समासहस्रम्.
5. There seems to be an unnecessary repetition of द्वे शुक्ले in a reverse manner.
6. It is not possible to trace the sources of these two stanzas नवम्यां शुक्लपक्षस्य etc. and दर्शे च माघमासस्य etc.
7. It is better to take तस्य for तस्या in view of the context.
8. This stanza is quoted in the *स्मृतिचंद्रिका-श्राद्धकाण्ड,* p. 96 and *श्राद्धप्रकाश,* p. 319; *श्राद्धमयूख,* p. 14, however, ascribes this stanza to अंगिरस्. This however is not found in the *अंगिरस स्मृति,* edited by A.N.K. Aiyangar (Madras).
9. *श्राद्धमयूख,* p. 14 ascribes this line to *वामनपुराण.*

'नेष्यते चोपवासश्च कैचिदप्यनद्वये[1] ।'१३। इति वचनद्वयेन गृहीणा[2] पुत्रिणा युगादित्रयोदश्यां श्राद्धं न कर्तव्यमिति कश्चित् । न अनाकरत्वादेतयो: साकारत्वेऽपि त्रयोदशे बहुपुत्रो धनमित्रो दर्शनीयापद्यो[3] स्वरमाविशश्च[4] भवन्ती[5]' सा आपस्तम्ब (२.७.१६-२०) वचनैकवाक्यतया त्रयोदश्युपरब्ध काम्यतिथिश्राद्धविषयत्वं भविष्यति । इदं च नित्यत्वे प्रमाणो[6] भवति । काम्यं आनुवादिकी पितृप्रीति: फलम् ।

1. The source of this line cannot be traced.
2. Grammatically the form may be emended as गृहिणा for गृहीणा.
3. *आपस्तम्ब धर्मसूत्र,* p. 77 reads ०अपत्यो for ०आपद्यो. Kullūka's reading is obviously corrupt.
4. *आपस्तम्ब धर्मसूत्र,* p. 77 reads युवमारिणश्च for स्वरमाविशश्च. It must be noted here that in the section on *काम्यतिथि श्राद्धकाण्ड,* p. 128 कुल्लूक records another reading स्वरमारिणश्च for स्वरमाविशश्च.
5. *Ibid.*, p. 77 reads भवन्ति for भवन्ती. Here again the reading in the ms. is grammatically wrong.
6. Grammatically it may be emended as प्रमाणं for प्रमाणो.

१०

अथ संक्रान्त्यादिः

विष्णुः[1] (७७.१-६)

आदित्यसंक्रमणं विषुवद्वयं[2] विशेषेणायनद्वयं व्यतीपातो जन्मर्क्षमभ्युदयञ्च ।

एतांस्तु श्राद्धकालान्वै नित्याना[3]ह प्रजापतिः ।
श्राद्धमेतेषु यद्दत्तं तदानन्त्याय कल्पते ॥१॥

अभ्युदयं विवाहादिः । आनन्त्याय आनन्तपितृतृप्तये । पितृतृप्तिर्वात्रार्थवादिकफलं रात्रि[5]सत्रन्यायात् । न त्वन्यत् स्वर्गादिकं कल्प्यम् ।

अत्र वदन्ति —

अयनद्वितये श्राद्धं विषुवद्वितये[6] तथा ।
संक्रान्तिषु च सर्वासु पिण्डनिर्वपणाहते ॥२॥
वैशाखस्य तृतीयायां नवम्यां कार्तिकस्य च ।
श्राद्धं कार्यं च शुक्लायां संक्रान्तिविधिना नरैः ॥३॥

इति पठेत् । मत्स्यपुराणवचनाभ्यां संक्रान्तौ युगादौ च पिण्डनिषेध इति संक्रान्तविधिना पिण्डदानेतरविधिना । तदसत् । एतयोरनाकरत्वात् । साकरत्वेऽपि

ततः प्रभृति संक्रान्तावुपरागादि पर्वसु ।
त्रिपिण्डमाचरेत् श्राद्धमेकोद्दिष्टं[7] मृता[8]हनि ॥४॥

इति मत्स्यपुराणात् (१८.२२ब-२३अ) । विकल्प एव पिण्डदाननिषेधयोः षोडशिग्रहणाग्रहणवत् । तत्र दाने फलभूमाकल्पनीयः ।

---

1. This is *विष्णुस्मृति*, p. 779.
2. *Ibid.*, p. 779 reads विषुवद् द्वयम् for विषुवद्वयम्. Which is corrupt.
3. *Ibid.*, p. 779 reads ०अभ्युदयश्च for ०अभ्यदञ्च.
4. *Ibid.*, p. 780 reads काम्यान्० for नित्यान्०.
5. This refers to *जैमिनि कृत पूर्वमीमांसा*, IV.3.8.17.
6. This may be emended as विषुवद् द्वितये for विषुवद्वितये.
7. *मतस्यपुराण*, reads ०एकोदिष्टे for एकोदिष्टम्.
8. *Ibid.*, reads मृते० for मृता०.

११

अथ काम्यतिथिश्राद्धकाल:

आपस्तम्ब: (२.७.१६.८-२२)

प्रथमेऽहनि क्रियमाणे स्त्रीप्रायमपत्यं[1] जायते । द्वितीयन्तेना[2]स्तृतीये ब्रह्मवर्चस्विन:[3]। चतुर्थे क्षुद्रपशुमानम्[4] । पञ्चमे पुमांसो बह्वपत्यो[5] न चानपत्य प्रमीयते । षष्ठेऽयं शीलोवृत्त: शालिश्च[6]। सप्तमे कृषिवृद्धि:[7]। अष्टमे पुष्टि: । नवमे एकखुरा: । दशमे व्यवहारसिद्धि:[8]। एकादशे कृष्णायसम् त्रपुसीसम्[9]। द्वादशे पशुमानम्[10]। त्रयोदशे बहुपुत्रो बहुमित्रो दर्शनीयापत्यो स्वरमारिणश्च[11] भवन्ति । चतुर्दशे आयुर्धनवृद्धि:[12]। पञ्चदशे पुष्टिश्च[13]।

स्त्रीप्रायं स्त्रीबहुलम् । लेना ब्रह्मवर्चस्विन: सुता: इति विशेष:[14]। एकखुरा: अश्वादय:। कृष्णायसं लौह: । त्रपुरङ्गं स्वरमारिण: पुत्रा भवन्तीति शेष: । प्रागुत्पन्ना एव पुत्रा स्वरा नो म्रियन्ते श्राद्धोत्पन्नो वा अस्वरमारिण[15] इति बोधे रिकारकल्पनापत्ते:[16]।

व्यक्तमाह कात्यायन:—

ज्ञातिश्रेष्ठं त्रयोदश्यां सुराणस्तत्र म्रियन्ते ।१।

---

1. *आपस्तम्ब धर्मसूत्र,* p. 77 reads ००अपत्ये for ००अपत्यम्.
2. *Ibid.*, p. 77 reads द्वितीयेस्तेना: for द्वितीयन्तेना:
3. *Ibid.*, p. 77 reads ०वर्चसिन: for ०वर्चस्विन:
4. *Ibid.*, p. 77 reads ०पशुमान् for ०पशुमानम्.
5. *Ibid.*, p. 77 reads in the foot-note भव्यापत्यो for बह्वपत्यो.
6. *Ibid.*, p. 77 reads षष्ठेध्वशीलोक्षशीलश्च for षष्ठेऽयं शीलोवृत्त: शीलश्च.
7. *Ibid.*, p. 77 reads कर्षे राद्धि: for कृषिवृद्धि:
8. *Ibid.*, p. 77 reads व्यवहारे राद्धि: for व्यवहारे सिद्धि:
9. *Ibid.*, p. 77 reads कृष्णायसं त्रपुसीसम् for कृष्णायसम् त्रपुसीसम्.
10. *Ibid.*, p. 77 reads पशुमान् for पशुमानम्.
11. *Ibid.*, p. 77 reads युवमारिणस्तु for स्वरमारिणश्च. The ms. also notes another reading स्वरमाविशश्च, p. 126.
12. *Ibid.*, p. 77 reads आयुषे राद्धि: and drops the word धन.
13. *Ibid.*, p. 77 drops च after पुष्टि: . Here कुल्लूक differs from हरदत्त.
14. हरदत्त on *आपस्तम्ब धर्मसूत्र,* p.180 states अचोरा: पुत्रा: भवन्ति.
15. This explanation of कुल्लूक is unintelligible because of स्वरमारिण:
16. The expression रिकारकप्लनापत्ते: is hopelessly corrupt.

महाभारते (१३.८७.१६)

ज्ञातीनां[1] च भवेत् श्रेष्ठं कुर्वन् श्राद्धं त्रयोदशीम् ।
अरण्यं[2] हि सुराणस्य[3] म्रियन्ते च[4] नरा गृहे ।।२।।

अतस्तेन्य अरमाषिद्धादयः पद्यदोषं स हिषेरपत्यमात्रार्थिनः[5]। तथा अन्यतर प्रोक्तं फलकामस्यापि द्वितीयां त्रयोदश्यां चाधिकार इति कल्पतरुः[6]। अपत्यनिन्दामुखेनापत्यार्थिनो निषेधात् अन्यतरोक्त फलकामस्यैवाधिकार इति हलायुधः[7]।

1. *स्मृतिचंद्रिका-श्राद्धकाण्ड,* p. 97 reads ज्ञानिनां for ज्ञातीनाम्.
2. *मनुस्मृति,* VIII.316 reads अवश्यं for अरण्यं; *स्मृतिचंद्रिका-श्राद्धकाण्ड,* p. 97 reads नावश्यं for अरण्यम्.
3. *स्मृतिचंद्रिका,* p. 97 reads युवानोऽस्य for सुराणस्य.
4. *Ibid.*, p. 97 reads प्रमीयन्ते for म्रियन्ते च.
5. This line defeats all attempts at editing.
6. *कृत्यकल्पतरु-श्राद्धकाण्ड,* p. 21 refers to त्रयोदश्यां; but there is no reference to the word द्वितीयाम्. Possibly कुल्लूक has a different ms. before him.
7. This work of हलायुष on *श्राद्ध* is not so far published.

१२

अथ श्राद्धवेला:

ब्रह्मपुराणे[1]—

पूर्वाह्णे[2] मातृकं श्राद्धमपरह्णे[3] तु पैतृकम् ।
एकोद्दिष्टं तु मध्याह्ने प्रातर्वृद्धि निमित्तकम् ॥१॥

मातृकमन्वष्टकाश्राद्धं यथा शङ्खः

पित्रादित्रय[4] पत्नीषु भोज्या मातृः प्रतिद्विजाः ।
स्त्रीणामेव तु तद्यस्मान्मातृश्राद्धमिहोच्यते ॥२॥

अपराह्णेतु पैतृकमिति कृष्णपक्षपार्वणविषयम्[5]।

यथाह विष्णुः[6] —

शुक्लपक्षस्य पूर्वाह्ण[7] श्राद्धं कुर्याद्विचक्षणः[8]।
कृष्णपक्षापराह्ण[9] च[10] रौहिणं तु न लङ्घयेत् ॥३॥

शुक्लपक्षविहितं युगादिश्राद्धं पूर्वाह्ण[11] कर्तव्यम् । पूर्वाह्णस्योत्तरावधिमपराह्णस्य पूर्वविधिमाह । रौहिणमिति नवमघटिका रौहिणीनक्षत्रमुहूर्तत्वात् ।[12] तन्न लङ्घयेत् । एतेन शुक्लपक्षे नवमघटिकोपरि

1. This stanza cannot be traced in the extant *ब्रह्मपुराण-श्राद्धतत्त्व,* p. 264 quotes this.
2. *श्राद्धतत्त्व,* p. 264 reads पूर्वाह्णे for पूर्वाह्ण.
3. *Ibid.*, p. 264 reads अपराह्णे for अपराह्ण.
4. *Ibid.*, p. 264 reads ००त्रिक० for ००त्रय०.
5. *Ibid.*, p. 264 expresses a contrary view 'अपराह्णे तु पैतृकम्' इति अन्वष्टकाशुक्लपक्ष-विहितपार्वणेतरपार्वणसपिण्डोपकरणम्.
6. *Ibid.*, pp. 264-65 ascribes this text of *विष्णु* to *वायुपुराण:; स्मृतिचंद्रिका-श्राद्धकाण्ड,* p. 81 ascribes this to *मार्कण्डेयपुराण.*
7. *श्राद्धतत्त्व,* p. 264 reads पूर्वाह्णे for पूर्वाह्ण.
8. *स्मृतिचंद्रिका-श्राद्धकाण्ड,* p. 81 reads द्विजोत्तम: for विचक्षण: .
9. *श्राद्धतत्त्व,* p. 265 reads अपराह्णे for अपराह्ण.
10. *स्मृतिचंद्रिका-श्राद्धकाण्ड,* p. 81 reads तु for च.
11. It should be emended as पूर्वाह्णे.
12. *श्राद्धतत्त्व,* p. 265 connects this मुहूर्त with the deity रोहिणी on the strength of astrology.

कृष्णे पक्षे नवमघटिकाया: प्राक् श्राद्धं न कर्तव्यम् । षष्ठैकोद्दिष्टपरतया रौहिणं तु न लङ्घयेदिति व्याख्यानं तत् पार्वणपरिचयेन । एतेन कृष्णपक्षेऽष्टमघटिकोपरि मुहूर्तचतुष्टयं पार्वणकाल: । नवमघटिकोपर्यश्च पराह्णे प्राशस्त्यम् ।

ननु एवं

उर्ध्वं मुहूर्तात्[1] कूतपातयन्[2]मुहूर्तचतुष्टम् ।
मुहूर्तपञ्चकं च[3] एतत्स्वेधां[4] भवनमिष्यते ॥४॥ इति ब्रह्मपुराणे[5]

कुतपस्याष्टमघटिका अपि श्राद्धकालत्वमुक्तम् । न च कुतपादूर्ध्वं मुहूर्तपञ्चकमिति व्याख्यानं युक्तम् ।

अपराह्णे तु संप्राप्ते अभिजिद्रोहिणीदये[6]।
यदत्र दीयते किञ्चित्तदक्षयमिहोच्यते[7]॥५॥ इति मत्स्यपुराण (२२.२)

विरोधात् । अभिजिदष्टमाघटिका । आ: सप्तममुहूर्तोपरि मुहूर्तपञ्चकं श्राद्धकालं इति । अत एन पार्वणप्रकरणे कुतपप्रशंसा—

ब्रह्मपुराणे[8]

पुराणे यति स्त्रिदण्ड: करुणा राजतं पात्रमेव च ।
दौहित्रं कुतप: काल: श्राद्धं कृष्णाजिनं तथा ॥६॥

अन्यथा तदप्रस्तुतं स्यात् । सत्यं मुहूर्तचतुष्टयपक्षादपकृष्टोऽयं कुतपादि मुहूर्तपञ्चक पक्ष इति न विरोध: । 'रात्रौ श्राद्धं न कुर्वीत'[9] इत्यादि वाक्येषु पर्युदासविधौ[10] रात्रिसम्बन्धेतराभावास्यादि कालस्यात्यन्तापकृष्णविषयत्वम् । येतु मन्यन्ते पूर्वाह्णो[11] वै देवानां माध्यन्दिनं मनुष्यानां[12] अपराहण: पितृणामिति श्रते:[13] पक्षा ते निर्वपत्तेभ्यो ह्यपराहणे तु धर्मविदिति यमवचनेति । अपराहणेच पैत्रिकमिति[14]

---

1. *स्मृतिचंद्रिका-श्राद्धकाण्ड,* p. 81 reads मूहूर्तं for मुहूर्तात्.
2. *Ibid.*, p. 81 reads कुतपाद्यन्० for कूतपातयन् ।
3. *Ibid.*, p. 81 reads हि for च: *श्राद्धतत्त्व,* p. 265 reads वापि for च.
4. *Ibid.*, p. 81 reads स्वधा for स्वेधां.
5. *श्राद्धतत्त्व,* p. 265 ascribes this stanza to *मत्स्यपुराण.*
6. *Ibid.*, p. 266 reads ०रोहिण उदये for ०रोहिणीदये. Which is wrong.
7. *मत्स्यपुराण,* p. 37 reads the 2nd line as यत्किंचिद्दीयते तत्र तदक्षयमुदाहृतम्. *श्राद्धतत्त्व,* p. 266 reads जन्तो: for किञ्चित्.
8. This stanza cannot be traced in the extant *ब्रह्मपुराण.*
9. This has a reference to the *मनुस्मृति,* III.280 and the text of *शातातप,* quoted in the *कृत्यकल्पतरु-श्राद्धकाण्ड,* p. 23.
10. *कुल्लूक on मनुस्मृति,* III.280 uses the principal of पर्युदास. *मेधातिथि,* p. 274 mentions two views and understands अर्थवाद in the word राक्षसी of *मनु,* III.280 *राघवानन्द,* p. 275 agrees with कुल्लूक.
11. This may be emended as पूर्वाह्णे.
12. This may be emended as मनुष्याणाम्.
13. This word श्रते: appears to be corrupt.
14. This may be emended as पैतृकमिति.

ब्रह्मपुराणवचनाच्चपराह्णे मुख्यः कल्पः । कुतपादूर्ध्वं मुहूर्तचतुष्टयमनुकल्पः । मुहूर्तपञ्चकेमापत्कल्पः ।[1] निषिद्धेतरश्च मुख्यकल्पनुकल्पवत् कल्पव्यतिरिक्तोऽत्यन्तावत्[2] कल्पः।

तदा च—

प्रभुः प्रथमकल्पस्य योऽनुकल्पेन वर्तते ।
न सांपरायिकं तस्य दुर्मतेर्विद्यते फलम् ॥७॥

गृह्यपरिशिष्टवचनात् । मुख्यभूतापराह्णलाभे शक्त्यान्यत्र फलं नास्त्येवेति विशेषः । तदशोभनम् । मुख्यकल्पानुकल्पत्वे प्रमाणाभावात् । फलातिशयानातिशयाभ्यामेव व्यवस्थासंभवात् । किं च सामान्यप्राप्तस्य विषतो[3] विधानमतिशयार्थमेव दृश्यते ।

यथाह विष्णुः (७७.१-२)

आदित्यसंक्रमणं विष्णुवद्वयमित्यादि।[4]

किं च नानामुनिवचने प्राशस्त्यश्रवणात् पूर्वोक्तवचनमन्याय्यमपि संशये प्राशस्त्यपराण्येव ।

यथा मनुः (३.२७८)

यथा चैवापरः पक्षः पूर्वपक्षाद्विशिष्यते ।
तथा श्राद्धस्य पूर्वाह्णदपराह्णो विशिष्यते ॥८॥

शातातपः[5]—

दर्शे श्राद्धं[6] तु यत्प्रोक्तं पार्वणं तदुदाहृतम्[7]।
अपराह्णे तु पितॄणां तु तत्र दानं प्रशस्यते ॥९॥

आपस्तम्बः (२.७.१६.४-५) —

मासि मास्य[8]परपक्षस्यापराह्णः श्रेयानिति ।

तदा चापराह्णो सद्भावेऽप्यन्यत्र फलमस्त्येव। किन्तु न तथा प्रकृष्टम् । तस्मात् फलप्रकर्षतारतम्यार्थमुत्तरोत्तर लघुकालोत्कर्षः । ननु रात्र्यादितरामावास्याकालसामान्य प्रतिपादकं वचनमपराह्णविशेषदर्शनात् विशेषपरमस्तु सर्वत्र सामान्यवचनस्य विशेषदर्शनाद्विशेष परत्वं दृष्टम् ।

1. This appears to be corrupt.
2. This portion appears to be corrupt and defies all attempts at editing.
3. This may be emended as विशेषतो for विषतो.
4. This is *विष्णुस्मृति,* p. 779.
5. The text of *शातातप* is quoted in the *स्मृतिचंद्रिका-श्राद्धकाण्ड,* pp. 80-81.
6. *स्मृतिचंद्रिका-श्राद्धकाण्ड,* p. 80 reads दर्शश्राद्धं for दर्शे श्राद्धम्.
7. *Ibid.*, p. 81 reads तत्प्रकीर्तितम् for तदुदाहृतम्.
8. *आपस्तम्ब धर्मसूत्र,* p. 76 reads कार्यं after मासि and before अपर. This word is dropped in our ms.

यथा

औरसक्षेत्रजौ पुत्रौ विधिना पार्वणेन तु ।
प्रत्यब्दमितरे कुर्युरेकोद्दिष्टं सुता दश ॥१०॥ इति जाबालवचनम्[1]।

यत्र यत्र प्रदातव्यं सपिण्डीकरणात्परम्।
पार्वणेन विधानेन देयमग्निमता सदा ॥११॥ इति मत्स्यपुराणदर्शनात्[2]।

साग्निकौरसक्षेत्रजपरमिति वक्ष्यते । तन्न । तत्र मुनिभेदात्तथास्तु । एकमुनिपक्षे तु तथात्वे सामान्यवचनवैयर्थ्यापत्तेः । इहत्वे केनैव मुनिना 'रात्रौ श्राद्धं न कुर्वीत' (मनु ३.२८०) इत्यभिधायापराह्णो विशिष्यत इत्युक्तम् । एवं मध्याह्नादि विधिरपि प्राशस्त्यपर एव ।

ननु मध्याह्नादि विधिविरोधात् 'रात्रौ श्राद्धं न कुर्वीत' (मनु ३.२८०) इति तीर्थे श्राद्धविषयस्तुनामावास्या पार्वणकोद्दिष्टविषयं न प्राशस्त्यपरतयोपपत्तौ प्रकरणबाधस्य न्याय्यत्वात् ।

उभयत मध्याह्नाप्राप्तौ श्राद्धलोपापत्तेः । तदा च प्रतिसंवत्सरमिति वीप्साबाधः। प्रातःकालादि विभागः उक्तो मत्स्यपुराणे (२२.८२-८४)

प्रातःकालो मुहूर्तास्त्रीन् सङ्गवस्तावदेव तु ।
मध्याह्नस्त्रिमूर्तः स्यादपराह्णस्ततः परम् ॥११॥
सायाह्नस्त्रिमूर्तः स्यात् श्राद्धं तत्र न कारयेत् ।
राक्षसी नाम सा वेला गर्हिता सर्वकर्मसु ॥१२॥
अह्नो मुहूर्ता विख्याता दश पञ्च च सर्वदा ।
तत्राष्टमो मुहूर्तो यः स कालः कुतपः स्मृतः ॥१३॥
मध्याह्ने सर्वदा यस्मान्मन्दी भवति भास्करः ।
तस्मादनन्तफलदस्तत्रारम्भो[3] विशिष्यते[4] ॥१४॥

राक्षसीति निन्दार्थम् । सर्वकर्मसु स्नानदानादिषु । अनापदीत्यर्थः । सोऽयं श्राद्धविषये पञ्चधा दिनभागः उक्तः । मध्याह्न इति अह्ने मध्यम् । मध्याह्न अष्टमघटिकेत्यर्थः। तत्र यस्मान्मन्दी भवति भास्करः स्थिरी भवति ।

अत एव शाम्बे जमदग्निवाक्यम् —

मध्याह्नेऽपि निमेषं हि स्थास्यसिद्धं दिवाकः[5]।
तत्र भेत्स्यामि सूर्य त्वां नामकार्या विचारणा[6]॥१५॥

अतस्तत्रारम्भो विशिष्यते ।

---

1. *कृत्यकल्पतरु-श्राद्धकाण्ड,* p. 262 quotes the first line of the text of जाबाल.
2. *Ibid.*, p. 262 quotes this stanza from the *मत्स्यपुराण.*
3. *मत्स्यपुराण,* p. 39 reads यदारम्भो for तत्रारम्भो.
4. *Ibid.*, p. 39 reads भविष्यति for विशिष्यते. *स्मृतिचंद्रिका-श्राद्धकाण्ड,* p. 83 reads विशिष्यते.
5. This may be emended as दिवाकरः .
6. This text of जमदग्नि cannot be traced.

१३

अथ श्राद्धनिषेधः

महाभारते (१३.१०७.११९-२०)

नक्षत्रे न च कुर्वीत यस्मिन्जातो भवेन्नरः ।
न प्रौष्ठपद्योः कार्यं न चाग्नेये च भारत ॥१॥
दारुणेषु च सर्वेषु प्रत्यरौ[1] च विवर्जयेत् ।
ज्योतिषेयानि प्रोक्तानि[2] तानि सर्वाणि वर्जयेत् ॥२॥

प्रोष्ठपदा भाद्रपदा । द्विनक्षत्रत्वात् द्विवचनम् आग्नेयं कृत्तिकां दारुणमुक्तं ज्योतिषे ।

'दारुणं चोरगं रौद्रं ऐन्द्रं नैतमेव च ।' उग्रनक्षत्रपरतया व्याख्यानमसङ्गतम् ।

'नक्षत्राणि तथैवात्र दारुणोग्राणि[3] वर्जयेत् ।' इति विष्णुधर्मोत्तरवचने भेदेनोपादानात् । ज्योतिषे यानि प्रोक्तानि निषिद्धतया भरण्यादीनि ।

तथा 'नन्दायां भार्गवदिने त्रयोदश्यां त्रिजन्मनि ।
अत्र श्राद्धं न कुर्वीत पुरदारधनक्षयात् ॥३[4]॥

एतच्च व्रीहियवपाकादिनिमित्तं सावकाशश्राद्धविषयम् ।

मनुः (३३.२८०)

रात्रौ श्राद्धं न कुर्वीत राक्षसी कीर्तिता हि सा ।
सन्ध्ययोरुभयश्चैव सूर्या[5]चैवचिरोदिते ॥४॥

राक्षसीति निन्दार्थम्[6]। अचिरोदते दिवसस्याष्टमघटिकायाम् ।

---

1. *महाभारत* (critical edition), reads प्रत्यहम्. *अपरार्क on याज्ञवल्क्य स्मृति*, p. 558 reads प्रत्यरे for प्रत्यरौ and explains प्रत्यरं as जन्मनक्षत्रात् पञ्चमं चतुर्दशं त्रयोविंशं च प्रत्यरम् ।
2. *महाभारत* (critical edition), reads चोक्तानि for प्रोक्तानि.
3. *वीरमित्रोदय-संस्कारप्रकाश*, p. 246 quotes the text of श्रीपति to indicate आर्द्रा, मूल, ज्येष्ठा and आश्लेषा as दारुणनक्षत्रs and पूर्वाषाढा, पूर्वाभाद्रपदा, मघा and भरणी as उग्रनक्षत्रs and this list does not agree with the text of कुल्लूक.
4. *पराशरमाधव*, Vol. I, p. 668 ascribes this text to गार्ग्य and reads एषु for अत्र and गृही पुत्रधनक्षयात् for पुरदारधनक्षयात्.
5. *मनुस्मृति*, III.280 reads सूर्ये for सूर्या.
6. *कुल्लूक on मनुस्मृति*, III.280 has raised the points of पर्युदास, प्रतिषेध and विकल्प and does not quotes *विष्णुस्मृति*, 77.8-9 which is quoted above.

विष्णु: (७७.८-९)

सन्ध्या रात्रयोर्न[1] कर्तव्यं श्राद्धं खलु विचक्षणै: ।
तयोरपि च कर्तव्यं यदि स्याद्राहूदर्शनम्[2]।।५।।
राहूदर्शनदत्तं हि श्राद्धमाचन्द्रतारकम् ।
गुणवत् सर्वकामीयं[3] पितॄणामुपतिष्ठते ।।६।।

यो चन्द्रतारकं यदुपतिष्ठतेऽतो रात्रावपि कर्तव्यमित्यर्थ: । सर्वकामीयं सर्वकामाय हितम् ।

यम:

स्नानं दानं तप: श्राद्धमनन्तं राहूदर्शने ।
आसुरी रात्रिरन्यत्र तस्मात्तां परिवर्जयेत्[4]।।७।।

राहूदर्शनेऽनन्तफलम् । यतोऽतोन्यत्रासुरी रात्रिरित्यर्थ: । स्नानादीनामप्यन्यत्र रात्रौ निषेधे प्रतिप्रसव: ।

देवल:

राहूदर्शनसंक्रान्ति विवाहात्ययवृद्धिषु ।
स्नानदानादिकं कार्यं निशिकाम्यव्रतेषु च[5]।।८।।

आदिशब्द: श्राद्धादिपर: । तेन रात्रौ रविसंक्रमणे स्नानदानश्राद्धादीनि कर्तव्यानि । रात्रौ विवाहे यदा प्रात:काले वृद्धिश्राद्धं न कृतं तदा रात्रावपि कार्यम् । एतेनासंभवे दिवसस्य भागान्तरेऽपि वृद्धिश्राद्धमवगम्यते । अव्यये मरणे रात्रौ स्नानतर्पणपिण्डदानादि कर्तव्यम् । 'वृद्धौ पुत्रजन्मनि रात्रौ स्नानमङ्गाशौचापगमार्थ दानं सहिरण्यतिलपात्रादिदानं' हारीतोक्तं वृद्धिश्राद्धं च कर्तव्यम् ।

अत्र केचित् वृद्धिश्राद्धं पुत्रजन्मान्तरं न कर्तव्यम् । शौचस्याधिकारि विशेषणत्वात् । किन्तु जातेष्टिन्यायादशौचापगम एव जातकर्मादिकं तु पुण्यार्थान् कुर्वन्ति । प्राङ्नालछेदादिति हारीतवचनात् । अनन्तरक्षण एव कर्तव्यम् । अत: पुत्रजन्मनि न रात्रौ वृद्धिश्राद्धम् । एतद्वचनादेव न भविष्यति इति चेत् । न । एतस्य यथासम्भवसम्बन्धात् तन्न जातकर्मसमकालविधानात् ।

यथा मार्कण्डेयपुराणे (२७.३ब-४अ)

नैमित्तिकमथो[6] वक्ष्ये श्राद्धमभ्युदयार्थिकम्[7]।
पुत्रजन्मनि तत्कार्यं जातकर्म समं नरै:।।९।।

तथा ब्रह्मपुराणे

---

1. *विष्णुस्मृति,* p. 781 readd रात्र्योर्न for रात्रयोर्न.
2. *Ibid.*, p. 781 reads राहु० for राहू०.
3. *कृत्यकल्पतरु-श्राद्धकाण्ड,* p. 23 reads सर्वकामोऽयं for सर्वकामीयम्.
4. This stanza, however, cannot be traced in the *यमस्मृति, लघुयमस्मृति* and *बृहद्यमस्मृति* in the *स्मृतिसंदर्भ,* Vol. IV.
5. The stanza of देवल, however, is not found in the *देवलस्मृति* in the *स्मृतिसंदर्भ* or *स्मृतिसमुच्चय* and *स्मृतिसङ्ग्रह.*
6. *मार्कण्डेय पुराण,* p. 148 drops the word अथ.
7. *Ibid.*, p. 148 reads ००तव for ००अर्थिकम्.

देवाश्च पितरश्चैव पुत्रे जाते द्विजन्मनाम् ।
आयन्ति यस्मात्तदहः पुरायं पष्ठं च सर्वदा[1] ॥१०॥

तत्र 'दद्यात्सुवर्णं च भूमिं गां तुरगं रथ'मित्यभिधाय 'जातश्राद्धेन दद्याच्च पक्वान्नं ब्राह्मणेष्वपी'त्यत्रापि तदहरिति सम्बन्धात् पक्वान्ननिषेधानुपपत्तेश्च ।

तथा विष्णुधर्मोत्तरे (१.१४२.१६ब-१७अ)

अच्छिन्ननाड्यां[2] कर्तव्यं श्राद्धं वै पुत्रजन्मनि ।
अशौचोपरमे[3] कार्यमथवापि नराधिप ॥११॥

न चास्य पूर्वपक्षोत्तर पक्षभावेन व्यवस्था । पूर्वार्द्धवैयर्थ्यापत्तेः । सौर्थकत्वे संभवति वैयर्थ्यस्यान्याय्यत्वात् । तस्माद्विकल्प एव शक्ताशक्तभेदेन उक्तः । तावत्कालं स्त्यन्यां प्रदाने पुत्रनाशप्रसंगात् साङ्गं वृद्धि कर्तुं न शक्यते इति चेत् । न । किञ्चिदङ्गविकलमेव भविष्यति । नित्ये हि किञ्चिदङ्गहानिर्न । काम्येऽभ्युदये श्राद्धे उक्तेति विशेषवचनाद्भविष्यति । को विरोधः । अतः सिद्धं रात्रौ वृद्धिश्राद्धमिति ।

अथञ्च[4] षष्ठिनाड्यावच्छिन्नामावास्यादि विधिपूर्वको रत्र्यादि निषेधः पर्युदासः । सर्वत्रसामान्यशास्त्रप्राप्तनिषेधस्य पर्युदासत्वात् ।

अथ पर्युदासः । ननु नञो निषेधे मुख्यत्वात् । पर्युदासपक्षे लक्षणापत्तेः । न चात्र लक्षणाबीजमस्ति। सामान्यशास्त्रप्राप्त्युपजीवो निषेधविधिर्वक्तव्यः । इतरथाभिधानादेव निषेधप्राप्तेरप्राप्तप्रापकत्वं रूपं विधित्वं न स्यात्तदा चोपजीव्यबाधापत्तेरेव विधानादेव । निषेधप्राप्तेरप्राप्तप्रापकत्वं रूपं विधित्वं न स्यात् । तदा चोपजीव्यबाधापत्तेरेव विधानासम्भवः । नान्तरिक्षेऽग्निश्चेतव्य इति वदनुवाद एव भविष्यतीति चेन्न । विधित्वसम्भवत्यनुवादायोगात् । अतो विधित्वानुपपत्तिरेव लक्षणाबीजं संकोचोऽयम् सामान्यशास्त्रस्य न बाधः । अत एव बाह्यावेक्षणाभ्यङ्गबाधभिया स्वर्गकामपदस्यान्धवधिरेव[5] तव स्वर्गकामपरत्वे संकोच एवेति चेन्न । निषेधविधौ सामान्यशास्त्रसंकोचे बाधस्यावश्यकत्वात् । तथा ह्यमावस्याशास्त्रस्य रात्रिमात्रपरत्वं दिवारात्रिपरत्वं वा उपजीव्य निषेधविधौ रात्रिज्ञानस्य बाध एव । दिवापरत्वं च नोपजीव्यं विधित्वविरोधात् । अत्र एव दिवारात्र्युल्लेखरहितं न सामान्ये ज्ञानमुपजीव्यं रात्रिपरत्वसंभावनयैव प्राप्तत्त्वेन विधित्वसंभवात् । स्वर्गकामपदस्य सामान्याधिकारिपरत्वादुपजीव्याङ्गविधौ न बाधः । अथोपजीव्यत्वान्निमित्तविधिरपराधत इति न्यायाग्रहणग्रहणवत् विकल्पो भविष्यति । न च विकल्पपरिहारार्थं क्वापि न लक्षणा दृष्टा । यजतिषु ये यजामहं कुर्यान्यायाजेष्ठित्यत्र विकल्पपरिहारार्थं लक्षणा दृष्टा इति चेन्न । तत्र संभूय समुच्चारणादेकवाक्यत्वावगमे वाक्यभेदभयादेव लक्षणाया उक्तत्वात् । गंगायां घोषेत्यादौ तथा दृष्टत्वात् । तदसत् । सामान्यविशेषवचनयोर्विकल्पादर्शनात् ।

---

1. This stanza, however, cannot be traced in the extant *ब्रह्मपुराण*. The portion 'पुरायं षष्ठं च सर्वदा' appears to be slightly doubtful.
2. *विष्णुधर्मोत्तरपुराण,* reads ०नाभ्यां for ०नाड्याम्. Which is corrupt.
3. *Ibid.*, reads आशौच० for अशौच०.
4. This may be emended as अथ च.
5. The expression ०००अन्धवधिरेव appears to be corrupt.

अत एव गौतम: (१.६)

तुल्यबलविरोधे विकल्प: ।

अन्यथा रागप्राप्ते निषेधेऽपि विकल्प: स्यात् । न तौ पशौ करोतीत्यतिदेश प्राप्तादयभाग भागद्वयनिषेधेऽपि विकल्प: कथं न भवेत् ।

अथोच्यते । एवमिति देशवत् रागवच्चान्यथा सिद्धत्वेन दुर्बलत्वात् । सामान्यशास्त्रस्य निषेधविधिनाऽन्यथा सिद्धत्वेन न बलीयसा बाध एव । भवतु लक्षणा नव: विकल्प: ।

अत एव नानाप्रामाण्यं तत्त्वदेवैकदेशे प्रामाण्यनिमित्तबाधोऽपि तत्त्वदेवाङ्गीकरणीय: । ग्रहणाग्रहणयोस्तु त्वयोरपि विशेषवचनत्वात् पक्षता बोध: ।

अत एव इदं रजतमिति भ्रान्तिज्ञानं नेदं रजतमिति ज्ञानेन बाध्यते । बाधश्च ज्ञानस्य संसर्गविषयत्वाभाव: । पूर्वज्ञानस्य संसर्गविषयत्वे कथमप्राप्त प्रापकविधित्वं तद्धि बाध्यते । यद् बाधे तत्वा[1] धतेयत्वाधे स्वयमबाधितं भवतीति चेन्न । तद्विधत्वमनपेक्ष्याप्राप्ति: ।

उच्यते । निमित्तस्यैव उपजीव्यत्वेन बलवत्त्वात् । पर्युदासेनाप्युपपत्ते: । अन्यथा सिद्धेश्चोभयत्र समानत्वात् । अतो निमित्तविरोधादेव नैमित्तिकमुख्यार्थ निषेधबाधानुपपत्ते: । पर्युदासलक्षणमुक्ता । अगत्या हि रागातिदेशयोर्बाध: पर्युदासासम्भवात् । पर्युदस्तेतर प्रतिपादकवचनान्तराभावात् । अत एव नातिरात्रं वाक्येन पर्युदासविधि: । अत एव दीक्षितो न ददाति अहरहर्दद्यादिति दीक्षितेतरपरत्वम् । यजतिषु ये यजामहं कुर्यान्वानुयाजेष्विति[2]। अन्नं यामेतरयाजकत्वम् । अत एवो पात्र[3] वसन्ति न वैश्वदेवे उत्तरवेदिमुपाकिरन्ति । नासीर्य इति वैश्वदेव सुनासुर्येतर पर्वपद्वय सर्वत्र निमित्तबाधादेव सिद्धम् । अन्ये तु विकल्पपक्षे सकृदुच्चरित्तस्य[4] सामान्यशास्त्रस्य नित्यानित्यविधाने वैषम्यापत्तिरिति वदन्ति ।

1. This portion seems to be corrupt.
2. This refers to *आपस्तम्ब श्रौत-सूत्र,* 24.13.5.
3. This refers to द्वयो: प्रणयन्ति न्याय used in the *मिताक्षरा on याज्ञवल्क्यस्मृति,* II.135-36.
4. This refers to *जैमिनि कृत पूर्वमीमांसा* & Also *cf. मीमांसा कोष,* Vol. VIII, p. 4067.

अथ आधिमासः

गृह्यपरिशिष्टम् —

मलिम्लुचस्तु मासो वै मलिनः पापसंभवः ।
गर्हितः पितृदेवेभ्यः सर्वकर्मसु तं त्येजत्[1] ।।१।।

मलिनः सकलमासमलत्वात् ।

तथा चोक्तम् —

'मलं वदन्ति कालस्य मासं कालविदौऽधिकम्[2]।' पापसंभव इति निन्दार्थम् । सर्वकर्मसु मलमासविहितेतर दैवपितृकर्मसु ।

मलमासबीज ज्योतिःशास्त्रे उक्तम् ।

दिवसस्य हरत्यर्कः षष्ठिभागंस्ततो ततः ।
करोत्येक महच्छेदं तथैवेकं तु चंद्रमाः ।।२।।

एवमर्द्धतृतीयानामद्धानामधिमासकम्।

'ग्रीष्मे जनयतः पूर्वं पञ्चाब्दान्ते तु पश्चिमम्[3]।३।

अस्यार्थः । दिवसस्यतिथेः षष्ठिभागं दण्डमेकं रविः प्रतिदिनमाकर्षति । एतेन ऋतौ मासद्वयात्मके षष्ठ्यहोरात्रैः षष्ठिनात्याकर्षत्तिथिरेकासूर्येण कृष्यते । एवं चन्द्रेणापि तेन प्रवृत्तिदिनद्वयाकर्षणेन द्वादश दिनानि लभ्यन्ते । एवं सार्द्धवत्सरद्वयेनाधिमासो निष्पद्यते । गमनक्रमादौ नित्यप्राप्तमिदम् । तिथिवृद्धिह्रसादिना न्यूनाधिकत्व दर्शनात् । इदं तु नियत एकस्मादधिमासादारभ्य तृतीयवत्सरे मलमासो भवतीति । ग्रीष्मे माधवादि षट्कपूर्वं पूर्वत्रिकपतितं पञ्चाब्दान्ते पश्चिममुत्तरत्रिकपतितं अधिमासं जनयतश्चन्द्रार्को ।

---

1. This stanza is quoted in *श्राद्धक्रियाकौमुदी,* p. 38. Also see *H.D.*, Vol. IV, p. 546.
2. This line is quoted from *गृह्यपरिशिष्ट* in the *स्मृतिचंद्रिका-श्राद्धकाण्ड,* p. 103 and it reads कालविदोऽधिकम् for कालविदौऽधिकम् which is corrupt.
3. This source of this cannot be traced.

अत्र को मासशब्दार्थ: । चान्द्र: सौरो वा । चन्द्र एव वा कीदृश: । को वा मलमास:?

इत्यत्राह लघुहारीत:—

इत्याग्नी[1] यत्र हूयेते मासादि: स प्रकीर्तित:[2]।
अग्निसोमौ[3] स्मृतौ मध्ये समाप्तौ पितृसोमकौ ॥४॥
तमतिक्रम्य तु[4] रविर्यदा[5] गच्छेत् कदाचन ।
आद्यो मलिम्लुचो ज्ञेयो द्वितीय: प्रकृत:[6] स्मृत: ॥५॥
तस्मिंस्तु प्रकृते मासि कुर्याच्छ्राद्धविधिं यथाविधि ।
तथैवाभ्युदयं कार्यं नित्यमेकं हि सर्वदा ॥[7]६॥

शुक्लप्रतिपदि इन्द्रमग्नियाग: । शुक्लप्रतिपदादि अग्निषोमयाग: । एतौ दर्शपूर्णमासान्तर्गतौ पितृविशिष्टसोमदेवताकोऽग्नौ करणहोम: पिण्डपितृयज्ञाङ्गभूतो दर्शे विहित: समादि:[8]समाप्तविति कीर्तनात् । शुक्लप्रतिपदादिदर्शान्तमास[9] शब्दार्थ: । चान्द्रोऽप्यथ मेवेति दर्शितम् ।

तथा ब्रह्मसिद्धान्त:[10]—

चान्द्र: शुक्लादि दर्शान्त: सावनस्त्रिंशतादिनै: ।
एकराशौ रविर्यावत् कालं मास: स भास्कर:[11]॥७॥

शुक्लादि: शुक्लप्रतिपदादित्यर्थ: । पक्षवाचित्वाच्शुक्लशब्दस्य । यत्तु ज्योतिषं दर्शादिदर्शश्चान्द्रस्त्रिंशत् दिवस सावनमास: । रविसंक्रान्तिषु चिह्न: सौरेऽपि निगद्यते । तत्र दर्शादित्यवधौ पञ्चमी । तेन शुक्लप्रतिपदादिरेव तिथिप्रचयो लभ्यते ।

अत्र वदन्ति —

अमावास्यापरिच्छिन्नं रविसंक्रान्तिवर्जितम् ।
मलमासं विजानीयाद्गर्हितं सर्वकर्मसु ॥[12]८॥
तस्यार्कौ दर्शकश्चैकराशौ दर्शत्वयातिग: ।

---

1. *स्मृतिचंद्रिका-श्राद्धकाण्ड,* p. 105 reads इन्द्राग्नी for इत्याग्नी, which is corrupt. Immediately ms. p. 140 gives इन्द्राग्नी as another reading.
2. *Ibid.*, p. 105 reads सम्प्रकीर्तित: for स प्रकीर्तित: .
3. *Ibid.*, p. 105 and *अपरार्क,* p. 547 read अग्निषोमौ for अग्निसोमौ.
4. *Ibid.*, p. 105 reads च for तु.
5. *Ibid.*, p. 105 reads अन्यस्मिन् मासे for रविर्यदा which is preferred by *अपरार्क,* p. 547.
6. *Ibid.*, p. 105 reads प्राकृत: for प्रकृत: .
7. This source of this stanza cannot be traced.
8. The word समादि: appears to be corrupt.
9. This is also found in *प्रमिताक्षरा* on *मुहूर्तचिन्तामणि,* III.20, p. 113.
10. This stanza from *ब्रह्मसिद्धान्त* is found quoted in the *श्राद्धतत्त्व,* p. 253 and *अपरार्क,* p. 546.
11. A line similar to this is quoted in *मुहूर्तचिन्तामणि,* p. 113 as 'चान्द्रो मास: ह्यसंक्रान्तो मलमास: प्रकीर्तित:।' This complete stanza is found quoted in *श्राद्धतत्त्व,* p. 253.
12. This stanza is found quoted in *मालमासतत्त्व,* p. 770.

अमावास्या द्वयं यत्र रविसंक्रान्तिवर्जितम् ॥[1]९॥
मलमासः स विज्ञेयो विष्णुः स्वपिति कर्कटे । १०।

इति ज्योतिःशास्त्रदर्शनाद्दर्शनादिश्चान्द्रःदर्शादित्ये हि तल्लंघने मलमासो भवति । अन्यथा प्रतिपल्लंघनमेवोच्यते ।

किं च 'अमावास्यायाममावास्याया[2] यजेतेति श्रुत्या दर्शस्य दर्शयागाङ्गतया विधानात्'। 'इन्द्राग्नी यत्र हूयेते' इति लघुहारीत[3]वचनादिप दर्शादित्वमेव गम्यते । न शुक्लप्रतिपदादित्वम् । तच्चिन्त्यम् ।

दर्शादित्ये दर्शान्तादित्ये वा मासस्य दर्शान्तेन तत्समाप्तावपरस्य तदादित्वाभावादमासत्वप्रसङ्गेऽवसरे षण्णां मासानां लोपः स्यात् । ततश्चामावास्याद्वयं यत्र रवि[4]संक्रान्तिवर्जितम् इति' । अत्र अमावास्यापदेन तदन्तो लक्ष्यते । संक्रान्तिशब्देन च क्रियाभिधीयते । प्रथमामावास्यान्त प्राक् क्षणे एव संक्रमणे प्रतिपदादेर्लङ्घितं संभवति । दर्शान्तक्षणे च क्रियोत्पत्तौ नैषा प्रक्रिया संभवति । दर्शान्तरविसंक्रान्तौ मलमासो न स्यात् इति चेत् । सत्यम् । तस्मात् प्रागेवेति ब्रूमः । अतः प्रतिपदादित्वेऽपि मासस्य दर्शद्वयस्य रविसंक्रान्ति वर्जितत्त्वमुपपन्नम् । अमावास्याममावास्यायेति वाक्यं यागारम्भमात्रार्थम् । यागस्तु प्रतिपद्येवापरस्मिन् दिवो । तथा च श्रुतिः 'द्वे ह वै पौर्णमास्यौ द्वे अमावास्ये[5]। तस्मात् प्रतिपद्युपर[6]सन्नेव[7] यजेता परेद्युरिति' ।

किं च

'इन्द्राग्नी यत्र हूयेते' इत्यनेन यदि दर्शोऽभिधीयते तदा तस्यैववान्तत्वति समाप्तौ पितृसोमकारित्वमनर्थकं स्यात् । स एवादिरन्तश्च ब्रूयात् । शुक्लप्रतिपत्परत्वे तु श्लाघ्यत एव । न च

'पर्वणो यश्चतुर्थोश आद्याः प्रतिपदत्रयः ।
यागकालः स विज्ञेयः प्रातरुक्तो[8] मरीचिभिः' ॥११॥

इति बौधायनवचनात्[9] पर्वतुयांशस्यापि यागकालत्वात् कथं शुक्लप्रतिपदादि नियम इति वाच्यम् ।

'पर्वणेंशे तुरीये तु कार्या इष्टि द्विजातिभिः ।
द्वितीया सहितां यस्मात् दूषन्त्याश्वलायना' ॥१२॥

इत्य[10]नुक्त्वात् ऋग्वेदिविषयत्वम् । बौधायनवचनस्य छन्दोगपरिशिष्टकृता च वेधेऽपि यागाद्युपगमात् ।

1. The stanza अमावास्या द्वयं यत्र etc. is found quoted in *मलमासतत्त्व*, p. 768.
2. The expression अमावास्याया appears to be unnecessary in view of the context and sense of the sentence.
3. The text of *लघुहारीत* gives इत्यग्नी as another reading for इन्द्राग्नी given here.
4. This line is found quoted in the *मलमासतत्त्व*, p. 769 and *स्मृतिमुक्ताफलम्*, p. 723 and it reads सूर्य for रवि.
5. The source of this श्रुति passage is found quoted in *मलमासतत्त्व*, p. 769.
6. इति indicates that this is a citation and found in *मलमासतत्त्व*, p. 769 and reads ०उपसवन् for ०उपरसन्.
7. *मलमासतत्त्व*, p. 769 drops एव.
8. *कृत्यकल्पतरु-श्राद्धकाण्ड*, p. 13 reads प्रातर्युक्तो for प्रातरुक्तो.
9. The text of *बाधायन* referring to the view of मरीचि is quoted in *कृत्यकल्पतरु-श्राद्धकाण्ड*, p.13.
10. The source of this stanza cannot be traced.

यथा पक्षादावेव कुर्वीत सदा पक्षादिकं चरुम् ।
पूर्वाह्णे एव कुर्वन्ति विद्धेप्यन्ये मनीषिणः ॥१३॥

तुरीयांशं व्यावृत्त्यमेवकारः सदाशब्दोपानाच्च[1]। तदा च ऋग्वेदिना ऐन्द्राग्नेययागाङ्गतिथेर-नियतत्वाच्छन्दोगानां च प्रतिपदो नियतत्वात् सैव लघुहारीतवचनेन गृह्यते । अतः सिद्धं शुक्लप्रतिपदादि दर्शान्तो मासश्चान्द्रः । स एव मलमासो न सौर इत्याह । तमतिक्रम्येति प्रकृत इति कर्माङ्गत्वात् ।

अत एव ज्योतिःशास्त्रम्[2]—

रविः शालालङ्घितो मासश्चान्द्र ख्यातो[3] मलिम्लुचः ।
तत्र यद्विहितं कर्म उत्तरे मासि कारयेत् ॥१४॥

तस्मिंस्तु प्रकृत इत्यादि श्राद्धममावास्या-पार्वण नवान्नापरपक्षादि । अभ्युदयं विवाहदि, श्राद्धाभ्युदयौ मलमासे न कर्तव्यावित्यत्र तात्पर्यं प्रकृते मासिकरणस्य तत्तद्विधिवाक्यैरेव प्राप्तत्वात् । नित्यमहरहः क्रियमाणं सन्ध्यास्नानपञ्चयज्ञादि सर्वदा मलमासेऽपि कर्तव्यम् । न त्वावश्यकत्वेन पार्वणादिकमपि एकपदेन नित्यनैमित्तिकाख्य पार्वणव्यवच्छेदात् ।

यथा मार्कण्डेयपुराणे (२७.१-३अ)

नित्यं नैमित्तिकश्चैव[4] नित्यनैमित्तिकं तथा ।
गृहस्थस्य च यत्कर्म[5] तन्निशामय पुत्रक ॥१५॥
पञ्चाश्रितं यज्ञाश्रितं[6] नित्यं यदेतत् कथितन्तर[7]।
नैमित्तिकं तथैवान्यत्[8] पुत्रजन्म क्रियादिकम् ॥१६॥
नित्यनैमित्तिकं ज्ञेयं पर्वश्राद्धादिपण्डितैः ॥१७॥

उपक्रमोक्त नित्यपरिभाषादार्ढ्यात् । लघुहारीतेनैव अहरहः श्राद्ध एव नित्यशब्दस्य प्रयुक्तत्वात् । यथा नित्यश्राद्धमदैवं स्यादर्घपिण्डविवर्जितम् । अन्यथाऽपरपक्षादीनामप्यनुष्ठानापत्तेः । अत एव काम्यमप्यहरहः क्रियमाणं गोहिरण्यादिदानं न कर्तव्यम् ।

अत एव ज्योतिषम् —

पक्षद्वयेऽपि संक्रान्तिर्यदि न स्यात् सितासिते ।
तदा तन्मासि विहितमुत्तरेमासि कारयेत् ॥[9]१८॥

---

1. This may be emended as ००उपादानाच्च for ००उपानाच्च.
2. This stanza is found quoted in the *श्राद्धतत्त्व*, p. 252. This stanza is, however, ascribed to पराशर in the *स्मृतिचंद्रिका श्राद्धकाण्ड*, p. 105.
3. *स्मृतिचंद्रिका-श्राद्धकाण्ड*, p. 105 reads ००आद्यो for ००ख्यातो.
4. *मत्स्यपुराण*, p. 148 reads नैमित्तिकं चैव for नैमित्तिकश्चैव.
5. *Ibid.*, p. 148 reads त्रिधाकर्म for च यत्कर्म.
6. *Ibid.*, p. 148 reads पञ्चयज्ञाश्रितं for पञ्चाश्रितं यज्ञाश्रितम्.
7. *Ibid.*, p. 148 reads कथितं तव for कथितन्तर which is corrupt.
8. *Ibid.*, p. 148 reads तथा चान्यत् for तथैवान्यत्.
9. The source of this stanza cannot be traced.

रविणा लंघितो मासश्चान्द्र ख्यालो मलिम्लुचः ।
तत्र यद्विहितं कर्म उत्तरे मासि कारयेत् ॥[1]१९॥

अभ्युदयं व्यनक्ति ज्योतिःपराशरः[2]—

अग्न्याधेयं प्रतिष्ठां च यज्ञदानव्रतानि च ।
वेदव्रत वृषोसर्ग[3] चूडाकरणमेखलाः ॥२०॥
माङ्गल्यमभिषेकं च मलमासे विवर्जयेत् ।२१।

दानं चात्र महादानम् । यदाह —

'वापीकूपतडागादि[4] प्रतिष्ठां[5] यज्ञकर्म च ।
न कुर्यात् मलमासे तु[6] महादाने व्रतानि च[7]॥'२२॥

महादानं षोडशतुल्यपुरुषादिव्रतस्यारम्भ एव निषिद्धः ।

यथा काश्यपः[8]—

राक्षैक[9]मन्दिरगतौ यदि जीवभानु शुक्रोऽस्तगःसुखरैकगुरुश्च सिंहे ।
नारभ्यते व्रतविवाह गृहप्रतिष्ठा क्षौरादिकर्म गमनागमनं च[10] धीरैः ॥२३॥

अत्र कालाशौचे[11] व्रताद्यारम्भो निषेधदर्शनात् । मलमासेऽपि तथा आरब्धव्रतं मलमासेऽपि कार्यम् । प्रतिष्ठा तु न कार्या ।

यथा रम्भातृतीयाव्रते शिवरहस्ये[12]—

---

1. This stanza is found quoted in the *श्राद्धतत्त्व,* p. 252 and *स्मृतिचंद्रिका-श्राद्धकाण्ड,* p. 105. Also see *मलमासतत्त्व,* p. 270, and *श्राद्धसागर,* p. 148.
2. This text of *ज्योतिःपराशर* is ascribed to वृद्धमनु in the *स्मृतिचंद्रिका-श्राद्धकाण्ड,* p. 110. Also see *अपरार्क,* p. 549.
3. *स्मृतिचंद्रिका-श्राद्धकाण्ड,* p. 110 reads वृषोत्सर्ग for वृषोत्सर्गम्.
4. This stanza is found ascribed to वृद्धवसिष्ठ in the *स्मृतिमुक्ताफलम्,* p. 734 and to वृद्धमनु in *अपरार्क,* p. 549. It reads तटाकानां for तडागादि.
5. *स्मृतिमुक्ताफलम्,* p. 734 and *अपरार्क,* p. 549 read प्रतिष्ठा for प्रतिष्ठाम्.
6. *अपरार्क,* p. 549 reads च for तु.
7. *स्मृतिमुक्ताफलम्,* p. 734 reads महादान०० for महादाने००.
8. The source of this stanza cannot be traced in the *काश्यपस्मृति* in *स्मृतिसंदर्भ,* Vol. IV. This, however, is quoted in *मलमासतत्त्व,* p. 851.
9. *मलमासतत्त्व,* p. 851 reads ऋक्षैक for राक्षैक.
10. *Ibid.*, p. 851 reads गमनागमनश्च for गमनागमनं च.
11. No information is available on this work *कालाशौच* in *H.D.*, Vol. I, Part II.
12. A reference to this work does not occur in *H.D.*, Vol. I, Part II, but found quoted in *मलमासतत्त्व,* p. 841.

'मासे मलिम्लुचेऽप्येवं यजेद्देवी सशंकरीम्[1]।
किन्तु नोद्यापनं कार्यमित्याह भगवाच्छिव:[2]॥'२४॥

यत्र व्रते द्वादशसु मासेषु मासविशेषोल्लेखेन कर्मविशेष उक्तस्तन्मलमासे न कर्तव्यमित्युक्तम् ।

वाशिष्ठ लिङ्गपुराणे —

प्रारब्धे तु व्रते पश्चात् सम्प्राप्ते त्वधिमासके ।
पूर्वमानेन तं त्यक्त्वा कार्यं द्वादशमाषिकम्[3]॥२५॥

मलिम्लुच शून्याब्दमानेन तं मलिम्लुचं त्यक्तेत्यर्थ: । द्वादशमासिकं द्वादशमासेषु कार्यं न मलमास इत्यर्थ: ।

ऋष्यशृंग:[4]—

अवषट्कार होमश्च[5]पर्वचाग्रयणं तथा ।
मलमासेऽपि कर्तव्यं काम्याइष्टी विवर्जयेत्[6]॥२६॥

अवषट्कार होम नित्य होम: । पर्व दर्शपौर्णमासयाग: । न पार्वणश्राद्धाष्टिसाहचर्यात् । आग्रयणं नवरात्रेष्टि: । एतत्वादुभयमहरहरक्रियमाणमपि वचनात् कर्तव्यम् । सामान्यत: श्राद्धनिषेधे उक्ते सपिण्डीकरणान्तस्य प्रसवमाह लघुहरीत:[7]।

प्रत्यब्धं द्वादशे मासि कार्या पिण्डक्रिया द्विजै:[8]।
क्वचित् त्रयोदयेऽपि स्यादास्यं[9]त्यक्त्वा[10]तुवत्सरम् ॥२७॥
चक्रवत् परिवर्तेत सूर्यकालवशाद्यत: ।
अत: सांवत्सरं श्राद्धं कर्तव्यं मासचिह्नितम् ॥२८॥
मासचिह्नं न कर्तव्यं पौषमाघाद्यमेव हि ।
यतस्तत्र विधानेन मास: स परिकीर्तित: ॥२९॥
असंक्रान्तेऽपि कर्तव्यमाब्दिकं प्रथमं द्विजै: ।
तथैव मासिकं पूर्वं सपिण्डीकरणं तथा ॥३०॥

---

1. *मलमासतत्त्व*, p. 841 reads सशंकराम् for सशंकरीम्.
2. *Ibid.*, p. 841 reads ०शिव: for ०शिश: .
3. It is better to emend this as ०मासिकम् for ०माषिकम् in view of grammer, and the reading द्वादशमासिकं preferred and explained immediately.
4. The text of *ऋष्यशृंग,* is ascribed to *गृह्यपरिशिष्ट* by *अपरार्क,* p. 549.
5. *अपरार्क,* p. 549 reads होमाश्च for होमश्च.
6. *Ibid.*, p. 549 reads इष्टीर्विवर्जयेत् for इष्टी विवर्जयेत्.
7. The text of *लघुहारीत* is quoted in the *स्मृतिचंद्रिका-श्राद्धकाण्ड,* p. 115 and *अपरार्क,* p. 549.
8. *अपरार्क,* p. 549 reads बुधै: for द्विजै: .
9. *स्मृतिचंद्रिका,* p. 115 and also *अपरार्क,* p. 549 reads ०आद्यं for ०आस्यम्.
10. *अपरार्क,* p. 549 reads मुक्त्वा for त्यक्त्वा.

गर्भे वार्द्धुषिकृत्ये च मृतानां पिण्डकर्मसु ।
सपिण्डीकरणाच्चैव नाधिमासं विदुर्बुधाः ॥३१॥
सपिण्डीकरणादूर्ध्वं यत् किंचित् श्राद्धिकं भवेत् ।
इष्टम्वाप्यथ पूर्वं वा तन्न कुर्यान्मलिम्लुचे[1]॥३२॥

प्रत्यब्दिकी या श्राद्धक्रिया सा द्वादशे मासि कर्तव्या इत्युत्सर्गः । क्वचिन्मलमासे पतितत्रयोदशे मासे अपि श्राद्धमाह विष्णुः[2]। संवत्सराभ्यन्तरे यद्यधिमासको भवेत् तदा मासिकार्थं दिनमेकं वर्धयेत् ।

तथा विष्णुधर्मोत्तरे (२.७७.१)

संवत्सरस्य मध्ये तु[3] यदिस्यादधिमासः[4]।
तदा त्रयोदशे मासि क्रिया प्रेतस्य वार्षिकी[5]॥३३॥

अतोऽधिककल्पः स्यात्। न एतयोर्मध्यश्रुतेर्मध्याधिमासविषयत्वात् । हारीत् वचनस्य सामान्यविषयत्वात् विषमशिष्ठत्वेन विकल्पायोगात् हेतुरत्र मध्याधिमासे द्वादशे प्रथमाब्दिकं न संभवति । मृताहाप्राप्तेरेवमादावपि । अतो हारीतवचनमन्ताधिमासविषयम् । न त्वमावास्याश्राद्धविषयत्वम् । विष्णु[6]वचनस्येति व्याख्यानं युक्तम् । विष्णुना प्रेतश्राद्धप्रकरणे पाठात् । यदा च मध्येऽधिमासस्तदा त्रयोदशमासिकश्राद्धानि कर्तव्यानि ।

यथा विष्णुधर्मोत्तरे (२.७७.८ब-९अ)

मध्ये चेदधिमासः[7] स्यात् कुर्यादप्यधिकं ततः ।
अथवा द्वादशाहेन सर्वमेतत्समाचरेत्[8] ॥३४॥

तथा च सत्यव्रतः[9]

संवत्सरस्य मध्ये तु यदि स्यादधिमासकः ।
तदा त्रयोदशे मासि श्राद्धं[10] तदधिकं भवेत् ॥३५॥

ननु सौरमासविषयचिह्ले मृताहे श्राद्धं विहितं सौरस्य च मासस्य राशिविशेषाविच्छन्न सूर्यविशेषत्वात् । त्रयोदशे मासि मृताह एव श्राद्धं न कृतं भवेत् । अत्राह चक्रवत् परिवर्तेतेति । राशिचक्रे

1. It may be mentioned here that all these stanzas from चक्रवत् etc. up to गर्भे etc. are not found in the extant *लघुहारीतस्मृति*. However, this stanza is found quoted in *श्राद्धतत्त्व*, p. 252. Also see *श्राद्धक्रियाकौमुदि*, p. 323.
2. This has a reference to the *विष्णुधर्मोत्तरपुराण*, II.77.9a.
3. *विष्णुधर्मोत्तरपुराण*, 2.77.9 reads चेत् for तु.
4. *Ibid*., eads ००अधिमासक: for ००अधिमासः.
5. *Ibid*., II.78.11a reads संवत्सरे समाप्ते तु श्राद्धं श्राद्धवदाचरेत् for 33b.
6. This has a reference to the *विष्णुधर्मोत्तरपुराण*, II.77.8.
7. *विष्णुधर्मोत्तरपुराण*, reads ०अधिवासः for ०अधिमासः .
8. *Ibid*., reads ००समापयेत् for ००समाचरेत्.
9. This stanza from the text of सत्यव्रत is found quoted in *श्राद्धतत्त्व*, p. 280.
10. *Ibid*., p. 280 reads ०त्रयोदश श्राद्धं कार्यं for ०त्रयोदशे मासि श्राद्धम्. *Ibid*., p. 289 however, reads त्रयोदये for त्रयोदश.

चक्रवत् परिक्रमेण सूर्यो गतेमन्दत्वात् कदाचिदेक राशिगत भोगसमाप्तावपि मृततिथिं न स्पृशति । तिथिद्वयं वा स्पृशति । यदा न स्पृशति तदा श्राद्धलोप: । यदा चोभयं स्पृशति तदा संशय: स्यात् । अत: सौरमासचिह्नितं श्राद्धं न कर्तव्यम् । किन्तु चान्द्रमासचिह्नितम् । चान्द्रमासस्यापि अनेकत्वात् । चिह्नमाह चिह्नान्विति । पौषमाघादिना लक्षितमित्यर्थ: । पौषादिपदप्रवृत्तिनिमित्तं चाह ब्रह्मगुप्त:[1]। मेषगरविसंक्रान्ति: शशिमासे भवति । यत्र तच्चैत्रं वैशाखाद्याश्चैवं वृषभिसंक्रान्तियोगेन । एतच्चाधिमासव्यापकम् । तत्रापि च द्विराषाढ: स विज्ञेय: । इत्यादावाषाढादिपदप्रयोगात् । तस्मादन्यदेवाधिमासव्याकं वृत्तिनिमित्तं वदन्ति । मीनस्थरविप्रारब्ध शुक्लप्रतिपदादि दर्शान्तिश्चान्द्रचैत्र इत्यादि । न च नक्षत्रेण युक्त: काल: यस्मिन् पौर्णमासीति पाणिनि[2]स्मरणात् । चित्रादिनक्षत्रयुक्ता पौर्णमास्यस्मिन् तिथिषूत्पत्त्या योगिकत्वम् । चैत्रादिशब्दानां नक्षत्रयोगस्य व्यभिचारात् ।

उक्तं च ज्योतिषे —

अन्त्योपान्त्यौ त्रिभौ ज्ञेयौ फाल्गुनस्य त्रिभो मत: ।
शेषा मासा द्विभाज्ञेया: कृत्तिकादिव्यवस्थायव्यलं बहुधा[3]॥३६॥

प्रकृतमनुसराम: । चान्द्रमासाङ्कितत्वे हेत्वन्तरमाह । यतस्तत्र विधानेनेति विधानेन शास्त्रेण चान्द्रमासा प्रकीर्तिता: । तच्च 'इन्द्राग्नी यत्र हूयेते' इत्याद्युक्तम् ।

अन्यदपि पठन्ति —

तथा पितामह:[4]—

आब्दिके पितृकार्ये तु मासश्चान्द्रमस: स्मृत:[5]।
विवाहादौ स्मृत: सौरो यज्ञादौ सावनोमत: ॥३७॥

पारस्कर:[6]—

विवाहोत्सव यज्ञेषु सौरं मानं प्रशस्यते ।
पार्वणेत्वष्टकाश्राद्धे चान्द्रमिष्टं तथाब्दिके ॥३८॥

ननु सौराङ्कित श्राद्धमाह सत्यव्रत:[7]—

यस्मिन् राशौ[8]गते भानौ विपत्तिं यान्ति मानवा: ।
तेषां तत्रैव कर्तव्या:[9] पिण्डदानोदकक्रिया:[10]॥३९।

---

1. This view of ब्रह्मगुप्त, cannot be traced.
2. This refers to *पाणिनि कृत अष्टाध्यायी,* IV.2.3 & 23.
3. This line seems to be metrically defective.
4. The text of पितामह is quoted in the *स्मृतिचंद्रिका-श्राद्धकाण्ड*, p. 376 (*JRG)* and *अपरार्क,* p. 546, *अपरार्क,* however, reverses the lines in this stanza.
5. This line is read slightly differently in the *स्मृतिचंद्रिका-श्राद्धकाण्ड*, p. 375 as 'दैवे कर्मणि पित्र्ये च मासश्चान्द्रमस: स्मृत: .
6. The text of पारस्कर is quoted in *मलमासतत्त्व,* p. 747.
7. The text of सत्यव्रत is quoted in *श्राद्धतत्त्व,* p. 281.
8. *श्राद्धतत्त्व,* p. 281 reads राशि for राशौ and connects it with गते. *अपरार्क,* p. 547 reads राशौ.
9. *Ibid.*, p. 281 reads कर्तव्या for कर्तव्या:; *अपरार्क,* reads कर्तव्यम्.
10. *Ibid.*, p. 281 reads ००क्रिया for ००क्रिया:.

न एतस्यामूलत्वात् । समूलत्वेऽपि प्रथमाब्दे द्वादशे मास्याधिमासपाते एकमासत्वान्मासद्वयस्य किं द्वादशश्राद्धं त्रयोदशे वा इति सन्देहे वचनमिदम् ।

एवं च

> वर्षे वर्षे तु यत् श्राद्धं मातापित्रोर्मृताऽहनि[1]।
> मलमासे[2]ऽपि तत्कार्यं व्याघ्रस्य[3] वचनमप्यमूलम्[4]॥४०॥

समूलत्वेऽपि निश्चितमूलहारीतवचन स्वरसावत्[5]। एतादृशी व्याख्या 'वर्षे वर्षे तु' इति प्रत्याब्दिकमित्यर्थः । एवं च प्रथमाब्दिकं मलमासेऽपि कार्यम् । प्रत्याब्दिकं श्राद्धं मलमासे पाते प्रकृते मासि कार्यमेव । न त्वमावास्याश्राद्धवन्निवर्त्तत[6] इत्यर्थः । अतश्चान्द्रमासाङ्कितत्वात् श्राद्धस्याधिमासपाते एकनामत्वान्मासद्वसस्य त्रयोदशेऽपि कृते मृताहे कृतं भवत्येवेति सिद्धम् । प्रथमाब्दिकं द्वादशे मासि कर्तव्यमित्युक्तम् । यत्तदन्ताधिमासविषयं न मध्याधिमासविषयमिति स्पष्टयति । असंक्रान्तेऽपि इति असंक्रान्ते रवौ मलमास इत्यर्थः । तथैवेति तथैवासंक्रान्त एव रवौ सपिण्डीकरणात्पूर्वं मासिकं कार्यम् । पूर्वपक्षं सपिण्डीकरणोत्तर पार्वणाख्य श्राद्धनिषेधार्थम् । गर्भे गर्भकृत्ये पुंसवनादौ वार्द्धुषिकृत्ये वैश्यानाङ्गीभिलाद्युक्ते[7] पिण्डकर्म प्रेत पिण्डदानं पुनः सपिण्डीकरणमपकृष्ट सपिण्डीकरणार्थं श्राद्धमेव । श्राब्दिकं स्वार्थे ढक् । यत् किञ्चिदित्यनेन नित्यश्राद्धमात्रस्य प्रतिप्रसवः । इष्टं यागदानादि तदपि नित्यं कर्तव्यमित्युक्तम् । पूर्तं वापी कूप तडागादि वा शक्तोऽग्न्याधेयमित्याह । ज्योतिः पराशरो[8]क्त कर्मनिषेधार्थः ।

ऋष्यशृंगः[9]—

> संवत्सरातिरेको वै मासश्चैव त्रयोदशः[10]।
> तस्मात्[11] त्रयोदशं[12] श्राद्धं न कुर्यान्नोपतिष्ठते[13]॥४१॥

---

1. The *व्याघ्रस्मृति,* reads क्षयेऽहनि for मृताऽहनि.
2. *Ibid.*, reads मासद्वये० for मलमासे०.
3. This appears to be a quotation from The *व्याघ्रस्मृति,* 315b-316a (of my critical edition).
4. This stanza from *व्याघ्रस्मृति* is found quoted in *स्मृतिचंद्रिका-श्राद्धकाण्ड,* p. 114 and 2nd line is read as मलमासे न कर्तयं व्याघ्रस्य वचनं यथा ।
5. This form appears to be doubtful.
6. This may be emended as निवर्तते for निवर्त्तत.
7. This expression appears to be corrupt.
8. This has a reference to the text of ज्योतिःपराशर aready quoted (p. 142) and ascribed to वृद्धमनु in the *स्मृतिचंद्रिका-श्राद्धकाण्ड,* p. 110.
9. The text of *ऋष्यशृंग* is quoted in the *श्राद्धतत्त्व,* p. 254, *स्मृतिचंद्रिका-श्राद्धकाण्ड,* p. 111 and *अपरार्क on याज्ञवल्क्य,* p. 548. Also see *Studies in the Dharma-Śastra,* p. 73.
10. *श्राद्धतत्त्व,* p. 254 reads मासो यः स्यात् त्रयोदश for मासश्चैव त्रयोदशः । *स्मृतिचंद्रिका-श्राद्धकाण्ड,* p. 111 agrees with the above ms. of *श्राद्धसागर.*
11. *Ibid.*, p. 254 and *अपरार्क,* p. 548 read तस्मिन् for तस्मात्.
12. *Ibid.*, p. 254 reads त्रयोदशे for त्रयोदशं.
13. *Ibid.*, p. 254 and *अपरार्क,* p. 548 read इंदुसंक्षये for नोपतिष्ठते. The *स्मृतिचंद्रिका-श्राद्धकाण्ड,* p. 111 also reads one more line 'असुराणां तु मासोसौ तस्माद्देवविगर्हितः' which is not quoted in our ms.

एतच्च प्रथमाब्दे द्वादशे मास्यधिमासपाते लघुहारीत समानविषयम् । न तु पार्वणनिषेधार्थमिदम् । कृतैक द्विकमात्रपार्वणपुरुषभेदेन त्रयोदत्वानुपपत्तेः । नवमध्यधिमाससमासिकविषयं तदा त्रयोदशे 'मासि दिनमेकं न तु वर्द्धयेत्' इति विष्णुवचनविरोधात् । मध्येऽधिमासातिक्रान्ते निषेधो भविष्यतीति चेत् । न । तस्य त्रयोदशत्वानुपपत्तेः । पद्मपुराणवत् भविष्यतीति चेत् । न । तदा त्रयोदशे श्राद्धं कार्यम् । तदधिकं भवेत् । तथैव मासिकं पूर्वमित्यादि वचनविरोधात् ।

बृहस्पतिः[1]—

नित्यं नैमितिके कुर्यात् प्रयतः सन्मलिम्लुचे[2]।
तीर्थस्नानं गजच्छायां प्रेतश्राद्धं तथैव च ॥४२॥

नित्यमहरहः कर्तव्यं स्नानश्राद्धहोमादि । न त्वावश्यकत्वेन पार्वणश्राद्धमप्युपक्रमोक्तं नित्यभाषा स्वरसात् । नैमित्तिकसहचरितस्य तथा व्युत्पत्तेश्च । गजच्छाया प्रेतश्राद्धयोश्च पृथगुपादानं वैयर्थ्याच्च । किं च बृहस्पतिनैवोपक्रमेऽहरहः क्रियमाणस्य नित्यपरत्वोक्तेः ।

यथा

नित्यं नैमित्तिकं काम्यं वृद्धिश्राद्धं तथैव च ।
पार्वणं चेति मनुना श्राद्धं पञ्चविधं स्मृतम् ॥[3]४३॥

नैमित्तिकं पारिभाषिकमप्येकोदिष्ट न ग्राह्यम् । प्रेतश्राद्धस्य पृथगुपादानवैयर्थ्यात् । किन्त्वभ्युदयम् ।

यथा मार्कण्डेयपुराणम् — (२७.३ब)

'नित्यनैमित्तिकमथो वक्ष्ये श्राद्धमभ्युदयात्मकम्[4]॥४४॥' इति ।

तथा च चन्द्रसूर्योपरागादिनिमित्तं श्राद्धादि । तथा अपाटवादिनिमित्तं शान्तिकर्मापि ग्राह्यम् ।

तथा च दक्षः[5] (२.५४ ब-५५अ)

नैमित्तिकानि काम्यानि निपतन्ति यथा यथा ।
तथा तथैव कार्याणि न कालस्तु विधीयते ॥४५॥

नैमित्तिककाम्यानि प्रायश्चित्तादीनि। तीर्थस्नानमप्यावृतम् ।

यथा ज्योतिषम् —

अनादि देवतां दृष्ट्वा शुचः स्युः नष्टभार्गवे ।
मलमासेप्यनावृत्तं तीर्थस्नानमपि त्यजेत् ॥४६॥

---

१. The text of बृहस्पति is quoted in the *स्मृतिचंद्रिका-श्राद्धकाण्ड*, pp. 105-06 and *अपरार्क on याज्ञवल्क्य*, p. 549.
2. *स्मृतिचंद्रिका-श्राद्धकाण्ड*, pp. 105-06 reads स० for सन्०.
3. This stanza is also quoted from the text of *बृहस्पति* in the section on *श्राद्धभेदाः*, p. 89 and is not found in the *स्मृतिसंदर्भ*, Vol. III.
4. *मार्कण्डेयपुराण*, 27.3b reads आभ्युदयं तव for अभ्युदयात्मकम्.
5. This stanza is found in the *दक्षस्मृति, स्मृतिसंदर्भ*, Vol. I, p. 56.

मलमासेप्यनावृत्तं तीर्थस्नानमपि त्यजेत् ।।४६।।

अनावृत्तं देवतादर्शनेऽपि संबध्यते ।

यथाज्योति:पराशर:[1]—

बाले वा यदि वा वृद्धे शुक्रे चास्तमुपागते ।
मलमास इवैतानि वर्जयेद्देवदर्शनम् ।।४७।।

मलमास इवेत्यनावृत्तमित्यर्थ: । अत्र मलमासेऽमावास्यायां पार्वणं कर्तव्यमिति केचित्तदयुक्तम् । 'सर्वकर्मसु तं त्यजेत्'[2] इति सपिण्डीकरणादूर्ध्वमिति । प्रति षेधात् । नित्यत्वेन प्रतिप्रसवस्य पूर्वं निरस्तत्वात् । न च सावकाशश्राद्धविषयोऽयं निषेध: । प्रमाणाभावात् ।

मलं वदन्ति कालस्य मासं कालविदोऽधिकम् ।
नेहेतात्र विशेषेद्याम[3]न्यत्रावश्यकाद्विधे: ।।४८।।

इति गृह्यपरिशिष्टवचनादिति चेत् । न । तस्यामूलत्वात् । समूलत्वेऽपि आवश्यकपदस्य निरावकाशवचनत्वाभावात् । किं च षष्ठया तु दिवसैर्मास: कथितो बादरायण: इतिमासैको न पार्वणस्यापि सकृद्विधानेन सावकाशात्वात् । सकृत् कृत: शास्त्रार्थ: इति न्यायात्[4]। प्रथम सांवत्सरिकवत् । अन्यथा प्रकृते मासि मृताहलाभात् द्वितीय सांवत्सरिक प्रसङ्ग: । किं च सन्ध्यापञ्चमहायज्ञादीनां निरवकाशत्वेन नि षेधावि षयत्वे नित्यत्वेन प्रतिप्रसवविधिर्न स्यात् ।

किं‌च

'रविणा लङ्घितो मासश्चान्द्रख्यातो मलिम्लुच: ।
तत्र यद्विहितं कर्म उत्तरे मासि कारयेत् ।।'[5]४९।।

इत्यनेनेति । क र्षुविधानादस्यापि सावकाशत्वात् । तन्त्रादेव प्रकृते मासि श्राद्धद्वयानुष्ठानात् । यत् किञ्चित् एतत् अपाटवाद्यशौचाख्यामपि पतितमेकोद्दिष्टमेकादश्यामशौचान्ते च मलमासपाते न कर्तव्यम् । किं च मलमासव्याप्त कृष्णैकादश्यामेवेति ।

---

1. The text of *ज्योति:पराशर,* is ascribed to वृद्धमनु by *स्मृतिचंद्रिका-श्राद्धकाण्ड,* p. 110 and is also quoted by *अपरार्क,* p. 549.
2. This line is quoted from *गृह्यपरिशिष्ट,* in the *श्राद्धक्रियाकौमुदी,* p. 38.
3. *स्मृतिचंद्रिका-श्राद्धकाण्ड,* p. 107 reads तु अशेषेज्याम् for विशेषेद्याम्.
4. This न्याय has a reference to शबर on *जैमिनि कृत पूर्वमीमांसा,* XI.1.28 and XII.3.10.
5. This stanza is ascribed to *पराशर* in the *स्मृतिचंद्रिका-श्राद्धकाण्ड,* p. 105 and reads ००आद्यो for ००ख्यातो. This is already noted (p. 142).

१५

अथ अमावास्या

मनुः (३.१२२)

पितृयज्ञं तु निर्वर्त्य विप्रश्चन्द्रक्षयेऽग्निमान् ।
पिण्डान्वाहार्यकं श्राद्धं कुर्यान्मासानुमासिकम् ॥१॥

चन्द्रक्षयेऽमावास्यायाम् । एतेनामावास्यायां प्रतिमासं पिण्डान्वाहार्यं संज्ञकं श्राद्धं साग्निना पिण्डपितृयज्ञानन्तरं कार्यम् । ननु पितृयज्ञपदं तर्पणपरमात्रम् ।

'पितृयज्ञं तु निर्वर्त्य तर्पणाख्यं द्विजोग्निमान्[1] ।
पिण्डान्वाहार्यकं श्राद्धं कार्यमिन्दुक्षये सदा[2] ॥'२॥

इति मत्स्यपुराण (१६.२१) वचनात् । न स्नानोत्तरभावित्वात् श्राद्धस्य तर्पणानन्तर्यस्यार्थ प्राप्तत्वेन विधातुमयोग्यत्वात् । ततो विधायकत्वानुरोधेन पिण्डपितृयज्ञपरता । मत्स्यपुराणे तु तर्पणान्तर्यस्यार्थ-वादस्तर्पण पार्वणयोः । पितृयज्ञार्थ नित्यश्राद्धव्युदासार्थः[3]। न च मत्स्यपुराणे बलिदानवत् श्राद्धोत्तरकर्मणि नित्यश्राद्धं विहितम् । पिण्डान्वाहार्यक समाख्याविवेचनव्याजेनापि पिण्डपितृयज्ञानन्तर्यमाह मनुः । (३.१२३)

पिण्डानां[4] मासिकं श्राद्धमन्वाहार्यं विदुर्बुधाः ।
तदामिषेण[5] कर्तव्यं प्रशस्तेन प्रयत्नतः ॥३॥
यतो मासिकं श्राद्धं पिण्डपितृयज्ञपिण्डनामनु ।
आद्रियते ततः पिण्डान्वाहार्यकं विदुः ॥४॥

मत्स्यपुराणेत्वन्यथान्वयो दर्शितः ।

यस्मादन्वाहृता[6] मात्रा भक्षयन्ति द्विजातयः ।
अन्वाहार्यकमित्युक्तं तस्माच्चन्द्रमसिक्षये[7] ॥५॥[8]

---

1. *मत्स्यपुराण,* p. 27 reads तु योऽग्निमान् for द्विजोऽग्निमान्.
2. *Ibid.,* p. 25 reads 2nd line as पिण्डान्वाहार्यकं कुर्याच्छ्राद्धमिन्दुक्षये सदा ।
3. *कुल्लूक on मनुस्मृति,* III.122 remarks 'अनेनास्य नित्यत्वमुक्तम् ।' Vol II, p. 133.
4. *मनुस्मृति,* III.123 reads पितॄणां for पिण्डानाम्.
5. *Ibid.,* III.123 reads तच्चामिषेण for तदामिषेण.
6. *मत्स्यपुराण,* p. 28 reads ०अन्नाद्धृता for ०अन्वाहृता.
7. *Ibid.,* p. 28 reads ०चंद्रसंक्षये for ०चन्द्रमासिक्षये.
8. This is *मत्स्यपुराण,* 16.43.

अन्वाहृता पिण्डेभ्यो मात्रा भाग: । बह्वृचानां ब्राह्मणभोजनात् प्राक् पिण्डदाने पिण्डमात्राभक्षणं[1] ब्राह्मणानामुक्तं मनुना[2]।

यथा

पिण्डेभ्यस्त्वल्पिकां मात्रां समादायानुपूर्वश: ।
तेनैव[3] विप्रानासीनान् विधिवत् पूर्वमाशयेत् ।।६।।

अथवा तत: प्रभृति पितर: पिण्डसंज्ञां लभेरन्निति मत्स्यपुराणवचनात् । पिण्डानां पितॄणां मासिकं श्राद्धं अन्वाहार्यं मासैकपितृजनक्रमत: । पिण्डान्वाहार्यकं छन्दोगपरिशिष्टं कात्यायन:[4] (१६.१)

पिण्डान्वाहार्यकं श्राद्धं हीणे राजनि शस्यते ।
वासरस्य तृतीयांशे[5] नातिसन्ध्या समीपत: ।।७।।

राजनि चन्द्रे तृतीयांशे त्रिधाविभक्तदिनस्य तृतीयभागे दशममुहूर्तादूर्ध्वमपि यावत् ।

अत एव श्रुति: ।

'पूर्वाह्णो वै देवानां मध्यन्दिनं मनुष्याणां अपराह्ण: पितॄणा'मिति । नातिसमीपत इति सन्ध्यासमीपमुहूर्त्त एव । आपद्यपि वर्जनीय इत्यर्थ: ।

सायाह्नस्त्रिमूर्त: स्यात् श्राद्धं तत्र न कारयेत् ।८।

इति मत्स्यपुराणे (२२.८३) सन्ध्योसन्निहितं मुहूर्तत्रयं निषिद्धम् । तथाप्यापत्काले मुहूर्तद्वयमनुपातमिति शब्द स्वरसात् ।

'त्रिमुहूर्ताऽपि कर्तव्या'[6] इति वक्ष्यमाण लघुहारीतवचनाच्च दर्शद्वैधे कथं श्राद्धमित्याह । स एवं यदा चतुर्दशीयामं तुरीयमनुपूरयेत् । अमावास्या क्षीयमाणा तदैव श्राद्धमिष्यते । यदुक्तं तदहस्तेन दर्शनं नैति चन्द्रमा: । तत: क्षयापेक्षया ज्ञेयं 'क्षीणे राजनि च'[7] इत्यपि । यच्चोक्तं[8] दृश्यमानेऽपि तच्चतुर्दश्यपेक्षया।

अमावास्यां प्रतीक्षेत तदन्ते वापि निर्वपेत् ।९।
अष्टमेंशे चतुर्दश्या: क्षीणो भवति चन्द्रमा: ।

---

1. This may be amended as पिण्डमात्र० for पिण्डमात्रा०.
2. This is *मनुस्मृति*, III.219.
3. *मनुस्मृति*, III.219 reads तानेव for तेनैव.
4. The text of *कात्यायन* is found in the *स्मृतिसंदर्भ*, Vol. III, p. 1356 and it completely agrees with our ms.
5. *स्मृतिमुक्ताफलम्*, p. 741 and *श्राद्धतत्त्व*, p. 218 quote *कात्यायन* and read तृतीयेंऽशे for तृतीयांशे.
6. *श्राद्धतत्त्व*, p. 268 ascribes this line to *हारीत* and reads it as 'त्रिमुहूर्ताऽपि कर्तव्या पूर्वा दर्शा बह्वृचै:। But *श्राद्धतत्त्व*, p. 273 ascribes this line to *लघुहारीत*.
7. This line is possibly quoted from the text of *कात्यायन* 16.1.
8. *श्राद्धतत्त्व*, p. 270 quotes this stanza from the text of *गोभिल*.

अमावास्याष्टमांशे तु[1] पुनः[2] किल लभेदनुः[3]॥[4]१०॥

आग्रहायण्यमावास्या तथा ज्येष्ठस्य या भवेत् ।

विशेषमाभ्यां ब्रुवते चन्द्राचारविदो[5] जनाः ॥[6]११॥

अत्रेन्दुराद्ये प्रहरेन तिष्ठते[7] चतुर्थभागो न कलावशिष्टः ।

तदन्त एव क्षयमेति कृत्स्नमेवं ज्योतिश्चक्रविदो वदन्ति ॥[8]१२॥

यस्मिन्नब्दे द्वादशैकश्च यव्यस्तस्मिन् तृतीया परिदृश्यो नोपजायते ।

एवं च[9] चारं चन्द्रमसो विदित्वा क्षीणे तस्मिन्नपराह्णेऽपि[10] दद्यात् ॥१३॥

संमिश्रा या चतुर्दश्या ह्यमावास्या[11] भवेत् क्वचित् ।

खर्वितां तां विदुः केचित् उपेध्यमिति[12] चापरे ॥१४॥

वर्द्धमानाममावास्यां लक्षयेदपरेऽहनि ।

यामांस्त्रीनाधिकान् वापि पितृयज्ञस्ततो भवेत्॥[13]१५॥

पक्षादावेव कुर्वीत सदा पक्षादिकं चरुम् ।

पूर्वाह्ने[14] एव कुर्वन्ति विद्धेप्यन्ये मनीषिणः ॥१६॥

यदा चतुर्दशी याममिति[15] तिथिद्वैधे अपरादिते तिथिप्रकार त्रितयान्यतमप्रकारा भवति । क्षीणा स्तम्भिता वर्द्धमाना च । अत्र क्षीणामावास्याविषयमिदम् । यदा पूर्वचतुर्दशी दिनस्य चतुर्थं प्रहरममावास्या पूरयेत् । प्रहरत्रयव्यापिनी चतुर्दशीत्यर्थः । अपरदिने पूर्वातिथ्यापेक्षया क्षीयमाणा भवति । तदा पूर्वदिन एवामावास्यावेलायां श्राद्धमेतच्चोभयतृतीयांशलाभेन तु क्षीयमाणेत्यस्य तृतीयांशव्यापिनीति व्याख्यानं युक्तम् । वासरस्य तृतीयांशे इत्यनेनैव प्राप्तत्वात् वैयर्थ्यापत्तेः । अत्र हेतुमाह । यदुक्तं[16] यदहस्त्वेवेति यदहस्त्वेवेव चन्द्रमा न दृश्येतताममावास्यां कुर्वीतेति । यद् गोभिलसूत्रं तत् क्षयाभिप्रायेण ज्ञेयम् । यस्मिन्नहनि चन्द्रक्षयो भवतीति तस्य सूत्रस्यार्थः कृतः । क्षयलक्षणेति चेत् । न । यदहश्चन्द्रमा[17] न दृश्यते ताममावास्यामिति पूर्वसूत्रेण[18] सह पौनरूक्त्यापत्तिरेव । लक्षणबीजमिति तत्रैव

1. *श्राद्धतत्त्व,* p. 271 reads च for तु.
2. *Ibid.*, p. 271 reads ततः for पुनः
3. *Ibid.*, p. 271 reads ०अणुः for ०अनुः which is corrupt.
4. *Ibid.*, p. 271 quotes this stanza from the text of *कात्यायन.*
5. *Ibid.*, p. 271 reads चन्द्रचारविदो for चन्द्राचारविदो.
6. *Ibid.*, p. 271 quotes this stanza from the text of *कात्यायन.*
7. *Ibid.*, p. 271 reads प्रहरेवतिष्ठते for प्रहरेन तिष्ठते, which is corrupt.
8. *Ibid.*, p. 271 quotes this stanza from the text of *कात्यायन.*
9. *Ibid.*, p. 272 ascribes this stanza to *कात्यायन* and drops च.
10. *Ibid.*, p. 272 reads च for अपि.
11. *Ibid.*, p. 272 drops हि० for हि०.
12. *Ibid.*, p. 272 reads उपेध्वं० for उपेष्यं०.
13. This stanza is quoted in *श्राद्धतत्त्व,* p. 273 and *कृत्यकल्पतरु-श्राद्धकाण्ड,* p. 11.
14. *कृत्यकल्पतरु-श्राद्धकाण्ड,* p. 11 reads पूर्वाह्ण एव for पूर्वाह्ने एव, which is grammatically wrong.
15. *Ibid.*, p. 11 quotes this line from *छन्दोगपरिशिष्टेकात्यायनः* (2.82).
16. *Ibid.*, p. 11 quotes this line from *छन्दोगपरिशिष्टेकात्यायनः* (2.83).
17. *श्राद्धतत्त्व,* p. 270 reads यदहस्तु एव for यदहः which omits तु एव.
18. *Ibid.*, p. 270 cites this as a quotation from *गोभिलसूत्र.*

व्याख्यातमस्माभिरपि । क्षीणे राजनि इत्युक्तं[1] चन्द्रक्षयस्य चतुर्दशी अष्टमी यामात् प्रभृति अमावास्या सप्तमं यामं यावदिति वक्ष्यति । अतश्चन्द्रक्षयानुरोधात् पूर्वदिने श्राद्धमिति तात्पर्यार्थः । यदहस्त्वेव चन्द्रमा न दृश्यतेति श्रुतिविरोध आशङ्का परिहृत इति कल्पतरु[2]व्याख्यानमयुक्तम् । दुर्बलस्मृतिविरोधेन बलवत्यां श्रुतौ लक्षणाया अयोगात् । अन्यथा विरोधाधिकरण[3]सिद्धान्तेऽपि औडम्बरी सर्वविष्ठयितव्येति स्मृतिविरोधादौडम्बरीं स्पृष्ट्वोद्गायेतेति श्रुतावुपस्पर्शलक्षणा स्यात् । तस्मान्वैतादृशी प्रत्यक्षश्रुतिरस्ति । अनुमीयमाना च स्मृत्यनुगुणैवानुमेयेति । तन्मतेनैव सूत्रेण सिनीवालीत्वेन पूर्वदिने दृश्यमाने चन्द्रमसो क्षयपुरस्कारेण श्राद्धस्योक्तत्वेति दृश्यमानेऽप्येकवदेति सूत्रमनर्थकमित्यत आह । यच्चोक्तं दृश्यमानेऽपी[4]ति पूर्वसूत्रममावास्यापदो पादानां च चन्द्रक्षये सत्यमावास्याविषयम् । इदं पुनरित्थं भूतचतुर्दशी विषयमिति नानर्थकम् । तदा च विकल्प इत्याहामावास्यां प्रतीक्षेत श्राद्धार्थम् । तदन्ते चतुर्दश्यन्ते वा निर्वपेत् । यदाऽमावास्याकालः श्राद्धयोग्यो न लभ्येत तदा चन्द्रक्षयानुरोधात् चतुर्दश्यन्त एव श्राद्धमित्यर्थः । अष्टमेंशे चतुर्दश्याः क्षीणो भवति इति चतुर्थभागो न कालावशिष्टता च क्षैरामं[5](?) वक्ष्यमाणवचनात् । अमावास्याष्टमे भागेऽनुरूपचन्द्रोऽत्यविधानात् । सप्तमे यामे निःशेष चन्द्रक्षयोऽवगम्यते । ननु कोऽयं क्षयः? सूक्ष्मता विनाशो वा । न तावदाद्यः । अमावास्योः सप्तमे यामे तदभावात् । न द्वितीयः । पूर्वायामेषु अव्याप्तेः । तुरीयो न कलावशिष्टानि विनाशः । इयमेवक्षयशब्दार्थ इति चेन्न । अनुगतैकरुपभावात् । अमावास्याष्टमे भागेऽप्यनुरूपत्वाच्चन्द्रमसः क्षयापत्तेः । इष्ट तत्र वा इति चेत् । न । एवममावास्यायां चन्द्रक्षयव्यभिचाराभावे क्षयस्य विशेषणत्वं प्रमत्तगीतं स्यात् ।

यथा गोभिलः[6] —

यदहस्त्वेव चन्द्रमा न दृश्यतेताममावास्यां कुर्वीत ।

मार्कण्डेयपुराणे — (२८.२०अ)

श्राद्धं कार्यममावास्यां मासि मासि उडूक्षये[7]।१७।

उच्यते । अन्त्यकालाया अवयव विनाशोत्पत्तिरेव क्षयः । सा च सूक्ष्मतायां विनाशेऽप्यस्तीति न विरोधः । विशेषमाह । आग्रहायण्यमावास्ये[8]ति चन्द्राचारविदो ज्योतिर्विदः । चन्द्र इति वैलक्षण्याद्वैलक्षण्यमित्यर्थः । चतुर्थभागो न कलावशिष्टः । क्षीणः मासान्तरे चतुर्दश्यष्टमे यामे क्षैण्यं एतयोरमावास्याप्रथमे यामे इति विशेषस्तदन्त एवामावास्याष्टमयामान्त एव कृत्स्नक्षयतेति । यतः अतस्तयोरमावास्याष्टमभागे एवापरदिने अपराह्णलाभे देयम् । यद्यपि पूर्वदिने अमावास्या प्रथमयामे चन्द्रक्षयो लभ्यते तथाप्यपरदिन एव कृत्स्नक्षयानुरोधादित्यर्थः । अत्रापि विशेषः । यस्मिन्नब्दे द्वादशैकादश्याः त्रयोदशमासा इत्यर्थः । तेन मलमासपाते न कलोभागत्रयावशिष्ठत्वममावास्या प्रथमयामे यदुक्तं तन्नभवतीति तात्पर्यम् । उभयत्रापराह्णलाभे स्तम्भिताया करस्थामाह संमिश्रेति । वृद्धिह्रासशून्या

---

1. *श्राद्धतत्त्व,* p. 270 cites this as a quotation from the text of *कात्यायन.*
2. This view of कल्पतरु is found with slight variations in the *कृत्यकल्पतरु-श्राद्धकाण्ड,* p. 12.
3. This has a reference to *जैमिनि कृत पूर्वमीमांसा,* I.3.2.3.
4. This refers to *छान्दोगपरिशिष्टे कात्यायनः,* (2.84) quoted in *कृत्यकल्पतरु-श्राद्धकाण्ड,* p. 11.
5. The reading क्षैरामं appears to be corrupt.
6. The text of *गोभिल* is quoted in the *श्राद्धतत्त्व,* p. 270.
7. *मार्कण्डेयपुराण,* p. 151 reads this line by changing the order of words cf. कार्यं श्राद्धममावास्यां मासि मास्युडुक्षये ।
8. *श्राद्धतत्त्व,* p. 271 ascribes this stanza to *कात्यायन.*

सती या चतुर्दश्यामिश्रामावास्या । तां खर्वितां नीचां निन्दितां केचिदाहु:[1]। अपरे[2] तामेव उपेध्वमुपगच्छतेति मन्यन्ते । अस्य व्यवस्था शाखिभेदेन इत्याह लघुहारीत:[3]—

त्रिमुहूर्ताऽपि कर्तव्या पूर्वादर्शा च बह्वृचै: ।
कुहूरध्वर्युभि: कार्या यथेष्टं सामगीतिभि: ॥१८॥

बह्वृचै: पूर्वदिने त्रिमुहूर्तव्यापिन्यपि कार्या । यजुर्वेदिभिरपरदिने । सामगीतिभिच्छन्दोगैर्यथेष्ट-मानियमेनेत्यर्थ: । यथेष्टं सामगीतिभिरित्यत्यभिधानात् । स्तम्भिता विषयमिदम् । क्षीयमानवर्द्धमानपक्षस्य विशिष्टकृता व्यवस्थाऽपि तत्त्वात् । उभयत्रापराह्णकालाभेऽपीयं व्यवस्था । वर्द्धमानामाह । वर्द्धमाना[4]मिति पूर्वदिने तुरीयं यामं पूरयित्वाऽपरदिने पूर्वतिथ्यपेक्षया क्षीयमानत्वस्यापि पूर्वतिथ्यपेक्षितत्वे वर्द्धमानत्वस्य तथैवान्याय्यत्वात् । ततश्च प्रहरत्रयमधिकं वा यदा वर्द्धमानाममावास्यां लक्षयेत्तदाऽपरदिने एव श्राद्धम् । चन्द्रक्षयालाभे वचनादेव एतदप्युभयत्रापराह्णलाभेनापि वचनादेव बोद्धव्यम् । ननु पूर्वदिने तुरीयं यामं पूरयित्वाह । परदिने प्रहरस्त्रयं यावदवतिष्ठमाना कथं वर्द्धमान स्यात्[5]। सत्यं तुरीयमनुपूरयित्वेत्य-पराह्णामात्रोपलक्षणार्थम् । अन्यथा दण्डाधिकतुरीय याम व्यापिन्यमावास्यापरदिने प्रहरत्रयमवतिष्ठमाना कथं वर्द्धमाना न स्यात् । ननु वर्द्धमानाममावास्या पक्षे प्रात:कालविहितस्य पक्षादिचरोर्न । तस्मिन् दिनेऽमावास्या प्रात:कालेऽनुष्ठानं पक्षादयोऽभियष्टव्या इति गोभिलविरोधात् । इतिनाप्यपरदिने द्वितीया विद्धत्वात् । द्वितीयावेधे एषा वै सुमनानामेष्टिरिति तैत्तिरीयश्रुतौ[6] निन्दाश्रवणाल्लोप एव पक्षादिचरो: स्यादित्याह । पक्षादावेव कुर्वीतेति । अपरदिने प्रतिपद्येव विद्धायामपिकर्तव्य इत्यर्थ: । वेधनिन्दा न बह्वृच विषयेति वक्ष्यते प्रसङ्गादिदमुक्तम् ।

लघुहारीत: —

पर्वणेंशे तुरीयेति कार्य इष्टि द्विजातिभि: ।
द्वितीयासहितं यस्माद्वृषयन्त्याश्वलायना: ॥१९॥

बह्वृचविधि विषयं चेदं वृषयन्त्याश्वलायना इत्याभिधानात् । छन्दोगपरिशिष्टकृता च । वेध एवेष्टैरुक्तत्वात् । क्षेत्र व[7] बौधायन: ।

पर्वणो यश्चतुर्थोंश आद्या: प्रतिपदस्त्रय: ।
यागकाल स विज्ञेय: प्रातर्युक्तो मनीषिभि: ॥२०॥

---

1. This view is found in *छन्दोगपरिशिष्टे कात्यायन:*, (II.89) and quoted in *कृत्यकल्पतरु-श्राद्धकाण्ड*, p. 11.
2. This view is found quoted in the *कृत्यकल्पतरु-श्राद्धकाण्ड*, p. 13, omitting the expression 'अर्थानुष्ठानार्थम्'. Also see *छन्दोगपरिशिष्टे कात्यायन:* (II.89) quoted in *कृत्यकल्पतरु-श्राद्धकाण्ड*, p. 11.
3. *श्राद्धतत्त्व*, p. 273 ascribes this stanza to *लघुहारीत* and on p. 268 ascribes this to *हारीत*.
4. This refers to *छन्दोगपरिशिष्टे कात्यायन:*, (II.90) quoted in *कृत्यकल्पतरु-श्राद्धकाण्ड*, p. 11.
5. This may be emended as वर्धमाना० for वर्धमान०.
6. This citation from *तैत्तिरीयश्रुति* is found quoted in *कृत्यकल्पतरु-श्राद्धकाण्ड*, p. 13.
7. This word व seems to be corrupt.

इति प्रसङ्गाद्दैवकृत्यतिथि व्यवस्थामाह लघुहारीत:[1]।

मध्याह्नव्यापिनी या तु पूर्वा वा यदि वापरा[2]।
तस्यां कर्म प्रकुर्वीत[3] क्षयवृद्धी न कारणम् ॥२१॥

ततो यत्र मध्याह्नलाभे व्यवस्थोक्ता विष्णुधर्मोत्तरे[4]—

नक्षत्रं देवदेवेश तिथिं चार्द्ध विनिर्गताम् ।
दृष्टोपवास: कर्तव्य: कथं शंकरजानता ॥२२॥

शंकर[5] उवाच ।

सा तिथिस्तदहोरात्रं यस्यामस्तमितो रवि: ।
तया कर्माणि कुर्वीत-ह्रासवृद्धिर्न कारणम् ॥२३॥
शुक्लपक्षे तिथिर्ग्राह्या यस्यामभ्युदितो रवि: ।
कृष्णपक्षे तिथिर्ग्राह्या यस्यामस्तमितो रवि: ॥२४॥

एतच्च युग्मवचनाव्याप्त दशम्यादि तिथिविषयमिति कल्पतरौ[6] दृष्टम् । विस्तरभयान्नेह स्थूयते । अन्यथा युग्मवचनविरोधात् ।

शुक्लपक्षविहित पार्वणैकोद्दिष्टयोरप्येतादृशी व्यवस्था । मध्याह्नसम्बन्धाविशेषात् । अमावास्याव्यतिरिक्त कृष्णपक्षविहित तिथिवैधे गृह्यपरिशिष्टम्[7]।

ययास्तं सविता[8] याति पितरस्तामुपासते।
तिथिं तेभ्यो पराह्णे हि स्वयंदत्त स्वयम्भुवा[9]॥२५॥

एतच्च नैकोद्दिष्ट शुक्लपक्षपार्वणविषयम् । अथ प्रतिमास पार्वणाशक्तस्य कर्तव्यं पार्वणश्राद्धमभिधायाह मनु: (३.२८१) ।

अनेन विधिना श्राद्धं त्रिरब्दस्येह निर्वपेत् ।
हेमन्त ग्रीष्मवर्षासु पाञ्चयज्ञिकमन्वहम् ॥२६॥

---

1. This stanza is found quoted in the *स्मृतिचंद्रिका-श्राद्धकाण्ड*, p. 32 with slight variations.
2. *Ibid.*, p. 32 reads तु तिथि: पूर्वा पराऽपि वा for तु पूर्वा वा यदि वापरा.
3. *Ibid.*, p. 32 reads तदह: कर्म कुर्वीत for तस्यां कर्म प्रकुर्वीत.
4. This stanza could not be located in the extant *विष्णुधर्मोत्तर पुराण*, but found in *तिथिविवेक*, p. 233 of *Poona Oerientalist*, Vol. VI, Nos. 3 & 4.
5. The veres in the mouth of शंकर can be traced in *तिथिविवेक*.
6. The view of कल्पतरु is not found in *कृत्यकल्पतरु-श्राद्धकाण्ड*.
7. *स्मृतिचंद्रिका-श्राद्धकाण्ड*, p. 31 quotes a stanza from the text of वृद्धमनु, which comes very near to this text.
8. *Ibid.*, p. 31 reads रवि: for सविता.
9. *Ibid.*, p. 31 reads यतो दत्तो ह्यपराह्ण स्वयंभुवा for पराह्णो हि स्वयंदत्त स्वयम्भुवा.

अयं च साग्निनिरग्निसाधारणः पक्षः । निरग्निविषयत्वे प्रमाणाभावात् । संवत्सरस्य मध्ये यत्रतिमासविहितं पार्वणं तद्‌द्रव्यासम्भवादेनिर्मित्ताद्दर्शान्तरेऽनावश्यकम् । पाञ्चयज्ञान्तर्गतं यत् श्राद्धं तत् प्रत्यहमुकादिनाऽपि कर्तव्यम्[1]। हेमन्तग्रीष्मवर्षास्विति यदुक्तं तत् कन्या कुम्भ-वृषस्थेऽर्के इति दर्शयति[2] मत्स्यपुराणे (१६.५७)

अनेन विधिना श्राद्धं त्रिरब्दस्येह[3] निर्वपेत् ।
न दर्शेन विना श्राद्धमाहिताग्नेर्द्विजन्मनः ॥२७॥

यज्ञात् पितृयज्ञाङ्गभूतोऽग्नौकरणहोमो न लौकिकेऽग्नौ विधीयते । किन्तु दक्षिणाग्नौ । स च दर्श एव विद्यते । दर्श एव तदुद्धरणस्य विहितत्वात् । अतस्तदङ्गबाधभिया न दर्शेन विना आहिताग्नेः श्रौताग्निमतः श्राद्धमेतत् । प्रतिमासविहित पार्वणाख्यमस्तीति अगत्याष्टकादौ यथा कथंचिद्विप्रपान्यादावग्नौ करणहोमः । यच्च दर्शनविनेत्यत्र दर्शपदेन पार्वणविधिर्लक्ष्यते । तेन दर्शेन विना पार्वणविधिना नाहिताग्नेः श्राद्धमिति हलायुध[4]व्याख्यानम्। तन्न युक्तं लक्षणाहेत्वभावात् । पूर्वार्द्धेन सहानन्वयात् वाक्यभेदापत्तेश्च । तस्मादयुक्तमेव व्याख्यानम् । पार्वणत्रयाशक्तेन द्विः सकृद्वा कर्तव्यमित्याह देवलः[5]।

अनेन विधिना श्राद्धं कुर्यात् संवत्सरं सकृत्[6]।
द्विश्चतुर्वा यथाशक्ति[7]र्मासे मासे दिने दिने ॥२८॥

सकृत्करणपक्षः कन्यायामिति प्रशस्तत्वात् । पार्वणश्राद्धाशक्तस्याहिताग्नेः । पिण्डदानमात्रं निरग्निना । ब्राह्मणभोजनमात्रं कर्तव्यमित्याह निगमः । आहिताग्नेः पित्र्यर्चनं पिण्डैरेव । ब्राह्मणान् भोजयेदिति पूर्वमनुदानम् ।

अशक्तनिरग्निविषये पार्वणश्राद्धमभिधाय आह विष्णुपुराणम् (३.१४.२४-२५) ।

अन्नेन वा यथाशक्त्या कालेऽस्मिन् भक्तिनम्रधीः ।
भोजयिष्यति विप्राणां तन्मात्र[8] विभवो नरः ॥२९॥
असमर्थोऽन्नदानस्य धान्यदानं स्वशक्तिभिः[9]।
प्रदास्यति द्विजाग्रेभ्यो[10] स्वल्पात्[11] वा पितृदक्षिणाम्[12]॥३०॥

---

1. *कुल्लूक on मनुस्मृति,* III.281 does not express this view.
2. *Ibid.*, III. 281 gives the same comments and does not quote *मत्स्यपुराण* in support but relies on *मनु,* III.83.
3. *मत्स्यपुराण,* p. 28 reads निरुद्धास्येह॰ for त्रिरब्दस्येह॰.
4. The view of *हलायुध* cannot be traced in *कृत्यकल्पतरु, श्राद्धमयूख, स्मृतिचंद्रिका* and *श्राद्धप्रकाश. श्राद्धप्रकाश,* p. 322 quotes the text of *देवल.*
6. *Ibid.*, p. 322 reads द्विजः for सकृत्.
7. *Ibid.*, p. 322 reads यथा श्राद्धं for यथाशक्तिः .
8. *विष्णुपुराण,* reads विप्राग्न्यांस्तन्मात्र for विप्राणां तन्मात्र.
9. *Ibid.*, reads स्वशक्तितः for स्वशक्तिभिः .
10. *Ibid.*, reads द्विजाग्न्येभ्यो for द्विजाग्रेभ्यो.
11. *Ibid.*, reads स्वल्पाल्पां for स्वल्पात्.
12. *Ibid.*, reads अपि दक्षिणाम् for पितृदक्षिणाम्.

अत्रापि असामर्थ्यमत: कराग्रगस्थिनां स्थिनान्[1]।

प्रणिपत्य द्विजाग्राय कस्मैचिदभूप दास्यति ।
एतै: सप्ताष्टभिर्वापि समवेताञ्जलाञ्जलीन् ।।३१।।
भक्तिनम्र: समुदिश्य भुव्यस्माकं प्रदास्यति ।
यत: कुतश्चित् संप्राप्य गोभ्यो वापि गवाह्निकम् ।।३२।।
अभावे प्रीणयन्नस्मान् श्रद्धायुक्त: प्रदास्यति ।
तिलै: सप्ताष्टभिर्वापि समवेताञ्जलाञ्जलीन् ।।३३।।
सर्वभावे वनं गत्वा कक्षामूलप्रदर्शक: ।
सूर्यादि लोकपालानामिदमुच्चै: पठिष्यति ।।३४।।
न मेऽस्ति वित्तं न धनं न चान्यत्
श्राद्धोपयोग्यं च पितॄन्नतोऽस्मि ।
तृप्यन्तु भक्त्या पितरो ममैतौ
कृतौ भुजौ वर्त्मदिन मारुतस्य ।।३५।।

अत्रानुमत: स्वर्ग: । पित्रोद्देशेन कर्तव्योऽस्माकमुद्दिश्येति वचनात् । पितृदक्षिणामिति पितृकर्मविहितां रजतादि दक्षिणाम् । एकोद्दिष्टाशक्तौ तु न ब्राह्मणभोजनम् । किन्त्वेकादशयामि[2]ति वक्ष्यति ।

---

1. The portion कराग्रगस्थिनां स्थिनान् appears to be corrupt.
2. The context permits one to emend ०एकोद्दिष्टं for ०एकादशयाम्.

१६

अथ पङ्क्तिपावनाः

तत्र मनुः (३.१८३-१८६)

अपाङ्क्तयोपहता पंक्तिः पाव्यते यैः द्विजेत्तमैः ।
तान्निबोधत कार्त्स्नेन[1] द्विजाग्न्यान् पंक्तिपावनान् ॥१॥

अग्न्याः सर्वेषु वेदेषु सर्वप्रवचनेषु च । श्रोत्रियानुयजाश्चैव विज्ञेयाः पङ्क्तिपावनाः ।

त्रिणाचिकेतः पञ्चाग्निस्त्रिसुपर्णः षडङ्गवित् ।
ब्रह्मदेयात्मसंतानो ज्येष्ठ सागम एव च ॥२॥
वेदार्थवित्प्रवक्ता च ब्रह्मचारी सहस्रदः ।
शतायुश्चैव विज्ञेया ब्राह्मणाः पंक्तिपावनाः ॥३॥

अग्न्या वेदपारगेषु ये करतलामलकवद्वेदं पश्यन्ति । प्रोच्यते एभिर्वेदार्थ इति प्रवचनान्यङ्गानि । त्रिणाचिकेतोऽध्वर्युर्वेदभागः तद्योगात् पुरुषोऽपि वेदार्थवित् । विनाप्यङ्गं प्रवक्ता[2] प्रकृष्टाध्यापकः । ब्रह्मदेयापतिश्चैव ब्राह्मणाः पंक्तिपावनाः ।

विष्णुः (८३.६-१९)

वेदाङ्गस्याप्येकस्य पारगः । प्रवासे[3]तिहास[4]पारगः । धर्मशास्त्रस्याप्येकदेशस्य[5] पारगः । तीर्थपूतः । यज्ञपूतः । तपः पूतः । सत्यपूतो मन्त्रपूतो गायत्रीजपनिरतो[6] जामाता दौहित्रश्चेति पात्रम् । विशेषेण[7] योगिनः ।

---

1. Other commentators read on *मनु,* III.183 कार्त्स्न्येन for कार्त्स्नेन.
2. *कुल्लूक on मनुस्मृति,* III.186 explains प्रवक्ता as वेदार्थस्यैव अनधीत्यापि वेदाङ्गानि गुरुपदेशाधिगतवेदार्थः। This is a slightly different explanation.
3. *विष्णुस्मृति,* p. 806 reads पुराणे for प्रवासे.
4. *Ibid.*, p. 806 reads व्याकरण after इतिहास, कुल्लूक omits व्याकरण.
5. *Ibid.*, p. 806 reads एकस्य for एकदेशस्य.
6. *कुल्लूक* reads from सत्यपूतो up to निरतो as one सूत्र. In the critical edition, however, each word is treated as a separate सूत्र.
7. *विष्णुस्मृति,* p. 807 reads च after विशेषेण, च is also droped in other Mss. ज and ठ of *विष्णुस्मृति.*

मत्स्यपुराणे (१६.११ब-१२अ)

> यश्च प्रकुरुते[1] वाचं[2] यश्च मीमांसतेऽध्वरम् ।
> सामस्वरविधिज्ञश्च पङ्क्तिपावनपावना: ॥४॥
> अष्टवर्षात्तु[3] या दत्ता श्रुतशीलसमन्विते ।
> सा गौरी मृतौ[4] गौर: पङ्क्तिपावन एव स: ॥५॥

वायुपुराणे (७९.५३-५५अ)

> यतिस्तु सर्वविप्राणां सर्वेषामग्रभुग्[5] भवेत्[6]।
> इतिहास पञ्चमान्वेदान्[7] पठेद्धि[8] द्विजोत्तम:[9]॥६॥
> अनन्तरस्तथायोगी[10] नियोक्तव्यो विजानता ।
> त्रिवेदोऽनन्तरं[11] तस्य द्विवेदस्तदनन्तरम्[12]॥७॥
> एकवेदस्तत: पश्चाद्विद्याध्यायी[13] तत: परम् ॥८॥

यतिरिति त्रिदण्डैकदण्डयोर्ग्रहणम्[14]।

> अलाभे ध्यानभिक्षुणां भोजयेद्ब्रह्मचारिणम् ।
> शिखिभ्यो धातुवक्तेभ्य: त्रिदण्डेभ्य: प्रदापयेत् । इति ॥९॥

वक्ष्यमाणवचनात् । तथा योगी यथा यतेरनन्तरमितिहास पञ्चमवेदपाठकं तथा योगीगृहस्थ एव । यथा युक्त: । ब्राह्मणोपवेशन क्रमोदयुक्त:[15]।

---

1. *मत्स्यपुराण,* reads व्याकुरुते for प्रकुरुते.
2. *अपरार्क on याज्ञवल्क्यस्मृति,* p. 441 reads वेदं for वाचं.
3. *Ibid*., p. 441 reads अष्टवर्षा तु for अष्टवर्षात्तु.
4. *कृत्यकल्पतरु-श्राद्धकाण्ड,* p. 70 reads सुतौ for मृतौ.
5. *वायुपुराण,* reads अग्न्य for अग्रभुग्.
6. *Ibid*., reads उत्सवे for भवेत्.
7. *Ibid*., reads वेदान्.
8. *Ibid*., reads य: befor पठेद्धि.
9. *कृत्यकल्पतरु-श्राद्धकाण्ड,* p. 70 reads द्विजसत्तम: for द्विजोत्तम:
10. *वायुपुराण,* reads अनन्तरं यथायोग्यं and *कृत्यकल्पतरु-श्राद्धकाण्ड,* p. 70 reads अनन्तरं यते सोऽयं for अनन्तरस्तथायोगी.
11. *कृत्यकल्पतरु-श्राद्धकाण्ड,* p. 70 reads त्रिवेदोऽनन्तरं तस्य for त्रिवेदोऽनन्तरस्तस्य.
12. *वायुपुराण,* reads अनन्तर: for अनन्तरम्.
13. *Ibid*., reads न्यायाध्यायी and *कृत्यकल्पतरु-श्राद्धकाण्ड,* p. 70 reads नित्याध्यायी for विद्याध्यायी.
14. Actually the line यतिरिति etc. is a gloss and should be read after प्रदापयेत् इति i.e. after Stanza No. 9 as per the practice of the निबन्ध writers. Hence the line यतिरिति etc. is an after thought of कुल्लूक.
15. The context permits one to prefer the reading अयुक्त: for अदयुक्त: .

ब्रह्मपुराणे

षडङ्गवित् ज्ञानयोगी यज्ञतन्त्रज्ञ[1] एव च ।
अयाचिताशी[2]विप्रो वा श्राद्धकल्पविदेव वा[3]।।१०।।
अष्टादशानां विद्यानामेकस्यामपि[4] पारगः ।।११।।

वायुपुराणे

गृहस्थानां सहस्रेण वानप्रस्थशतेन च ।
ब्रह्मचारिसहस्रेण एको योगी[5] विशिष्यते ।।१२।।

यमः

अभावे[6] ध्यानभिक्षूणां भोजयेद्ब्रह्मचारिणम् ।
तदभावेप्युदासीनं गृहस्थमपि भोजयेत् ।।१३।।[7]

ध्यानभिक्षुर्ध्यानप्रधानो भिक्षुरेकदण्डः । उदासीनमसम्बधिनमिति मुख्यकल्पः ।

अनुकल्पमाह मनुः (३.१४७-१४८)

एष वै प्रथमः कल्पः प्रदाने हव्यकव्ययोः ।
अनुकल्पस्त्वयं ज्ञेयः सदा सद्भिरनुष्ठितः ।।१४।।
मातामहं मातुलं च स्वस्रीयं[8] श्वशुरं गुरुम् ।
दौहित्रं विट्पतिं बन्धुमृत्विग्याज्यौ च भोजयेत् ।।१५।।

एष गुणवदसम्बन्धि ब्राह्मणभोजनः लक्षणः । विट्पतिः जामाता[9]।

वशिष्ठः (११.१८)

शिष्यानपि गुणवतो भोजयेत् ।१६।

---

1. *कृत्यकल्पतरु-श्राद्धकाण्ड*, p. 70 reads तत्त्वज्ञ for तन्त्रज्ञ.
2. *Ibid.*, p. 70 reads अयाचितार्थी for अयाचिताशी.
3. *Ibid.*, p. 70 reads च for वा.
4. *Ibid.*, p. 70 reads ००अपि तु for ००अपि.
5. *Ibid.*, p. 71 reads योगी त्वेको for एको योगी; *स्मृतिचंद्रिका-श्राद्धकाण्ड*, p. 158 reads यो योगी स for एको योगी.
6. *पराशरमाधव*, Vol. I, p. 680 reads अलाभे for अभावे. The reading अलाभे suits the context.
7. *स्मृतिचंद्रिका-श्राद्धकाण्ड*, p. 157 ascribes the text 'अभावे' etc. of *यम* to *ब्रह्माण्डपुराण*.
8. *कृत्यकल्पतरु-श्राद्धकाण्ड*, p. 71 reads स्वकीयं for स्वस्रीयं adopted by other commentators of *मनु*.
9. रामचन्द्र, explains this as पितृगृहे कन्या तस्याः विट्पतिं भगिनीपतिमित्यर्थः . *मनुस्मृति*, Vol. II, p. 159. नीलकण्ठ in his *श्राद्धमयूख*, p. 38 quotes the opinion of मेधातिथि and माधव as अतिथिरिति मेधातिथिमाधवौ.

कात्यायन:

अभावे शिष्यान् भोजयेदिति प्रक्रम्य

देवल:[1]

अज्ञातीन् समानार्षान्[2] मुख्यानपि[3] शक्तित: ।१७।
गुणवतोऽन्यस्याभावे,
गुणवन्तं सपिण्डमपि भोजयेदित्याह ।१८।

बौधायन: (२.८.१४.३-४)

'तदभावे रहस्यवित् ऋचो यजूंषि सामानीति श्राद्धस्य महिमा । तस्मादेवंविधं सपिण्डमप्याशयेत् ।' रहस्यं उपनिषद् । एवंविधं वेदविदम् ।

आपस्तम्ब: (२.७.१७.४-६)

भोजयेद्ब्राह्मणान्[4] ब्रह्मविदो योनिगोत्रान्ते[5] वास्य सम्बन्धात्[6]। गुणहाराय[7] तु परेषां समुदित: सोदर्यो[8] भोजयितव्य: ।

एतत् पुरूषत्रयादूर्ध्वं[9] त्रिभ्यो गुणवन्तमिति गौतम (१५.२०-२१) वचनात् ।

ननु विष्णुसूत्रात्[10] (८३.१७-१८) जामातृ दौहित्रयोरूपादानं मुख्यकल्पे । मनुना गौणकल्पे तयोरुक्तं सत्यं साग्निनिरग्निविषयम् । मुख्ये यजूषां गौणमेव इति कल्पतरुकार:[11]। अस्मद्गुरुचरणास्तु[12] सविद्य निर्विद्य भेदे विचार: ।

---

1. The text of *देवल* is untraced in the *स्मृतिसंदर्भ,* Vol. III. This however, is found quoted in the *श्राद्धचंद्रिका,* p. 19.
2. *श्राद्धचंद्रिका,* p. 19 reads असमानार्षान् for समानार्षान्.
3. *Ibid.,* p. 19 reads अयुग्मान् for मुख्यानपि.
4. *आपस्तम्ब धर्मसूत्र,* II.7.17.4 reads प्रयत: प्रसन्नमना: सृष्टो before भोजयेत् ब्राह्मणान्.
5. Bühler locates the expression मन्त्र after गोत्र and before अन्ते. The reading मन्त्र is also adopted by *कृत्यकल्पतरु-श्राद्धकाण्ड,* p. 72.
6. *आपस्तम्ब धर्मसूत्र,* p. 78 reads संबन्धान् for सम्बन्धात्.
7. *Ibid.,* p. 78 and *कृत्यकल्पतरु-श्राद्धकाण्ड,* p. 72 read गुणहान्यां for गुणहाराय.
8. *Ibid.,* p. 78 reads अपि after सोदर्यो.
9. The expression एतत् पुरुषतायादूर्ध्वं is not found in the *गौतमधर्मसूत्र.* Besides, कुल्लूक joins *गौतमधर्मसूत्र,* 15.20 and 15.21 together.
10. *विष्णुस्मृति,* p. 807 reads जामाता । दौहित्रश्चेति पात्रम् ।
11. This view of कल्पतरु, however, is not found or traced in the *कृत्यकल्पतरु-श्राद्धकाण्ड.*
12. The revered teacher of कुल्लूकभट्ट cannot be identified.

१७

अथ वर्ज्याः

मनुः (३.१३८-१४०.१४४)

न श्राद्धे भोजयेन्मित्रं धनैः कार्योऽस्य संग्रहः ।
नारिं न मित्रं यं विद्यात्तं[1] श्राद्धे भोजयेद्द्विजम् ॥१॥
यः संगतानि कुरुते मोहाच्छ्राद्धेन मानवः ।
संबन्धाच्च्यवते[2] लोकाच्छ्राद्धमित्रो द्विजाधमः ॥२॥
कामं श्राद्धेऽर्चयेन्मित्रं नाभिरूपमपि त्वरिम् ।
द्विषता हि हविर्भुक्तं भवति प्रेत्य निष्फलम् ॥३॥

मित्रमित्रमरिं च पूर्वसिद्धं धनैर्धनान्तरैः संग्रहो विच्छेदः । संगतं मित्रभावम् । स्वर्गात् कामान्तरार्जितात् काममिति । गुणवद्ब्राह्मणाभावे सगुणं मित्रं भोजयेत् । न योग्यमपि रिपुम् । गुणवन्मित्रप्रतिप्रसवार्थमिदम्[3]।

ब्राह्मणो ह्यनधीयानस्तृणाग्निरिव शाम्यति ।
तस्मै हव्यं न दातव्यं न हि भस्मनि हूयते[4] ॥४॥

आरित्वनिषेधार्थ निन्दामाह —

मनुः(३.१३३)

यावतो ग्रसते पिण्डान् हव्यकव्येष्वमन्त्रवित् ।
तावतो ग्रसते प्रेतो[5] दीप्तान्[6]शूलच्यतेगुडान्[7] ॥५॥

---

1. *स्मृतिचंद्रिका-श्राद्धकाण्ड,* p. 162 reads विन्द्यात् for विद्यात्.
2. *मनुस्मृति,* III.139 reads स्वर्गलोकाच्च्यवते for संबन्धाच्च्यवते.
3. Also read *कुल्लूक on मनुस्मृति,* III.140 'यथोक्त पात्रासंभवे मित्रप्रतिप्रसवार्थमिदम् ।
4. This is *मनुस्मृति,* III.168.
5. Other commentators on *मनुस्मृति,* III.133 read प्रेतो. But in the *श्राद्धसागर* in the कुल्लूक reads प्रेत्य. In the *मनुस्मृति,* we also get the reading प्रेत्य by कुल्लूक.
6. *मनुस्मृति,* III.133 reads दीप्त for दीप्तान्.
7. *Ibid.,* reads शूलर्ष्टर्ययोगुडान्. *कृत्यकल्पतरु-श्राद्धकाण्ड,* p. 75 ascribes this stanza to *मनुयमशातातप.*

प्रेत्य ग्रसतेऽस्तु ।

प्रस्तुत: श्राद्धकर्ता वसिष्ठ: (३.१२)

विद्वद्भोज्यान्यविद्वांसो येषु राष्ट्रेषु[1] भञ्जते ।
तान्यनावृष्टिमृच्छन्ति[2] महद्वा जायते भव्यम्[3]॥६॥

तानि राष्ट्रान् ऋच्छन्ति प्राप्नुवन्ति । इच्छन्तीति पाठे तान्यन्वतीसम्बन्ध: ।

---

1. *कृत्यकल्पतरु-श्राद्धकाण्ड,* p. 75 reads श्राद्धानि for राष्ट्रेषु.
2. *वसिष्ठधर्मसूत्र,* III.12 also reads ऋच्छन्ति and also notes another reading. *हेमाद्रि-श्राद्धकाण्ड,* p. 460 reads प्राप्नुवन्ति for इच्छन्ति. This stanza is also quoted in the *कृत्यकल्पतरु-श्राद्धकाण्ड,* p. 75. The reading इच्छन्ति noted by कुल्लूक has escaped the notice of Bühler.
3. *वसिष्ठधर्मसूत्र,* III.12 reads भयम् for भव्यम्. The reading भव्यम् noted by कुल्लूक does not convey any good sense.

अथ निमन्त्रणम्

मनुः (३.१८७)

पूर्वेद्युरपरेद्युर्वा श्राद्धकर्मण्युपस्थिते ।
निमन्त्रयेत्[1] त्र्यवरान् सम्यग्विप्रान्यथोदितान् ॥१॥

त्रयोऽवरा निकृष्टकोटिर्येषां ते त्र्यवरान्तान् पूर्वदिनापरदिनयोर्न व्रीहियवबाहुल्यवत् विकल्प इत्याह देवलः[2]।

श्वः कर्तास्मीति निश्चित्य दाता विप्रान् निमन्त्रयेत् ।
निरामिषं सकृत् भुञ्ज्वा[3] सर्वसुप्त[4]जने गृहे ॥२॥
असंभवे परेद्युर्वा ब्राह्मणस्तान्निमन्त्रयेत् ।
अज्ञातीन्[5] समानार्षान्[6] मुख्यानमपि[7] शक्तितः ॥३॥

निरामिषं सकृत् भुक्त्वेति अपरदिनेऽपि संबध्यते ।

तथा मार्कण्डेयपुराणे (२४.३०ब-३४ब)

निमन्त्रयीत पूर्वेद्युः पूर्वोक्तान् द्विजसत्तमान् ।
अप्राप्तौ तद्दिने वापि[8] हित्वा[9] योषित् प्रसङ्गिनम्[10]॥४॥

---

1. *मनुस्मृति,* III. 187 reads निमन्त्रयीत for निमन्त्रयेत्.
2. *पराशरमाधव,* Vol. I, pp. 696-97 quotes he text of *देवल.*
3. *Ibid*., p. 697 reads भुक्त्वा for भुञ्ज्वा.
4. *Ibid*., p. 696 reads ०भुक्त० for ०सुप्त०.
5. *Ibid*., p. 697 reads अज्ञातान् for अज्ञातीन्.
6. *Ibid*., p. 697 reads असमानार्षान् for समानार्षान्.
7. *Ibid*., p. 697 reads आयुष्मानात्म for मुख्यानमपि.
8. *मार्कण्डेयपुराण,* p. 152 reads चापि for वापि.
9. *Ibid*., p. 152 reads वर्ज्या for हित्वा.
10. *Ibid*., p. 152 and *पृथ्वीचन्द्र-श्राद्धप्रकाश,* VI.7, p. 116 read प्रसङ्गिनः for प्रसङ्गिनम्.

यमः —

> योनिक्रियावरोधाद्यै गुणैर्युक्तानलोलुपान् ।
> प्रार्थयेत[1] प्रदोषान्ते भुक्त्वान्नं शयितान्[2] द्विजान् ॥५॥
> सर्वमासविनियुक्तैः कामक्रोधविवर्जितैः ।
> भवद्भिर्भवितव्यं नः श्वो भूते श्राद्धकर्मणि ॥६॥
> ततस्तथेत्य विघ्नेन याति चेद्रजनीमुखम् ।
> यथाश्रुतं प्रतीक्षेरन् श्राद्धकालमतन्द्रिताः ॥७॥

प्रार्थयेत तान् निमन्त्रणपूर्वं नियममर्थयेदित्यर्थः । तन्नियममाह सर्वायासेत्यादि ते ब्राह्मणास्तं निमन्त्रयितारं तथेत्यूचुरिति शेषः । तदहर्वामन्त्रणपक्षे तु नान्यमन्त्रस्य पाठः । असमवेतार्थत्वात् श्वपदस्य । न च श्वः पदस्थानेऽद्य पदेह कार्यव्रीहिपदस्थाने निवारपदोवदिति वाच्यम् । अन्यथोपत्तेः प्रकृतावूहकल्पनाया अयोगात् । व्रीहिमन्त्रस्य एव यवे ।

अत एव कात्यायनः ।

न प्रकृतावपूपत्वात् ऊह इत्यर्थः । वचनात्तु क्वचित् प्रकृतौ अपि ऊहो[3]।

यथा छन्दोगपरिशिष्टम्—

> मातामहानामप्येवं श्राद्धं कुर्याद्विचक्षणः ।
> मन्त्रोहेन[4] यथान्यायं शेषाणां मन्त्रवर्जितम् ॥८॥

किं च

> अक्रोधनैः शौचपरैः सततं ब्रह्मचारिभिः ।
> भवितव्यं भवद्भिश्च मया ते[5] श्राद्धकर्मणि ॥९॥

इति मत्स्यपुराणोक्तं समवेतार्थ मन्त्रसद्भावेन ऊहकल्पनाऽन्याय्या नाप्यसमवेतार्थमन्त्रपाठो युक्तः । अत एवास्मात्त्वमभिजातोसीति मन्त्रस्य लिङ्गात् साग्न्यस्वि[6] प्रकाशकस्य निरविषये निवृत्तिः[7]। किन्तु कृत्वा तु दुष्करमिति वराहपुराणीय मन्त्रस्यैव पाठः । अतो व्यवस्थितविकल्पोऽयम् । पूर्वदिने सर्वायासपाठस्तदहरक्रोधनै[8]रिति ।

---

1. *श्राद्धप्रकाश,* p. 105 reads प्रार्थयीत for प्रार्थयेत.
2. *Ibid.*, p. 105 reads भुक्तानशयितान् for भुक्त्वान्नं शयितान्.
3. It may be emended as ऊहः for ऊहो.
4. *कृत्यकल्पतरु-श्राद्धकाण्ड,* p. 105 quotes *मत्स्यपुराण* and reads मयात्र for मयाते.
5. *Ibid.*, p. 237 quotes this stanza and reads मन्त्रोहेण for मन्त्रोहेन.
6. This word appears to be corrupt.
7. The portion from प्रकाशकस्य up to निवृत्तिः is not intelligible.
8. This stanza from *मत्स्यपुराण* is quoted in *कृत्यकपतरु-श्राद्धकाण्ड,* p. 237.

मत्स्यपुराणे[1]—

'दक्षिणं जानुं आलभ्य त्वं मयात्र निमिन्त्रतः ।'१०।

एवं निमन्त्रितनियमान् श्रावयेत् पैतृकान् बुधः ।

अत्र केचित् अस्मद्ववचनात् श्वः कर्तव्यत्वन्मयात्र निमन्त्रित इति निमन्त्रणवाक्यं वर्णयन्ति । तदसङ्गतम् । निमन्त्रित इत्यस्यातीत निमन्त्रणप्रकाशकत्वात् । निमन्त्रणाय च वर्तमानत्वात् । वर्तमानक्तस्य वृद्धयर्थादि[2] धातुविशेषनियतत्वात्, असमवेतार्थत्वेनादृष्टार्थत्वापत्तेः । हुँ फडादिव[3]दृष्टार्थत्वैव कुतो न भवेदिति चेत् । न । निमन्त्रणबाधापत्तेः । अनुमितिफलकः कर्मकरणार्थम् । बोधनभेदो निमन्त्रणं यतः । किं च निमन्त्रितोऽस्मीत्यनुमतिरपि बाध्येत । तथा विष्णुमित्रपुत्राय तुभ्यं यज्ञदत्तपुत्री सम्प्रदत्तेति बह्वृच-गृह्यपरिशिष्टवचनात् । कन्यासम्प्रदानमपि तथा स्यात् । दृष्टार्थत्वात् । पुंवचसां उक्तप्रयोगाविवक्षायाः प्रकृतेऽपि तुल्यत्वात् । तस्मात् श्राद्धं कर्तुं त्वामहं निमन्त्रय इति लङ्तन्त्येत्वामन्त्रय[4] इति वदन्ति तदयुक्तम् । निमन्त्रण आमन्त्रणयोर्भेदात् । विधिनिमन्त्रणाधीष्टेत्यादिसूत्रे यत्र प्रत्याख्याने प्रत्यवायस्तन्निमन्त्रणम् । यत्र कामचारस्तदा मन्त्रणमिति भेदस्य निरुक्तत्वात् । श्राद्धे च अनिन्द्येनामन्त्रितो नापक्रमेदिति कात्यायन[5]वचने प्रत्यवायश्रवणान्निमन्त्रणमेव । किं च उक्तप्रत्यवायस्य असमवेतार्थत्वे तावन्मात्रस्य हानिर्युक्ता न प्रकृतेरपि । अपि च मन्त्रादिवचनेषु बहुषु निमन्त्रणावगतेर्यदल्पीयसां मुनीनामामन्त्रणप्रयोगः स गौणः । यत्तु 'जन्म शारीरलक्षणगुणोपेतान् ब्राह्मणानुपामन्त्रये[6] तथा[7]ऽद्येति वा श्राद्धमाचरिष्येति[8] शङ्ख[9]वचनात् श्राद्धं युस्मास्वहमाचरिष्येति इति निमन्त्रणवाक्यं तदनुग्रहरूपम् । पूर्वदिने निमन्त्रणासंभवे निवेदनं कर्तव्यम् । तथा पूर्वदिनामन्त्रण तदहरामन्त्रणे वा श्राद्धदिने निमन्त्रणानन्तरमनुज्ञाग्रहणं कर्तव्यमित्याह आपस्तम्बः[10] (२.७.१७.११-१३) पूर्वेद्युर्निवेदनमपरेद्युर्द्वितीयं तृतीयमामन्त्रणम् ।

निवेदन—श्वो मया श्राद्धं कर्तव्यं तत्र भवन्तो निमन्त्रणीया इति[11]। ब्राह्मणबोधन इति लक्षणम् । द्वितीयमामन्त्रणं मत्स्यपुराणोक्तं[12] तृतीयं शंखलिखितोक्तमनुज्ञाग्रहणलक्षणं द्वित्व त्रित्व बोधनापेक्षया ।

अत एव ब्रह्मपुराणम्[13]—

---

1. This line from the *मत्स्यपुराण* is quoted in *पराशरमाधव,* Vol. I., p. 698.
2. The expression वर्तमानक्तस्य वृद्धयर्थादि is hopelessly corrupt.
3. The expression फडादिव is hopelessly corrupt.
4. The expression लङ्तन्त्येत्वामन्त्रय is corrupt and defies all attempts at purification.
5. *स्मृतिमुक्ताफलम्,* p. 779 quotes the text of *कात्यायन* as अनिन्धेनामंत्रितो नापक्रमेच्छक्तेन न प्रत्याख्यातं कर्तव्यम् ।
6. *कृत्यकल्पतरु-श्राद्धकाण्ड,* p. 103 reads आमन्त्रयेत् for उपामन्त्रये.
7. *Ibid.,* p. 103 reads श्वः०० for तथा००.
8. The word इति appears to be redundant.
9. *कृत्यकल्पतरु-श्राद्धकाण्ड,* p. 103 ascribes this text to शंखलिखित.
10. This is *आपस्तम्ब धर्मसूत्र,* p. 79.
11. This passage is also quoted in *कृत्यकल्पतरु-श्राद्धकाण्ड,* p. 105 and our ms. drops सर्वेष्वेव विप्रेषु before श्वो मया.
12. *कृत्यकल्पतरु-श्राद्धकाण्ड,* p. 105 quotes *मत्स्यपुराण* which is quoted in *हेमाद्रि श्राद्धकाण्ड,* p. 1258.
13. *पृथ्वीचंद्र-श्राद्धप्रकाश,* VII.102, p. 147 quotes *ब्रह्मपुराण.*

उपविश्य जपेत् धीमान् गायत्रीं तदनुज्ञया ॥११॥

अनुज्ञासामर्थ्यात्तद्ग्रहणलक्षणं प्रश्नवाक्यमप्याक्षिप्तम् ।

तथा मत्स्यपुराणम् (१६.२९ब-३०अ)

आसनेषूपक्लृप्तेषु दर्भवत् सुविधानतः[1]।
उपस्पृष्टोदकान् विप्रानुपविश्या[2]नुमन्त्रयेत् ॥१२॥

निमन्त्रणाच्च दैवादिक्रमेण कर्तव्यम् ।

तथा मनुः (३.२०४-२०५)

तेषामारक्षभूतेन्तु[3] पूर्वदैवं[4] नियोजयेत् ।
रक्षांसि हि विलुम्पन्ति[4] श्राद्धमारक्षवर्जितम् ॥१३॥
दैवाद्यन्तं तदीहेत पित्राद्यन्तं न तद्भवेत् ।
पित्राद्यन्तं त्वीहमानः क्षिप्रं नश्यति सान्वयः ॥१४॥

देवलः[6] —

यत्र यत्[7] क्रियते कर्म पैतृके ब्राह्मणान् प्रति ।
तत्सर्वं तत्र कर्तव्यं वैश्वदैवत्यपूर्वकम् ॥१५॥

शातातपः[8] —

सदैव भोजयेत् श्राद्धं तत्पूर्वं च प्रवर्तयेत् ।
अन्यथा त्ववलुम्पन्ति सदैवासुरराक्षसाः ॥१६॥

विष्णुधर्मोत्तरे प्रथमकाण्डे (१.१४०.१५-१६अ)

वैश्वदेवोपविष्टानां[9] चरमं हस्तधावनम् ।
विसर्जनं च निर्दिष्टं तेषु रक्षा यतःस्थितिः ॥१७॥
सर्वमन्यत् प्रकर्तव्यमा[10]दौ तेषां नराधिप ।१८।

---

1. *मत्स्यपुराण,* p. 28 reads दर्भवत्सु विधानवत् for दर्भवत् सुविधानतः. .
2. *Ibid.,* p. 28 reads ०उपवेश्य० for ०उपविश्य०.
3. *मनुस्मृति,* Vol. II, p. 209 reads ००भूतं तु for ००भूतेन्तु.
4. *Ibid.,* p. 209 reads पूर्वं दैवं for पूर्वदैवम्.
5. *Ibid.,* p. 209 reads विप्रलुम्पन्ति for हि विलुम्पन्ति.
6. The text of *देवल* is quoted in *कृत्यकल्पतरु-श्राद्धकाण्ड,* p. 142, but untraced in the *स्मृतिसंदर्भ,* Vol. III.
7. *कृत्यकल्पतरु-श्राद्धकाण्ड,* p. 142 reads तु for यत्.
8. This stanza cannot be traced in the extant *शातातपस्मृति.*
9. *विष्णुधर्मोत्तरपुराण,* reads ०निविष्टानां for ०उपविष्टानाम्.
10. *Ibid.,* reads प्रदातव्यं० for प्रकर्तव्यं०.

हस्तधावनमाचमनम् । एतेन आचमन विसर्जने पितृपूर्वे दर्शिते ।

अत्र पाञ्च

आपादसेचनात्पूर्वं कुर्याद्दैव द्विजन्मम् ।१९।

इति विष्णुपुराणवचनादापादसेचनादिति विशेषस्वरसात् । पादप्रक्षालनादावेव दैवादित्वमिच्छन्ति । न निमन्त्रणादौ तथा पूर्वलिखितानेकवचनस्वरसाद्दक्षिणाया अपि दैवादित्वमिति । तदसङ्गतम् । पूर्वलिखितानेकवचनस्वरसान्निमन्त्रणादौ दैवाददित्व प्रणीतेः । आपादसेचनादित्यस्य स्वायोगव्यवच्छेदार्थत्वात् । अन्ययोगव्यवच्छेदस्वरसानुरोधेन नानावचनार्थबाधास्तैरयोगात् । दक्षिणा च पितृपूर्वमेव दैवाद्यन्तमिति मनुवचने (३.२०५)ऽन्तत्वेन दक्षिणायाः परिग्रहणात् । न च विसर्जनमेवान्तः दक्षिणाया एव सर्वसाधारणान्तत्वात् । अन्यथा प्रदक्षिणीकरण पिण्डप्रतिपत्त्यादीनामेवान्ततो न विसर्जनस्य ।

अत एव छन्दोगपरिशिष्टम्[1]—

ब्राह्मणे दक्षिणा देया यत्र परिकीर्तिता ।
कर्मान्तेऽनुच्यमानायां पूर्णपात्रादिका भवेत् ॥२०॥
निमन्त्रणाञ्च कुशमय ब्राह्मणपक्षे निवर्तते ।२१।

अनुमति प्रकाशकलक्षणावश्यबाधितत्वात् वीहिमन्त्र इव यवे । एवं नियमश्रवणमपि अनुज्ञाग्रहणलक्षणां च कर्तव्यमेव । ब्राह्मणान्तरादपि तत् सम्भवात् । ननु कुशमयब्राह्मणपक्षो न युक्तः । प्रमाणाभावात् । अंगभूतब्राह्मणस्याभावे श्राद्धस्य लोप एव प्राप्नोति । तन्न । ब्राह्मणाभावेऽपि श्राद्धस्य दर्शनात् ।

यथा वशिष्ठः (११.३०-३१)

यद्येकं भोजयेत् श्राद्धे दैवं तत्र कथं भवेत् ।
अन्नं पात्रे समुद्धृत्य सर्वस्य प्राकृतस्य[2] तु ॥२२॥
देवतायतने कृत्वा ततः श्राद्धं[3] प्रवर्तयेत् ।
तदन्नं प्रक्षिपेदग्नौ[4] दद्याद्वा ब्रह्मचारिणे ॥२३॥

देवतायतने वैश्वदेवस्थाने ।

यथा शङ्खः[5] (४.१०)

भोजयेदथवाप्येकं ब्राह्मणं पङ्क्तिपावनम् ।
दैवे कृत्वा तु नैवेद्यं पश्चात्तस्य विनिर्वपेत्[6] ॥२४॥

एतयोश्च ब्राह्मणप्रतिनिध्यधिकरणे दर्शितत्वात् । छन्दोगपरिशिष्टकृतादर्शितत्त्वाच्च ।

---

1. The source of the text of छन्दोगपरिशिष्ट cannot be traced.
2. *वशिष्ठ धर्मसूत्र,* p. 30 and *पराशरमाधव,* Vol. I, p. 700 read प्रकृतस्य for प्राकृतस्य.
3. *पराशरमाधव,* Vol. I, p. 700 reads यथाविधि for ततः श्राद्धम्.
4. *Ibid.*, p. 700 and *अपरार्क,* p. 464 read प्रास्येदन्नं तदन्नं तु for प्रक्षिपेदग्नौ. *वसिष्ठ धर्मसूत्र,* p. 31 reads प्रास्येदग्नौ तदन्नं वा for प्रक्षिपेदग्नौ.
5. The text of शंख is found in *स्मृतिसंदर्भ,* Vol. III , p. 1439.
6. *Ibid.*, p. 1439 reads पश्चात् वह्नौ तु तत् क्षिपेत् for पश्चात्तस्य विनिर्वपेत् । *अपरार्क,* p. 464 and *A.B.O.R.I.*, Vol. VIII, p. 95 read पश्चात् तस्य तु निर्वपेत्.

यथोक्त वस्त्वसम्पत्तौ ग्राह्यं तदनुकारि यत् ।
यवानामिव गोधूमा व्रीहिणामिव शालयः ॥२५॥

ब्राह्मणप्रतिनिधिश्च दर्भबटुर्दृष्टौ ।

यथा गोभिलः —

यदि उभयं चिकीर्षेत् धौत्रं ब्रह्मत्वं च तेनैवकल्पेन छत्रमुत्तरासङ्गं कमण्डलुं वासन्ते दर्भबटुं वा निधायेति ।

तथा कुशमयीं प्रतिकृतिमाह पैठीनसिः —

कुशमयीं प्रतिकृतिं तीर्थवारि निमज्जयेत् ।
मज्जयेत्तु यमुद्दिश्य अष्टभागं लभेत सः ॥२६॥

तथोपकर्मणि छन्दोगपरिशिष्टम् —

'कौषान् षीन्[1] स्थूलस्थानगन्धमाल्यधूपैः सत्कृत्य' इति । अतोऽत्राप्याकाङ्क्षया ब्राह्मणप्रतिकृतिदर्भ-पुत्रकसिद्धिः । अत एव श्राद्धे सत्यव्रतः —

निधायाथ दर्भचयमासनेषु समाहितः ।
पैषानुपैषसंयुक्तं विधानं प्रतिपादयेत् ॥२७॥

न चास्यानाकरत्वाशङ्का । वशिष्ठशंखाभ्यामेव तदर्थस्य स्वहस्तिततत्त्वात् । पैषानुपैषसंयुक्तमिति विशेषणादर्भ ब्राह्मणपक्षे निमन्त्रणादेः पैषानुपैषसंयोगाभावन्निवृत्तिः । अत एव होमे दर्शमयब्रह्मपक्षे दृष्टद्वाराभावाद्धरणनिवृत्तिः । नन्वेवं ब्राह्मणनत्यनुत्वाद्दक्षिणायाः कुशमयब्राह्मणपक्षे । तदभावाद्बाधः स्यात् । अत एव सत्रे ये यजमानास्त एव ऋत्विज इति ऋत्विक् कार्ये यजमानविधौ आनति लक्षणस्य दृष्टस्याभावाद्दक्षिणाया बाध उक्तः । तन्न । अदृष्टाया अपि दक्षिणायाः सत्त्वात् ।

यथा बृहस्पतिः[2]—

तस्मात् पणं काकिनीं[3] वा फलं पुष्पमथापि वा ।
प्रदद्यात् दक्षिणामन्ते[4] तया स सफलो[5] भवेत् ॥२८॥

पुष्पादीनामानर्थत्वाभावात् । अत एव स्वयं कर्तृपक्षे अदृष्टार्थत्वाद्दक्षिणामाह छन्दोगपरिशिष्टम् ।

विदध्याद्धौत्रमन्यश्चेद्दक्षिणार्द्धहरो भवेत् ।
स्वयंश्चेदुभयं कुर्यादन्यस्मै प्रतिपादयेत् ॥२९॥

सत्रेऽप्यतिदेशागत दृष्टार्थ दक्षिणाया बाधो नादृष्टार्थदक्षिणायाः ।

1. This word appears to be corrupt.
2. *कृत्यकल्पतरु-श्राद्धकाण्ड*, p. 246 quotes this text.
3. *Ibid.*, p. 246 reads काकिणी for काकिनीम्.
4. *Ibid.*, p. 246 reads ०यज्ञे for ०अन्ते.
5. *Ibid.*, p. 246 reads समफलो for सफलो.

११

अथ ब्राह्मणसंख्या

याज्ञवल्क्य: (१.२२७-२२८)

दैवे युग्मान्[1] यथाशक्ति:[2] पित्रे युग्मांस्तथैव[3] च ।
परिस्तृते शुचौ देशे दक्षिणाप्रवणे तथा ।।१।।
द्वौ दैवे[4] पित्र्ये[5] उदगेकैकमेव वा ।
मातामहानामप्येवन्त[6] वैश्वदेविकम् ।।२।।

परिस्तृते सर्वत आवृते । प्राक् प्राङ्मुखौ । उदक् उदङ्मुखा: । एकैकमेव वा इति एकं दैवे पित्रादि त्रिके चैकम् । तन्त्रं वेति वा शब्दो विकल्पार्थो नावधारणार्थ: ।

मातामहानामप्येवं दैवपूर्वं श्राद्धं कुर्यादिति गोभिलवचनात् । वचनान्न्यायसिद्धयोरपि तन्त्रतयावृत्तिर्विकल्पेन । आवृत्तिपक्षे च फलभूमाकल्पनीय: ।

गौतम: (१५.७-८)

'नवावरान् भोजयेदनुयुजो[7] वा यथोत्साहम्[8]।' नव अवरे निवृष्ट[9] कृष्टा येषां तान् पित्रादीनां त्रयाणामेकैकं प्रति त्रींस्त्रीनित्यर्थ: ।

अत एव आश्वलायन: (४.७.२)

त्रीन् त्रीन्[10] वेति । रक्षति अयुजो वा सप्त पञ्च त्रीन् वा न तु नवाधिकार: । तेषामवरग्रहणेनैव ग्रहणात् ।

---

1. *याज्ञवल्क्यस्मृति,* p. 77 reads युग्मान् दैवे for दैवे युग्मान्.
2. *Ibid.*, p. 77 reads यथाशक्ति for यथाशक्ति: .
3. *Ibid.*, p. 77 reads ०अयुग्मान्०० for ०युग्मान्००.
4. *Ibid.*, p. 78 reads प्राक् त्रय: after दैवे.
5. *Ibid.*, p. 78 reads पित्र्ये for पित्रे.
6. *Ibid.*, p. 78 reads ००एवं तन्त्रं वा for ००एवन्त and our ms. omits तन्त्रं वा.
7. *गौतमधर्मसूत्र,* p. 250 reads ०अयुजो for ०अनुयुजो.
8. *Ibid.*, p. 250 reads वा after यथोत्साहम्.
9. The word निवृष्ट appears to be corrupt.
10. *आश्वलायन गृह्यसूत्र,* p. 123 reads स्त्रीन् for त्रीन्.

आश्वलायनगृह्यम् (४.७.२-४)

एकैकमेकैकस्य द्वौ द्वौ त्रींस्त्रीन् वा वृद्धौ फलभूयस्त्वं न त्वेकैकं सर्वेषाम् । पिण्डे[1] व्याख्यातं काममनास्ते[2]।

एकैकस्य पित्रादेरेकैकं द्वौ द्वौ दैवे वीप्सा तन्त्रता । भावपक्षे एकैकस्य पित्रादे स्त्रीन् त्रीन् वा पक्षः । अस्मिन् पक्षे फलविशेषः । कल्पतरौ[3] तु द्वौ द्वावित्यभ्युदयश्राद्धे[4] विषयं व्याख्यातम् । अथातः पार्वणश्राद्धे काम्ये आभ्युदयिक[5] इत्यनेनाभ्युदयिकस्याप्युपक्रान्तत्वात् । न त्वेवैकं सर्वेषां त्रयाणां पित्रादीनां पिण्डैर्व्याख्यातमिति[6]। यथा त्रयाणामेको पिण्डो न भवति तथा ब्राह्मणोऽपि कामं यथेष्टं एकमपि वा सर्वेषां कुर्यात् । अनाद्ये सपिण्डीकरणव्यतिरिक्ते आदिः सपिण्डीकरणमित्याश्वलायनेन तस्यादित्वाभिधानात्। अदनीयाभावो वा अन्नाद्यशब्दार्थः । तदापि सकलगुणोपेतो निर्दोष एकः कर्तव्य इत्याह वशिष्ठः (११.२९-३१)

अपि वा भोजयेदेकं ब्राह्मणं वेदपारगम् ।
श्रुतशीलोपसंपन्नं सर्वालक्षणवर्जितम् ॥३॥
यद्येकं भोजयेत् श्राद्धे दैवं तत्र कथं भवेत् ।
अन्नं पात्रे समुद्धृत्य सर्वस्य प्रकृतस्य तु ॥४॥
देवतायतने कृत्वा ततः श्राद्धं प्रकल्पयेत्[1]।
प्रास्येदग्नौ तदन्नं तु दद्याद्वा ब्रह्मचारिणे ॥५॥

कृत्वा निवेदनमिति शेषः ।

तथा शङ्खः (४.१०)

भोजयेदथवाप्येकं ब्राह्मणं पंक्तिपावनम् ।
दैवे[8] कृत्वा तु नैवेद्यं पश्चात्तस्य तु निर्वपेत् ॥६॥

बृहस्पतिः[9] (८६.८८)

यद्येकं भोजयेत् श्राद्धे स्वल्पत्वात् प्रकृतस्य तु ।
स्तोकं स्तोकं समुद्धृत्य तेभ्योऽन्नं विनिवेदयेत्[10] ॥७॥

---

1. *आश्वलायन गृह्यसूत्र*, p. 125 reads पिण्डैः for पिण्डे and treats this as IV.7.4.
2. *Ibid.*, p. 125 reads काममनाद्ये for काममनास्ते.
3. The view of कल्पतरु is found in the *कृत्यकल्पतरु-श्राद्धकाण्ड*, p. 122.
4. *Ibid.*, p. 122 reads ००आभ्युदयिक श्राद्ध० for ००अभ्युदयश्राद्धे०.
5. अथातः up to आभ्युदयिक appears to be a citation from *आश्वलायनगृह्यसूत्र*, IV.7.1, p.123.
6. This appears to be a portion from the *आश्वलायनगृह्यसूत्र*, IV.7.2. and 4 and the expression काममनाद्ये is omitted here.
7. *वसिष्ठ-धर्मसूत्र*, p. 31 and *कृत्यकल्पतरु-श्राद्धकाण्ड*, p. 125 read प्रवर्तयेत् for प्रकल्पयेत्. विश्वरूप on *याज्ञवल्क्यस्मृति*, I.225 supports the reading प्रकल्पयेत् of our manuscript.
8. *कृत्यकल्पतरु-श्राद्धकाण्ड*, p. 125, *श्राद्धचंद्रिका*, p. 32 and *अपरार्क*, p. 464 read दिव्ये for दैवे.
9. The text of *बृहस्पति*, is quoted by *अपरार्क*, p. 464, and *कृत्यकल्पतरु-श्राद्धकाण्ड*, p. 125.
10. *अपरार्क*, p. 464 reads अन्नं च निवेदयेत् for अन्नं विनिवेदयेत्.

प्रकृतस्य श्राद्धोचितद्रव्यस्य स्तोकं स्तोकं समुद्धृत्य एकस्मिन्नेव पात्रे पित्रादिभ्यो दद्यात् । अन्नं विभज्य संकल्पयेदित्यर्थः ।

मनुः (३.१२५)

द्वौ दैवे पितृकृत्ये त्रीनेकैकमुभयत्र वा ।
भोजयेत् सुसमृद्धेऽपि न प्रसज्येत[1] विस्तरे ॥८॥

एकैकमिति देवपित्रादि त्रिकापेक्षया उभयत्र दैवे पित्रे च न मातामहापेक्षयोभयत्वम् । तेषामप्रकृतत्वात्। अत एवैकैकमिति पितृपितामहप्रपितामहापेक्षया ज्ञेयम् । पित्रादीनां सन्निधानात् न त्वेकमिति । पित्रादि त्रिकापेक्षया न त्वेवैकं सर्वेषामित्याश्वलायनगृह्यविरोधादिति मेधातिथिव्याख्यानम्[2] पास्तम् । उभयशब्दात् पूर्वोक्त दैवपितृकृत्यप्रतीतेः । गृह्य एव काममनाद्य इत्यनेनैक ब्राह्मणोपवेशनपक्षाभिधानात् । अपि च शंख-वशिष्ठ-बृहस्पतिभिरत्यन्ताशक्तौ पितृपितामहप्रपितामहापेक्षयैवैक ब्राह्मणोपवेशनपक्षाभिधानात् । अपि च द्वौ द्वौ पितृकृत्ये त्रीनेकैकमुभय एवेत्यभिधाय —

'उपस्थाः[3] पितरस्तस्य वामपार्श्वे पितामहाः ।
प्रपितामहा दक्षिणतः पार्श्वनः[4] पिण्डभक्षकाः[5] ॥९॥

इति बौधायने[6]नैक ब्राहाण एव पित्रादि त्रिकाधिष्ठानस्योक्तत्वात् । पिण्डभक्षकाः पिण्डलेपभागिनः ।

तथा ब्रह्मपुराणे[7]

देशकालधनाभावादेकैकमुभयत्र वा ।
शिष्यान्[8] वित्तानुसारेण भोजयेदन्यवेश्मनि ॥१०॥
यथा[9] ब्राह्मणबाहुल्याद्दोषो बहुतरो भवेत् ।
श्रद्धानाशो[10] मौननाशः श्राद्धतन्त्रस्य विस्मृतिः ॥११॥
उच्छिष्टोच्छिष्टसम्प[11] निन्दादात्रनु[12]भोक्तृषु ।
वितण्डया परिवादो[13] जलस्पास्ते ते पृथक् पृथक्[14] ॥१२॥

1. *मनुस्मृति,* Vol. II, p. 136 reads प्रवर्तेत for प्रसज्येत.
2. कुल्लूक's criticism of मेधातिथि's view is also found in *मन्वर्थमुक्तावली,* Vol. II., pp. 136-37. This also proves that the author of *मन्वर्थमुक्तावली* and *श्राद्धसागर* is identical.
3. *कृत्यकल्पतरु-श्राद्धकाण्ड,* p. 121 reads उरस्थाः for उपस्थाः.
4. *Ibid.*, p. 121 reads पृष्ठतः for पार्श्वनः which is corrupt.
5. *Ibid.*, p. 121 reads ०तर्ककाः for ०भक्षकाः.
6. *बौधायन* is quoted in *Ibid.*, p. 121.
7. The text of *ब्रह्मपुराण* is quoted in *Ibid.*, p. 121.
8. *Ibid.*, p. 121 reads शेषान् for शिष्यान्.
9. *Ibid.*, p. 121 reads यस्मात् for यथा.
10. *Ibid.*, p. 121 reads श्राद्ध० for श्रद्धा०.
11. This ००सम्प is corrupt and some letters are missing. *कृत्यकल्पतरु-श्राद्धकाण्ड,* p. 121 reads ००संस्पर्शो for ००सम्प.
12. *Ibid.*, p. 121 reads ०दात्रन्न० for दात्रनु०.
13. *Ibid.*, p. 121 reads परीवादो for परिवादो.
14. *Ibid.*, p. 121 reads विषाः for पृथक्.

अत्र संक्षेपार्थः । युग्मान् यथाशक्तीत्यनेन चतुः षडित्यादयः पक्षाः सूचिताः । अयुग्मान् यथाशक्तीत्यनेन पञ्चसप्तनवेत्यादयः ।

अत एव पैठीनसिः[1]—

श्वः श्राद्धं[2] संकल्प्य ब्राह्मणान् सप्त पञ्च नव[3] वा श्रोत्रियान्निमन्त्रये[4]दित्यादि पञ्चोपवेशनपक्षे पितरि ब्राह्मणाः पितामहप्रपितामहयोरेकैकः । सप्तपक्षे पितृत्रयो पितामहयोस्त्रयस्त्रयः । प्रपितामहस्यैकः । नवपक्षे एकैकस्मिंस्त्रयस्त्रयः । एतच्च शक्तेन फलभूमार्थिना कर्तव्यम् ।

अत एव वृद्धौ फलभूयस्त्वमित्युक्तम् । द्वौ दैवे त्रयः पित्र इति शक्तमात्रविषयम् ।

अत एव

'देशकालधनाभावादेकैकमुभयत्र वा ।'१३। इति ब्रह्मपुराण[5]वचनम् । एकब्राह्मणपक्षस्त्वहयन्ताशक्त-विषयः ।

ननु

'भोजयेत् सुसमृद्धोऽपि न प्रसज्येत विस्तरे ।'१४।

इति मनु (३.१२५) वचनम् ।

'यस्मात् ब्राह्मणबाहुल्यादोषो बहुतरो भवेत् ।'१५।

इति ब्रह्मपुराण[6]वचनाभ्यामत्यन्तशक्तपक्षेऽपि बहुतर ब्राह्मणोपवेशन पक्षस्य निषिद्धत्वात् । कथं पञ्चसप्तनवाद्युपवेशनपक्षः?

उच्यते ।

सत्क्रियां देशकालौ च शौचं ब्राह्मणसम्पदः ।
पञ्चैतान् विस्तरो हन्ति तस्मान्नेहेत विस्तरम् ।।१६।।

इति मनुवचने (३.१२६) । 'यस्मात् ब्राह्मणबाहुल्यादि'त्यादि ब्रह्मपुराणवचने च सत्काराद्यसम्भवस्य हेतुत्वेनाभिधानात् । बहुतरसत्कारादि शक्तविषयं गौतमवचन[7]मिति न किंचिदनुपपन्नम् । अथ मातामहपक्षे निर्देशदर्शनमाह जिकनानां[8] मतम् ।

दौहित्रो द्विविधः । पुत्रिकासुतोऽपुत्रिकासुतश्च। पुत्रिकापुत्रोऽपि द्विविधः । मातामहपक्षमात्र स्वधाकरः ।

---

1. The text of पैठीनसि is quoted in *कृत्यकल्पतरु-श्राद्धकाण्ड*, p. 123.
2. *Ibid*., p. 123 reads करिष्यामीति after श्राद्धं and before संकल्प्य.
3. *Ibid*., p. 123 omits नव.
4. *Ibid*., p. 123 reads निमन्त्र्य for निमन्त्रयेत्.
5. The line from *ब्रह्मपुराण* is quoted in *कृत्यकल्पतरु-श्राद्धकाण्ड*, p. 121.
6. The text of *ब्रह्मपुराण* is quoted in *कृत्यकल्पतरु-श्राद्धकाण्ड*, p. 121.
7. This has possibly a reference to the *G.D.S.* 15.7.8 already quoted at the beginning of this chapter, p. 169.
8. This view of जिकन cannot be traced.

पक्षद्वयस्वधाकरश्च यथा यमं च कुर्यात् । मातामहश्राद्धं नियमात् पुत्रिकासुतः । उभयोरथ सम्बन्धः कुर्यात्तदुभयोरपि । अपुत्रिकापुत्रोऽपि द्विविधः । रिक्थहरोऽरिक्थहरश्च । एवं च द्वारो[1] दौहित्रो भवन्ति । तत्रोभयोः पुत्रिकापुत्रयोः रिक्थहरस्य च । पुत्रिकापुत्रस्य नियतः पिण्डदानाधिकारः । रिक्थाग्राहिणः पुत्रिकापुत्रव्यतिरिक्तस्य त्वनियतः ।

यथा मनुः (९.१३६)

> अकृता वा कृतावापि यं विन्देत् सदृशात् सुतम् ।
> पौत्री मातामहास्तेन[2] दद्यात् पिण्डं हरेद्धनम् ॥१७॥

अकृतेत्यपुत्रिकाकृता पुत्रिका ।

> 'दौहित्रो[3] ह्यनिखिलं[4] रिक्थं अपुत्रस्य पितुर्हरेत् ।
> स एव दद्यात् द्वौ पिण्डौ पित्रे मातामहाय च ॥१८॥

अत्र धनग्रहणपिण्डदानयोः समानाधिकरण्यमवगम्यते । अत्र मध्यपठितस्यैवकारस्योभयत्र सम्ब[5]न्धात् । स एव दद्यादेवेत्यन्वयः । अतो धनहार्यवश्यं दद्यादिति वचनान्तरस्यानियमः । किं च सर्वेषां नियताधिकारे पुत्रिकाकरणमनर्थकं स्यात् । तदसङ्गतम्। अकृते[6]त्यस्यापुत्रिकापरत्वे पौत्रीमातामह इत्यनन्वयापत्तेः । पुत्रत्वे हि पुत्रिकायास्तयास्तत्[7] पुत्रेण मातामहः पौत्री भवति । अतोऽवाक् कृताभिः सन्धिकृतेति । यावत् अत एव गौतमः (२८.१९) 'आभिसन्धिमात्रात् पुत्रिकेत्यकेषाम्' । अतो मनुवचनद्वयं प्रकरणात् पुत्रिकापुत्रविषयम् । तदधिकारज्ञापकम् । अन्यदेवापुत्रिका पुत्रधिकारज्ञापकमनुस्मरणीयम् । तत्तु मातामहादीनां चैवं दैवपूर्वं श्राद्धं कुर्वीतेति गोभिलसूत्रम् ।

तथा

> पितृमातामहानां[8] च भोजयेच्चाप्युदन्मुखान् ॥१९॥

इति विष्णुपुराणम् (३.१५.१६ब) ।

मातामहानां न प्येव[9]मिति याज्ञवल्क्यवचनम् (१.२४३अ) ।

पितॄन्मातामहांश्चैव श्राद्धे यत्नेन भोजयेत्[10]। श्राद्धहीनो पशुतामाप्नोति मनुरब्रवीत् ।

---

1. The word द्वारो appears to be corrupt.
2. *मनुस्मृति,* IX.136 reads मातामहस्तेन for मातामहास्तेन.
3. This stanza No. 18 has a reference to the *मनुस्मृति,* IX.132.
4. *मनुस्मृति,* IX.132 reads ह्यखिलं for ह्यनिखिलं which is corrupt.
5. It may be noted here that this point ofintroduced by कुल्लूक on *मनु,* IX.132, Vol. II, p. 388.
6. This refers to *मनुस्मृति,* IX.136.
7. The portion 'पुत्रिकायास्तयास्तत्' appears to be corrupt.
8. *विष्णुपुराण,* reads ०पैतामहानां for ०मातामहानाम्.
9. *याज्ञवल्क्यस्मृति,* p. 83 reads मातामहानामप्येवं for मातामहानां नप्येवम्.
10. This line has possibly a reference to the *मनुस्मृति,* III.148.

पितरो यत्र पूज्यन्ते तत्र मातामहा ध्रुवम् ।
अविशेषेण कर्तव्यं विशेषान्नरकं व्रजेत् ॥२०॥

इति वृद्ध[1]याज्ञवल्क्यनाम्ना वचनं पठितम् ।

पितृभ्यः स्वधोच्यतां पितामहेभ्यः स्वधोच्यतां प्रपितामहेभ्यः स्वधोच्यतां मातामहेभ्यः स्वधोच्यतामित्यादि कात्यायन[2]वचनं च । अत्र हि सर्वत्र पित्रादि मातामहादि वर्गद्वय श्राद्धमवगम्यते । न च मातामहादिवर्गस्य श्राद्धे पुत्रिकापुत्रस्याधिकारः सम्भवति ।

मातुः प्रथमतः पिण्डं निर्वपेत् पुत्रिकासुतः ।
द्वितीयं तु पितुस्तस्यां[3] तृतीयं तु[4] पितुः पितुः ॥२१॥

इति मनुवचन (९.१४०) विरोधात् । तस्मादेतानि वचनान्यपुत्रिकापुत्राधिकारः प्रतिपादकानि ।

न चैतेषु धनहारित्वेन विशेषः श्रूयते । अत्र एव द्वयोरपुत्रिकापुत्रयोर्दौहित्रयोर्नियतोऽधिकारः । मनुवचनद्वयं तु पुत्रिकापुत्र मात्राधिकारे प्रमाणं प्रकरणात् । किं च दौहित्रो धनं हरेत् पिण्डं दद्यादित्यवगम्यते । न तु यो धनहारी स एव पिण्डं दद्यात् । न वा धनग्रहणस्य पिण्डदानहेतुत्वमवगम्यते । अन्यथा धनग्राहिणः पुत्रस्य पिण्डदातृत्वं न स्यात् । स एव इत्येवकार पुत्रिकापुत्रस्य परिपाटी विशेषविशिष्ट पिण्डदानाधिकारः नियमार्थः ।

अतः 'मातुः प्रथमतः पिण्डमि'ति मनुनोक्तं[5] एवकारस्य च तत्परसम्बन्धे प्रमाणं नास्ति । पूर्वेणैव सम्बन्धदर्शनात् । किं च चतुर्थस्य दौहित्रस्य पिण्डत्रयदातृत्वे षट्संख्यानियमस्मृतिविरोधः ।

तथा छन्दोगपरिशिष्टम्[6]—

कर्षु समन्वितं[7] मुक्त्वा तथाद्य[8] श्राद्धषोडशम् ।
प्रत्याब्दिकं च शेषेषु पिण्डाः स्युः षडितिस्थितिः ॥१२॥

तथा वृद्धिश्राद्धे षड्भ्यः पितृभ्यस्तदनु श्राद्धदानमुपक्रमेत् । अत्र षट्संख्यान्यूनाधिक व्यवच्छेदिकाङ्गमवगम्यते —

तथा शातातपः[9]

मातृणामग्रतः कुर्यात्[10] पितृणां तदनन्तरम् ।
ततो मातामहानां च वृद्धौ श्राद्धत्रयं भवेत्[11]॥२३॥

---

1. The text of *वृद्धयाज्ञवल्क्य* is not found quoted in any श्राद्ध work.
2. The text of *कात्यायन* is quoted in *कृत्यकल्पतरु-श्राद्धकाण्ड*, p. 11.
3. *मनुस्मृति*, IX.140 reads ०तस्याः for ०तस्याम्.
4. *Ibid*., IX.140 reads तत् for तु.
5. This refers to *मनुस्मृति*, IX.1110.
6. This stanza is quoted in *श्राद्धमयूख*, p. 13.
7. *Ibid*., p. 13 reads कर्षूसमन्वितं. for कर्षु समन्वितम्.
8. *Ibid*., p. 13 reads ०आद्यं for ०आद्य.
9. The text of *शातातप* is quoted by *मिताक्षरा* on *याज्ञवल्क्यस्मृति*, I.250.
10. *Ibid*., I. 250 reads मातुः श्राद्धं तु पूर्वं स्यात् for मातृणामग्रतः कुर्यात्.
11. *Ibid*., I.250 reads स्मृतं for भवेत्.

अत्र मातामहान्तर्भावात् त्रित्वमवगम्यते । न च धनहारित्वेन विशेषः श्रूयते । पुत्रिकाकरणं च मृते मातामहे जीवत्यपि पितरि पार्वणाधिकारार्थमिति न कंचिदनुपपन्नम् । अतश्चतुर्णामिव दौहित्राणां नियतोऽधिकारो । नियतत्वं मातामह ब्राह्मणोपवेशनमिति तस्यापुत्रस्य दत्तकसत्वे तेषां भवति न वेति संदेहो विशेषादग्रे विवरणीयम् । अत्र ब्राह्मणोपवेशन विशेषेणोक्तम् ।

२०

अथ दर्भः

तत्र हारीतः —

श्वो भूते श्राद्धकर्मणि दक्षिणां दिशं गत्वा दक्षिणादिक् प्रणतान् समूलान् कुशान् हरेत् ।

ब्रह्मपुराणे[1]—

हरिताः सपिञ्जलाः[2] स्निग्धाः पुष्टाः समाहिताः ।
गोकर्णमात्रां तु[3] कुशाः सकृच्छिन्नाः समूलकाः ।।१।।
पितृतीर्थेन देयाः स्युर्देवो श्यामाक एव वा[4]।
काशा कुशाः बल्बजोश्च[5] तथान्ये तीक्ष्णरोमशाः ।।२।।
मौञ्जश्च[6] शाद्वलश्चैव[7] षड्दर्भाः परिकीर्तिताः ।
श्राद्धवर्ज्याः[8] प्रयत्नेन ह्युसपाः सगवेधुकाः[9]।।३।।

सपिञ्जलाः शाग्राः[10] स्युः स्निग्धाः अकर्कशाः पुष्टाः । न सूक्ष्माः समाहिता निर्दोषाः[11]। नामिकाः परिमाणः । तीक्ष्णरोमशा इति बल्बजानी[12] विशेषणम् ।

गोभिलेन तु तदितरबल्बजनिषेधः । मुञ्जः शरस्तद्भवं मौञ्जम् । शाद्वलमिति पूर्वादीनां सर्वेषां

---

1. The *ब्रह्मपुराण* is quoted in the *श्राद्धतत्त्व*, p. 201 and *कृत्यकल्पतरु-श्राद्धकाण्ड*, p. 114.
2. *Ibid.*, p. 201 reads सपिञ्जलाश्च हरिताः for हरिताः सपिञ्जलाः of our ms. which drops च.
3. *Ibid.*, p. 201 reads गोकर्णमात्राश्च for गोकर्णमात्रां तु.
4. *Ibid.*, p. 201 reads ०च for ०वा.
5. *Ibid.*, p. 201 reads बल्बजाश्च for बल्बजोश्च.
6. *Ibid.*, p. 201 reads मौञ्जाश्च for मोञ्जश्च. पृथ्वीचंद्र-*श्राद्धप्रकाश,* V.143, p. 110 reads मौजं for मौञ्जश्च.
7. *Ibid.*, p. 201 reads शाद्वलाः०० for शाद्वलः०० पृथ्वीचंद्र-*श्राद्धप्रकाश,* V.143, p. 110 reads शाङ्वलम्००.
8. *कृत्यकल्पतरु-श्राद्धकाण्ड,* p. 114 reads श्राद्धे वर्ज्याः for श्राद्धवर्ज्याः .
9. *Ibid.*, p. 114 reads ह्युलपक्षुपबल्बजाः for ह्युसपाः सगवेधुकाः .
10. *श्राद्धतत्त्व,* p. 201 reads साग्राः for शाग्राः which is corrupt.
11. *Ibid.*, p. 201 treats this as the view of गोभिल.
12. Grammatically it may be emended as बल्बजानां for बल्बजानी.

विशेषणम् । दुर्वादिषु दर्भशब्दो गौणस्तत्कार्यकरत्वज्ञापनार्थः । कुशकार्यकरत्वादेव हरितत्वादि तद्धर्मप्राप्तौ यत् शाद्वलग्रहणं तत्सूल[1]त्वादिधर्मनियमार्थम् । उसपस्तृणभेदः । गवेधूका गण्डू यस्य प्रसिद्धिः ।

छन्दोगपरिशिष्टम् —

हरिता यज्ञिया दर्भाः पीतकाः पाकयज्ञियाः[2]।
समूलाः पितृदैवत्याः कल्मषा वैश्वदेविकाः ॥४॥

कल्मषाः कृष्णपाण्डवः । पितृदैवत्ये मूलनियमादन्यत्रानियमः ।

मूले विशेषमाह गोभिलः[3]

बर्हिरूप मूललूनाः[4] पितृभ्यः । तेषामलाभे शूकदृशा[5] शरशीर्य बल्वजः । उत[6] वनलशुश्च[7] सतृणानि[8] । मूलसमीपे लूनाः कुशाः बर्हिसंज्ञाः । तदपि मूलस्य नोर्ध्वदेशे । किन्तु अधोदेशे ।

समूलस्तु भवेद्दर्भः पितॄणां श्राद्धकर्मणि ।
मूलेन लोकाञ्जनयति[9] शक्रस्य च[10] महात्मनः ॥५॥

इति वचनात्[11] समूलत्वप्रतीतेः । शूलतृणं शूकमुक्ततृणं[12] धान्यादिशरशीर्यबल्वज उत वनलशुश्चास्तृणजातिभेदास्तत्र देशप्रसिद्धाः[13]।

वायुपुराणे (७५.३८ब-३९अ)

अरत्निप्रमाणाः[14] शस्तावै पितृतीर्थेन संस्कृताः ।
उपमूले[15] तथा लूनाः[16] प्रस्तरार्थे कुशोत्तराः[17]॥६॥

1. It may be emended as सूक्ष्म for सूल.
2. पृथ्वीचन्द्र-*श्राद्धप्रकाश*, V.139, p. 109 reads ०यज्ञिकाः for ०यज्ञियाः
3. *कृत्यकल्पतरु-श्राद्धकाण्ड*, p. 113 quotes गोभिल, I.5.17-19.
4. *Ibid*., p. 113 reads बर्हिः उपमूललूनाः for बर्हिरूप मूललूनाः .
5. *Ibid*., p. 113 reads तृण for दृशा.
6. *Ibid*., p. 113 connects उत with बल्बज and reads बल्बजमुत.
7. *Ibid*., p. 113 reads वनलशुष्ठवर्जं for वनलशुश्च which is corrupt.
8. *Ibid*., p. 113 reads सर्वतृणानि for सतृणानि.
9. *Ibid*., p. 113 reads जयति for जनयति.
10. *Ibid*., p. 113 reads तु for च.
11. *Ibid*., p. 113 ascribes this stanza to *यम*. Also *हेमाद्रि-श्राद्धकाण्ड*, p. 1171.
12. *Ibid*., p. 114 reads शूकवत्तृणं for शूकमुक्ततृणम्.
13. This explanation comes very close to the explanation of *कृत्यकल्पतरु-श्राद्धकाण्ड*, p. 114.
14. *वायुपुराण, कृत्यकल्पतरु-श्राद्धकाण्ड*, p. 114 and *श्राद्धतत्त्व*, p. 201 read रत्निप्रमाणाः for अरत्निप्रमाणाः
15. *वायुपुराण*, reads उपम्मूले for उपमूले.
16. *कृत्यकल्पतरु-श्राद्धकाण्ड*, p. 114 reads लूनाः for लूना
17. *Ibid*., p. 114 reads कुशोत्तमाः for कुशोत्तराः

तथाप्यन्त्रा[1] श्राद्धे क्षीरकुशा बल्वजा गन्धकी तथा ।
वीरणाद्योणपाश्चैव नववह्याश्च यत्नत:[2]।।७।।

संस्कृताः सक्रदंष्टाः[3]? प्रस्तरोऽत्र पिण्डप्रस्तरः । प्यन्त्रा स्वस्तकः[4]। क्षीरकुशाः प्रत्यगजाताः[5]। गन्धकी गन्धतृण[6] (तृण) । निलम्बाः[7] उक्तप्रमाणाधिकाः कुशा एव दीर्घाः[8]।

गृह्यपरिशिष्टम्[9]—

दर्भाः कृष्णाजिनं मन्त्रा ब्राह्मणा हविरग्नयः ।
अयातयामान्येतानि नियोज्यानि पुनः पुनः ।।८।।

अयातयामानि[10] अजीर्णानि ।

छन्दोगपरिशिष्टम्[11] —

पिण्डार्थं ये स्तृता दर्भास्तर्पणार्थं तथैव च[12]।
घृतैः कृते च विन्मूत्रे[13] त्यागस्तेषां विधीयते ।।९।।

घृतैरिति उपलक्षणे तृतीया ।

हारीतः—

चितौ दर्भाः[14] पथि दर्भाः ये दर्भाः यज्ञभूमिषु ।
स्तरणासनपिण्डेषु षट्कुशान्[15] परिवर्जयेत् ।।१०।।
पिण्डार्थं ये स्तृता दर्भाः यैः कृतं पितृतर्पणम् ।
मूत्रच्छिष्ट[16]प्रलोपेषु तेषां त्यागो विधीयते ।।११।।

---

1. *कृत्यकल्पतरु-श्राद्धकाण्ड,* p. 114 reads गुन्द्रा for तथाप्यन्त्रा.
2. *Ibid.,* p. 114 reads वीरणाश्चोलपश्चैव लम्बा वर्ज्याश्च नित्यशः as the second line for 7b.
3. Is it likely to be emended as संसृष्टाः on the strength of *कृत्यकल्पतरु-श्राद्धकाण्ड,* p. 114 ?
4. This is corrupt.
5. This may be emended as प्रत्यग्रजाताः on the strength of *कृत्यकल्पतरु-श्राद्धकाण्ड,* p. 114.
6. *कृत्यकल्पतरु-श्राद्धकाण्ड,* p. 114 explains it as गन्धतृणानि.
7. *Ibid.,* p. 114 reads लम्बाः for निलम्बाः .
8. *Ibid.,* p. 114 gives the same explanation of this entire passage. *कुल्लूक* has borrowed.
9. *गृह्यपरिशिष्ट* is quoted in *श्राद्धमयूख,* p. 35.
10. *नीलकंठ-श्राद्धमयूख,* p. 35 explains this differently.
11. *H.D.,* Vol. IV, p. 418 quotes this stanza from *गोभिलस्मृति,* I.22 and is quoted by *अपरार्क,* p. 458, *हेमाद्रि,* p. 640. *श्राद्धक्रियाकौमुदि,* p. 49.
12. *श्राद्धतत्त्व,* p. 201 reads यैः कृतं पितृतर्पणं for तर्पणार्थं तथैव च and ascribes to *हारीत.*
13. *Ibid.,* p. 201 reads विण्मूत्रे for विन्मूत्रे.
14. चितौ दर्भाः etc. is ascribed to संग्रह in *श्राद्धकल्पलता,* p. 65.
15. *श्राद्धतत्त्व,* p. 201 reads षट्दर्भान् for षट् कुशान्.
16. *Ibid.,* p. 201 reads ०उच्छिष्ट० for ०च्छिष्ट० which is corrupt.

नीवीमध्ये च ये दर्भा ब्रह्मसत्रे[1] च कृता:[2]।
पवित्रान् तान् विजानीयात् यथो[3] कायस्तथा कुशाः ।।१२।।

पितृतर्पणमिति विशेषणाद्देवाद्यर्थ कृततर्पणेन पितृतर्पणं कर्तव्यम् । मूत्रच्छिष्टप्रलोपे सतीत्यर्थः । घृतै कृते चेत्यस्यापवादः । 'नीवीमध्ये तु ये दर्भाः' इति ।

विष्णुः (७९.२)

कुशाभावे कुशस्थाने काशं[4] दूर्वां च[5] दद्यात् ।१३।

वायुपुराणे (७५.५९ब-६०अ)

अञ्जनाभ्यञ्जनं गन्धः मूल[6]प्रणयनन्तथा ।
काशैः पुनर्भवैः कार्यमश्वमेधफलं लभेत[7]।।१४।।[8]

विष्णुधर्मोत्तरे (१.१४१.९ब-१०अ)

पिण्डनिर्वपणं कार्यं कुशाभावे[9] विचक्षणैः ।
काशेषु राजन्[10] दूर्वासु[11] पवित्रे परमे मते[12]।।१५।।

काशदूर्वयोः प्रतिनिधित्वेन प्राप्तो यो नियमविधिरयं यदि सोमं न विद्यते । पूतिकामभिषुश्वयादितिवत् । ननु नात्र प्रतिनिधिकरणन्यायेन[13] प्राप्तिरस्ति । यत्र हि विहितव्यक्तीनामवघातादिना विनाशेऽवयवपर्यंतः शास्त्रार्थस्तत्रावयवानां प्रतिनिधीभूतव्यक्त्यन्तरे प्रत्याभिज्ञानमस्तीति प्रतिनिधी-अधिकरणसिद्धान्ते युक्तिः । नात्र व्यक्तेर्विनाशः । नापि यथोक्तवस्तु सम्पत्तौ ग्राह्यं तदनुकारि यत् । यवानामिव गोधूमा व्रीहिनामिव शालयः इति छन्दोगपरिशिष्टवचनात् प्राप्तिः । तस्यापि कल्पनालाघवेन प्रतिनिध्यनुकरणन्यायमूलत्वात् उच्यते । काण्डमूलपर्णपुष्पफलप्ररोह रसगन्धादिना

1. *श्राद्धतत्व,* p. 202 reads ब्रह्मसूत्रे for ब्रह्मसत्रे.
2. *Ibid.*, p. 202 reads ये धृताः for कृताः .
3. *Ibid.*, p. 202 reads यथा for यथो.
4. *विष्णुस्मृति,* p. 789 reads काशान् for काशम्.
5. *Ibid.*, p. 789 reads वा for च.
6. पृथ्वीचंद्र-*श्राद्धप्रकाश,* V.144, p. 111 reads सूत्र for मूल.
7. *Ibid.*, p. 111 reads तथा for लभेत.
8. *वायुपुराण,* reads अञ्जनाभ्यञ्जने चैव पिण्डसंवपनं तथा ।
अश्वमेधफलेनैव तत्स्मृतं मन्त्रपूर्वकम् ।। for St. 14.
9. *विष्णुधर्मोत्तरपुराण,* reads कुशालाभे for कुशाभावे.
10. पृथ्वीचंद्र-*श्राद्धप्रकाश,* V.145, p. 111 reads राज for राजन्.
11. *विष्णुधर्मोत्तरपुराण,* reads सर्वासु for दुर्वासु.
12. *Ibid.*, reads पवित्रे ते परे मते for पवित्रे परमे मते.
13. This refers to *जैमिनि कृत पूर्वमीमांसा,* III.6.14.37.

सादृश्येन प्रतिनिधिं कुर्यात इति पैठीनसिवचनात् प्राप्तिः । न चास्य न्यायमूलता । रसगन्धादिना सादृश्येन प्रतिनिधिविधानात् । अतोऽनेन वचनेन अवयवपर्यन्ताभावेऽपि यथा कथंचित् सादृश्येन प्रतिनिधिरुक्तः ।

अत एव मैत्रायणीय परिशिष्टम् —

दक्षिणाभावेन मूलानां भक्षणान् दक्षिणान् ददातीति प्रतिनिधिनियमः । ननु कथमत्र निर्णयः सर्वतृणानीति गोभिलविरोधात् । न एतयो विशेषोपादानात् प्रतिनिधौ मुख्य कल्पार्थोऽयं नियमः । प्रतिनिधिष्वपि मुख्यानुकल्पयोर्दृष्टत्वात् । यथा मैत्रायणीय परिशिष्टम् । दर्भास्तरणार्थे काशः प्रतिनिधिः । तदभावे पर्ववतीभिः काण्डवतीभिः ओषधीभिः स्तरणार्थान् कुर्वन्ति । एतच्च प्रतिनिधिकाशादीनामुपादानं न काम्यविषयम् । प्रतिनिधौ किञ्चिदङ्गविकलमनुष्ठानम् । तच्च काम्ये सर्वशक्ताधिकरणे[1] निरस्तम् ।

---

1. P.V. Kane. *H.D.*, Vol. V, Part II, p. 1350 points out that this is the same as यथाशक्तिन्याय which has a reference to *जैमिनि कृत पूर्वमीमांसा*, VI.3.1-7. Also see *धर्मद्वैतनिर्णय*, p. 105 and *एकादशी तत्त्व*, pp. 18, 26.

२१

अथ श्राद्धदेवता:

बृहस्पति:[1] (श्राद्धकाण्ड ९१-९४)

क्रतुदक्षो[2] वसु: सत्य: कालकामस्तथैव च ।
धृतिश्च लोचनश्चैव तथा चैव पुरोरवा:[3]॥१॥
माद्रवाश्च[4] दशैवैते[5] विश्वेदेवा: प्रकीर्तिता: ।
इष्टिश्राद्धे क्रतुर्दक्ष: सत्यो नान्दीमुखे वसु: ॥२॥
नैमित्तिके कालकामो काम्ये च धूरिलोचनौ[6]।
पुरोरवामाद्रवाश्च[7] पार्वणे समुदाहृतौ ॥३॥
उत्पत्तिं नाम चैतेषां न विदुर्ये द्विजातय: ।
अयमुच्चारणीया[8]स्तै: श्लोक: श्रद्धासमन्वितै: ॥४॥
आगच्छन्तु महाभागा विश्वेदेवा वरप्रदा:[9]।
ये यत्र[10] विहिता:[11] श्राद्धे सावधाना भवन्तु ते ॥५॥

इष्टिश्राद्धं इच्छाश्राद्धम् । रुचिश्राद्धमित्यर्थ: । नैमित्तिकमेकोद्दिष्टम् । ननु मात्र विश्वेदेवा इति देवतानिषेधात् कथं कालकामयोर्देवतात्वम् । अत्र कल्पतरू[12]प्रभाकर-कमलाकरभट्टा[13] साम्वत्सरिकं यदा साग्निना पार्वणविधिना क्रियते तदा विश्वेषां देवानां संभव इति । तदसङ्गतम् । त्रैपुरूषिकत्वेन

---

1. *बृहस्पति,* is quoted in *कृत्यकल्पतरु-श्राद्धकाण्ड*, p. 142.
2. *Ibid*., p. 142 reads क्रतुर्दक्षो for क्रतुदक्षो.
3. *Ibid*., p. 142 reads पुरुरवा: for पुरोरवा:
4. *Ibid*., p. 142 reads मार्द्रवश्च for माद्रवश्च.
5. *Ibid*., p. 142 reads दशैते तु for दशैवैते.
6. *Ibid*., p. 142 reads धुरि० for धूरि०.
7. *Ibid*., p. 142 reads पुरुरवा मार्द्रवश्च for पुरुरवा माद्रवाश्च.
8. This is emended as उच्चारणीय:० for उच्चारणीया:०.
9. *स्मृतिचंद्रिका-श्राद्धकाण्ड,* p. 288 quotes शंख and reads महाबला: for वरप्रदा:
10. *Ibid*., p. 288 reads ह्यत्र for यत्र.
11. *Ibid*., p. 288 reads विहिता: *कृत्यकल्पतरु-श्राद्धकाण्ड*, p. 142 reads योजिता: for विहिता: .
12. This view is found in *कृत्यकल्पतरु-श्राद्धकाण्ड*, p. 143 with a slightly different wording.
13. For this view of कमलाकरभट्ट, see *निर्णयसिन्धु,* pp. 395-96.

तस्यैकोद्दिष्टत्वाभावात् । उच्यते ।

नवश्राद्धं दशाहानि नवमिश्रन्तु षड् ।
अतः परं पुराणं वै त्रैविधं श्राद्धमिष्यते ॥६॥
यस्मिन्नवे पुराणे वा विश्वेदेवा न लेभिरे ।
आसुरं तद्भवैः[1] श्राद्धं वृषलं मन्त्रवर्जितम्[2] ॥७॥

इत्याश्वालायनगृह्यपरिशिष्टवचनात् । दशाहमध्ये क्रियमाणे नववश्राद्धसंज्ञके द्वादशमासिकश्राद्धे च नवमिश्रसंज्ञके एकोद्दिष्टे विश्वेषां देवानां संभवात् । न चास्य त्रैपुरुषिकत्वं संभवति । प्रेतश्राद्धत्वात् ।

असपिण्डीकृतं प्रेतं एकोद्दिष्टे न[3] तर्पयेत् ।८।

इति जाबाल[4]वचनात् । एतच्च बह्वृचानामेव बह्वृचपरिशिष्टकारेणोक्तत्वात् । कात्यायनादिभिरेकोदिष्टे नात्र विश्वेदेवा इति देवतानिषेधाच्च एकादशाह श्राद्धस्यापि नवश्राद्धसंज्ञामाह यमः ।

चतुर्थे पञ्चमे चैव नवमैकादशे तथा ।
यदत्र दीयते जन्तोस्तन्नवश्राद्धमिष्यते ॥९॥

वृषलं वृषस्य धर्मस्यालमसाधकमित्यर्थः ।

यत्तु ब्रह्मपुराणीय[5]मिति — कृत्वा पठन्ति —

विश्वेदेवौ क्रतुदक्षौ[6] सर्वस्विष्टिषु विश्रुतौ[7]।
नित्यं नान्दीमुखे श्राद्धे वसुरुत्यौ[8] च पैतृके ॥१०॥
नवान्नलाभने[9] देवौ कालकामौ सदैव हि ।
अपि कन्यागते सूर्ये काम्ये च धूरिलोचनौ[10]॥११॥

गौडमैथिलमयूख[11]भट्टाः संदिग्धमूलम् । वयं च ब्रूमः । अथर्वणघण्टाशाखिनां कर्मणीति । ननु पुरोरवादीनामन्तर्गणा द्वादशयुग्मं तु द्वयोरेव श्रुत्यादीनामेकवचननिर्दिष्टत्वात् एक एव उच्यते । वसुमत्यौ विश्वदेवौ न नान्दीमुखमुदाहृतौ इति वृद्धमनुवचनात् ।

---

1. *श्राद्धतत्त्व,* p. 200 reads ०भवेत् for ०भवैः .
2. This complete stanza No. 7 is quoted in *श्राद्धतत्त्व* for *गृह्यपरिशिष्ट.*
3. पृथ्वीचंद्र-*श्राद्धप्रकाश,* XVIII.17, p. 432 reads एकोद्दिष्टेन for एकोद्दिष्टे न.
4. *Ibid.,* p. 432 quotes the text of *जाबाल.*
5. *श्राद्धचंद्रिका,* p. 28 quotes this stanza from *हेमाद्रि* who ascribes this stanza to *आदित्यपुराण.*
6. *श्राद्धचंद्रिका,* p. 28 reads क्रतुर्दक्षः for क्रतुदक्षौ.
7. *Ibid.,* p. 28 reads कीर्त्तितौ for विश्रुतौ.
8. *Ibid.,* p. 28 reads वसुमत्यौ for वसुरुत्यौ.
9. *Ibid.,* p. 28 reads ००लम्भने for ००लाभने.
10. *कृत्यकल्पतरु-श्राद्धकाण्ड,* p. 142 reads धुरि० for धूरि०.
11. This has possibly a reference to *नीलकण्ठ कृत श्राद्धमयूख,* p. 11 which attributes this stanza to *आदित्यपुराण.*

अत एव वाक्ये वसुसत्यौ[1] विश्वेदैवो इमावर्घ्यौ नम: । सामगेतरास्तु एतावधोवां[2] नम: । तन्न । लिङ्गसंख्याकालश्चातन्त्राणि भवतीति न्यायात् इति शाब्दिका: । अप्रधानं शाब्दबोधे एकवचननिर्दिष्टे दित्वबहुत्वावगते: । अत एव प्राचामाराचो[3] दुराचारो निष्प्रमाणक एव ।

1. This may be emended as वसुमत्यौ.
2. This expression appears to be corrupt.
3. This can be emended as ०आचारो.

२२

अथ उपवीतः

प्राचीनावीतिना[1] सम्यगपसव्यमतन्त्रिणा[2]।
पित्र मा निधनात्[3] कार्यं विधिवद्दर्भपाणिना ॥१॥

इति मनुना (३.१८९) श्राद्धे प्राचीनावीतित्वमुक्तम् । तत्रोपवीतित्व प्राचीनावीतित्वे गोभिलेनोक्ते[4]। यथा गोभिलः

दक्षिणं बाहुमुद्धृत्य शिरोवधाय सव्यंशे प्रतिष्ठापयति । दक्षिणं कक्षमनुवलमुम्भवति । एवं यज्ञोपवीती भवति । सव्यं बाहुमुद्धृत्य शिरोवधाय दक्षिणेंशे प्रतिष्ठा भवति । तदर्थमुपवीतं निरूप्यते। उपवीतमाह गोभिलः ।

यज्ञोपवीतं कुरुते सूत्रं वस्त्रं वा अपि कुशरज्जुमेव । यज्ञोपवीतं विशिष्टविन्यास धारणकर्मतया कुरुते ' किन्तत्र[5] सूत्रं विशेषयति ।

छन्दोगपरिशिष्टे[6]—

ऊर्ध्वन्तु त्रिवृतं कार्यं तन्तुत्रयमधोवृतम् ।
चोपवीतं[7] स्यात्तस्यैको ग्रन्थिरिष्यते ॥२॥

वामावर्तवलितः । तन्तुत्रयं त्रिगुणं कृत्वा दक्षिणावर्तवलितं कार्यम् । तदेव त्रिसवमुपवीतं स्यात् । एको ग्रन्थिरिति नानात्वनिषेधार्थः ।

तथा बौधायनः (१.५.८.५)

कौष सौत्रितं[8] त्रिवृतं यज्ञोपवीतमलाभे[9]।

---

1. This is *मनुस्मृति,* III. 189.
2. *Ibid.,* reads ००अतन्द्रिणा for ००अतन्त्रिणा.
3. *Ibid.,* reads पित्र्यमानिधनात् for पित्र मा निधनात्.
4. This may be emended as गोभिलेनोक्ते: .
5. This may be emended as किन्त्वत्र.
6. कुल्लूक on *मनु.,* II.244 quotes *छन्दोगपरिशिष्ट.*
7. *Ibid.,* reads त्रिवृतं before चोपवीतम्, which is omitted in our manuscript.
8. *बौधयन धर्मसूत्र,* p. 46 reads सूत्रं for सौत्रितम्.
9. *Ibid.,* p. 46 reads अनाभे: for अलाभे.

कौषं कृमिकोषोद्भवं पट्टं सूत्रमयमित्यर्थः । सूत्रं कार्पायसोद्भवम् । तथा मनुः (२.४४)

> कार्पायसमुपवीतं स्याद्विप्रस्योद्धर्व[1]वृतं त्रिवृत् ।
> शणसूत्रमयं राज्ञो वैश्यस्याविक सौत्रिकम् ॥३॥

त्रिस्त्रिवृतमित्युक्तत्वन्मनुवचनेऽपि त्रिसत्वेन विशेष्यम् ।

यत्तु पैठीनसिवचन —

कार्पायसमुपवीतं षट्तन्तु त्रिवृतं ब्राह्मणस्य क्षौमेयं राजन्यस्याविकं वैश्यस्य तन्नवतन्त्वसम्भवे षट्तन्तु विधायकम् ।

नवतन्तुत्वं व्यक्तमाह देवलः[2]।

> यज्ञोपवीतं कुर्वीत सूत्राणि नवतन्तवः ।
> एकेन ग्रन्थिना तन्तु द्विगुणा त्रिगुणेऽथवा ॥४॥

एकेन ग्रन्थिना युक्त इति शेषः । द्विगुणस्त्रिगुणोऽथवेति । तन्तुर्वलने द्विसव-त्रिसवोऽवाथकर्तव्यः । द्विसवत्वं त्रिसवत्वासम्भवे । गोभिले वा शब्दः विकल्पार्थः । अपि शब्दो वस्तु कुशरज्वोः सूत्रानुकल्पत्वप्रदर्शनार्थः । द्वितीयो वा शब्दोऽनुक्तमुञ्जगोवालादि-समुच्चयार्थः[3]। एवकार त्रिसत्व व्यवच्छेदार्थः ।

तथा निगमपरिशिष्टम् —

वाससा यज्ञोपवीतं कुरुते । तदभावे त्रिवृतासूत्रेण कुशमुञ्जवाल प्रतिसवा रज्जुभिर्वा । वालोऽत्र गोवालः ।

यथा देवलः[4]—

> कार्पासक्षौमगोवाल वृणवल्कसवोद्भवम् ।
> यदा सम्भवतो धार्यमुपवीतं द्विजातिभिः ॥५॥

तदभाव इति करणाद्वस्त्राभावे कुशरज्जुरिति बौद्धव्यम् । नन्वेवं सूत्रमयमुपवीतं वस्त्राभावे स्यात् । न त्रिवृता सूत्रेति त्रिवृत् सूत्रस्य एकसवस्य वस्त्राभावे विधानार्थम् । त्रिवृत् सूत्रस्य तु त्रिसवस्य सर्वमुख्यस्यत्वमेव । छन्दोगपरिशिष्टकृता तत्रोपवीतस्य संकेतितत्वेन मुख्यत्वात् । वस्त्रादौ गौणत्वात् । एकस्य रूपस्याभावेऽनेकशक्तिकल्पना प्रसङ्गाच्च । न च मुख्यस्य गौणानुकल्पत्वं युक्तम् ।

ननु उपवीतस्थानाविहित कुशरज्वादीनामुपवीत धर्मास्त्रिसवत्वादयो भवेयुः । व्रीहिधर्माः प्रोक्षणादय इव यवे अत्र कल्पतरु[5]कामधेनुकृता-यज्ञोपवीतानीत्युत्तरीये गौणं तद्धर्मविन्यासविशेषमात्रप्राप्त्यर्थम् ।

---

1. *मनुस्मृति,* II.44 reads ००ऊर्ध्व ० for ००ऊद्धर्व०, which is corrupt.
2. कुल्लूक on *मनुस्मृति,* II.44 quotes only the first line of the text of *देवल,* i.e. 4a.
3. It may be noted here that कुल्लूक on *मनुस्मृति,* II.44 does not introduce the *Mīmāṁsā* points of विकल्प and समुच्चय.
4. The text of *देवल* cannot be traced in the *स्मृतिसंदर्भ,* Vol. III.
5. This view of कल्पतरु could not be traced.

तन्निर्मुक्तिकम् । त्रिसवत्वादेऽपि तद्धर्मत्वाविशेषात् । अन्ये तु त्रिसवत्वादि विशिष्टस्य उपवीतार्थत्वे तद्धर्मत्वाभावात् । न हि व्रीहिधर्मः प्रोक्षणादिवदत्र सम्बन्धः । न सूत्रं वस्त्रं वापि कुशरज्जुमेवेति सूत्रस्थाने वस्त्रादिविधिरूपवीतस्थाने । किं च वाससा यज्ञोपवीतानीति तृतीयया यज्ञोपवीतखङ्गत्वेन वासो विधीयते । न यज्ञोपवीत कार्याङ्गत्वेन लक्षणाप्रसङ्गात् । अतः सूत्र कार्यकारत्वात् कथं सूत्रधर्माः त्रिसत्वादयो भवेयुः । पवित्रानुष्ठाने कुशधर्मा इव कश्मादिषु द्विदलत्वादयः । खले वाली यूपो भवतीति यूपकार्ये खले वालीविधानादष्टा । त्रिकरणादीनां यूपपदार्थत्वान्मा भवतु । खले वाली सम्बन्धः । उच्यते । वाससो यज्ञोपवीत साधकत्वासम्भवात् तन्तुमये यज्ञोपवीतत्वशब्दस्य संकेतितत्वेन मुख्यत्वात् यज्ञोपवीतशब्दे तत्कार्यलक्षणा । अतो यज्ञोपवीतकार्यकरे वाससि त्रिसत्वादीनां यज्ञोपवीतधर्मत्वाभावान्न सम्बन्धः ।

२३

अथ अर्घ्यः

अत्र केचित्

विश्वान् देवान् यवैः पुष्पैरभ्यर्च्यासनपूर्वकम् ।
पूरयेत् पात्रयुगमं तु स्थाप्य दर्भपवित्रके ।।१।।

इति मत्स्यपुराण[1]वचनदर्शनात् अर्घ्यद्वयं देवे नित्यमिति वर्णयन्ति । तदसङ्गतम् ।

यवैरन्नवकीर्याथ भाजने सपवित्रके ।
इति[2] शन्नो देव्या पयः[3]क्षिप्ता यवोसीति यवांस्तथा ।।२।।

इति याज्ञवल्क्य (१.२३०) वचनादेकत्वावगतेः । विभक्ति संख्याया अप्यङ्गत्वस्य पश्वधिकरणे पशुना यजेतेत्यत्र दर्शितत्वात् । अर्घद्वयवचनं देवा श्राद्धस्य तन्त्रत्वाभावे वर्णनीयम् । यद्वा पुरोरवीमाद्रव सोरुभयत्वादर्घभयत्वं तत् प्रीत्यतिशयार्थम् ।

अत्र केचित् प्रथमे पात्रे संश्रवानसीय[4] पितृभ्यः स्थानमसीति न्युब्जं पात्रं करोतीति[5] कात्यायनादि-वचने पिधानश्रवणात् । पिधानरहितस्य एव न्युब्जीकरणमिति वदन्ति । तदसारम् ।

दश्वार्घ[6] संस्रवांस्तेषां पात्रे कृत्वा विधानतः ।
पितृभ्यः स्थानमसीति न्युब्जं पात्रं करोघ[7] ।।३।।

इति याज्ञवल्क्य (१.२३५) वचनादधः स्थितं पात्रं न्यूब्जं[8] करोतीत्यन्वयानुपपत्त्या पिधानपात्रापेक्षति।

---

1. This stanza from *मत्स्यपुराण* is quoted in *कृत्यकल्पतरु-श्राद्धकाण्ड*, p. 144.
2. *कृत्यकल्पतरु-श्राद्धकाण्ड,* p. 145 quotes *याज्ञवल्क्यस्मृति*, I.230 which drops इति before शन्नो.
3. *Ibid.*, p. 145 reads अपः for पयः which however, is preferred by विश्वरूप and विज्ञानेश्वर on *याज्ञवल्क्यस्मृति.*
4. *कृत्यकल्पतरु-श्राद्धकाण्ड,* p. 147 quotes कात्यायन and reads संस्रवान् समवनीय for संश्रवानसीय which is corrupt.
5. *Ibid.*, p. 147 reads निदधाति० for करोति०.
6. *Ibid.*, p. 145 reads ०अर्घ्यं for ०अर्घ which is corrupt.
7. *Ibid.*, p. 145 reads करोत्यधः for करोघ which is corrupt.
8. This may be emended as न्युब्जम्.

अत एवाधोभूमाविति कल्पतरु[1]व्याख्यानमयुक्तम् । एतेन निरस्ता हर्षणभट्टादयः । सांगप्रधानार्थतया वेदैः क्लृप्तत्वात् । तदा च पिधा[2]मित्याकांक्षायां प्रपितामहपात्रेण पिधाय प्रतिष्ठापयतीति शौनक[3]वचनमप्रतिष्ठितम् ।

नन्वेतस्य धर्मत्वात् छन्दोगयजुर्वेदिनः स्वगृह्ये नाभिधानात् । कथं ताभ्यामनुष्ठानम् ।

तथा च गृह्यपरिशिष्टम् —

बह्वल्पं वा स्वगृह्योक्तं यस्य कर्म प्रकीर्तितम् ।
तस्य तावति शास्त्रार्थे कृते सर्वः कृतो भवेत् ॥४॥

तथा छन्दोगपरिशिष्टम् —

स्वशाखाश्रयमुत्सृज्य इत्याभिधानात् स्वशाखोक्तकर्मपरित्यागेन पारशाखिककर्मानुष्ठानं न कारीत्यर्थः । यथा पिण्डे नमो वः पितर इत्यञ्जलिकरणं गोभिलेनोक्तं गोभिलीयानां अधिकं च परोक्तमविरोधि कर्तव्यमेव ।

यथा छन्दोगपरिशिष्टम् —

यन्नाम्नातं स्वशाखायां परोक्तमविरोधिता ।
विद्वद्भिस्तदनुष्ठेयमग्निहोत्रादि कर्मवत् ॥५॥

इति परोक्तविरोधिन कर्तव्यमेव । यथा श्राद्धे ब्राह्मणभोजनस्य गोभिलीयैः अग्निहोत्रादिकर्मवदिति ।

यथा छन्दोगादीनामनुक्तोऽपि यजुर्वेदविहितो अग्निहोत्रविधिः क्रियते ।

नन्वेवं बहूनां शाखान्तरोक्तानां मन्त्राणामनुष्ठानं स्यात् । यथा पिण्डे पिण्डवाहनादि गोभिलोक्तं यजुर्वेदिनां न विरोचेति । चकारादाकांक्षित एव परोक्तो गृह्यतः । यथा अग्निहोत्रं जुहोतीति वाक्येनाविशेषात् सर्वशाखिनामधिकार बोधिते विध्यपेक्षायां यजुर्वेदिकाग्निहोत्रविधेः सर्वशाखिसम्बन्धः । अत एव गोभिलेन-मनूक्त मनुष्य प्राशनकर्म गोभिलीयैः कर्तव्यमेव । गोतमा[4]दिभिर्गर्भाधानादि चत्वारिंशत् संस्कारेष्वनप्राशनस्य विशेषात् सर्वशाखिसम्बन्धप्रतिपादनात् । प्रकृते पिधानं केन क्रियतामित्यापेक्षया विद्यत एव । गृह्यपरिशिष्टवचनाकांक्षित धर्मत्यागपरम् । तथा यमवचनादपि प्रपितामहतोऽन्यत्र नोद्धरेन्न चालयेत् पात्रेण पिधानम् ।

यथा यमः[5] —

पैतृकं प्रथमं पात्रं तस्मिन् पैतामहं न्यसेत् ।
प्रपितामहं ततोऽन्यत्र[6] नोद्धरेन्न[7] चालयेत् ॥६॥

---

1. This view of कल्पतरु is traced in the *कृत्यकल्पतरु-श्राद्धकाण्ड*, p. 146.
2. Is it possible to take पिधानं०० for पिधां००?
3. This view of शौनक is also referred to in *श्राद्धतत्त्व*, p. 213.
4. This may be emended as गौतमादिभिः for गोतमादिभिः.
5. *स्मृतिचंद्रिका-श्राद्धकाण्ड*, p. 311 and *स्मृतिमुक्ताफलम्*, p. 799 ascribe this text of यम to कात्यायन.
6. *Ibid.*, p. 311 reads ०अन्यस्य for ०अन्यत्र.
7. *Ibid.*, p. 311 reads च before चालयेत् and after नोद्धरेन्न.

पात्रद्वयेन पिधानं विकल्पार्थम् । न च पैतामहमिति संस्रवपरं पैतृकं प्रथमपात्रमिति स्ववाक्योपात्तश्रवणात् ।

अत्र महार्णवोपाध्यायः —

पितृपात्रे मातामहादि संश्रवग्रहणे वचनाभावात् । मातामहपात्रे मातामहादिकसंभवं गृहीत्वा पृथक् मातामहपात्रस्य न्युब्जीकरणमाहुः तदसत् ।

आवृतास्तत्र तिष्ठन्ति पितरः शौनको[1]ऽब्रवीत् ।७।

इति अर्थवादस्वरसात् पितृभ्यः स्थानमसीति[2] मन्त्रलिङ्गाच्च पितृरक्षणमेव न्युब्जीकरणकार्यम् । तच्च सकृत् कृतेनैव न्युब्जीकरणेन मातामहादीनामपि कृतम् । अतः प्रयाजादितन्त्रता न्युब्जीकरणतन्त्रतापि शास्त्रार्थः । अत एवावाहनं तन्त्रेणैव क्रियते । मातामहादीनामपि पितृशब्दवाच्यत्वात् । न्युब्जीकरणमन्त्रस्यापि तन्त्रतैव । न्युब्जीकरणं च —

'पितृपात्रे[3] निधायाश्च[4] न्युब्जी[5]मुत्तरतो न्यसेत्' ।८।

इति मत्स्यपुराणवचनादुत्तरस्य कर्तव्यम् ।

अन्योपविष्टब्राह्मणस्योत्तरस्यां दिशि हेमकरभट्टकल्पतरु[6]कारौ ।

ब्राह्मणानां वामपार्श्व इति हलायुधः । आख्यानात् कर्तुः सन्निहितत्वास्यैव वामपार्श्व इति परमार्थः । तीर्थश्राद्धे चार्घ्यावाहने न कार्ये ।

यथा देवीपुराणे[7]—

श्राद्धं तत्र कर्तव्यमर्घ्यावाहन वर्जितम् ।
श्राद्धं तत्तीर्थकं प्रोक्तं पितॄणां तुष्टिकारकम् ।।९।।
अकालेऽप्यथवा काले तीर्थश्राद्धं तु सदा[8] नरैः ।
प्राप्तैरेव सदा कार्यं कर्तव्यं पितृतर्पणम् ।।१०।।
विलम्बो नैव कर्तव्यो न च विघ्नं समाचरेत् ।।११।।

तीर्थप्राप्तिनिमित्तार्थमिदं तीर्थकानि पदोपादानात् ।

---

1. This view of शौनक is quoted in *कृत्यकल्पतरु-श्राद्धकाण्ड*, p. 148 where the first line is read as 'नोद्धरेत् प्रथमं पात्रं पितृणामर्घ्यपातितम् ।'
2. 'पितृभ्यः स्थानमसि'। has a reference to the *याज्ञवल्क्यस्मृति*, I.235.
3. *कृत्यकल्पतरु-श्राद्धकाण्ड*, p. 146 quotes *मत्स्यपुराण* and reads ०पात्रं for ०पात्रे.
4. *Ibid.*, p. 146 reads निधायाथ for निधायाश्च.
5. *Ibid.*, p. 146 reads न्युब्जं० for न्युब्जीं०.
6. This view of कल्पतरु is found in *कृत्यकल्पतरु-श्राद्धकाण्ड*, p. 146 as 'उत्तरतः' 'उपविष्ट ब्राह्मणादुत्तरस्यां दिशि ।' with a change of ब्राह्मणात् for ब्राह्मणस्य.
7. The text of *देवीपुराण* is quoted by पृथ्वीचंद्र-*श्राद्धप्रकाश*, XII.8, p. 295.
8. पृथ्वीचंद्र-*श्राद्धप्रकाश*, XII.8, p. 295 reads तथा for तु सदा.

२४

अथ अग्नौकरणम्

किमेतद्दैवकृत्यं पितृकृत्यं वेतिसंशयः । दैवकृत्ये उपवीतित्वादयः । पितृकृत्ये प्राचीनावीतित्वादयः । ननु कथं संशयः। सोमादि पदानां देवता — वाचित्वेन पितृत्वाभावात् । न सोमादीनामपि पितृत्वश्रुतेः ।

यथा हारीतः[1]—

सोमो यमोऽङ्गिराश्चैव सोमपाः पितरस्तथा ।
बर्हिषदोऽग्निस्वाता[2]श्च[3] हुतादयः[4] षड्विधो गणः ।।१।।

अत्र छन्दोगपरिशिष्टम्[5]—

अग्नौकरणहोमश्च[6] कर्तव्यः[7] उपवीतिना ।
प्राङ्मुखे नैवादरेभ्यो[8] जुहोतीति श्रुतिः श्रुतेः[9] ।।२।।
अपसव्येन वा कार्यो[10] दक्षिणाभिमुखेन तु[11]।
निरूप्य हविरन्यस्य[12] अन्यस्मै न हि हूयते ।।३।।

दैवकृत्यत्वे हेतुमाह देवेभ्य इति ।

तथा माध्यन्दिनी श्रुतिः —

---

1. The text of *हारीत* is quoted in *कृत्यकल्पतरु-श्राद्धकाण्ड*, p. 111.
2. *Ibid.*, p. 111 reads अग्निष्वाता बार्हिषदो for बर्हिषदोऽग्निस्वाता.
3. *Ibid.*, p. 111 omits च.
4. *Ibid.*, p. 111 reads हुतादः for हुतादयः .
5. The text of *छन्दोगपरिशिष्ट* is quoted in *श्राद्धकल्पलता*, pp. 76-77, *स्मृतिचंद्रिका-श्राद्धकाण्ड*, p. 321 and *कृत्यकल्पतरु-श्राद्धकाण्ड*, p. 171.
6. *स्मृतिचंद्रिका-श्राद्धकाण्ड*, p. 321 reads तु for च.
7. *श्राद्धकल्पलता*, p. 75 reads कर्तव्यं for कर्तव्यः .
8. *Ibid.*, p. 75 reads प्राङ्मुखेनैव देवेभ्यो for प्राङ्मुखे नैवादरेभ्यो which is corrupt.
9. *कृत्यकल्पतरु-श्राद्धकाण्ड*, p. 171 reads श्रुतिश्रुतेः for श्रुतिः श्रुतेः .
10. *Ibid.*, p. 171 and *श्राद्धकल्पलता*, p. 76 read कार्यो for कार्यो.
11. *श्राद्धकल्पलता*, p. 76 reads वा for तु.
12. *कृत्यकल्पतरु-श्राद्धकाण्ड*, p. 171 reads ०अन्यस्मात् for ०अन्यस्मै.

स उद्वास्याग्नौ द्वे आहुयती[1] जुहोति देवेभ्य इत्यादि पितृकृत्यत्वे हेतुमाह । निरूप्येति अग्निमान्निर्वपेत् पित्र्यं चरूः वासमयस्य मुष्टिभिः ।

पितृभ्यो निर्वपामीति[2] सव्यं दक्षिणतो न्यसेत् ॥४॥

इति मत्स्यपुराण (पृ० २६) वचनात् पितृभ्यस्त्वामुष्टं निर्वपामीति वाक्येन चर्वन्नं पित्र्युद्देशेन व्रीहिमुष्टि निर्वपे कृते होमोऽपि पित्र्युद्देशेन कार्य इति निर्वपहोमयोः समानदेश्यकत्वात् । अन्यथा निर्वापस्य होमार्थत्वानुपपत्तेः ।

ननु तथापि तदवल्क[3] एव संशयः । द्वयोरेववचनार्थत्वात् । अत्र जिकनप्रभृतयः पूर्ववचनेन पूर्वपक्षमभिप्रायोत्तरवचने सिद्धान्तो दर्शित इत्याहुः । तदसङ्गतम् । पूर्ववचनवैयर्थ्यापत्तेः। पूर्वोक्तश्रुतिविरोधाच्च । किं च स्मृतिविरुद्धोऽयं पक्षः ।

यथा बैजवाप्यगृह्यम्[4]—

यज्ञोपवीताग्नौकरणं पिण्डपितृयज्ञवृता सर्वमनुक्रमेत्[5]।

मत्स्यपुराणे (१६.३४)

यज्ञोपवीत[6] निर्वर्त्य ततः पर्युक्षणादिकम् ।
प्राचीनावीतिना कार्यमतः सर्वं विजानता ॥५॥

पैठीनसिः[7]—

देवान् पितृंश्चावाहयिष्य इत्यनुज्ञाप्या[8]ग्नौ करिष्यामीत्यनुज्ञाप्य कुरुष्वेत्यादि अग्नौदेवतानामावाहनमग्नौकरणहोमार्थमवगम्यमानमदृष्टार्थं स्यात् ।

निरूप्य हविरन्यस्मा इति हेतुवन्निगदो । न मुख्यार्थः । किन्तु स्तुतिनिन्दापरमित्युक्तं हेतुवन्निगदाधिकरणे । मुख्यार्थत्वे देवश्राद्धत्रमपि पित्र्यर्थेन हविषा न स्यात् ।

गंगेश्वरमतानुयायिनो वदन्ति । अथोपवीतिसोमं पितृमन्तमग्निं कव्यवाहन याजेति लिखितसूत्रबलात् सोमसूत्रबलात् सोमपूर्वाहुतिद्वये उपवीतित्वं अग्निपूर्वाहुतित्रयपक्षे एव प्राचीनावीतित्वदर्शनात् ।

यथा शौनकः —

प्राचीनावीतिव्धमुपसमाधाय प्रेक्षणे ना वद यो न दानसम्पदा जुहुयात् । सोमाय पितृमते स्वधा नमः

---

1. This may be emended as आहुती for आहुयती.
2. *मत्स्यपुराण,* p. 28 reads यज्ञोपवीती निर्वर्त्य for पितृभ्यो निर्वपामीति.
3. This word appears to be corrupt.
4. This is quoted in *कृत्यकल्पतरु-श्राद्धकाण्ड,* p. 162.
5. *Ibid.,* p.162 quotes this line as यज्ञोपवीत्यग्नौ for करवाणीत्यामन्त्र्याग्नौकरणं पिण्डपितृयज्ञवत् । आवृतो वा सर्वमनुक्रमेत् ।
6. *मत्स्यपुराण,* reads यज्ञोपवीती for यज्ञोपवीत.
7. The text of *पैठीनसि* is quoted in *कृत्यकल्पतरु-श्राद्धकाण्ड,* p. 167.
8. *Ibid.,* p. 167 reads सौम्याः सन्त्वित्युक्त्वा after अनुज्ञाप्य and before अग्नौ. These words however, are omitted in our manuscript.

इति । किं साग्निपूर्वाहुतित्रयपक्ष एव उपवीतित्वं दृश्यते ।

यथा मत्स्यपुराणे (१६.३३)

अग्नेः सोमाय समाम्याञ्च कुर्यादाप्यायनं बुधः[1] ॥६॥

इति अभिप्रायः ।

'यज्ञोपवीति[2] निर्वर्त्य ततः पर्युक्षणांदिकम्[3]।
प्राचीनावीतिना कार्यमतः सर्वं विजानता' ॥७॥

विकल्पोऽयं शाखाभेदेन व्यवस्थित इति कल्पतरु[4]प्रभृतयः ।

वस्तुतस्तु पितृकृत्यत्वं दैवकृत्यत्वं च द्वयमपि वचनस्वरसादवगम्यते । अतः इच्छा विकल्पः ।

यथा श्रुतिः —

अग्नौकरणे प्राचीनावीति हूत्वेत्यादि ।

तथा मनुः — (३.२१४)

अपसव्यमग्नौ कृत्वा सर्वमादवृत्[5] परिक्रमम् ।
अपसव्येन हस्तेन निर्वपेदुदकं भुवि[6]॥८॥

यमः —

पितृना वाहयिष्यामि इत्युक्त्वा तु प्राञ्जलिः शुचिः ।
ये ममेका इति पुनः सम्यगावाहयेत् पितृन् ॥९॥

ततः संतीर्य दर्भाणां संस्तरं दक्षिणामुखम् ।

शंखलिखितौ[7]—

सघृतमन्नमनुज्ञाप्य[8] दर्भैर्दक्षिणाग्रै[9]रग्निं परिस्तीर्य जुहुयात् ।

---

1. *मत्स्यपुराण*, p. 28 reads this line as अग्नीषोमयमाभ्यां तु कुर्यादाप्यायनं बुधः ।
2. *Ibid.*, XVI.34 reads यज्ञोपवीती for यज्ञोपवीति.
3. *Ibid.*, XVI.34 reads पर्युक्षणादिकं for पयुक्षणां दिकम्.
4. The view of कल्पतरु is found in *कृत्यकल्पतरु-श्राद्धकाण्ड*, p. 171 as सव्यापसव्यविकल्प स्वगृह्यानुसारेण शाखाभेदव्यवस्थितो बोद्धव्यः ।
5. *मनुस्मृति*, III.214 reads ०आवृत् for ०आदवृत् which is corrupt.
6. *Ibid.*, reads शुचि for भुवि .
7. *शंखलिखित*, is quoted in *कृत्यकल्पतरु-श्राद्धकाण्ड*, p. 162.
8. *Ibid.*, p. 162 reads ००समनुज्ञाप्य for ००अनुज्ञाप्य.
9. *Ibid.*, p. 162 reads ०दक्षिणामुखैः for ०दक्षिणाग्रैः.

ब्रह्मपुराणे[1] —

> घृताक्त[2] समिधो हुत्वा दक्षिणाग्रा[3] समन्त्रकाः ।
> तथा पलाशः समिदर्थे तु नियोज्यः पितृकर्मणि ॥१०॥

इत्यादि शौनकः प्राचीनावीतीध्वमुपसमाधौ येत्यादि एतेषु वचनेषु प्राचीनावीतित्वेऽपि त्रि आवाहन दक्षिणामुखत्व दक्षिणाग्रदर्भास्तरण दक्षिणग्रशमिद्दाना पित्र्यकर्मशब्दनिर्देशाः पित्र्यचिह्नान्यवगम्यन्ते । पूर्वोक्त माध्यन्दिनश्रुति बैजवापगृह्य मत्स्यपुराणवचनस्वरसादक्षिणोपवीतित्वं गोभिलसरसाच्च ।

अथाग्नौकरणान्तरं गोभिलः —

अत उर्ध्वं प्राचीनावीतिनावश्येतेन कृत्यम् । अग्नौकरणादूर्ध्वं प्राचीनावीतित्वमभिदधत् पूर्वमुपवीतित्वं दर्शयति । अतः श्रुत्योर्विरोधे द्वयोरेव धर्मत्वादिच्छाविकल्पः ।

अत एव मनुः (२.१४)

> श्रुतिद्वैधं च[4] यत्र स्यात्तत्र धर्मावुभौ स्मृतौ ।
> उभावपि हितौ धर्मौ सम्यगुक्तौ मनीषिभिः ॥११॥

तथोक्त स्मृतीनामपि तुल्यबलविरोधाद्विकल्पः[5]।

तथा गौतमः (१.६)

तुल्यबलविरोधे विकल्पः ।

एकेनैव मुनिना छन्दोगपरिशिष्टकृता द्वयोरेव स्वहस्ति तत्त्वाच्च । ननु गोभिलसूत्रकृता उपवीतित्वमात्राभिधानापरिशिष्टस्वरसाद्विकल्पः ।

उच्यते — अत ऊर्ध्वं प्राचीनावीतिनेत्यभिधानादुपरिष्टादग्नौकरणेऽनियमोवगम्यते इति भट्टभाष्यव्याख्यानीदय[6] एवानियमः । सूत्रस्वरससिद्धोऽव्यक्तोव्यक्तीकृतः परिशिष्टकृतेति सर्वमनाकुलम् ।

---

1. The text of *ब्रह्मपुराण* is quoted in *कृत्यकल्पतरु-श्राद्धकाण्ड*, p. 168.
2. *Ibid.*, p. 168 reads घृताक्ताः for घृताक्त.
3. *Ibid.*, p. 162 reads दक्षिणाग्राः for दक्षिणाग्रा.
4. *मनुस्मृति,* II.14 reds तु for च.
5. कुल्लूक, in his *मन्वर्थमुक्तावली,* II.14 also introduces the same मीमांसा points and quotes the text of गौतम.
6. The expression ०व्याख्यानीदय seems to be corrupt.

२५

हुतशेषदानम्

दैवपात्रेऽपि हुतशेषं देयं प्रदद्यात्तु भाजनेषु समाहित:[1]। १।

इति । हुतशेषं दत्वा पात्रमालभ्य जपतीत्यादि याज्ञवल्क्या[2]दिभि: कात्यायनदिभि: सामान्येनाभिधानात् ।

न तु

> यत्र यत्[3] क्रियते कर्म पैतृके ब्राह्मणान् प्रति ।
> तत् सर्वं तत्र[4] कर्तव्यं वैश्वदैवत्यपूर्वकम् ॥२॥

इति देवलवचनाद्येव पात्रेऽपि तद्देयम् इति समाधानमुक्तमेतस्य प्राप्तयोग: क्रममात्रपरत्वात् ।

अन्यथा दैवे पिण्डप्राप्तिरपि स्यात् ।

अत्र लोल्लभट्टकमण्डनभट्टादय: —

> अग्नौकरण शेषं तु पित्रे तु[5] प्रतिपादयेत् ।
> प्रतिपाद्य पितॄणां तु न दद्याद्वैश्वदेविके ॥३॥

इति यमवचनाद्दैवे हुतशेषौ न देयमित्याहु: । तदसत् । क्रमविशेषनिषेधपरत्वात् । क्रमान्तरेण तु दानसिद्धमेव । अन्यथा प्रतिपाद्येति विशेषणवैयर्थ्यापत्ते: ।

किं च नायं हुतशेषनिषेधविधि: । शास्त्रत: प्राप्त्यप्राप्तिकल्पाभ्यां गतार्थत्वात् । वैश्वदेवेतरस्मिन् हुतशेषं देयमिति पर्युदास एवायमिति चेत् । न । सामान्यप्राप्तेऽपि पर्युदासविधि: ।

'यजतिषु ये यजामहं कुर्यान्नायाजेष्विति इह तु पित्र्योत्पत्तिविशेषण एव प्राप्तेरन्यथाऽनुवादापत्ते: । क्रमपर्युदासस्तु युक्त: । स्ववाक्येऽपि त्विति दैवपित्र्य हुतशेषदानयो: सामान्यप्राप्ते: । पित्र्येपीति पाठेऽपि

---

1. This line is quoted in *श्राद्धतत्त्व*, p. 220 as हुतशेषं प्रदद्यात्तु भाजनेषु समाहित: ।
2. This line is quoted from the *याज्ञवल्क्यस्मृति,* I.237.
3. *कृत्यकल्पतरु-श्राद्धकाण्ड,* p. 142 reads तु for यत्.
4. *Ibid.*, p. 142 reads तस्य for तत्र.
5. *Ibid.*, p. 172 reads तु and notes the reading *पित्र्येषु* in the foot-note. This is also quoted in *हेमाद्रिकृत श्राद्धकाण्ड,* p. 1362.

शब्दो दैवपरिग्रहणार्थो ज्ञेय: । पितृपदेनैव मातामहादीनां सद्रं[1] इति विप्रपाणानग्नौ करणपक्षे तत्पात्रे हुतशे षं न देयम् ।

यथाछन्दोगपरिशिष्टम्[2]—

पित्र्ये य: पंक्तिमूर्द्धरायस्तस्य पाणावनग्निमान् हुत्वा मन्त्रवदन्येषां तूष्णीं पात्रेषु नि:क्षिपेत् । अत्र अन्येषमिति ग्रहणात्तु ।

1. The reading सद्रं appears to be corrupt.
2. The text of *छन्दोगपरिशिष्ट* is quoted in *कृत्यकल्पतरु-श्राद्धकाण्ड*, p. 172 as *छन्दोगपरिशिष्टे कात्यायन:* and the verse runs thus:

पित्र्ये य: पङ्क्तिमूर्धन्यस्तस्य पाणावनग्निक: ।
दत्वा मन्त्रवदन्येषां तूष्णीं पात्रेषु निक्षिपेत् ॥

२६

अन्नादिसंकल्पः

शांखायनसूत्रम्[1] (४.१.८)

अन्नं चासावेतत्त इत्यनुद्दिश्यं[2] भोजयेत् ।

कात्यायनः —

असावेषत्तेर्घ्यं इति पिण्डपितृयज्ञाधिकारे स एव यथावनिक्तं पिण्डं दद्यादसावेतत्त इति । असानीति संबोधनपदोपलक्षणम् ।

तथा गोभिलः —

असावेषते पिण्डो ये चान्नत्वामनुजांश्च त्वमनुतस्मै ते स्वधेति असावेतत्रे[3] तिलोदकं असावेत्ते सूत्रं इत्यादि स्वधान्तम् ।

ब्रह्मपुराणे[4]—

ततो मधुघृताक्त[5] सोष्ममन्नं तिलान्वितम् ।
गृहीत्वा देवतीर्थेन प्रणवेणैव[6] तत् पुनः ॥ १॥
एतद्वोऽन्नमित्युक्त्वा वैश्वदेवाश्च[7] संयजेत्[8]।
पितृभ्यश्च ततो दद्यादन्नमामन्त्रणे[9] च[10]॥२॥
अमुकामुक गोत्रे तत्तु[11]भ्यमत्रं स्वधा नमः ।३।

1. The *शांखायनसूत्र* is quoted in *कृत्यकल्पतरु-श्राद्धकाण्ड*, p. 183.
2. *Ibid.*, p. 183 reads ०अनुद्दिश्य for ०अनुद्दिश्यम्.
3. This may be emended as ००ते for ००त्रे.
4. The text of *ब्रह्मपुराण* is quoted in *कृत्यकल्पतरु-श्राद्धकाण्ड*, p. 184 and पृथ्वीचन्द्र-*श्राद्धप्रकाश*, IX.51, p. 210.
5. *Ibid.*, p. 184 and पृथ्वीचन्द्र-*श्राद्धप्रकाश*, IX.51 p. 210 read ०घृताक्तं for ०घृताक्त.
6. *Ibid.*, p. 184 and पृथ्वीचन्द्र-*श्राद्धप्रकाश*, p. 210 read प्रणवेनैव for प्रणवेणैव.
7. *कृत्यकल्पतरु-श्राद्धकाण्ड*, p. 184 reads वैश्वदेवांश्च for वैश्वदेवाश्च.
8. *पृथ्वीचन्द्र-श्राद्धप्रकाश*, IX.52, p. 210 reads संजपेत् for संजयेत्.
9. *कृत्यकल्पतरु-श्राद्धकाण्ड*, p. 184 reads ००आमंत्रणेन for ००आमंत्रणे.
10. *Ibid.*, p. 184 reads तु for च and पृथ्वीचंद्र-*श्राद्धप्रकाश*, IX.52, p. 210 reads मधु for च.
11. *Ibid.*, p. 184 reads गोत्रैतत् for गोत्रे तत्.

नम इति स्त्रीशूद्रविषयम् । एतेनामुक गोत्रामुक शर्मन्नेत्तेऽन्नं स्वधेति यजुर्वेदिनामुत सर्गवाक्यम् । अमुकगोत्र पितरमुकदेवशर्मन्नेत्तेऽन्नं ये चान्नत्वामनुजांश्च त्वमनु तस्मै ते स्वधेति छन्दोगानाम् । अमुकगोत्र पितरमुकदेवशर्मन्नेतदन्नं तुभ्यं स्वधेति सामान्यधर्म: पौराणिकत्वात् । पुराणकात्यायनवचनयोरेकवाक्यतया एत्तेऽन्नं तुभ्यं स्वधेति वाक्यकल्पना न प्रामाणिकी । द्वयोरेव निराकांक्षत्वात् तुभ्यमिति पदयो पर्यायंयो: । युगपत् प्रयोगानर्थक्याच्च । शूद्रेण तु विशेषत: पौराणिक एव विधि: कर्तव्य: ।

यथा भविष्यपुराणे —

ब्राहाणादिषु सर्वेषु त्रिषु वेदा: प्रतिष्ठिता: ।
मन्वादीनि च शास्त्राणि तथांगानि समन्तत: ।।४।।
शूद्राश्चेमेदृशं दीनां प्रतिभान्ति मम द्विज ।
कण्ठेषामागम: प्रोक्त: पुरो द्विज मनीषिभि: ।।५।।
त्रिवर्गप्राप्तये ब्रह्मणश्रेयसे च तथोभयो: ।६।

सुमन्तुरुवाच —

साधु साधु महाबाहो शृणु मे परमं वच: ।
चतुर्णामपि वर्णानां यानि प्रोक्तानि श्रेयसे ।।७।।
धर्मशास्त्राणि राजेन्द्र शृणुतानित्युपोत्तम ।
विशेषतं तु शूद्राणां पावनानि मनीषिभि: ।।८।।
अष्टादश पुराणानि चरितानि राघवस्य च ।
रामस्य कुरुशार्दूल धर्मकामार्थं सिद्धये[1] ।।९।।
यथोक्त भारतं वीर पाराशर्येण धीमता ।
वेदार्थं सकलं योह्यं धर्मशास्त्राणि वै प्रभो ।। १०।।

ननु गोत्रसम्बन्धनाम्नां क्रमनियमो निष्प्रमाणक: । प्रत्युतानियमेन मुनीनां प्रयोगो दृश्यते ।
यथा विष्णु: (७३.१४)

नामगोत्राभ्यामुदङ्मुखेषु ।[2]

ब्रह्मपुराणे —

अमुकामुकगोत्रैतत्तुभ्यमन्नं स्वधा नम: ।
तथा प्रदक्षिणं तु निनिह्याद् गोत्रनामान्नमन्त्रितम्[3] ।।११।।

छन्दोगपरिशिष्टम् —

---

1. This may be emended as धर्मकामार्थसिद्धये for धर्मकामार्थं सिद्धये to remove metrical irregularity.
2. *विष्णुस्मृति,* p. 765 reads पित्रे पितामहाय प्रपितामहाय च before नामगोत्राभ्यामुदङ्मुखेषु ।
3. The 2nd line of the stanza No. 11, however is not found in the *कृत्यकल्पतरु-श्राद्धकाण्ड,* p. 184.

गोत्रनामभिरामन्त्र्य पितॄनर्घ्यं प्रदापयेत्[1]।१२।

सम्बन्धापंकपद प्रयोगोप्यप्राणिकः।

उच्यते। गोत्रसम्बन्धयोर्नामविशेषणत्वात् विशेषणविशेष्यक्रमस्य नागृहीतविशेषणन्यायलब्धत्वात्। गोत्रसंबंधयोः क्रमनियमः कुत इति चेत्। न। गोत्रसंबन्धोल्लेखस्य गोभिलादि वचनसिद्धत्वात्। तत् क्रमस्य तत्पाठसिद्धत्वात्।

यथा गोभिलः

> गोत्रं स्वरान्तं सर्वत्र गोत्रस्याक्षरस्य कर्मणि।
> गोत्रस्तु तर्पणे प्रोक्तं कर्ता एवं न मुह्यति ॥१३॥
> सर्वत्रैव पितुः प्रोक्तं पिता तर्पणकर्मणि।
> पितुरक्षस्य काले च अक्षयां तृप्तिमिच्छता ॥१४॥
> शर्मन्नर्घ्यकि कार्यं शर्मा तर्पणकर्मणि।
> कर्मणोक्षय्य काले तु पितॄणां दत्तमक्षयम् ॥१५॥

तथा पारस्करप्रचेतो नाम्ना वचनद्वयं पठयते।

> अर्घ्यदाने त्वसंकल्पे पिण्डदाने तथाक्षये।
> गोत्रसम्बन्धनामानि यथावत् परिकीतयेत् ॥१६॥
> गोत्रसम्बन्धनामानि पितॄणां परिकीर्तयन्।
> एकैकस्य च विप्रस्य अर्घ्यदानं विनिःक्षिपन् ॥१७॥
> पिण्डदाने त्रिभिरामन्यासेवेत्तनः।१८।

इति त्रिभिर्गोत्रसम्बन्धनामभिस्तदेवं पूर्वोक्त शांखायनादिवचनैः श्राद्धे दैवपित्र्योत्सर्गवाक्ये सम्बोधनान्तपदोपात्तयोर्दैवपित्र्योश्चतुर्थ्यपदोपात्तयोर्दैवपित्र्योश्चतुर्थ्यन्तपदेन निद्देश इत्येवैकश्रुतिः सर्वशाखि-साधारणी कल्पनीया। अपरो विशेषः शाखाभेदव्यवस्थित इति प्रागुक्तम्। अक्षय्यदाने तु षष्ठ्यन्ततामाह गोभिलः —

शर्मणोऽक्षय्यकाले त्विति।

छन्दोगपरिशिष्टम्[2]—

> अक्षय्योदकदानं तु र्घ्य[3]दानवदिष्यते।
> षष्ठयैव नित्य[4]तत् कुर्यान्न चतुर्थी[3]कदाचन ॥ १९॥

1. This line is found quoted in *कृत्यकल्पतरु-श्राद्धकाण्ड*, p. 273 from the text of *गोभिल*, I.256.
2. This text is quoted in *कृत्यकल्पतरु-श्राद्धकाण्ड*, p. 274.
3. *Ibid.*, p. 274 reads अर्घ०० for अर्घ्य००.
4. *Ibid.*, p. 274 reads नित्यं for नित्य.
5. *Ibid.*, p. 274 reads चतुर्थ्यां for चतुर्थीं.

अर्घ्यदानवदिति ज्येष्ठोत्तरकरत्वमतिदिश्यते ।

ननु चतुर्थ्यन्त वाक्यमाह विष्णुः (७३.१३.१४)

नमो विश्वेभ्यो देवेभ्य इति अर्घ्यमादौ[1] प्राङ्मुखयोर्निवेद्य[2] पित्रे पितामहाय प्रपितामह[3]-गोत्राभ्यामुदङ्मुखेषु । न पूर्वोक्तानेकवचनं विरोधान्नाम इति विश्वेभ्यो निवेदयेदिति भिन्नक्रमेण योजना कार्या । अन्यथा नमो विश्वेभ्यो देवेभ्य इत्यापि क्रमः स्यात् । किं च पित्रे पितामहाय प्रपितामहाय च निवेदयेदिति सम्बन्धे न चतुर्थ्यन्तता लभ्यते । विश्वेभ्य इत्यस्यापि निवेदयति नासम्बन्धः ।

ननु समानं गोत्रमस्येति सगोत्रशब्दव्युत्पत्तौ प्रकमेऽर्घ्यसंगतिर्न स्यात् । न गोत्रपदस्य गोत्रपर्यन्तत्वात् ।

यथा महाभारते (१२.३०८.२४)

पराशरगोत्रस्य[4] वृद्धस्य च महात्मनः[5]।
भिक्षोः पञ्चशिखस्याहं शिष्यः परमधार्मिकः[6]॥२०॥

याज्ञवल्क्यः (२.८५)

समामस[7] तदर्द्धंशि[8] नामजानी[9] सगोत्रकैः ।
सब्रह्मचादिकात्मीय पितृनामादि चिह्नितम् ॥२१॥

इति लेख्यं कुर्यादिति सम्बन्धः । अत गोत्रसगोत्रयोः विकल्पः ।

---

1. *कृत्यकल्पतरु-श्राद्धकाण्ड,* p. 183 reads अन्नमादौ for अर्घ्यमादौ.
2. *Ibid.*, p. 183 reads निवेदयेत् for निवेद्य.
3. *Ibid.*, p. 183 reads च नाम after प्रपितामह and before गोत्राभ्यां००.
4. *Mbh.*, p. 1708 reads पाराशर्यसगोत्रस्य for पराशरगोत्रस्य.
5. *Ibid.*, p. 1708 reads सुमहात्मनः for च महात्मनः .
6. *Ibid.*, p. 1708 reads ०संमतः for ०धार्मिकः .
7. *याज्ञवल्क्यस्मृति,* p. 191 reads समामास for समामस.
8. *Ibid.*, p. 191 reads तदर्धाह for तदर्द्धंश.
9. *Ibid.*, p. 191 reads नामजाति for नामजानि

२७

अथ ब्राह्मणभोजनम्

प्रधानं पिण्डदानमुभयं वा । ब्राह्मणभोजनं प्रधानमिति गौडगोविन्दराजः[1]। फलश्रुतेः फलवत् तदङ्गमिति न्यायात्[2] पिण्डदानमङ्गम् ।

यथा मनुः (३.१२९)

एकैकमपि विद्वांसं दैवे पित्र्ये च भोजयेत् ।
पुष्कलं फलमाप्नोति नामन्त्रज्ञान्बहूनपि ॥ १॥

पिण्डदानमन्तरेणापि मघादौ श्राद्धदर्शनाच्च । गयादौ तु पिण्डदानमात्रदर्शनात् पिण्डदानं प्रधानमिति कैयटभट्टः[3]।

तथा ह्यशक्तौ पिण्डदानमाह निगमः —

आहिताग्नेः पित्र्यर्चनं पिण्डैकेन । भीष्मस्य पिण्डदाने शान्तनोरुत्तानकरदर्शनाच्च । उभयमुक्तेरुभयं प्रधानमिति भट्टनारायणप्रभृतयः[4]।

तथा च श्लोकाः

प्राधान्यं पिण्डदानस्य केवलस्य विधानतः ।
भीष्मस्य ददतः पिण्डान् हस्तोत्तान श्रुतेरपि ॥२॥
भोजनस्य प्रधानत्वं वदन्त्यन्ये महर्षयः ।
ब्राह्मणानां परीक्षायां महायत्नस्य दर्शनात् ॥३॥
महाफलविधेश्चैव पङ्क्तिपावन दर्शनात् ।
अपङ्क्त्यभोजने दातुर्महानर्थप्रदर्शनात् ॥४॥
आमश्राद्धं विधानस्य विना पिण्डक्रियाविधेः ।

---

1. *गोविन्दराज* on *मनुस्मृति,* III.129 observes ब्राह्मणस्य भोजनमत्र प्रधानं पिण्डदानादि तु अङ्गमित्यवसीयते । *मनुस्मृति,* Vol. II., p. 142.
2. This has a reference to the मीमांसा maxim फलवत् संनिधौ अफलं तदङ्गम् । Also see *शबर.*
3. On *जैमिनि कृत पूर्वमीमांसा,* IV.4.19, IV.4.34; IV.4.7. Also *कुल्लूक* on *मनुस्मृति,* II.101-02; *जैमिनीय न्यायमालाविस्तर,* IV.3.16.37; Also read *आचारमयूख,* p. 58.
4. This view of भट्टनारायण cannot be traced in the *नारायणभट्टी.*

तदालभ्याप्यनध्याय इत्येवं श्रवणादपि ।।५।।
विधिद्वैधमुपादाय ममत्वे तन्मतं पुनः ।
प्राधान्यमुभयोर्यस्मात् तस्मादेव समुच्चयः ।।६।।
वस्तुतस्तु यद्यपि 'अग्नौ हुतेन देवस्था पितृस्था द्विजतर्पणैः ।
नरकस्थाश्च तृप्यन्ति पिण्डैर्दत्तैः स्त्रिभिर्भुवि[1] ।।७'।।

इति वचनात् ब्राह्मणभोजनपिण्डदानयोः फलश्रुतेः द्वयोः प्राधान्यं नानुपन्नम् । असोमयाजिपक्षे दधिपयोयागवत् । तथापि नित्यश्राद्धमदैवं स्यादर्घ्यपिण्डविवर्जितमिति ।

तत्रापि महती पूजा कर्तव्या पितृदैवते ।

ऋक्षे पिण्डप्रदानं च ज्येष्ठपुत्री[2] विवर्जयेत् ।।८।। इति हारीतदेवीपुराणाभ्यां पिण्डदाननिषेधोऽवगम्यते। न चाप्राप्तस्यापि निषेधो घटते । न चातिदेशान्तरमन्तरेण प्राप्तिरस्ति । अतिदेशश्चांगत्वेन युज्यते । न तु प्राधान्येन प्रधानस्यातिदेशात् । उपकारकत्वेनैवातिदेशस्य सप्तमाध्याये दर्शितत्वात् । अतो ब्राह्मणभोजनं प्रधानमंगं पिण्डदानम् । अङ्गे च फलश्रुतिरर्थवाद[3] एव । पिण्डदानविधिस्तु अङ्गभूतपिण्डदानात् कर्मान्तरमेव प्रकरणान्तरस्यादिति सिद्धम् ।

---

1. This stanza is quoted in the *कृत्यकल्पतरु-श्राद्धकाण्ड*, p. 222 from the text of *बृहस्पति* (श्राद्ध ११०).
2. *कृत्यकल्पतरु-श्राद्धकाण्ड*, p. 21 quotes this stanza from the *देवीपुराण* and reads ०पुत्रो for ०पुत्री.
3. This has a reference to *जैमिनि कृत पूर्वमीमांसा*, IV.3.1. Also see कुल्लूक on *मनुस्मृति*, III.129 'वयं तु ब्रूमः—पितृद्देशेन द्रव्यत्यागं ब्राह्मणस्वीकारपर्यन्तं श्राद्धशब्दवाच्यं प्रधानंब्रूमः । *मनुस्मृति*, Vol. II. p. 141. Also see *समयमयूख*, p. 47 for the use of this maxim.

२८

अथ श्राद्धशेषभोजनम्

देवल:[1]—

पश्चात् स्वयञ्च पनीभि:[2] पिण्डशेष्[3]मुदाहरेत् । १।

उदाहरेदभ्यवहरेत्।

उशना [4]—

तैरनुज्ञात: शेषमिष्टेभ्यो दद्यात् स्वयं वा भुञ्जति । वा शब्द: समुच्चये[5]।

याज्ञवल्क्य: — (१.२४९अ)

प्रदक्षिणमनुव्रज्य भुञ्जीत पितृसेवितम् ।२।

ननु भुञ्जीतेति न भोजनस्वरूपविधि: । अप्राप्तविषयत्वाद्विधेर्भोजनस्य रागप्राप्तत्वात् ।

तथा चोक्तम्—

विधिरत्यन्तमप्राप्तौ नियम: पाक्षिके सति ।
तत्र चान्यत्र च प्राप्तौ परिसंख्येति गीयते[6] ॥३॥

न च परिसंख्या विधेया । पितृसेवितमेव भुञ्जीत नान्यदित्येवं लक्षणा हि सा । सा चान्नार्थहानि[7] स्वार्थकल्पना[8] प्राप्तबाधलक्षणा दोषत्र[9]यदुष्टा ।

न च नियमविधिनागतौ सम्भवन्त्यां दोषत्रयमभ्युपगन्तुं युज्यते ।

---

1. The text of *देवल* is quoted in *कृत्यकल्पतरु-श्राद्धकाण्ड*, p. 225.
2. *Ibid.*, p. 225 reads पत्नीभि: for पनीभि: which is corrupt.
3. *Ibid.*, p. 225 reads पितृ०० for पिण्ड००.
4. *Ibid.*, p. 227 quotes the text of उशना verbatim.
5. The explanation of कुल्लूक is taken from *कृत्यकल्पतरु-श्राद्धकाण्ड*, p. 227.
6. This is तन्त्रवार्तिक I.2.4.
7. This may be emended as श्रुतहानि.
8. This may be emended as अश्रुनकल्पना for स्वार्थकल्पना.
9. This expression is corrupt.

अत एव

कालाभिगामी स्यादिति मनुवचन (५.१८) चेत् नियमविधिरुक्तः । एवं पञ्चनखपरिसंख्या न स्यादिति चेत् । न ।

श्वाविधं शल्यकं गोधां खड्ग कूर्मशशांस्तथा ।
भक्ष्यान् पञ्चनखेष्वाहुरनु[1]श्चैक तोदत ॥४॥

इति मनुवचने (५.१८) एते भक्ष्या इत्यनेन विधौ सिद्धौ यत् पञ्चनखग्रहणं तत्परिसंख्यार्थमिति । पञ्चनखेष्विति निर्द्धारणसप्तमीवशाच्च । अत्र तु परिसंख्यायां प्रमाणाभावान्नियमविधिः । पितृसेवितं भुञ्जीतैवेत्यर्थः । न च दृष्टार्थे कर्मणि वचनशतेनापि नियमो बाधयितुं शक्यते । अतः श्राद्धाङ्गतया दृष्टार्थोऽयं नियमः । तथाचोपवासवासरेऽपि श्राद्धशेषभोजनप्रसङ्गः । किं च अमावास्याष्टकावपि मांसभोजनमिष्टं स्यात् । मांसव्यतिरिक्तभोजनेऽपि शेषशब्दार्थहानिरिति चेत् । न । सर्वस्माद्[2] ग्रासाववार्द्धमी[3] स्नी यदित्यापस्तम्बवचने[4] बहुकृत्स्नत्वादि सर्वशब्दश्रुतेः । इष्यत एवेति चेन्न । पर्वणि तद्भक्षणनिषेधात् । दृष्टार्थभक्षणाविषयो भक्षणनिषेधो भविष्यति । हिंसानिषेधविधित्वे वा दृष्टार्थं यागादि पशुहिंसाव्यतिरिक्त इति चेत् । न । यावज्जीवनिरामिष प्रतिज्ञायामपि मांसभोजनप्रसङ्गात् । तेन मांसं न देयमिति चेत् । न । मांसाष्टकायां मांसस्य प्राधान्यात् तदसम्भवात् । सागनेरप्यमावास्याश्राद्धे 'तदा मिश्रेण[5] कर्तव्यमिति' मनु[6]वचनाच्च ।

उच्यते ।

'दर्शे च औपनसार्थकमन्नं दम्पती भुञ्जीयाताम्' इति गोभिले भोजननियमदर्शनाच्च ।

उच्यते ।

भक्ष्यं भोज्यं तथा पीयं यत् किंचित् पच्यते गृहे ।
न भोक्तव्यं पितृणान्तादनिवेद्य कथंचन ॥५॥
यत् किंचित् पच्यते गेहे भक्ष्यं भोजनम[7]थापि[8] वा ।
अनिवेद्य न भुञ्जीत[9] पिण्डमूले कथञ्चन ॥६॥

इति यमशंखाभ्यां पितृसेवतिमेव भुञ्जीतेत्यवगम्यते । तदेकवाक्यतया परिसंख्याविधिरयम् । नियमात्वेधौ मूलभूतश्रुतिकल्पनाप्रसङ्गात् । यान्तेर[10]कल्पभिया गंगाघोषादौवस्वार्थहानेश्च दृष्टत्वात् । अत एव

---

1. *मनुस्मृति*, V.18 reads ००अनुष्टान्० for ००अनु च०. Here in our manuscript some word is missing.
2. *आपस्तम्ब धर्मसूत्र*, p. 79 reads सर्वतः समवदाय शेषस्य for सर्वस्मात्.
3. *Ibid*., p. 79 reads ग्रासावराध्यं for अग्रासाववार्द्धम् which is corrupt.
4. This is *आपस्तम्ब धर्मसूत्र*, II.7.17.16.
5. In view of context, this may be emended as ०अमिषेण for ०अमिश्रेण which is corrupt.
6. This is *मनुस्मृति*, III.123.
7. *कृत्यकल्पतरु-श्राद्धकाण्ड*, p. 211 quotes the text of शंख, and reads भोज्य for भोजनम्.
8. *Ibid*., p. 211 reads एव for अथापि.
9. *Ibid*., p. 211 reads भोक्तव्यं for भुञ्जीत.
10. This expression seems to be corrupt.

रागप्राप्तबाधोऽपि न दूषणं वचनान्तरेणैव बाधितत्वात् । प्रोक्षितं भक्षयेन्मांसमितिवत् । तदापि नाद्याद् विधिना मांसविधिज्ञोनापदि द्विज इति वचनैकवाक्यतया प्रोक्षितमेव मांसं भक्ष्यं नान्यदिति परिसंख्योक्ता । अत एव

स्वदारनियतः सदेत्य परदारान्न गच्छेत् ।७।

इत्येकवाक्यतया परिसंख्योक्ता ।

अस्तु वा नियमविधिः । तथामक्षास्योपभुक्ते शेषप्रतिपङ्क्तिरूपत्वात् प्रतिपत्तेश्च सत्येव शेषेऽङ्गविरोधात् । ततश्चोपवासरे पर्वणि च यावज्जीवनिरामिषप्रतिज्ञायां चोपवासादि धर्मानुरोधादनुमांसादीनां तथोपयोगः कर्तव्यो यथा श्राद्धमिष्टभोज्यं च निष्पाद्यापरम् । किंचिद् भक्षणार्थं नावशिष्येते भक्षणरूपप्रतिपत्ति अनुरोधादेव स्थास्यामिति चेन्न । गुणभूतत्वात् । प्रतिपत्तेर्गुणस्य च प्रधानाप्रयोजकत्वात् । अत एवाग्निसोमीये[1] पशौ सकृन्निरस्यति लोहितं निरस्यति । गुदेनोपयजतीत्यादीनामुपभुक्तशेषप्रतिपत्तिरूपाणां दैवमलोहितादीनां विनाशे लोहिताव्यर्थं पश्वन्तरप्रयोजकत्वं निरस्तम् । एवं भक्षणरूपस्यांगस्य हानिः स्यादिति चेन्न । यदि काण[2]वोपेनांगत्वविधानात् । यदि अवशिष्येत तदा किं कर्तव्यमित्याकांक्षायां प्रतिपत्तिर्विधानात् । ततश्च रथन्तरसामसोमः स्यात् । तदैन्द्रवायव्यानग्रहान् गृह्णातीतिवन्नाङ्गत्वहानिः । यदि कारणोपेने[3] च विधानान्नियमविधिरभ्युपपन्न इति ।

1. This may be emended as अग्निषोमीये.
2. This expression appears to be corrupt.
3. This expression seems to be corrupt.

२१

अथ श्राद्धम्

मत्स्यपुराणे — (१८.२७)

आमश्राद्धं यदा कुर्याद्विधिज्ञः श्राद्धदः सुतः[1]।
ते नाग्नौकरणं[2] कुर्यात् पिण्डांस्तेनैव निर्वपेत् ॥१॥

तेनान्नेनैव न पक्वान्नेनैव ।

ननु आमश्राद्धस्य तीर्थे निमित्तेन विधानादम्मान्नं पिण्डेऽपि प्राप्तम् । पिण्डदानस्यापि श्राद्धत्वात् । तेनैवेत्यनर्थकम् ।

सर्वस्मात् प्रकृतादन्नात् पिण्डान्मधुतिलान्वितान्[3]।२।

इत्यादि वचनैः प्रकृतान्नप्राप्तेश्च । नयेदित्यशक्तपरम् । अतो ब्राह्मणभोजनार्थं प्रचुरतर अन्नपाकासमर्थेन पिण्डदानार्थमल्पपाकसमर्थेनापि पाकाङ्गबाधाय पिण्डार्थं पाको न कर्तव्य इत्यत्र तात्पर्यम् ।

आमश्राद्धं कदा कर्तव्यमित्याह उशना[4]—

आत्मनो देशकालानां विप्लवे समुपस्थिते ।
आमश्राद्धं द्विजैः[5] कार्यं[6] शूद्रेन[7] तु सदैव हि ॥३॥

आत्मनो विप्लवः पाककारणासामर्थ्यं कर्तव्यम् । देशविप्लवोऽतिवृष्ट्यादिना । कालविप्लवः परचक्रादिभयेन पाककालत्ययः । एतेन मुख्यभूतश्राद्धानुरोधायाङ्गबाधः । प्रकृतावपि वचनादित्युक्तम् ।

---

1. *मत्स्यपुराण,* p. 32 reads ०तदा for ०सुतः .
2. *Ibid*., p. 32 reads तेनाग्नौकरणं for ते नाग्नौकरणम् .
3. *कृत्यकल्पतरु-श्राद्धकाण्ड,* p. 204 quotes this line from the text of *बृहस्पति.*
4. The text of *उशनस्* is found in the *औशनसस्मृति,* V.82 in *स्मृतिसंदर्भ,* Vol. III., p. 1585.
5. *Ibid*., p. 1585 reads द्विजः for द्विजैः .
6. *Ibid*., p. 1585 reads कुर्यात् for कार्यम्.
7. *Ibid*., p. 1585 reads वृषलः for शूद्रेन.

व्यासः —

यद्यत् विप्रेभ्यो श्रुतं वा यदि वाश्रुतम् ।
तेनाग्नौकरणं कुर्यात् ब्राह्मणस्य विधानतः ।।४।।[1]

हस्ते विप्रहस्ते । एतच्च साग्निकविषयम् । निरग्नेर्विप्राणामेव होमान्यप्राप्तत्वात् ।

तथा मनुः (३.२१२अ)

अग्न्यभावे तु विप्रस्य पाणावेवोपपादयेत् ।।५।

एतदशक्तावामान्नविधानमतिदिष्टमप्येकोद्दिष्टे न कर्तव्यमित्याह लघुहारीतः ।

श्राद्धविघ्ने द्विजातीनामामश्राद्धं प्रकीर्तितम् ।
अमावास्यादि नियतं माससंवत्सरादृते। ।६।।[2]
एकोद्दिष्टं तु कर्तव्यं पाकेनैव सदा स्वयम् ।
अभावे पाकपात्राणां तदहः समुपोषणम् ।।७।।[3]
अमावास्यादि नियतं प्रोषिते सहचारिणी ।[4]
पत्नौ तु कारयेन्नित्यमन्येमप्यद्विजादिना ।।८।।

अमावास्यादीत्यादिशब्दः समस्तपार्वणकालपरः । माससंवत्सराहत एकोद्दिष्टमात्रप्रदर्शनार्थमित्याह एकोद्दिष्टन्तु इति । अत्रविशेषित द्विजातिग्रहणं ब्राह्मणक्षत्रियवैश्यैः साग्निनिरग्निसाधारणैर्विघ्नं विना पाकाङ्गवामेव पार्वणं कर्तव्यामिति प्रतीयते । हलायुधस्तु प्रचेतो वचनदर्शनात् साग्निकविषयं निरग्निना सर्वदा आमान्नेनैव तत् कार्यम् ।

यथा बृहत्प्रचेताः[5]—

आपद्यनग्नौ तीर्थे च चन्द्रसूर्यग्रहे तथा[6]।
आमश्राद्धं द्विजैः कार्यं शूद्रेण तु सदैव हि ।।९।।

अत्र ह्यनग्नीरित्यग्न्यभावे आमन्नविधिरवगम्यते । ततश्च द्विजातीनामिति साग्निकपरत्वात् 'एकोद्दिष्टं तु कर्तव्यं' इत्यपि साग्निकपरमेव । निरग्निना तु एकोद्दिष्टं पार्वणाच्चामान्ने न कर्तव्यम् । साग्निना तु शक्तौ पाकाङ्गकमेव पार्वणमेकोद्दिष्टं पाकेनैव ।

कल्पतरौ[7] तु पाकाङ्गश्राद्धमुक्त्वा ।

---

1. This stanza, however, is not found in the *वेदव्याससमृति*.
2. This stanza is not found in the *लघुहारीतस्मृति*. This stanza No. 6, however, is ascribed to *हारीत* in *श्राद्धमयूख*, pp. 17-18.
3. This stanza No. 7 ascribed to *लघुहारीत* is found quoted in *श्राद्धमयूख*, p. 72.
4. The first line of stanza No. 8 is found ascribed to *हारीत* in *श्राद्धमयूख*, p. 72.
5. This text of *बृहत्प्रचेतस्* is ascribed to *जाबाल* in *श्राद्धमयूख*, p. 72.
6. *श्राद्धमयूख*, p. 72 reads ग्रहणे चन्द्रसूर्ययोः for चन्द्रसूर्यग्रहे तथा.
7. This view of *कल्पतरु* is found with some changes in the *कृत्यकल्पतरु-श्राद्धकाण्ड*, p. 235.

एतच्चानुपनीतोऽपि कुर्यात् सर्वेषु पर्वसु ।
श्राद्धं साधारणं नाम सर्वकामफलप्रदम् ॥१०॥
भार्याविरहितोप्येतत् प्रवासस्थोऽपि नित्यशः[1] ।
शूद्रोऽप्यमन्त्रवत् कुर्यादनेन विधिना बुधः ॥११॥

इति मत्स्यपुराण (१७.६४) वचनात् ।

एतच्छब्दात् प्रकृतवाचिनः सन्निहितपाकाङ्गकश्राद्धप्रतीतेः । अत्र चानुपनीतभार्याविरहितप्रवासस्थानामधिकारबोधान्निरग्निनापि पाकाङ्गकमेव श्राद्धं कर्तव्यम् । अनग्नाविति पाकसामर्थ्याग्न्यभावपरमिति व्याख्यानम् । तदसङ्गतम् । आपदि इत्यननैव लब्धत्वादनग्निवित्यस्यानर्थकत्वापत्तेः । किं च एतदिति सांगसमानाधिकरणतया पाकांगकत्वाभावात् पाकस्य च श्राद्धशब्दानर्थकत्वात् । वस्तुतस्तु 'आमश्राद्धं द्विजैः कार्यामित्युशन[2]सो प्रचेतवचनयोः श्राद्धविघ्ने द्विजातीनामिति हारीत[3]वचने च अविशेषितद्विजातिग्रहणात् । पाकांगश्राद्धमभिधाय 'अनेन विधिने'ति मत्स्यपुराण[4]वचनाच्च निरग्नेरपि पाकांगकमेव श्राद्धम् । अत एव अनुपनीतादीनां सर्वेषामेव पाकांगकश्राद्धप्राप्तौ शूद्रस्यापि प्रशस्तौ तस्यैव निषेधो दर्शितः ।

मत्स्यपुराणे (१७.७०) एवम् ।

शूद्रस्यापि सामान्यं वृद्धिश्राद्धं च सर्वदा ।
नमस्कारेण मन्त्रेण कुर्यादामान्नवद्[5] बुधः ॥१२॥

प्रचेतोवचने त्वनग्निशब्दः पाकसामग्न्यभावपरः । आपदीत्यपि संभवत्यपि पाके कालात्ययात् श्राद्धपदमभिधत्ते । अतो न विरोधः । एतेन निरग्निनापि विघ्नाद्यभावे पाकान्नेनैव पार्वणमेकोद्दिष्टं च कर्तव्यम् । शूद्रेण तु आमान्नेनैव दाशाहिकपिण्डदेवतानैवेद्यादिकमप्यान्नेनैव तुल्यन्यायात् ।

आम शूद्रस्य पक्वान्नं पक्वमुच्छिष्टमुच्यते ।१३।

इति वचनाच्च ।

जातश्राद्धं तु द्विजातीनाप्यामान्ननैव कर्तव्यम् ।१४।

जातश्राद्धेन दद्याच्च ब्राह्मणेष्वपि इत्यादिपुराणवचनात् आमश्राद्धमिति समाख्यानात् ।
तथा विष्णुः — (७३.५)

आमश्राद्धे[6]षु प्रथमपञ्चकेनाग्निं हुत्वेत्यादि ।

---

1. *कृत्यकल्पतरु-श्राद्धकाण्ड*, p. 235 and *मत्स्यपुराण* reads भक्तिमान् for नित्यशः .
2. The text of *उशनस्* is found in *औशनसस्मृति*, V.82 *स्मृतिसंदर्भ*, Vol. III, p. 1585.
3. It may be noted here that the manuscript ascribes this stanza to *लघुहारीत* in stanza No. 6, p. 206 while here it is ascribed to हारीत.
4. This line from *मत्स्यपुराण* is found quoted in *कृत्यकल्पतरु-श्राद्धकाण्ड*, p. 235.
5. *मत्स्यपुराण*, p. 31 reads ०आमान्नतः for ०आमान्नवद्.
6. *विष्णुस्मृति*, p. 762 reads काम्येषु after आमश्राद्धेषु.

अत्र आमश्राद्धं जातश्राद्धमिति व्याख्यातम् ।

अभावे पाकपात्राणामिति पाकपात्राभावे पाकाभावात् श्राद्धलोपे विहितातिक्रमजनितपापक्षयार्थं प्रायश्चित्तं स्वयमित्यनेनैकोद्दिष्टं स्वयमेव कार्यं नान्यद्वारा । अमावास्यादि निर्णयं तु पार्वणं सहचारिणी पत्नी प्रोषिते पत्यौ ऋत्विगादिद्वारा वा कुर्यात् । अपि शब्दात् "ऋत्विकपुत्रो गुरुर्माता भागिनेयीऽथ विट्पतिः ।

एभिरेव हुतं यत् स्यात् तत्तत् कृतं स्वयमेव हि ॥"१५॥

इति वचनात् पुत्रादय उह्याः। स्वयमशक्तावेकोद्दिष्टं गोत्रजद्वारा कर्तव्यम् ।

यथा प्रेतक्रियां प्रकृत्य ब्रह्मपुराणेन
कदाचित् सगोत्राय श्राद्धं देयमगोत्रजैः ।१६।

अत्र अन्यगोत्रजस्य साक्षात्कर्तृत्वं निषिद्धयते । सगोत्रायेत्यसम्बन्धापत्तेः । तस्माद् गोत्रजैर्द्वारभूतैः सगोत्राय सगोत्रेण न कर्तव्यमित्यस्यार्थः । तदा च पर्युदासपक्षे सगोत्रजद्वाराऽपि कर्तव्यमिति सुव्यक्तमेव । प्रसह्यपक्षे गोत्रजस्वरसाद् गोत्रजलाभः । प्रेतश्राद्धधर्मग्राहित्वात् सांवत्सरिकमपि तथा । पार्वणं तु असगोत्रज ऋग्त्वादिद्वारापि कर्तव्यमित्यमावास्यादिवचनस्यार्थः ।

३०

अथ जीवत्पितृकश्राद्धम्

मनुः (३.२२०-२२३)

ध्रियमाणे तु पितरि पूर्वेषामेव निर्वपेत् ।
विप्रवत् वापि तं श्राद्धं[1] स्वकं पितरमाशयेत् ॥१॥
पिता यस्य निवृत्त[2]स्याज्जीवेद्वापि पितामहः ।
पितुः स्वनाम[3] संकीर्त्य कीर्तयेत् प्रपितामहम् ॥२॥
पितामहो वा तत् श्राद्धं भुञ्जीतेत्यब्रवीन्मनुः ।
कामं वा तदनुज्ञातः[4] स्वयमेव समाचरेत् ॥३॥
तथा त्रयाणामुदकं कार्यं त्रिषु पिण्डः प्रवर्तते ।
चतुर्थः सम्प्रदातैषां पंचमी नोपपद्यते[5] ॥४॥

ध्रियमाणे जीवतीत्यर्थः । पूर्वेषां पितुः पितुः पूर्वेषां[6] पुरूषत्रयाणामित्यर्थः । अथवामुक[7]पितराशयेत् विप्रवदिति गन्धाद्यर्चनपूर्वकमित्यर्थः । तेन जीवन्तमेव पितरमादितो भोजयित्वा पुरुषद्वयस्य भोजयित्वादूर्ध्वं[8] पुरुषत्रयस्य श्राद्धं कर्तव्यमिति हलायुधस्य व्याख्यानमादरणीयम् ।

पितरं भोजयित्वा तु पिण्डो निर्घृणुयात् परौ ॥५॥

इति यज्ञपार्श्वपरिशिष्टवचनात् । पिता यस्य तु इत्यादि पितर्यविद्यमाने पितामहे जीवति । पक्षद्वयं नाम संकीर्तनं श्राद्धोपलक्षणं कीर्तयेत् । प्रपितामहमित्यत्र वृद्धप्रपितामहकीर्तनमपि ज्ञेयम् । 'यस्य पिता[9]

---

1. *मनुस्मृति,* p. 224 reads श्राद्धं for श्राद्धे.
2. *Ibid.*, p. 226 reads वृत्तः००० for निवृत्तः०००.
3. *Ibid.*, p. 226 reads स नाम for स्वनाम.
4. *Ibid.*, p. 226 reads समनुज्ञातः for तदनुज्ञातः.
5. This complete stanza is not found in the extant *मनुस्मृति*.
6. The expression पितुः पूर्वेषां appears to be redundant.
7. In view of the *मनुस्मृति,* III.220, i.e., stanza No. 1 above, this may be emended as अथवास्वकं for अथवामुक.
8. This may be emended as भोजनादूर्ध्वं for भोजयित्वादूर्ध्वम्.
9. *विष्णुस्मृति,* p. 775 reads प्रेतःस्यात् after पिता. This expression is omitted here.

प्रपितामहश्च' प्रेतौ स्यातां[1] प्रेत: स्यात् स पित्रे पिण्डं निधाय पितामहात्परं द्वाभ्यां दद्यादिति विष्णु (७५.४) वचनात् । 'कामं वेति तदनुज्ञात:[2]' पित्र्यनुज्ञात: काममभिलषितं वा समाचरेत् । भोजनपक्षात् पक्षान्तरमिति यदा पूर्वेषां तदा किमित्यपेक्षायामाहत्रयाणामुदमिति ।

विष्णु:(७५.१.२.३-७)

पितरि जीवति य: श्राद्धं कुर्यात्[3]। पितरे[4] पितामहे[5] जीवति येषां पितामह: । पितरि पिता मे[6] प्रपितामहे च[7] नैव कुर्यात् । यस्य पिता प्रेत: स्यात् स पवित्रे[8] विष्णु[9] निधाय प्रपितामहापरं[10] द्वाभ्यां दद्यात् । यस्य पितृपितामहौ[11] प्रेतौ स्यातां स ताभ्यां पिण्डं दत्वा पितामहप्रपितामहाय[12] दद्यात् । यस्य पितामह: प्रेत:[13] स तस्मै पिण्डं निधाय प्रपितामहात् परं द्वाभ्यां दद्यात् ।

मातामहानामप्येवं श्राद्धं कुर्याद्विचक्षण: ।
मंत्रोहेन[14] यथान्यायं शेषाणां मन्त्रवर्जितम् ।।६।।

पितरि जीवति इति साधारणोऽयं निर्देश: ।

पितर्येव जीवनतीर्थ: । अत एव त्रिषु जीवत्सु नैव कुर्यादित्युक्तम् । एवमन्यत्रापि य: श्राद्धमिति यच्छब्दोपादानादकरणपक्षोऽपि सूचित: । मातामहानामप्येवमिति यथा पितरि जीवति येषां पिता कुर्यात् तेषां कुर्यात्तथा मातामहे जीवति । येषां मातामह: कुर्यात्तेषां यथा पित्रादिषु त्रिषु जीवत्सु नैव कुर्यात् तथा मातामहादिषु त्रिषु जीवत्सु मातामहपक्षं नैव कुर्यात् इत्यादि सर्वमतिदेश्यम् । किन्तु पितृपदवत् मात्रे पितृपदस्थाने मातामहपदोह: कार्य इति विशेष: । यथान्यायमिति ऊहोऽपि क्रियमाणो न्यायानुसारेण कार्य: । दृष्टार्थो हि मन्त्रो असमवेतार्थपदवत्तया प्रयुज्जमाणो दृष्टार्थो न भवेत् । अत: समवेतार्थ पदप्रक्षेपेण दृष्टार्थो प्रयोज्य: । अग्नये त्वामुष्टं निर्वपामीति मन्त्र: सौर्ये चरु सूर्यपद-प्रक्षेपेण प्रयोज्य: । अग्निहोत्राधिकरणन्याय:[15]। तदनुसारेणात्रापि 'शुन्धन्तां पितर: शुन्धन्तां पितामहा: शुन्धन्तां प्रपितामहा' इति मन्त्रस्य पित्रादिपदस्थाने मातामहादि पदोह: कार्य: । ननु एवममीदन्त: पितर इत्यादौवप्यूहप्रसङ्ग: ।

---

1. *विष्णुस्मृति,* p. 775 in the foot-note reads पितामह: प्रपितामहश्च जीवेत् for प्रपितामहश्च प्रेतौ स्याताम्.
2. This refers to *मनुस्मृति,* III.223.
3. *विष्णुस्मृति,* p. 775 reads स येषां पिता कुर्यात् तेषां कुर्यात् after कुर्यात्. This is omitted here.
4. *Ibid.*, p. 775 reads पितरि for पितरे.
5. *Ibid.*, p. 775 reads च before जीवति.
6. *Ibid.*, p. 775 reads पितामहे for पिता मे which is corrupt.
7. *Ibid.*, p. 775 reads जीवति after च.
8. *Ibid*, p. 775 reads पित्रे for पवित्रे, which is corrupt.
9. *Ibid.*, p. 775 reads पिण्डं for विष्णुम्.
10. *Ibid.*, p. 775 reads पितामहात्परं for प्रपितामहापरम्. It is strange that at two places, the manuscript gives two different readings.
11. *Ibid.*, p. 775 reads पिता पितामहश्च for पितृपितामहौ.
12. *Ibid.*, p. 775 reads ०पितामहाय for ०प्रपितामहाय.
13. *Ibid.*, p. 775 reads स्यात् after प्रेत: and before स तस्मै.
14. *Ibid.*, p. 775 reads मन्त्रोहेण for मन्त्रोहेन.
15. This refers to *जैमिनि कृत पूर्वमीमांसा,* VI.2.23-26.

न द्वेधा पितृपदप्रवृत्तिः । जनकत्वोपाधिना पितृलोकप्राप्त्या च दृश्यते ।

यथा विष्णुपुराणम् — (३.१३.३६अ)

प्रेते पितृत्वमापन्ने सपिण्डीकरणादान्विति ।७।

यथा हारीतः[1]

ततः प्रभृति वै प्रेतः पितृसामान्यमाप्नुयात् ।८।

तदत्र मातामहादीनामपि सपिण्डीकरणेन पितृलोकप्राप्तेर्जातत्वात् । पितृलोकप्राप्त्युपाधिना पितृपदस्य समवेतार्थत्वमेव । 'शुन्धन्तां पितर' इत्यादौ तु जनकत्वोपाधिनैव पितृपदप्रवृत्तिः । पितृलोकप्राप्त्युपाधिना प्रवृत्तौ 'शुन्धन्तां पितामहा' इत्यनर्थकं स्यात् ।

न च पितृभ्यः स्वद्योवाच्यतामिति कात्यायन-गोभिलादिभिरभिधानात् । न च श्रुतस्य पदस्योहः सम्भवति । न च पितरे तत्तेऽर्घ्यं पितामहे तत्तेऽर्घ्यं इत्यादौ मातामहादिपदोहः इति वाच्यम् । एतस्याभिलाप-मात्रपरत्वेन मन्त्रात्वाभावात् मन्त्रत्वे च 'शेषाणां मन्त्रवर्जितम्[2]' इत्युत्सर्गवाक्यस्यापि वर्जनप्रसंगात् ।

अयमेव विधिः प्रोक्तः शूद्राणां मन्त्रवर्जितः ।८।

इति वराहपुराणवचने च शूद्रस्योत्सर्ग-वाक्य-निषेधापत्तेश्च । तस्मादपौरुषेय ग्रन्थविशेष एव मन्त्रशब्दो मुख्योऽन्यत्र गौणः । 'शेषाणां मन्त्रवर्जितमिति' शेषाणां पितृव्यमातुलादीनामेकोद्दिष्टे ऊहयोग्य पितृपदवन्मन्त्र एव न प्रयोज्य न तूहः कर्तव्यः । न तु पितृपदरहितोप्यप्रयोज्योऽप्रवृत्तत्वात् ।

छन्दोगपरिशिष्टम् —

स पितुः पितृकृत्येषु अधिकारी[3] न विद्यते ।
जीवन्तमतिक्रम्य किंचिदद्यादिति श्रुतिः ॥९॥
पितामहे ध्रियमाणे पितुः प्रेतस्य निर्वपेत् ।
पितुस्तस्य च वृत्तः[4] जीवेच्चेत्[5] प्रपितामहः ॥१०॥
पितुः पितुः पितुश्चैव तस्यापि पितुरेव च[6]।
कुर्यात् पिण्डत्रयं यस्य संस्थितः प्रपितामहः ॥११॥
जीवन्तमपि दद्याद्वा प्रेतायान्नोदके द्विजः ।
पितृभ्यो[7] वा दद्यात् स पितेत्यपरा श्रुतिः ॥१२॥

पितृकृत्ये षुपिण्डपितृयज्ञपार्वणतर्पणादि षुजीवत्पितृकस्याधिकारो नास्ति । हेतुमाह । जीवन्तमिति

१. The text of हारीत is also quoted in पृथ्वीचन्द्र-*श्राद्धप्रकाश,* 20.63, p. 48 and *कृत्यकल्पतरु-श्राद्धकाण्ड,* p. 256.

2. This refers to *विष्णुस्मृति,* 75.7.

3. *कृत्यकल्पतरु-श्राद्धकाण्ड,* p. 239 reads अधिकारो for अधिकारी.

4. *Ibid.,* p. 239 reads वृद्धस्य for वृत्त; *बालंभट्टी-आचार,* p. 576 reads वृत्तस्य for वृत्तः .

5. *Ibid.,* p. 239 omits चेत्.

6. *Ibid,* p. 239 reads पितुः स नाम सङ्कीर्त्य कीर्तयेत् प्रपितामहम् before stanza No. 11a of our text.

7. *Ibid.,* p. 239 reads पितु before पितृभ्यो in stanza No. 12b.

जीवतोऽदत्वा किंचिन्न देयमित्येतादृशी श्रुतिरस्ति । पितामहे ध्रियमाणे इति सावधारणनिर्देशः । पितामह एव ध्रियमाण इत्यर्थः । पितुश्च प्रेतस्य निर्वपेत् । पितुरेव न जीवन्त पितामहमतिक्रम्य प्रपितामहस्यापीत्यर्थः ।

तथा हारीतः —

पितामहे[1] जीवे[2] वै पितर्येव समापयेत् । १३।

पितुर्जनकस्य । पितुः पितुः प्रपितामहस्येत्यर्थः। एतेन जीवन् पित्रादित्रय एव पिण्डत्रयं कुर्यादिति पक्षः । पक्षान्तरमाह । जीवन्तमतिदद्याद्वा इति हेतुमाह । स पिता पितुः पितृभ्यो दद्यादित्यपरा श्रुतिरस्ति।

यतः अतः एव हारीतः —

जीवे[3] पितरि वै पुत्रः श्राद्धकालं विवर्जयेत् ।
येषां वापि पिता दद्यात्तेषामेके[4] प्रचक्ष्यते[5] ।।१४।।

नन्वेवं विरोधः स्यात् । उच्यते। पूर्ववचननित्याधिकारः नि षेधार्थमुत्तरवचनमुपकारकत्वेनानावश्यकर्तव्यतापरम् । अथवा पतित प्रव्रजित जीवत्पितृकवि षयं उत्तरवचनम् ।

अत एव कात्यायनः[6]—

ब्राह्मणादि हते[7] जाते पतिते संगवर्जिते ।
व्युत्क्रमाच्च मृते देयं येभ्य एव ददात्यसौ[8]।।१५।।

आदिशब्दाच्चण्डालादीनां ग्रहणम् । पतिते ताते जीवत्यपि संगवर्जिते प्रव्रजिते जीवतीत्यर्थः। व्युत्क्रमादुदरभेदादिनादृते पुत्रजन्मादिनिमित्त वृद्धिश्राद्धवि षयं वा उत्तरवचनम् । न तु पितुरशक्तौ तदनुज्ञावि षयमिति व्याख्यानं युक्तम् । तदानीमृत्तिकतुल्यत्वेनाधिकारात । एवं पितुराज्ञापक्षे पितुरेव मातामहपक्षाधिकारे स्वमातामह इति विशे षः ।

हारीतः—

जीवे[9] पितरि वै पुत्रः श्राद्धकालं विवर्जयेत् ।
येषां वापि पिता दद्यात्तेषामेके[10] प्रचक्ष्यते[11] ।।१६।।

---

1. *कृत्यकल्पतरु-श्राद्धकाण्ड,* p. 237 reads च before जीवे and after पितामहे.
2. *पृथ्वीचंद्र-श्राद्धप्रकाश,* XIX.20, p. 461 and निर्णयसिंधु, p. 502 read जीवति वै for जीवे वै.
3. *बालंभट्टी-आचार,* p. 576 reads जीवेत् for जीवे.
4. *कृत्यकल्पतरु-श्राद्धकाण्ड,* p. 237 reads ००एव for ००एके.
5. *Ibid.*, p. 237 reads प्रचक्षते for प्रचक्ष्यते.
6. The text of *कात्यायन* is quoted in *मिताक्षरा* on *याज्ञवल्क्यस्मृति,* I.253-54 and *पृथ्वीचन्द्र-श्राद्धप्रकाश,* XIX.30, p. 465.
7. *बालंभट्टी-आचार,* p. 574 reads ब्राह्मणाभिहते for ब्राह्मणादि हते.
8. *Ibid.*, p. 574 reads 15b as येभ्य एव पिता दद्यात्तेभ्यो दद्यात् स्वयं सुतः ।
9. *Ibid.*, p. 576 reads जीवेत् for जीवे.
10. *कृत्यकल्पतरु-श्राद्धकाण्ड,* p. 237 reads ००एव for ००एके.
11. *Ibid.*, p. 237 reads प्रचक्षते for प्रचक्ष्यते.

पितामहे जीवे वै पितर्येव समापयेत् ।
उदकाञ्जलिं[1] प्रदीपं[2] च अञ्जनं च प्रयत्नतः ॥१७॥

व्याख्यातार्थमिदं उदकाञ्जलिमिति पिण्डाङ्गसामग्रीप्रदर्शनार्थम् ।

यज्ञपार्श्वपरिशिष्टम्[4] —

होमान्तः पितृयज्ञः स्याज्जीवे पितरि नामतः[4]।
पितरं भोजयित्वा तु पिण्डौ विवृणुयात्[5] परावितिं[6]॥१८॥
येभ्यः पिण्डान् पिता दद्यात् तेभ्यः पुत्रोऽपि दापयेत् ।
न जीवन्तमपि दद्यात्[7] इत्येषा नैगमी श्रुतिः ॥१९॥
जीवेत् पितामहो यस्य पिता चान्तरितो भवेत् ।
पितुरेकस्य दातव्यमेवमाहुर्मनीषिणः ॥२०॥
त्रीन् वा पिण्डान् समारोप्य मध्यमन्त्रेन[8] भोजयेत् ।
द्वौ[9] पिण्डौ निवृणुयात् पूर्वो[10] भोजयेत् प्रपितामहम् ॥२१॥
ब्राह्मणे[11] दद्यात् अग्नाम्भसि[12] वा क्षिपेत् ।
उभौ यदि[13] व्यतीतौ तु जीवेच्चेत् प्रपितामहः ॥२२॥
पिण्डौ निर्वृणुया[14] पूर्वो[15] भोजयेत् प्रपितामहम् ॥२३॥

होमाजीवतृ पित्रदीनान्मतदन्तोष्ठीवत् मात्रं कर्तव्यम् । नान्नोत्सर्गं पिण्डदानादिकं कर्तव्यमित्यर्थः । व्यक्तमपरम् ।

निगमः[16] —

1. *कृत्यकल्पतरु-श्राद्धकाण्ड,* p. 237 reads च after उदकाञ्जलिम्.
2. *Ibid.,* p. 237 reads दीपं for प्रदीपम्.
3. The text of *यज्ञपार्श्वपरिशिष्ट* is quoted in *कृत्यकल्पतरु-श्राद्धकाण्ड,* p. 238 and *निर्णयसिंधु,* p. 499.
4. *कृत्यकल्पतरु-श्राद्धकाण्ड,* p. 238 reads जानतः for नामतः.
5. *Ibid.,* p. 238 reads निपृणुयात् for विवृणुयात्.
6. *Ibid.,* p. 238 omits ०इति.
7. *Ibid.,* p. 238 reads ०अतिदद्यात् for ०अपि०.
8. *Ibid,* p. 238 reads मध्यमं तेन, for मध्यमन्त्रेन which is corrupt.
9. *Ibid.,* p. 238 reads द्वौ before पिण्डौ. Here some lines are dropped in our manuscript.
10. *Ibid.,* p. 238 reads पूर्वां for पूर्वो which is corrupt.
11. *Ibid.,* p. 238 reads द्वौ पिण्डौ before ब्राह्मणे.
12. *Ibid.,* p. 238 reads अग्नौ चाम्भसि for अग्नाम्भसि.
13. *Ibid.,* p. 238 reads यस्य for यदि.
14. *Ibid.,* p. 238 reads निपृणुयात् for निर्वृणुया.
15. *Ibid.,* p. 238 reads पूर्वां for पूर्वो.
16. The text of *निगम* is quoted in *कृत्यकल्पतरु-श्राद्धकाण्ड,* p. 238.

यो वा जीवति पितॄणान्तं[1] भोजयेत् स्वपिण्डस्थाने[2] इत्येके । जीवतामजीवतां च देयमिति[3] हिरण्यकेतुः । तथा कस्मिन्नपि जीवत्यदानमित्यपि[4] कात्यायनः । पिण्डस्थान इत्यनेन पिण्डेन देयस्तत् स्थाने भोजनपात्रं विधीयते । जीवतामित्यनेन जीवतामपि पिण्डादिकमुत्सृज्य देयमिति हिरण्यकेतुराह । एतच्च शाखिभेदव्यवस्थितम् । पितृपितामह-प्रपितामहाधिकारे आश्वलायनगृह्यपरिशिष्टं न परेभ्यो नाधिकारान्न प्रत्यक्षं न जीवेभ्यो निवृणुयात् । न जीवान्तरितेभ्यो जुहुयात् जीवेभ्यः सर्वहुतं सर्वजीवनो नामान्यविद्वांस्तत् पितृ-पितामह-प्रपितामह इति न परेभ्यो न जीवतः पित्रादेः परेभ्यः न प्रत्यक्षः न जीवतीत्यर्थः । न जीवेभ्यो निवृणुयात् न जीवान्तरितेभ्य इति श्रुतिरिति शेषः । कर्तव्यमाह जुहुयाज्जीवेभ्यः जीवन्तां होमः कर्तव्य इत्यर्थः । सर्वजीविनः पित्रादिजीविनः सर्वहुतं त्रयाणां होम इत्यर्थः । नाम्नोऽज्ञानेऽमुकपितृपितामह प्रपितामह इति कृत्वा दद्यात् निवृणुयान्निर्वपेत् । तदेषः संक्षेपः ।

जीवति पितरि चत्वारः पक्षाः । एकः पितृकृत्यानधिकारः । पितामहादीनां दातव्यमित्यपरः । पितरं भोजयित्वा पितामह प्रपितामहयोर्देयः इति भट्टभाष्यः । होममात्रं कर्तव्यमिति भट्टरत्नाकरः ।

पितृमात्रोपरतौ चत्वारः पक्षपितुरेवदेयमिति नारायणोपाध्यायः । पित्रे दत्वा पितामह-प्रपितामहौ भोजनीयौ । होमो वा पित्रे दत्वा प्रपितामहात् परं द्वाभ्यां देयमिति कमलाकरभट्टः[5]। पितृपितामहौ परस्तावपि चत्वारः पक्षाः । पितृपितामहयोर्देयमिति गोविन्दभट्टः । तयोर्दत्वा प्रपितामहौ यौ जानीयौ होमो वा तयोर्दत्वा प्रपितामहपित्रे देयमिति सर्वनिगमः । पितामहमात्रे जीवत्यपि चत्वारः पक्षाः । पितृपितामहयोर्देयम् । पितृपितामहयोर्दत्वा पितामहो भोजनीयः । तयोर्दत्वा प्रपितामहपित्रे देयम् । होमो वा पितामहस्य ।

---

1. *कृत्यकल्पतरु-श्राद्धकाण्ड*, p. 238 reads पितॄणां तं for पितॄणान्तम्.
2. *Ibid.*, p. 238 reads सपिण्डानित्येके for स्वपिण्डस्थाने इत्येके.
3. *Ibid*, p. 238 and *निर्णयसिंधु*, p. 499 read ०एव० for देयमिति.
4. *Ibid.*, p. 238 gives a more elaborate quotation from कात्यायन.
5. This view comes near to the *निर्णयसिन्धु*, p. 499.

३१

अथ अभ्युदयश्राद्धम्

हारीतः[1]—

मृते पितरि वै पुत्र पिण्डं[2] समाचरेत् ।
अन्नं कुम्भं च विप्राय प्रेतनिद्देश[3] धर्मतः ॥१॥

पिण्डदानमिदं शाखिभेदव्यवस्थितम् । पिण्डमप्येके निगृणन्ती[4]ति पारस्कर (३.१०.५५) दर्शनात् । प्रेतनिर्देशत इति प्रेतशब्दोच्चारणं कर्तव्यमिति हलायुधव्याख्यानमयुक्तम् । सपिण्डीकरणत्वात् । प्रेतकृत्यस्य प्रेतशब्दोच्चारणस्य प्राप्तत्वात् । वस्तुतस्तु प्रेतनिर्देशः प्रेतैकोद्दिष्टं तद्धर्मातस्तद्धर्मातिदेशः कार्यः इत्यर्थः । नन्वतिदेशप्राप्तार्थबाधः कुतः? पिण्डनिषेधादर्घबाध इति चेन्न । हेत्वभाववति मघाश्राद्धेऽप्यर्घ निषेधापत्तेः । न नित्यं तावत् प्रवक्ष्यामि । अर्घ्यावाहनवर्जितमिति मत्स्यपुराणवचनात् । नित्यश्राद्धमदैवं स्यात् । अर्घपिण्डनिषेधात् । अम्बुघटमपि नित्यश्राद्धमेव अहरहः क्रियमाणत्वात् ।

तथा भविष्यपुराणम् —

अहन्यहनि यत् श्राद्धं तन्नित्यमित्यभिधीयते[5] ।२।

ये त्वम्बुघटस्य श्राद्धत्वं नेच्छन्ति ये निरस्ताः । हारीतपारस्करादिभिः श्राद्धप्रकरणे पाठात् प्रागुक्तलक्षणाक्रान्तत्वाच्च । पिण्डदानश्रुतेः अत्र सर्वेष्वेव वचनेष्वम्बुघटस्य च स्वातन्त्र्येणोपादानात् । स्वतन्त्र्योरेवोत्सर्गवाक्ये निवेशः । एषोऽम्बुघटः एतदन्नमित्येवं रूपं सर्वत्रैवाम्बुघटदानश्रुतेर्घटस्याप्युत्सर्गः ।

पारस्करः — (३.१०.५४.५५)

अहरह हवनमस्मै[6] ब्राह्मणायान्नं[7] च दद्यात् । पिण्डमप्येके निगृह्णन्ति ददातीत्यर्थः ।

अम्बुघटश्राद्धफलमाह मत्स्यपुराणे (१८.२६)

---

1. The text of *हारीत* is quoted in the *कृत्यकल्पतरु-श्राद्धकाण्ड*, p. 252.
2. *Ibid*., p. 252 reads पिण्डमब्दे for पिण्डं which is metrically defective.
3. *Ibid*., p. 252 reads प्रेतनिर्देश for प्रेतनिद्देश.
4. *Ibid*., p. 252 reads निगृह्णन्ति for निगृणन्ति.
5. *Ibid*, p. 6 reads कीर्तितं for अभिधीयते.
6. *Ibid*., p. 252 reads अहरहरन्नमस्मै for अहरह हवनमस्मै.
7. *Ibid*., p. 252 reads ०उदकुम्भं for ०अन्नम्.

यावदब्दं च यो दद्यादुदकुम्भं विमत्सरः ।
प्रेतयान्नं[1] समायुक्तं सोऽश्वमेधफलं लभेत्[2]॥३॥

तथा पठन्ति —

प्रेतलोके च वसतिर्नृणां वर्षं प्रकीर्तितम् ।
क्षवृष्टे प्रत्यहं तत्र भवति भृगुनन्दनः ॥४॥
तदर्थमिह दातव्यं जलान्नमिह वत्सरम् ॥५।

याज्ञवल्क्यः (१.२५५)

अर्वाक् सपिण्डीकरणं यस्य संवत्सराद्भवेत् ।
तस्यान्नं[3] सोदकुम्भं दद्यात् संवत्सरं[4] द्विजे[5]॥६॥

संवत्सरादर्वाक् सपिण्डीकरणं वृद्धयादि निमित्तेनेति वक्ष्यति । सपिण्डीकरणान्त प्रेतश्राद्धापकर्षेऽन्यापकर्षप्राप्तौ वचनम् ।

उशना[6] —

एकोद्दिष्टं न कुर्वीत न्यासिनां चैव सर्वदा ।
अहन्येकादशे प्राप्ते पार्वणं तु विधीयते ॥७॥
सपिण्डीकरणं तेषां न कर्तव्यं सुतेन वै ।
त्रिदण्डग्रहणादेव प्रेतत्वं नैव जायते ॥८॥

अत्र प्राञ्चः —

व्यासोक्त नारायणबलिदानं यतीनां कर्तव्यम् ।

उदकानर्हाणां चाण्डालादिहतानां व्यासेन तथा विधानात् । यतेवप्युदकानर्हत्वात् ।

तथा मनुः — (५.८९)

वृथा संकरजातानां प्रव्रज्यासु च तिष्ठताम् ।
आत्मनस्त्यागिनां चैव निवर्तेतोदकक्रिया ॥९॥

आदिपुराणे[7]—

त्रयाणामाश्रमाणां च[8] कुर्याद्दाहादिकां क्रियाम् ।
यतेः किंचिन्न कर्तव्यं न चान्येषां करोति सः ॥१०॥

---

1. *मत्स्यपुराण*, p. 32 reads प्रेतायान्नसमायुक्तं for प्रेतायान्नं०.
2. Grammatically this may be emended as लभेत.
3. *याज्ञवल्क्यस्मृति*, reads तस्याप्यन्नं for तस्यान्नम्.
4. *Ibid.*, reads वर्षं for संवत्सरम्.
5. *Ibid.*, reads द्विजन्मने for द्विजे.
6. This text of *उशनस्* is not found in the *स्मृतिसंदर्भ*, Vol. III.
7. The text of *आदिपुराण* is ascribed to *विष्णुपुराण* by *कृत्यकल्पतरु-श्राद्धकाण्ड*, p. 266.
8. *Ibid.*, p. 266 reads तु for च.

बलिदानमाह व्यासः —

शुक्लैकादश्यां दशपिण्डान् दद्यात्

तद् यथा —

प्रथमे विष्णवे दत्वा ब्रह्मणे व शिवाय च ।
यमाय परिवाराय चतुर्थं पिण्डमुत्सृजेत् ॥११॥
मृतसंकीर्त्य मनसा गोत्रपूर्वमतः परम् ॥१२॥

तन्न । उशनोवचने न्यासिनां विशेषतः पार्वणविधानात् उदकानर्हता सामान्येन नारायणबलिदानकल्पनायोगात् । किं च यतेर्दाहक्रियानिषेधदि शब्देन दशपिंडदाननिषेधात् प्रेतत्वभावेन प्रेतकारीरपूरकपिण्डदानयोगाच्च । ननु नैष्ठिकानां यतीनां नियतात्मनां नाशौचं कीर्त्यते । सद्भिः पतिते च तथा मृते कूर्मपुराणे[1] वचने —

नाशौचाभावादेकादशे श्राद्धं निर्मुक्तिकम् ।
सत्यं यतीनां वचनादेवेति ब्रूमः ॥१३॥

अत एव सद्यः शौचेऽपि कर्तव्यं श्राद्धमेकादशेऽहनीति पठितमेताद्विषयमेव अस्मादेव वचनात् । प्रत्यब्दिकमपि यतीनां पार्वणविधिनैव कार्यम् । ननु प्रव्रजितस्य पार्वणानिषेधः । श्रूयते यथाशक्तौ कालान्तरमपि द्रष्टव्यमिति तात्पर्यार्थः । एतेन पूर्वोक्तकालानां मुख्यत्वं दर्शितम् । अथवा अनावश्यकवृद्धिनिमित्तेन षोडशापकर्षानकार्य इति तात्पर्यम् ।

मरीचिः [2]

मुख्यं श्राद्धं मासि मासि अपर्याप्तावृत्तं प्रति ।
द्वादशाहेन वा कुर्यादैकाहे द्वादशाथवा ॥१४॥

मासि मासि श्राद्धं कर्तव्यमिति मुख्यः कल्पः । अपर्याप्तसामर्थ्ये तु प्रति ऋतुर्मासद्वयं तेन प्रतिमासं श्राद्धकरणासामर्थ्ये मासद्वयेन श्राद्धं कर्तव्यम् । तन्नाप्यशक्तौ द्वादशभिर्दिनैर्मासिकश्राद्धानि कार्याणि । तदसंभवे एकेन दिनेन द्वादशश्राद्धसमाप्तिम् ।

छन्दोगपरिशिष्टं कात्यायनः[3]

पितामहपिण्डः पश्चात् पञ्चत्वं यदि गच्छति ।
पौत्रेणैकादशाहादि कर्तव्यं श्राद्धषोडशम् ॥१५॥
नैतत्पुत्रेण कर्तव्यं पुत्रवांश्चेत् पितामहः ॥१६॥

पितृमरणात् पश्चात् यदि पितामहमरणं भवति तदा पौत्रैणैकादशाहादि श्राद्धं षोडशं कर्तव्यम् ।

1. This stanza, however, is untraced in the critical edition of *कूर्मपुराण*.
2. This text of *मरीचि* cannot be traced.
3. This text of *छन्दोगपरिशिष्टं कात्यायनः* cannot be traced.

षोडशमिति विशेषणं जीवत्यपि पितरि पितामहमरणे षोडशवर्थ[1]हिर्भूतपार्वणाद्यनुज्ञानार्थं तेनोभयथैव पौत्रस्य पार्वणाधिकारः । षोडशश्राद्धाधिकारे विशेषे पितृमरणानन्तरं पितामहे मृते षोडशश्राद्धप्राप्तेः पुत्रवत्यप्राप्तत्वान्नैतत् पौत्रेणेति निषेधोऽनुपपन्न एव सज्ज[2] जीवत्पुत्रस्य पौत्रेण श्राद्धषोडशं कर्तव्यमित्येवं लक्षणम् । स च प्राप्तत्वानुविधेयः ।

उच्यते । पितृव्यसद्भावे पौत्रस्य षोडशश्राद्धानधिकार ज्ञापनार्थमिति सर्वमनुपपन्नम् ।

1. This word is corrupt.
2. This word appears to be corrupt.

३२

अथ एकोद्दिष्टम्

तस्य कालमाह छन्दोगपरिशिष्टं कात्यायनः[1]—

श्राद्धमग्निमतः कार्यं दाहादेकादशेऽहनि ।
ध्रुवाणि तु प्रकुर्वीत प्रमीताहनि सर्वदा ।।१।।

तदवधिना तस्याशौचस्मरणात् ।

यथा शंखः[2]—

मरणादेव कर्तव्यं संयोगो यस्य नाग्निना ।
दाहादूर्ध्वमशौचं स्यात् यस्य वैतानिको विधिः ।।२।।

अत्राग्नि वैतानिकग्रहणाच्छ्रौतोऽग्निपरम् । वैतानिकः श्रौतहोमः । एकादशेऽहनीत्यशौचान्तोपलक्षणन् । अथाशौच व्यपगमे सुस्नात इत्यादि विष्णुवचन[3] (२१.१)

क्षतादि सूतकान्ते तु भोजयेदयुतो द्विजान् ।३।

इति मत्स्यपुराण[4]वचनाभ्यामेकवाक्यत्वात् । अतः क्षत्रियदीनामप्यशौचान्त एव श्राद्धं कर्तव्यं नैकादशाहे । एवं वक्ष्यमाणान्यप्येकादशाहश्राद्धविधायकानि च नान्यशोचान्तपराण्येव । प्रमीताहनीति मृततिथावपराण्यपि श्राद्धानि कर्तव्यानि । तानि ध्रुवाणि । नित्यानि प्रमीताहनि सर्वदेत्यनेन प्रेतसंस्कारकानि श्राद्धानि स्वकाल एव कार्याणीति दर्शयति । प्रेतसंस्कारकाणि षोडशश्राद्धानि गणयति द्वादशप्रतिमास्यानीति । ननु मासि भवं मास्यम् । न च मासिकश्राद्धं तथा अतीते मासि एकत्रिंशद्दिने मृताहे क्रियमाणत्वात् ।

अत एवैकोद्दिष्टमभिधाय विष्णुः[4]—(२१.११)

एवं मृताहे प्रतिमासं कुर्यात् ।

---

1. This text is quoted in *कृत्यकल्पतरु-श्राद्धकाण्ड*, p. 251.
2. This stanza cannot be taced in *स्मृतिसंदर्भ*, Vol. III.
3. This is *विष्णुस्मृति*, p. 345.
4. This is *मत्स्यपुराण*, quoted in *कृत्यकल्पतरु-श्राद्धकाण्ड*, p. 244.
5. This is *विष्णुस्मृति*, p. 348.

अत्र महार्णवोपाध्याय:[1]—

मासेन निमित्तेन अन्तरतिथौ क्रियत इति मास्यशब्दव्युत्पत्ति: । एवं त्रैपक्षिक सांवत्सरिकादीनां न एवमेकाहे न तु षण्मासा इत्यनेन मृताहपूर्वदिने षण्मासिकानुपपत्ते: ।

अनन्तभट्टस्तु एवं मृताहे प्रतिमासं कुर्यादिति बहुवचने ।

मृताहनि[2] त कर्तव्यं प्रतिमासं तु वत्सरम् ।४।

याज्ञवल्क्यवचने (१.२५६अ) एकादिनाधिके माससंवत्सरप्रयोगात् दण्डिन्यायात् अजहत्स्वार्थलक्षणया एकदिनाधिकमाससंवत्सरपरत्वम् । माससंवत्सरयोरिति तच्चिन्त्यम् । द्वितीयादि मासानामेकादिनाधिकत्वसंभवात् । तिथिवृद्धिह्रासाभ्यां तदसंभवात् । किन्तु त्रिंशत्तिथ्यात्मकश्चान्द्र एव ।

तथा च

सूर्यसिद्धान्त:[3]

तत् त्रिंशता भवेन्मास:[4] सावनार्को दोष[5]स्तथा ।
ऐन्द्रव तिथि[6]स्तावत्[7] संक्रान्त्या[8] सौर उच्यते ।।५।।

अत एव तिथिनैकेन दिवसश्चान्द्रमाने प्रकीर्तित इति प्रागुक्तम् । तेन मृततिथि यावच्चान्द्रं मृततिथेरित्यवधौ पञ्चमी । एवं मृताहे प्रतिमासमिति वचनात् अनन्तमृततिथे: पूर्वमासशब्दार्थत्वं न पूर्वतिथेरुत्तरमास शब्दार्थता । अतो न विरोध: । आद्यमेकादशाह श्राद्धषाण्मासिक कालमाह एकाहेनत्विति । एकाहन्यूने षण्मासशब्दो गौण: । एवं चतुर्थाह त्रैपाक्षिक द्वादशाहानां षोडशश्राद्धान्तमान: ।

त्रैपक्षिकमुक्तं ब्रह्मपुराणे (२२०.६४)

सूतकान्ते गृह[9]श्राद्धमेकोद्दिष्टं प्रचक्षते ।
द्वादशेऽहनि मासे च त्रिपक्षे च तत: परम् ।।६।।

त्रैपक्षिकग्रहणे प्रातश्चित्ताच्च[10] तदपि सिद्धम् ।

यथा शंख:[11] —

---

1. This view cannot be traced.
2. *याज्ञवल्क्यस्मृति*, p. 91 reads मृतेऽहनि for मृताहनि.
3. This text is quoted in पृथ्वीचन्द्र-*श्राद्धप्रकाश*, XX.35, p. 473.
4. *Ibid.*, p. 473 reads ०मासो for ०मास: .
5. *Ibid.*, p. 473 reads ००दयै:० for ००दोष:०.
6. *Ibid.*, p. 473 reads ऐंदवास्तिथिभि: for ऐन्दव तिथि: .
7. *Ibid.*, p. 473 reads तद्वत् for तावत्.
8. *Ibid.*, p. 473 reads संक्रान्तौ for संक्रान्त्या.
9. *ब्रह्मपुराण*, p. 1302 reads गृहे for गृह.
10. This may be emended as प्रायश्चित्ताच्च for प्रातश्चित्ताच्च.
11. The text of शंख cannot be traced in *स्मृतिसंदर्भ*, Vol. III.

चांद्रायणं नवश्राद्धं[1] पराको मासिको मतः ।
पक्षत्रयेति कृच्छ्रः स्यात् षण्मासे कृच्छ्र एव हि[2]॥७॥
आब्दिके पादकृच्छ्रः स्यादेकाहः पुनराब्दिके ।८।

तथा च पठन्ति —

त्रैपक्षिकं त्रिपक्षे तु वृत्ते स्यात्तदनन्तरम् ।९।

ब्रह्मपुराणे [3] —

नृणां च[4] त्यक्तदेहानां श्राद्धः षोडशसंख्यया ।
चतुर्थे पञ्चमे चैव[5] नवमेकादशे[6] तथा ॥१०॥
ततो द्वादशभिर्मासैः श्राद्धा द्वादशसंख्यया ।
कर्तव्या शुचिभिस्तेषां तत्र विप्रांस्तु तर्पयेत् ॥११॥

श्राद्धा इति पुल्लिंगं छान्दसः । एतच्च षोडशश्राद्धं शाखिभेदे व्यवस्थितम् ।

बौधायनः [7]—

एकादश्यां द्वादश्यां वा श्राद्धकर्म ।

वा शब्दः समुच्चयार्थः । एकादशाहश्राद्धमभिधाय द्वितीयेऽह्नि पुनस्तदेकोद्दिष्टं समाचरेदिति वक्ष्यमाणमत्स्यपुराणवचनात् । यज्जिकाले[8]नोक्तं विकल्पार्थोऽयं वा शब्दः । अत एव श्राद्धमेकं दिनद्वय इति पठन्ति । तत् प्रत्युक्तम् ।

पैठीनसिः [9]—

मृतस्य मासिकश्राद्धं[10] कुर्वीत संवत्सरान्ते विसर्जनम् । नवमास्यमित्येके ।

पारिजातादयः—

विसर्जनं सपिण्डीकरणं नवमे मासि च सपिण्डीकरणमशक्तविषयम् ।

यमः[11]

---

1. *A.B.O.R.I*, Vol. VIII, p.126, reads नवश्राद्धे for नवश्राद्धं.
2. *Ibid.*, p.126, reads तु for हि.
3. This is quoted in पृथ्वीचन्द्र-*श्राद्धप्रकाश,* XX.26, p. 471. Also *कृत्यकल्पतरु-श्राद्धकाण्ड,* p. 251.
4. *Ibid.*, p. 471 reads तु for च.
5. *कृत्यकल्पतरु-श्राद्धकाण्ड,* p. 251 reads वाऽथ for चैव.
6. *Ibid.*, p. 251 reads नवमैकादशे for नवमेकादशे, which is corrupt.
7. The text of *बौधायन* cannot be traced in extant *बौधायन धर्मसूत्र.*
8. Is it possible to emend this as यज्जिकनेनोक्तम् ?
9. The text of *पैठीनसि* is quoted in *कृत्यकल्पतरु-श्राद्धकाण्ड,* p. 252.
10. *Ibid.*, p. 252 reads मासि मासि० for मासिक०.
11. The text of *यम* cannot be traced in the extant *यमस्मृति.*

चतुर्थी पंचमे चैव नवमैकादशे तथा ।
यदत्र दीयते जन्तोस्तन्नवश्राद्धमुच्यते ॥१२॥
यस्य सञ्चयनादर्वागाहिताग्नेर्द्विजन्मनः ।
अयुग्मान् भोजयेद्विप्रान् तन्नवश्राद्धमुच्यते ॥१३॥

पञ्चमे नवमे च श्राद्धं प्रेतोपकारार्थम् अनावश्यकम् । नवश्राद्धसंज्ञा एतदग्रहायणप्रायश्चितप्रदर्शनार्थः । आहिताग्नेरस्थिसंचयनादर्वाक् श्राद्धान्तरमस्तीति दर्शितम् । षोडशश्राद्धानां प्रमाणमभिहितम् ।

फलमाह देवलः[1]—

एकादशादिभिः श्राद्धैर्मृतस्याप्यायनं चरेत् ।
सम्यक् संवत्सरे पूर्णे पितॄणां स्थानमृच्छन्ति ॥१४॥

अप्यायनं तुष्टिः । प्रेतः शरीरपरिहारः । संवत्सरे पूर्णे इति संवत्सरविहित सपिण्डनस्य पितृत्वप्राप्तिफलमित्यर्थः । एतेन प्रेतत्व परीहारः[2]। षोडशश्राद्धफलं पितृलोकप्राप्तिः । सपिण्डनस्येत्युक्तम् । प्रेतत्वपरीहारमिति व्यक्तफलमाह यमः[3]।

यस्यैतानि न दीयन्ते प्रेतश्राद्धानि षोडश ।
पिशाचत्वं ध्रुवं तस्य दत्तैः श्राद्धशतैरपि ॥१५॥

शंखः[4]—

ततः श्राद्धमशुद्धौ तु कुर्यादेकादशे तथा ।
कर्तुस्तात्कालिकी शुद्धिरशुद्धः पुनरेव सः ॥१६॥

अशुद्धौ चतुर्थाहादौ तथैकादशे कर्तव्यम् । कथमशुद्धौ श्राद्धं शोचस्याधिकारिविशेषणत्वं कालशौचाधिकारे दर्शितमित्याह । कर्तुस्तात्कालिकी शुद्धिरिति श्राद्धविधानाक्षेवापात्त[5] मात्रनिष्ठा शुद्धिः कल्प्यते । न पुनरशुद्धकर्मान्तर इति शेषः ।

व्याघ्रः [6]—

एकादशे चतुर्थे च मासि मासि च वत्सरम् ।
प्रतिसंवत्सरश्चैव एकोद्दिष्टं मृताहनि ॥१७॥

संवत्सरं व्याप्य मासि मासि कार्यमित्यर्थः ।

1. The text of देवल is quoted in *कृत्यकल्पतरु-श्राद्धकाण्ड*, p. 252.
2. This may be emended as परिहारः .
3. This text of *यम* cannot be traced in the extant *यमस्मृति*.
4. The text of *शंख* cannot be traced.
5. The expression ००क्षेवापात्त appears to be corrupt.
6. This stanza No. 17 from the text of *व्याघ्र* is not found in the manuscript of *व्याघ्रस्मृति*, edited by me.

मत्स्यपुराणे[1]—

तत्रै[2]कादशाहे तु द्विजानैकादशैव तु ।
क्षत्रियादि:[3] सूतकान्ते तु भोजयेदयुजो द्विजान् ॥१८॥
द्वितीयेऽह्नि पुनस्तत्वदेकोद्दिष्टं[4] समाचरेत् ।१९।

एकादशाद्विभोजनं फलातिशयार्थम् । एकादशाहे श्राद्धं न क्षत्रादिविषयमित्याह । क्षत्रादिरिति क्षत्रादि पुनरशौचान्ते श्राद्धं कुर्यात् । अन्तशब्दः समीपवचनः ।

अत एव विष्णुः — (२१.१)

अथाशौच व्यपगमत[5] इति ।

एकादशाहे श्राद्धविधायकानि यानि वचनानि तानि ब्राह्मणविषयकानि अशौचान्तोपलक्षकानि वा मत्स्यपुराणवचनैकवाक्यत्वात् । न च मुख्यैकादशाहे चातुर्वर्ण्यं श्राद्धविधायकानि मत्स्यपुराण विष्णुपुराणवचनविरोधात् । किं च —

राज्ञां च दशमः पिण्डौ द्वादशेऽहनि दीयते ।
वैश्यस्य पञ्चदशमे ददातु दशमं तथा ॥२०॥
शूद्रस्य दशमः पिण्डो मासे पूर्णेऽह्नि दीयते ।२१।

इत्यादि पुराणवचनात् ।

पिण्डःशूद्राय दातव्यो दिनान्यष्टौ न वाथवा ।
संपूर्णे तु ततो मासे पिण्डशेषं समापयेत् ॥२२॥

इति प्रचेतोवचनाच्च ।

द्वादशपञ्चदशत्रिंशद्दिनेषु क्षत्रियवैश्यशूद्राणां दशमपिण्डदानमवगतेषामप्यशौचान्त एव श्राद्धयुज्यते । एवं चैकादशाहश्रुतेरशौचान्तोपलक्षकत्वे त्र्यहैकादशाहाशौचेप्यशौचान्त एव । श्राद्धान्तेन मुख्यदशाह एव दशमपिण्डदानं समाप्य चतुर्भिरेव वर्णैः संपूर्णत्र्यहैकाहा[6]शौचिभिरेकादशाह एवं ॱॱद्धं निवर्त्त्यत इति प्राचामाचारो दुराचारो निष्प्रमाणक एव ।

इदानीमेकोद्दिष्टेतिकर्तव्यतामाह ।

एकोद्दिष्टं तु यच्छ्राद्धं तन्नैमित्तिकमुच्यते ।
तदप्यदैवकं कर्तव्यमयुग्मान् भोजयेद्द्विजान्[7] ॥२३॥

1. The text of *मत्स्यपुराण* is quoted in *कृत्यकल्पतरु-श्राद्धकाण्ड*, p. 244.
2. *Ibid.*, p. 244 reads तत॰ for तत्र॰.
3. *Ibid.*, p. 244 reads क्षत्रादि for क्षत्रियादि: .
4. *Ibid.*, p. 244 reads ॰तद्वत्॰ for ॰तत्वत्॰.
5. *विष्णुस्मृति,* p. 245 reads व्यपगमे for व्यपगमत.
6. This expression appears to be corrupt. It may be emended as ॰॰एकादशाह॰ for ॰॰एकाह॰.
7. The stanza No. 23 in quoted from *भविष्यपुराण* in *कृत्यकल्पतरु-श्राद्धकाण्ड,* p. 6.

अदैवं कर्तव्यमिति अप्राप्तदैवश्राद्धनिषेधानुपपत्त्या दर्शपौर्णमासधर्मातिदेशवत् ।

कात्यायन: —

एकोर्घ्य: एकं पवित्रं एक: पिण्डो नावाहन: । नाग्नौकरणं नात्र विश्वेदेवा: स्वादितमिति प्रश्न: सुस्वदितमित्यनुज्ञया तं उपतिष्ठतामित्यक्षय्य स्थानेऽभिरम्यतामिति विसर्गोऽस्मिन् तस्म इत्यवरे ।

नन्वेवं पवित्रमित्यत्र न पवित्रविधि: । अतिदेशात्तत् प्राप्तावप्राप्तप्रापकत्वलक्षणस्य विधिद्वयस्यायोगात् । अतिदेशत: प्राप्ते विलंबितत्वात् द्वादग्र[1] तत्र चोपदेशस्य विधित्वमिति चेन्न । यत्र तद्विधित्वमनपेक्ष्यान्यत: प्राप्ति: पश्चादपि स्यात् । न तत्र विधित्वमिति । तदर्थशास्त्रादि दर्शितत्त्वात् । अप्राप्तप्रापको विधिरित्यत्रौक्तप्रत्ययस्य अविवक्षित भूतकालत्वात् । न चातिदेशातपवित्रषट्क प्राप्तावेपत[2]द्विधि: । एककरणसाध्ये एकोद्दिष्टपूर्वे एककरणधर्माकांक्षाया एकस्यैव पवित्रस्यातिदेशतो लाभात् । अत एवाष्टमिक विकृत्याधिकरणे[3] सौर्यं चरूं निर्वपेत् ब्रह्मवर्चसकाम इत्यत्र षट्ककरणसाध्य दर्शपौर्णमासापूर्वस्यैककरण धर्मातिदेश: उक्त: । एतत् सिद्धान्तन्यायमूला पवित्रैकत्वस्मृतिरिति चेन्न । तथापध्यैकत्वात् । पवित्रैकत्वप्राप्तौ विधित्वं न स्यात् । न च पवित्रशब्देन स्वावयवभूत कुद्ध[4]लक्षणा कार्या । अनुपपत्यभावात् न च दले मुख्यत्वं विशिष्टद्विदलवाचित्त्वात् पवित्रशब्दस्य ।

यथा छन्दोगपरिशिष्टम् —

अनन्तगर्भिनं साग्रं कोशं द्विदलमेव च ।
अप्रदेशमात्रं विज्ञेयं पवित्रं यत्र कुत्रचित् ॥२४॥

उच्यते । यत् एतत् वैयर्थ्यं स्यात् । अत एव पवित्रशब्दो लक्षणया उच्यते । किं च प्रकृते विधौ मन्त्रे च पवित्रशब्दस्य दले प्रवृत्तत्वात् निरूढलक्षणेयम् । निरूढलक्षणा च मुख्यतुल्येत्युक्तं सपिण्डमधिकरणे ।

तथा च प्रकृते गोभिल: —

तत एव बर्हिष: प्रादेशमात्रे पवित्रे कुरूते ओषधिमन्तर्धाय छिनत्ति । न नरवेव पवित्रे स्थो वैष्णव्याविति । अथैते अद्भिरनुमाष्टि विष्णो मनसा पूतेस्थ इति । अत्रापि सांकेतिक पवित्रपरत्वमिति चेन्न । पवित्रे कुरुते इति विधौ छेदनादि मन्त्रे च द्विवचनानुपपत्ते: प्रादेशविधानानर्थक्याच्च । पारस्करोप्यर्थवदुपस्तीर्य पवित्रे कृते इति दर्भपरतैव कुतो न भवतीति चेन्न । बर्हिष इति षष्ठ्या अवयवावयविसम्बन्धप्रतीते: । अनन्तगामित्व साग्रत्वादय: परिशिष्टवचनावलभ्यन्ते । होमप्रकरणपठितमिदं पार्वणे पात्रेषु पवित्रान्तर्हितेषु इत्येतावन्मात्रमेव श्रूयते इति चेन्न । आकांक्षया पार्वणे होमांगपवित्रधर्मातिदेशात् । इतरथा तन्न सांकेतिकपवित्रधर्मानुष्ठाने मार्जनमन्त्रछेदनमन्त्रादीनामनुष्ठानं न स्यात् । अतिदेशपरम्परागतदलरूपपवित्रप्राप्तौ तद्विधित्वस्यापि प्राप्तत्वात्तद्बाधेनदलगत एकत्वमेकोद्दिष्टे विधीयते इति कल्पतरुकार:[5]। तन्न । होमविधौ मन्त्रे पवित्रस्य द्विवचनानुरोधेन श्रुतिबलादेकोद्दिष्टेऽपि दलगतैकत्वं विधीयते । अन्यथा पार्वणादौ तु प्रत्येकं पुरूषं एकदलगतविशिष्टग्रहणं स्यात् । अन्यच्च

1. This expression द्वादग्र is corrupt.
2. This expression is corrupt.
3. This has a reference to *जैमिनि कृत पूर्वमीमांसा,* XI.1.38-39.
4. This expression is corrupt.
5. The view of *कल्पतरु* cannot be traced in *कृत्यकल्पतरु-श्राद्धकाण्ड.*

अनन्तगामिनं साग्रं कौशं द्विदलमेव च ।
प्रादेशमात्रं विज्ञेयं पवित्रं यत्र कुत्रचित् ॥[1] २५॥

एवकारस्वरसात् यत्र कुत्रचिदित्युपादानात्[2] सर्वेषु श्राद्धादिषु ज्ञेयम् ।

श्रुतिरपि पार्वणैकोद्दिष्टे चरुपाककरणे द्विदलवाचि पवित्रं मुख्यं मुधपर्कादौ च इति होवाच । तथा च मृगयजुषां आश्वलायनशाखायां द्वौ दर्भौ पवित्रे समूलौ सामग्रौ दर्भद्वयमान्नमत्रपवित्रमित्यर्थः । यथा बहुतरदुर्वातण्डुलादिभिरर्घ्यं क्रियते । मुख्यत्त्वात्तस्याप्येकत्वस्यावगतेरिति महाभाष्यप्रभृतिभिः । एकदलस्य विशिष्टकर्मणि न तात्पर्यग्राहकं भवति इति भट्टनारायणः । लिंगसंख्याकालश्च तेस्त्राणि भवन्तीति न्यायात्।

'एतद्वः पितरो वास' इति[3] लिंगसंख्यादि गौणमेवाचरणामिति वक्ष्यति । अत एवास्माभिरप्येवं मतमनुसरणीयम् ।

मिश्रास्तु मधुपर्कादौ पवित्रमन्तरेणार्घशब्दप्रयोगाज्जलकुसुमगन्धादि युक्त एवार्घशब्दार्थः ।

तथा कात्यायनः —

सपवित्रेषु हस्तेष्वित्यभिधायायासावेषतेऽर्घं इति पवित्रसहितमेवार्घमाह । अतः कथं पवित्रकत्वे प्राप्ति तन्नाष्टांगप्यर्घे गन्धपुष्पं विना अर्घशब्दप्रयोगात् ।

तथा ब्रह्मपुराणे[4]—

एषतेऽर्घ[5] इति प्रोक्ता तेभ्यो दद्यात्तथ[6]ष्टधा ।
जलं क्षीरं दधिघृतं तिलतण्डुलसर्षघान्[7]॥२६॥
कुशाग्राणि च सर्वाणि[8] दत्वा चामेत्ततः[9] परम्[10]।२७।

भविष्यपुराणे—

आपः क्षीरं कुशाग्राणि दध्याज्यमधुतण्डुलाः ।
तिलाश्च सर्षपाश्चैव अर्घोऽष्टांग प्रकीर्तितः ॥२८॥

तस्माज्जलमेवार्हणार्ह द्रव्यसहितमर्घशब्दार्थः । तच्च द्रव्यं विधानानुसारात् त्र्यभ्यं पार्वणे च

1. The source of this stanza cannot be traced.
2. This may be emended as उपादानात्.
3. *कृत्यकल्पतरु-श्राद्धकाण्ड*, p. 215 quotes the complete stanza as —
   यथेहं पुरुषं तं च मन्त्रं जप्त्वा कृताञ्जलिः ।
   एतद्वः पितरो वास वासस्त्विति जल्पन् पृथक् पृथक् ॥ from *ब्रह्मपुराण*.
4. The text of *ब्रह्मपुराण* is quoted in *कृत्यकल्पतरु-श्राद्धकाण्ड*, p. 152.
5. *Ibid.*, p. 152 reads ०अर्घ्यं for ०अर्घम् .
6. *Ibid.*, p. 152 reads ०अथ० for ०तथा०.
7. *Ibid.*, p. 152 reads ००सर्षपाः for ०सर्षघान्, which is corrupt.
8. *Ibid.*, p. 152 reads पुण्यानि for सर्वाणि.
9. *Ibid.*, p. 152 reads दत्वाऽऽचामेत्० for दत्वाचामेत्ततः
10. *Ibid.*, p. 152 reads स्वयं for परम्.

पवित्रविधानात् सपवित्रार्घोऽतिदेशप्राप्तौ विकृतावनूद्यते । प्राप्त्यनुसारित्वादनुवादस्येति । अन्यथा

नित्यश्राद्धमदैवं स्यादर्घपिण्डविवर्जितम् ।२९।

इति । अर्घवाधे पवित्रवाधो वा न स्यात् । सपवित्रेष्वित्यत्र हस्तस्थ पवित्रसहितस्यैवार्घस्योत्सर्गः । अभिरिता स्म इत्यु[1]परेमोक्त ब्राह्मणा ब्रूयुरिति शेषः ।

षोडशश्राद्धाधिकारे ब्रह्मपुराणे —

भवद्भिः स्वदितं कश्चिदिति चामन्त्रयेत् द्विजान् ।
सुस्वदितमिति विप्राः प्रीतयोऽक्षय्यमस्तु ॥३०॥

इति सुस्वदितमितिः तृप्ताः स्थ ।

प्रश्नस्थाने कार्यमेकोद्दिष्टे मत्स्यपुराणे[2] —

स्वदितं विकिरे कुर्याद्विसर्गे चाभिरम्यताम् ।३१।

विकिरे विकरणे सतीत्यर्थः ।

आश्वलायनगृह्यपरिशिष्टम्[3]—

प्रेतश्राद्धेषु[4] सर्वेषु न स्वधामभिरम्यताम्[5]।
स्वस्त्यस्तु विसृजेदेवं सकृत् प्रणववर्जितम्[6]॥३२॥
एकोद्दिष्टस्य पिण्डेषु[7] अन्[8] शब्दो न युज्यते ।
पितृशब्द न युञ्जीत[9] पितृहा चोपजायते ॥३३॥

न स्वधेति न स्वधावाचन कुर्यादित्यर्थः[10]। न च हविस्त्यागादिवाक्येषु स्वधापर निषेध इति हलायुधवचनमादरणीयम् । स्वधोच्यतामिति वाचं विसृजेदित्याश्वलायनगृह्योक्तेः नाभिरम्यतामिति बह्वृचधर्मोऽयं बह्वृचानामेव प्राप्तत्वेन निषेधोपपत्तेः ।

तथा पार्वणे हारीतः —

अभिरम्यतामित्येके । अभिरम्यतामिति विसर्गः इति कात्यायनविरोधाच्च । प्रेतैकोद्दिष्टविषयमिदं

1. This line is quoted from the text of *हारीत* in *कृत्यकल्पतरु-श्राद्धकाण्ड,* p. 204.
2. *कृत्यकल्पतरु-श्राद्धकाण्ड,* p. 245 quotes this line from *मत्स्यपुराण.*
3. *Ibid,* p. 245 quotes *आश्वलायन गृह्यपरिशिष्टं* with slight variations.
4. *Ibid.,* p. 245 reads **एकोद्दिष्टेषु** for **प्रेतश्राद्धेषु**.
5. *Ibid.,* p. 245 reads स्वधा नाभिरम्यताम् for स्वधामभिरम्यताम्.
6. *Ibid.,* p. 245 reads ०वर्जितः for ०वर्जितम्.
7. *Ibid,* p. 245 reads पिण्डे तु for पिण्डेषु.
8. *Ibid.,* p. 245 reads अनु for अन्.
9. *Ibid.,* p. 245 reads कुर्वीत for युञ्जीत.
10. This explanation agrees well with that of *कृत्यकल्पतरु-श्राद्धकाण्ड,* p. 245.

परिशिष्टवचनम् । कात्यायनादिवचनमितरैकोद्दिष्टविषयमिति — कल्पतरु:[1]। तदसत् । अभिरम्यतामिति विसर्जनमभिधाय एतत् प्रेतश्राद्धमिति गोभिलेनाभिधानात् ।

किं च बृह्वृचानामेव पार्वणेऽभिरम्यतामित्यनेन प्राप्तत्वाद्विसर्जनस्य सर्वशाखिगोचरनिषेधानुपपत्ते: । अत: शाखिभेदव्यवस्थितोऽयं प्रेतश्राद्धेष्वभिधानात् । कथं सांवत्सरिकादौ निषेध इति चेदतिदेशादिति ब्रूम: । एवं स्वधावाचननिषेधोऽपि अनुशब्दो ये चात्र एवेति मन्त्रोपलक्षणार्थ: । पितृशब्दं न प्रयुञ्जीतेति सम्बन्धकीर्तनपरमिदमिति रत्नाकरभट्टादय: । तन्न । एवमनुशब्दवत् सांवत्सरिकेऽपि पितृपदनिषेधापत्ते: । प्रेतश्राद्धे पितृपदवन्मन्त्रप्रयोग कार्य इति हलायुध: । नातिदेशात् सांवत्सरिकेऽपि तन्निषेधापत्ते: । वस्तुतस्तु एतत् प्रेतश्राद्धमिति वचनात् प्रेतपदत्वेन देवतत्वात् पितृपदस्थाने प्रेतपदविधानात् । उत्सर्गवाक्ये मन्त्रे च पितृपदनिवृत्तिरिति न्यायमूलमिदं वचनमतो न सांवत्सरिके तत्प्रसंगे । अत एव प्रेतपिण्डोऽप्यस्य विषय: ।

विष्णु: — (२१.१-११)

अथाशौच व्यपगमे सुस्नात: सुप्रक्षालित पाणिपाद आचान्त[2]स्त्वेवं विद्वान्[3] ब्राह्मणान् यथाशक्ति उदङ्मुखान् गंधमाल्यवस्त्रालंकारादिभि: पूजितान् भोजयेत् । एकवन्मन्त्राहे[4]तैकोद्दिष्टे । उच्छिष्टसन्निधावेकमेव तन्नामगोत्राभ्यां निर्वपेत्[5] । भुक्तवत्सु विप्रेषु दक्षिणयाति[6]पूजितेषु प्रेतनामगोत्राभ्यां दत्ताक्षय्योदकेषु[7] चतुरङगुलपृथ्वीस्तावदन्तरा च[8] तथा च[9] स्वातीवितस्त्यायता[10]स्तिस्र: कर्ष्णु:[11] कुर्यात् । कर्षूसमीपेऽग्नित्रयमुपाधाय[12] परिस्तीर्य तथैकस्मिन्नाहुतित्रयं जुहुयात् । सोमाय पितृमते स्वधा नम: । अग्नये कव्यवाहनाय स्वधा नम: । यमाय अंगिरसे स्वधा नम: । स्थानत्रये[13] प्राग्वत् पिण्डनिर्वपनं[14] कुर्यात् । ततो[15] दधिमधुघृतमांसै: कर्षूत्रयं पूरयित्वा एतत्तु[16] इति जपेत् । एवं मृताहे प्रतिमासि[17] कुर्यात् ।

अथाशौचे व्यपगमे इति सर्वेषां वर्णानामेकाहाद्यशौचेप्यशौचान्ते श्राद्धं दशयति ।[18]

---

1. This view of *कल्पतरु* is traced in *कृत्यकल्पतरु-श्राद्धकाण्ड*, p. 245.
2. *विष्णुस्मृति*, p. 345 reads स्वाचान्त:०० for आचान्त:००.
3. *Ibid.*, p. 345 reads विधानेव for विद्वान्.
4. *Ibid.*, p. 345 reads ००अनूहेत्० for ००अहेत० which is corrupt.
5. *Ibid.*, p. 345 reads पिण्डं before निर्वपेत्.
6. *Ibid.*, p. 347 reads ०अभि० for ०अति०.
7. *Ibid.*, p. 347 reads ००उदक: for ००उदकेषु.
8. *Ibid.*, p. 347 omits च.
9. *Ibid.*, p. 347 drops तथा च.
10. *Ibid.*, p. 347 reads तावदध: खाता: वितस्त्यायता: for स्वातीवितस्त्यायता: which in corrupt.
11. *Ibid.*, p. 347 reads कर्षू: for कर्ष्णु: which is corrupt.
12. *Ibid.*, p. 347 reads ००उपसमाधाय for ००उपाधाय.
13. *Ibid.*, p. 348 reads च after स्थानत्रये and before प्राग्वत्.
14. *Ibid.*, p. 348 reads निर्वपणं for निर्वपनम्.
15. *Ibid.*, p. 348 drops ततो and reads अत्र in place of ततो.
16. *Ibid.*, p. 348 reads एतत्त० for एतत्तु०.
17. *Ibid.*, p. 348 reads प्रतिमासं for प्रतिमासे.
18. These comments of कुल्लूक on *विष्णुस्मृति*, XXI.1 substantially differ from the comments of नन्दपण्डित in his *केशववैजयन्ती*, p. 345. Here it may be noted that this section on एकोद्दिष्ट is repeated in the manuscript and from herewards the matter differs. Hence that matter will be treated as an additional section.

एकोदिष्टम्-अ[1] ।

सुस्नातः शिरस्नातः । एवंविधान् पङ्क्तिपावनादीन् मन्त्रान् बहुवचनान्तानेकवचनस्वमृहैत[2] विकृतान् कुर्यात् । एकस्मिन् पितरि बहुवचनस्यामवेतार्थत्वात् । अप्रकृतावर्थप्रकाशनाख्य दृष्टप्रयोजनस्य मन्त्रस्य विकृतौ बहुवचनस्य स्थाने एकवचनस्योहः कार्य इति न्यायमूलमिदं वचनम् । अत एव 'एतद्वः पितरौ वास'[3] इति मन्त्रस्य बहुवचनस्य स्थाने नैवोह इति प्रकृतावेकैकत्र पित्रादौ प्रयुक्तस्य तथानर्थकत्वात् ।

तथा ब्रह्मपुराणे —

एतद्वः पितरो वासः इति जल्पन् पृथक् पृथक् ।१।

अत एव दैक्षेपशावककवचान्तः पाशमन्त्रो बहुवचनान्तः श्रुतस्तत्रैकवचनान्तस्य प्रकृतावर्थवत्त्वात् । द्विकापाशिकायां[4] विकृतौ द्विवचनोहः कार्यः । बहुवचनान्तस्य प्रकृतावपि नोहः । किन्तु बहुवचनान्तस्यैव प्रयोग इत्युक्तः ।

बृहस्पतिः[5]—

एकोद्दिष्टविधानेन यद्येकस्य[6] प्रदीयते ।
आवाहनाग्नौकरणरहितं दैववर्जितम् ॥२॥
वस्त्रालंकारशय्याघ्यं[7] पितुर्यद्वाहनायुधम् ।
गन्धमल्यैः समभ्यर्च्य श्राद्धमेतत्तर्पयेत्[8] ॥३॥
भोजनं चानेकविधिस्कारयेभ्यञ्जनानि च[9]।
यथाशक्तया प्रदद्याच्च् गोभूहेमादिकं तथा ।।४।
तृतीया[10] भोजनीयास्तु नवसप्त[11]त्रयोदश ।
ज्ञातयो बान्धवा निःस्वास्तथा चातिथयोऽपरे ॥५॥

---

1. The portion of this chapter is copied doubly in the manuscript by a scribe. Hence the portion that is common to both the chapters is included in the previous chapter. And the matter that is uncommon is treated as additional chpters 'अ' and 'ब'. Here chapter 'अ' is started.
2. The expression ऋहेत appears to be corrupt.
3. This मन्त्र is quoted from the *ब्रह्मपुराण* in the *कृत्यकल्पतरु-श्राद्धकाण्ड*, p. 215.
4. This expression appears to be corrupt.
5. The text of *बृहस्पति* is quoted in *कृत्यकल्पतरु-श्राद्धकाण्ड*, p. 246.
6. *Ibid.*, p. 246 reads यदेकस्य for यद्येकस्य.
7. *Ibid.*, p. 246 reads ०००आद्यं for ०००अघ्यम्.
8. *Ibid.*, p. 246 reads श्राद्धभोक्ते तर्पयेत् for श्राद्धमेतत्तर्पयेत्।
9. *Ibid.*, p. 246 reads चानेकविधं कारयेद्व्यञ्जनानि च for चानेकविधिस्कारयेभ्यञ्जनानि च which is corrupt.
10. *Ibid.*, p. 246 reads श्रोत्रिया for तृतीया.
11. *Ibid.*, p. 246 reads ०सप्तं० for ०सप्त०.

प्रदद्याद्दक्षिणां तेषां सर्वेषामनुरूपत: ।
हतमश्रोत्रियं श्राद्धं हतोयज्ञ[1]स्त्वदक्षिण:[2]।।६।।
तस्मात्पणं काकिनीं[3] वा फल[4]पुष्पमथापि वा ।
प्रदद्यात् दक्षिणां५ यज्ञे तथा स सफलो[5] भवेत् ।।७।।

गोभूहेमादिकमपि श्राद्धदक्षिणा । भोजनीयास्त्वित्यनेन भोज्यं दानमुक्तं प्रदद्यादित्यनेन दक्षिणा भोज्ये विहिता । काकिनी पणतुरीयांशा: । फलं पुष्पमथापि वा इत्यनेन यद्यप्यानतीकरी दक्षिणा तथापि तदशक्ता-वदृष्टार्थापि दक्षिणा देयेति दर्शितम् ।

एकोद्दिष्टमभिधाय वराहपुराणे[7]—

अयमेव विधि: प्रोक्त: शूद्राणां मन्त्रवर्जित: ।
अमन्त्रस्य तु शूद्रस्यतु विप्रो[8]मन्त्रेण गृह्यते ।।८।।

अयमेव श्राद्धविधि: शूद्राणामुक्त: किन्तु मन्त्ररहित: । मन्त्रजन्यादृष्टसिद्धिस्तु सामान्यप्राप्तनमस्कारेण ।

यथा शूद्राधिकारे गौतम: — (१०.६३)

अनुमतो[9]ऽस्य नमस्कारो मन्त्र: ।

अनुष्ठेयप्रकाशनं तु ब्राह्मणपठितमन्त्रादित्याह । विप्रो मन्त्रेण गृह्यते संबध्यत इत्यर्थ: । अमन्त्रस्य शूद्रस्येति परिभाषेयम् । न च परिभाषा प्रकरणेन नियम्यते । तेन शूद्रस्य स्नानदानदानादावपि ब्राह्मणेन मन्त्र: पठनीय: । अन्यथा प्रकरणादेकोद्दिष्ट एव ब्राह्मणस्य मन्त्रपाठ: स्यात् । न पार्वणादौ ।

अत एव

पित्रे तु द्विगुणा दर्भा इति कात्यायनवचनं न प्रकरणश्राद्धमात्रविषयम् । किन्तु परिभाषात्वात् पितृकृत्यमात्रविषयम् । अमन्त्रस्येति विशेषणोपादानं यावदमन्त्रव्यापनार्थम् । तेन स्त्रिया अपि क्रियमाणे श्राद्धे ब्राह्मणस्य मन्त्रपाठस्तुल्यन्यायात् । यदार्थप्रकाशनाख्यदृष्टमनुक्रमस्य ध्यानादिना भवति, तदा मन्त्रपाठेन काचित् क्षति: । ब्राह्मणपाठमन्त्रस्य अदृष्टमात्रजनकत्वात् । अदृष्टस्य नमस्कारेण जनितत्वात् ।

'विप्रौ[10] मन्त्रेण गृह्यते' इति पाठे उपविष्टब्राह्मणेन मन्त्र: पठनीय: । ब्राह्मणान्तरपाठस्य प्रतिनिधित्वमेति ।

---

1. *कृत्यकल्पतरु-श्राद्धकाण्ड,* p. 246 reads हतायज्ञा: for हतोयज्ञ: .
2. *Ibid.*, p. 246 reads ०००अदक्षिणा: for अदक्षिण: .
3. *Ibid,* p. 246 reads काकिणी for काकिनीम्.
4. *Ibid.*, p. 246 reads फलं००० for फल००० but below we find the reading फलम्.
5. *Ibid.*, p. 246 reads दक्षिणां for दक्षिणा.
6. *Ibid.*, p. 246 reads समफलो for स सफलो.
7. This stanza could not be traced in the *वराहपुराण* brought out under *Bibliotheca Indica Series.*
8. We have another reading विप्रौ for विप्रो in the gloss of *कुल्लूक* on the text of *वराहपुराण.*
9. *गौतम धर्मसूत्र* p. 175 reads अनुज्ञात:० for अनूमत:०.
10. In the stanza No. 8 we have the reading विप्रो for विप्रौ.

अत्र हरिदेवभट्टाः —

वैदिकमन्त्रपाठनिषेधोऽयम् । पौराणिकमन्त्रस्तु शूद्रेण पठनीय एव ।

यथा पद्मपुराणे —

न हि वेदेष्वधिकारः कश्चित् शूद्रस्य विधीयते ।
पुराणेष्वधिकारिभिर्दर्शितो ब्राह्मणैरिह ॥९॥

न एतस्य सूताधिकारप्रतिपादकत्वात् । सूतस्य संस्कारजातित्वेन शूद्रान्यत्वात् ।

यथा याज्ञवल्क्यः (१.९३अ)

'ब्राह्मण्यां क्षत्रियात् सूत' इति यत्रानुलोमस्याधिकारस्तत्र शूद्रस्य सुतरामिति न्यायाच्छूद्रस्याधिकार इति वचनान्यस्य दुर्बलत्वात् ।

यथा पुराणमधिकृत्य भविष्ये —

अध्येतव्यं न चान्येन ब्राह्मणं क्षत्रियं विना ।
श्रोतव्यमिह शूद्रेण नाध्येतव्यं कदाचन ॥१०॥
तथा श्रौतं च स्मार्तं च वैधव्यं प्रोक्तमस्मिन् नरोत्तम ।
तस्माच्छूद्रैर्विना विप्रं न श्रोतव्यं कदाचन ॥११॥

किं च प्रतिलोमजत्वेऽपि सूतस्य विशिष्टतेजोमयत्वात् अधिकारो युक्तः ।

अत एव शूद्रापुत्रस्यापि विदुरस्य धर्मोपदेशकत्वं धर्मावतारदेहत्वादुपपन्नम् । तपोबलविहीनानां दुर्वाचां संकरजातीनां शूद्राणां वा कथमधिकारो भवतु ।

तथा आपस्तम्बः[1]—

तेषां च विधानतः चक्रे द्वादशिकं श्राद्धं त्रयोदशिकमेव च ।

ततश्चोदिश्य पितरं ब्राह्मणेभ्यो धनं ददौ ।
महार्णानि च रत्नानि गाश्च वाहनमेव च ॥१२॥
यानादि दासी दासांश्च वेश्मनि च महान्ति च ।
भूषणानि च मुख्यानि राज्ञस्तस्योर्ध्वदेहिके ॥१३॥

दशाहग्रहणमशौच कालोपलक्षणार्थम् । द्वादशिकं द्वादशाहेन निर्वृत्तं त्रयोदशाहे विधेयमित्यर्थः । एवं त्रयोदशिकं चतुर्दशाहे विधेयं और्ध्वदेहिकश्राद्धे ।

अत एव राजधर्मे वसिष्ठः (१९.२९.३०)

---

1. This passage cannot be traced in *आपस्तम्ब धर्मसूत्र,* possibly the stanza Nos. 12 and 13 are quoted from *आपस्तम्ब-स्मृति.*

राजनि[1] प्रेते दद्यात् । प्रासंगिकमेतेन मातृपितृ[2]वृद्धि[3] व्याख्याता ।

प्रसंगो विषयोपभोगः । तदर्थं शय्यासनादिप्रासंगिकं मातापित्रोर्वृद्धि मातापित्रोरपि श्राद्धं प्रासंगिकशय्यासनादि दानेन वर्द्धयितव्यम्[4]।

देवलः[5]—

> एकोद्दिष्टस्य[6] शेषं च ब्राह्मणेभ्यः समुत्सृजेत् ।
> पश्चात्[7] स्वयं च भुञ्जीत पुनर्मंगलभोजनम् ॥१४॥

पुनर्मंगलभोजनं एकोद्दिष्टशेषं प्राश्य पुनः पाकान्तरेण भोक्तव्यम् । प्रेतश्राद्ध[8] शेषस्यामांगलिकत्वात्। अत्रैकोद्दिष्टे हुतशेषभावात् तदंगकं समन्त्रकपात्रालम्भनबाधः । अंगत्वं च कात्यायन-गोभिलयोर्हुतशेषं दत्वा पात्रमालभ्य जपति इति श्रुतिदर्शनात् । उपनीयाध्यापयेदितिवत् तथा मृतं जुहोमि इति मन्त्रलिंगाच्च हुतशेषांगत्वं अमृतं हुतशेषमित्यर्थः । संग्रवग्रहणन्युब्जीकरणेन च न कर्तव्ये पिधानपात्राभावेन संश्रवरक्षणस्य कार्यस्याभावात् । न पात्रमालभ्य जपति नाशिषः प्रार्थयेदिति । प्रचेतोनाम्नालिखितवचनान्नाशिषः प्रार्थनमिति वदन्ति मैथिलरत्नाकरगौडवाचस्पतिभट्टाचार्याः ।

एकोद्दिष्टम् ब[9] ।

न मृत सं र्य[10]पुत्रदुहितृविषयत्वादभ्युदयशब्दस्य महागुरौ प्रेतीभूते कथं वृद्धिश्राद्धार्थं कर्मेत्याकांक्षायामपकर्षवचनम् । न च भ्रातु मातामहगुरुसपिण्डस्य वा सपिण्डः ।

ननु वृद्धौ वृद्धिश्राद्धार्थं सपिण्डनस्यापकर्षः पितृत्वभावेन तत् पितृपदेन देवतात्वसंभवात् । तदा च मातृसपिण्डनापकर्षो निर्युक्तिकः । छन्दोगव्यतिरिक्तानां मातुरपि वृद्धिश्राद्धे अन्तर्भावोऽस्तीति चेन्न। छन्दोगानामपकर्षप्रसंगात् ।

न महागुरौ प्रेतीभूते वृद्धिकार्यं न युज्यते इति वृद्ध्यर्थमेव सपिण्डनाय कर्षपूर्वोक्त गोभिल-लघुहारीतवचनेष्ववगम्यते । न वृद्धिश्राद्धार्थम् ।

---

1. *वसिष्ठ धर्मसूत्र,* p. 56 reads च after राजनि and before प्रेते.
2. *Ibid.*, p. 56 drops पितृ.
3. *Ibid.*, p. 56 reads वृत्तिः for वृद्धि.
4. This explanation of कुल्लूक differs from that of *बालंभट्टी-आचार,* p. 622.
5. The text of *देवल* is quoted in the *कृत्यकल्पतरु-श्राद्धकाण्ड,* p. 225.
6. *Ibid.*, p. 225 reads एकोद्दिष्टेषु for एकोद्दिष्टस्य.
7. *Ibid.*, p. 225 reads ततः for पश्चात्.
8. This may be emended as प्रेतश्राद्धम्.
9. This is an additionl chapter 'ब' to the एकोद्दिष्टम् of the manuscript. The chapter on एकोद्दिष्टम् is found doubly copied. Hence whatever portion is uncommon to chapter 'अ' is presented here as chapter 'ब'.
10. This expression is corrupt and lacking in some letters.

किं च

एकादशाहं निर्वर्त्य अर्वाग् दर्शनात् यथाविधि ।
प्रकुर्वीत अग्निमान् पुत्रो मातापित्रोः सपिण्डनम् ॥१॥

इति छन्दोगपरिशिष्टवचने पिण्डपितृयज्ञार्थं मातृसपिण्डनापकर्षोऽवगम्यते । अतः सिद्धं वृद्ध्यर्थं मातापित्रोः सपिण्डनापकर्ष इति साग्नेः पुत्रस्य पितृयज्ञोप्यकर्षनिमित्तमित्याह जाबालः[1]।

नासपिण्डाग्निमान्[2] पुत्रः पितृयज्ञं समाचरेत् ।
पापी भवत्यकुर्वन्[3] हि पितृहा चोपजायते ॥२॥
सपिण्डीकरणं कुर्यात् पूर्णे दर्शेऽग्निमान् सुतः ।
परतो दशरात्रस्य पूर्णेऽब्दे तथेतरः ॥३॥

अकरणे निन्दावदन् पितृयज्ञस्यावश्यकतामाह । पापी भव्तीति अशौचापगमे दर्शात् प्राक् सपिण्डनं साग्निना सुतेन कार्यमित्याह । सपिण्डीकरणमिति इतरोऽनग्निः पूर्णेऽब्दे कुर्यात् बैजवापः ।

अथ सपिण्डीकरणं संवत्सरमेकं पिण्डमुद्दिश्य समाप्ते संवत्सरे चत्वार्युदकपात्राणि प्रयुनक्ति । तत्रैकं प्रेताय त्रीणि पितृभ्यः प्रेतपात्रं पितृपात्रेष्वासिञ्चति ये समाना इति द्वाभ्यामेवं पिण्डानामथाष्टिपि[4]मिभृषति । एष वोनुगतः प्रेतः पितरस्तं दधामिव । शिवमास्त्विति शेषाणां जायन्तां चिरजीविनः समानीव धीहृतिः समाना हृदयानिव समानमस्तु । वो मनो यथावः सुसहासत इति । संगच्छध्वं संवदध्वं संनो मनांसि जानतां देवामागं यथापूर्वे संजानान्य उपासन इति । अभिशप्तपतित भूणघ्नः[5] स्त्रीं व्यभिचारिणीं मादिशेत्[6]।

ऋध्यर्थं शातातपः[7]—

पितृनेवाशयेत्तत्र पुनः प्रेतं च निर्दिशेत् ।
निरूप्य चतुरः पिण्डान् पिण्डदः पितृनामतः[8]॥४॥
ये समाना इति[9] द्वाभ्यामाद्यस्तु[10] विभजेत् त्रिधा ।
एष[11] एव विधिः पूर्वमर्घपात्रचतुष्टये ॥५॥
आसिञ्चेत् पितृपात्राणि प्रेतपात्रेषु[12] मन्त्रवित् ।६।

---

1. The text of *जाबाल* is quoted in *पृथ्वीचन्द्र-श्राद्धप्रकाश,* XXI.9, p. 490.
2. *Ibid.*, p. 490 reads नासापिण्डयाग्नि(मान्) for नासण्डाग्निमान्.
3. *Ibid.*, p. 490 reads ०कुर्वन् for ०अकुर्वन्.
4. This expression appears to be corrupt.
5. This word is corrupt.
6. This may be emended as व्यभिचारिणीमादिशेत् for व्यभिचारिणीं मादिशेत्.
7. The text of *शातातप* is quoted in *कृत्यकल्पतरु-श्राद्धकाण्ड,* p. 253.
8. *Ibid.*, p. 253 reads प्रतिनामतः for पितृनामतः .
9. *Ibid.*, p. 253 reads समानामिति for समाना इति.
10. *Ibid.*, p. 253 reads ०आद्यं तु for ०आद्यस्तु.
11. *Ibid.*, p. 253 reads एकः for एषः .
12. *Ibid.*, p. 253 reads प्रेतपात्रेण for प्रेतपात्रेषु.

पितृनेव इत्येवकारोमातामह इति कैयटभट्टः । तदसंगतम् ।

प्रेतविप्रस्यहस्ते तु चतुर्भागं जलं क्षिपेत् ।७।

इति ब्रह्मपुराण[1]विरोधात् । पुनःशब्दस्य का गतिरति चेत् । श्राद्धार्थनिर्देशमात्रस्य वृत्तिरिति ब्रूमः । विशेषस्य प्रेतश्राद्धस्यावृत्तिः । पक्षान्तरेऽपि नास्ति आश्वलायनगृह्यसूत्रम् ।

1. The text of ब्रह्मपुराण is quoted in कृत्यकल्पतरु-श्राद्धकाण्ड, p. 256.

३३

अथ श्राद्धाधिकारिण:

अथाधिकारिणो निरूप्यन्ते —

मृते पितरि पुत्रेण क्रिया कार्या विधानत: ।
बहव स्युर्यदा पुत्रा: पितुरेकत्रवासिन:।।[1]१।।
सर्वेषां तु मतं कृत्वा ज्येष्ठेनैव तु[2]यत् कृतम् ।
द्रव्येण चाविभक्तेन सर्वैरेव कृतं भवेत् ।।२।।

पुत्रेणत्यविशेषात् सपिण्डदत्तकेन सर्वेषां पुत्राणामधिकार: । पुत्रेणेत्येकवचनमविवक्षितम् ।

प्रमीतस्य पितु:[3] पुत्रै: श्राद्धं[4] देयं विधानत:[5]।३।

इति वक्ष्यमाण बृहस्पति[6]वचनात् । सर्वेषां पृथगनुष्ठानप्राप्तावाह । बहव: स्युरिति एकत्रवासिनोऽविभक्तधना: । एकत्रवासिन इत्यनेन प्राप्ते द्रव्येन[7] च अविभक्तेन इति ग्रहणम् । विभक्तधनानामपि श्राद्धीय द्रव्येन[8] अविभक्तेन पुन: कृतसंश्लेषणेनापृथगेव श्राद्धं दर्शितम् ।

अत एव शंख:[9]—

यद्येकजाता बहव: पृथक् क्षेत्रा: पृथक् जना:[10]।
एकपिण्डा: पृथक् शौचा: पिण्डं[11] त्वावर्तते त्रिषु ।।४।।

---

1. The stanza Nos. 1 and 2 are ascribed to *मरीचि* in *कृत्यकल्पतरु-श्राद्धकाण्ड*, p. 263.
2. *Ibid.*, p. 263 reads जेष्ठेनैकेन for ज्येष्ठेनैव तु.
3. *Ibid.*, p. 264 reads पिण्डं for पितु: which is also adopted by *पराशरमाधव-आचार*, p. 785.
4. *Ibid.*, p. 264 reads श्राद्धे for श्राद्धम्.
5. *Ibid.*, p. 264 and *पराशरमाधव-आचार*, p. 785 read प्रयत्नत: for विधानत: .
6. This is *बृहस्पति-श्राद्ध*, 150 quoted in *कृत्यकल्पतरु-श्राद्धकाण्ड*, p. 264.
7. This may be emended as द्रव्येण.
8. This may also be emended as द्रव्येण.
9. The text of *शंख* is quoted in the *कृत्यकल्पतरु-श्राद्धकाण्ड*, p. 263.
10. *Ibid.*, p. 263 reads ०धना: for ०जना: .
11. *Ibid.*, p. 263 and *A.B.O.R.I.*, Vol. VIII, p. 98 reads पिण्ड: for पिण्डम्.

पृथक् क्षेत्राः विजातीयमातृजाता[1]। एकपिण्डा एकमेव पिण्डं दद्युः इत्यर्थः । पृथक् शौचा विजातीयमातृसम्बन्धेन[2] पृथगशौचभागिनः । पिण्डं त्वावर्तते त्रिष्विति सपिण्डता त्रिषु पुरुषेषु एव भवतीत्यर्थः ।[3]

अतश्च विभक्तधनानां पुत्राणां सर्वामत्यापि[4]।

अन्नं दद्याच्च देवेन तीर्थेनैव[5] जपन् स्वधाम् ।५।
कच्चित् संपन्नमेतन्मेतान् पृच्छेत्[6] प्रहर्षितान्[7]।
सुसंपन्नं च ते ब्रूयुः सर्वं सिद्धि[8] ततः क्षिपेत् ॥६॥
नान्दीमुखेभ्यश्चाक्षय्यमिदमस्त्विति संश्चपन्[9]।
प्राङ्मुखा[10]स्त्वथदर्भांश्च[11] दद्यात् क्षीरावनेजनम् ॥७॥
दत्वानान्दीमुखेभ्यश्च प्राचीं गच्छेत्[12] दिशं क्रमात् ।
शाल्यन्नं दधिमध्वक्तं बदराणि यवास्तथा[13]॥८॥
मिश्रीकृत्य च चत्वारि पिण्डान् श्रीफलसंयुतान्[14] ।
दद्यान्नान्दीमुखेभ्यश्च पितृभ्यो विधिपूर्वकम् ॥९॥
अर्घ्यपुष्पं[15] च धूपश्च प्रशस्तमनुलेपनम् ।
वासश्चाप्याहतं[16] वस्त्रं[17] देयं च सदशं समम् ॥१०॥
द्राक्षामलकमूलानि यवांश्चाथ निवेदयेत् ।
तान्येव[18] दक्षिणार्थन्तु दद्यात् विप्रेषु सर्वदा ॥११॥
अथाक्षय्योदकस्थाने दत्वा क्षीरयवोदकम् ।
प्रपितामहसंज्ञाश्च[19] नान्दीमुखश्च[20] मातरः ॥१२॥

---

1. *कृत्यकल्पतरु-श्राद्धकाण्ड,* p. 263 reads ००जाताः for ००जाता.
2. *Ibid.*, p. 263 reads पृथक् शुद्धयः after ००सम्बन्धेन.
3. This explanation agrees substantially with that of *कृत्यकल्पतरु-श्राद्धकाण्ड*, p. 263.
4. This expression is corrupt.
5. *कृत्यकल्पतरु-श्राद्धकाण्ड,* p. 269 quotes this stanza from *ब्रह्मपुराण* and reads ०च for ०एव.
6. *Ibid.*, p. 269 reads च after पृच्छेत्.
7. *Ibid.*, p. 269 reads प्रहर्षयन् for प्रहर्षितान्.
8. *Ibid.*, p. 269 reads सर्वसिद्धिं for सर्वं सिद्धि which is corrupt.
9. *Ibid.*, p. 269 reads संजपेत् for संश्चपन which is corrupt.
10. *Ibid.*, p. 269 reads प्राङ्मुखांस्त्वथ for प्राङ्मुखास्त्वथ.
11. *Ibid.*, p. 269 reads दर्भास्तु for दर्भांश्च.
12. *Ibid.*, p. 269 reads गच्छन् for गच्छेत्.
13. *Ibid.*, p. 269 reads यवांस्तथा for यवास्तस्था.
14. *Ibid.*, p. 269 reads ०सन्निभान् for ०संयुतान्.
15. *Ibid.*, p. 269 reads अर्घं० for अर्घ्य०.
16. *Ibid.*, p. 269 reads ०००अहतं for ०००आहतम्.
17. *Ibid.*, p. 269 reads युग्मं for वस्त्रम्.
18. *Ibid.*, p. 269 reads तथैव for तान्येव.
19. *Ibid.*, p. 269 reads ०संज्ञेभ्यो for ०संज्ञाश्च.
20. *Ibid.*, p. 269 reads नान्दीमुख्यश्च for नान्दीमुखश्च.

मातामह्य[1] पितामह्य प्रपितामह्य एव च[2]।
प्रमातामहसंज्ञेभ्यो विद्वद्भिश्च[3] स्वधोच्यताम् ॥१३॥
अस्तु स्वधेति ते तत्र[4] जपन्ति[5] प्रसहाः[6] स्वयम् ।
विश्वेदेवाश्च प्रीयन्तामिति दत्वा[7] ब्रवीति च[8]॥१४॥
प्रीता भवन्ति[9] ते तत्र[10] जपन्ति[11] मधुराक्षरम् ।
येषामृषा[12]वाजिनमिति पठंस्तांस्तु[13] विसर्जयेत् ॥१५॥

जपन् स्वधामिति शाखिभेदव्यवस्थितम् । नवद्या प्रयुञ्जीतेति कात्यायन[14]-गोभिलदर्शनात् । सर्वं सिद्धस्ततः क्षिपेदित्यर्थं विकरणमुक्तम् । नान्दीमुखेभ्यश्चाक्षय्यमित्यपि शाखिभेदव्यवस्थितम् । नान्दीमुखाः पितरः प्रीयन्तामिति कात्यायनदर्शनात् । क्षीरावनेजनमिति फलातिशयार्थम् । अतः क्षिपेन्मूलदेश इति छन्दोगपरिशिष्टदर्शनात् । मातामहीशब्देन माता लक्ष्यते । स्वधोच्यतामस्तु स्वधेति स्वधावाचनं शाखिभेदव्यवस्थितम् । नान्दीमुखाः पितरः प्रीयन्तामिति पितॄनावाहयिष्ये इति पृच्छति नान्दीमुखाः पितरः पितामहाः प्रपितामहाश्च प्रीयन्तामिति न स्वधा प्रयुञ्जीतेति कात्यायनदर्शनात् ।

छन्दोगपरिशिष्टं कात्यायनः[15]

असकृत् यानि कर्माणि क्रियेव न[16] कर्मकारिणा[17]।
प्रतियोगं नैव स्युर्मातरः[18] श्राद्धमेव[19]॥१६॥
आपान[20]होमयोश्चैव वैश्वदेवे तथैव च ।
बलिकर्मणि दर्शे च पौर्णमासे तथैव च ॥१७॥

1. *कृत्यकल्पतरु-श्राद्धकाण्ड*, p. 269 reads मातामही० for मातामह्य०.
2. *Ibid.*, p. 269 reads हि for च.
3. *Ibid.*, p. 269 reads भवद्भिश्च for विद्वभिश्च. Here in our manuscript one line as dropped.
4. *Ibid.*, p. 270 reads तं च for तत्र.
5. *Ibid.*, p. 270 reads जल्पन्ति for जपन्ति.
6. *Ibid.*, p. 270 reads प्रहसाः for प्रसहाः .
7. *Ibid.*, p. 270 reads दाता for दत्वा.
8. *Ibid.*, p. 270 reads तान् for च.
9. *Ibid.*, p. 270 reads भवन्तु for भवन्ति.
10. *Ibid.*, p. 270 reads तं च for तत्र.
11. *Ibid.*, p. 270 reads वदन्ति for जपन्ति.
12. *Ibid.*, p. 270 reads तमूषु for येषामृषा.
13. *Ibid.*, p. 270 reads पठंस्तांश्च for पठंस्तांस्तु.
14. *Ibid.*, p. 270 quotes the text of *कात्यायन* as 'नान्दीमुखाः पितरः पितामह्य प्रपितामह्य' इत्यादि.
15. *Ibid.*, p. 270 ascribes this text to *गोभिलः* .
16. *Ibid.*, p. 275 reads क्रियेरन् for क्रियेव न.
17. *Ibid.*, p. 275 reads कर्मकारिभिः for कर्मकारिणा.
18. *Ibid.*, p. 275 reads ० मातरं for ० मातरः.
19. *Ibid.*, p. 275 reads च after श्राद्धमेव.
20. *Ibid.*, p. 275 reads आधाने for आपान.

नवयज्ञे च यज्ञज्ञा[1] वदन्ति एवं मनीषिण: ।
एवमेव[2] भवेत् श्राद्धमेतेषु न पृथक् पृथक् ॥१८॥
नार्कासु[3] भवेत् श्राद्धं न श्राद्धे श्राद्धमिष्यते ।
न सोष्यन्ती जातकर्म प्रोषितागतकर्मसु ॥१९॥
विवाहादि[4] कर्मगुणो उक्तो गर्भाधानं शुभ्रम[5]यस्य[6] चान्ते ।
विवाहादावेकमेवात्र कुर्याच्छ्राद्धं नादौ कर्मण:[7] स्यात् ॥२०॥
प्रदोषे श्राद्धमेकं स्यात् दोनिष्कान[8] प्रवेशयो: ।
न श्राद्धं युज्यते कर्षं[9] प्रथमे पुष्टिकर्मणि ॥२१॥
हलामि[10]योगादिषु तु षट्सु कुर्यात् पृथक् पृथक् ।
प्रतियोगमन्येषामादावेकं[11] च कारयेत् ॥२२॥
बृहत्पत्र क्षुद्रपशु स्वस्त्यर्थं परिवेश्यतो:[12]।
सूर्येन्द्वो: कर्मणी ये तु तयो: श्राद्धं न विद्यते ॥२३॥
न दशाग्रन्थिकेनैव विषवद्दुष्टकर्मणि ।
कृमिदष्टचिकित्सायां नैव शेषेषु विद्यते ॥२४॥
गणश: क्रियमाणे तु[13] मातृभ्य: पूजनं सकृत्[14]।
सकृदेव भवेत् श्राद्धमादौ न पृथगादिषु ॥२५॥
यत्र यत्र भवेत् श्राद्धं तत्र तत्र तु[15] मातर: ।
तथा[16] स्वपितृभ्य:[17] दद्यात् सुतसंस्कारकर्मसु ॥२६॥
पिण्डानोद्वाहनात्तेषां तस्याभावेऽपि[18] तत् क्रमात् ।
असकृदिति प्रतिदिनं प्रतिमासं प्रतिसंवत्सरं च क्रियते ॥२७॥

---

1. *कृत्यकल्पतरु-श्राद्धकाण्ड* p. 275 reads यज्ञे च for यज्ञज्ञा.
2. *Ibid.*, p. 275 reads एकमेव for एवमेव.
3. *Ibid.*, p. 275 reads नाष्टकासु for नार्कासु.
4. *Ibid.*, p. 275 reads विवाहादि: for विवाहादि.
5. *Ibid.*, p. 275 reads शुश्रुम for शुभ्रम.
6. *Ibid.*, p. 275 reads य: स for यस्य.
7. *Ibid.*, p. 275 reads कर्मण: after कर्मण: and befor स्यात् i.e., twice.
8. *Ibid.*, p. 275 reads गोनिष्कास for गोनिष्कान.
9. *Ibid.*, p. 275 reads कर्तुं for कर्षम्.
10. *Ibid.*, p. 275 reads हलादि० for हलामि०.
11. *Ibid.*, p. 275 reads ००० एकत्र for ००० एकम्.
12. *Ibid.*, p. 275 reads परिविश्यतो: for परिवेश्यतो: .
13. *Ibid.*, p. 275 reads क्रियमाणेषु for क्रियमाणे तु.
14. *Ibid.*, p. 275 reads सदा for सकृत्.
15. *Ibid.*, p. 275 reads च for तु.
16. *Ibid.*, p. 276 omits the word तथा in stanza No. 26b.
17. *Ibid.*, p. 276 reads पिता after स्वपितृभ्य: and before दद्यात्.
18. *Ibid.*, p. 276 reads तु after ००० and before तत्.

यानि वैश्वदेव-बलिकर्मा दर्शपौर्णमास श्रावण्याग्रहायण्यानि तेषु प्रथमप्रयोग एव श्राद्धम् । मातृपूजा च प्रत्यहमेव येन पशुयागादिर्न क्रियते । तेनापि प्रथमप्रयोग एव श्राद्धं कर्तव्यम् । विशेषमाधान इति आधाने अग्न्याधाने होमयो: सायंप्रातर्होमयो: नवयज्ञ आग्रहायणेष्टि: । एतेष्वाधानादिषु प्रतियोगमिव प्रतिकर्मापि श्राद्धं न कर्तव्यम् । किन्त्वाधानादौ कृते सर्वेष्वेव कृतं स्यात् । तेनान्यत्र श्रावण्यादौ प्रतिकर्मैव श्राद्धमित्युक्तम् । अपवादमाह । नाष्टकाष्विति अष्टकेष्टिसु तिसृषु श्राद्धे पार्वणादौ आसन्नप्रसवाया वध्वा: सुखप्रसवार्थं गोभिलोक्ते: । व्रीहय: पिष्टेन कुमारजिह्वामार्जनाख्ये जातकर्मणि गोभिलोक्ते: । प्रवासादागतस्य गृहपते: कुमारमूर्द्धाभिघ्राणरूपे प्रोषितागतकर्मणि गोभिलोक्ते: श्राद्धं न कार्यम् । विवाहादिरिति समहानीयचरु-होम-गृहप्रवेश यानारोहण चतुष्पाद्यामन्त्रणाक्षमंग समाधानार्थ होमे चतुर्थो होमदानादिशब्देन ग्रहणम् । एषु विवाहादि गर्भाधानान्तकर्मसु एकमेवश्राद्धं कुर्यात् । प्रदोषे श्राद्धमिति गोभि: शरणप्रवेशकर्मणो गोभिलोक्तेरंगत्वेन प्रदोषे प्रवेशादौ तन्त्रेणैकं श्राद्धम् । गवां पुष्टिकर्मत्रये गोभिलोक्ते: प्रथमपुष्टिकर्माणि श्राद्धं न कर्तव्यम् । हलाभियोगादिषु हलस्यामिक्षख्येन[1] योग: । पक्वसु धानेषु शीतायज्ञकृष्टक्षेत्रमध्ये खलयज्ञे खले प्रवर्षणं बीजवपनं प्रलवनं धान्यछेदनं पर्यवनं धान्यादीनागृहगमनम् । एषु हलाभियोगदिषु षट्सु कर्मसु एकैककर्मणि पृथक् प्रतियोगश्च कार्यम् । अन्येषां श्रावणीकर्माणामादावेकं श्राद्धं कार्यम् । बृहत्पत्रेति बृहत्पत्रम् । हस्त्यश्वादिक्षुद्रपशुरजाव्यादि: । तयो: स्वस्त्यर्थं परिविश्वमानयो: सूर्येन्द्वो: ये कर्माणि गोभिलोक्ते: तयो: श्राद्धं न कार्यम् ।

यथा गोभिल: —

वृक्ष इवेति पञ्च च इति प्रकृतिद्वितीयया आदित्य परिविश्वमाणे दाततण्डुलान् जुहुयात् । बृहत्पत्रस्वस्त्ययनकाम: एतेन यदुक्तं केनचित् छन्दोगवाजसनेयिनोर्निष्क्रामणकर्मणि गृहायां च प्रदर्शनादित्यदर्शनयो: विहितत्वात् । सूर्येन्दुकर्मणि निष्क्रामणकर्मग्रहणं तत् परिविश्यतो: सूर्येन्द्वोविल्वन्यया[2] परामर्शात् । गोभिलसूत्रार्थज्ञानाच्च न दशाग्रन्थिक इति प्रतिभये ध्वनि वस्त्रदशायां ग्रन्थीन् बध्नीयात् । उपेत्यवसन[3]वसनवत: स्वाहाकारान्तिया मैघीर्मा मरिष्यतीति विषयवतादष्टमद्भिरमभ्युक्षं जपेत् ।

इतस्तेजग्रिणा कृमिरिति कृमिमन्तं देशमद्भिरभ्युक्ष जपेत् इति गोभिलसूत्रस्योक्ते: कर्मत्रये शेषेष्विति अर्हणीय ऋत्विकादीनां पाद्यार्घं विष्टरमधुपर्कदानादिषु श्राद्धं नास्ति । गणश इति यथा यजनीयेऽहनि नवयज्ञ वास्तुगमन गोयज्ञान्ययज्ञेषु समुदायेन क्रियमाणेषु मातृपूजा श्राद्धं च सकृदेवगणादौ न कर्मसंख्यानुसारेण । यत्र यत्रेति न त्वकर्मादौ षड्भ्य पितृभ्य इत्यनेन श्राद्धं विहितं कर्मादिषु च सर्वेष्विति नाद्यपूजाविहिता इति पुनरुक्ति: । न कर्मादौ हि मातृपूजापूर्वमुक्ता । अनेन पुत्रजन्मादौ कर्मादित्वाभावेऽपि श्राद्धनिमित्तत्वादेव विधीयते ।

अथवा यत्र यत्र श्राद्धं भवेत्तत्र तत्रैव मातर इति वचनार्थ: । तेनाष्टकादौ श्राद्धनिषेधे मातृपूजानिषेध: । स्वपितृभ्य इति सुतसंस्कारकर्मत्व नामकरणादिषु श्राद्धं दद्यात् ।

तथा विष्णुपुराणे[4]—

1. This expression appears to be corrupt.
2. This expression ०विल्वनया appears to be corrupt.
3. Here one word वसन appears to be redundant.
4. This text of *विष्णुपुराण* agrees well with the extant *विष्णुपुराण*, III.13.1 in substance.

जातस्य कर्मादि क्रियाकाण्डमशेषत: ।
पुत्रस्य कुर्वीत पिता श्राद्धं चाभ्युदयात्मकम्[1] ॥२८॥

आङ[2]द्वहनादित्यमिविधावाङ्मर्यादाभि विधिसंशये कार्यान्वयानुरोधेनामिविधिरेव न्याय्यत्वात् । विशेषणोपलक्षसंदेहे विशेषणवत् कन्यापुत्रविवाहेषु इति वचनाच्च । स्वशब्द: स्वमातामहादि व्यवच्छेदार्थ: । तस्याभावे पितुरभावे अन्य: संस्कार्य: सपिण्डादेर्वा तत् क्रमात् संस्कार्यपुत्रदुहितृपितृक्रमात् तेषां पितॄणां दद्यादिति शेष: ।

तेन भ्राता वा भ्रातृपुत्रो वा सपिण्ड: । शिष्य एव वा इत्यनेन सपिण्डपुत्रकन्यासंस्कारकर्मणि सपिण्डानां वृद्धिश्राद्धाधिकारे सपिण्डपुत्रकन्यापितृपक्षमातामहपक्षयोरेवश्राद्धं कार्यम् । न स्वपितृपक्षस्य नरा संस्कार्य पितु: पितृगणमातामहगणयोस्तत् क्रमादित्यन्वयापत्ते: ।

अत एव कन्यापुत्रविवाहेष्विति विष्णु[3]पुराणवचनात् ।

तत् सर्वानन्दसन्तानें[4] यज्ञोद्वाहादिमंगले ।२९।

इति मत्स्यपुराण (१७.६५ब) वचनाच्च विवाहे वरपितृकन्यापितॄणामधिकार इति निरस्तम् । पितुरभावे संस्कारकर्मणि अन्यस्याधिकारप्रतिपादनात् न वरपितृकन्यापित्रोरेवाधिकार इति ।

1. The *विष्णुपुराण,* reads the text as —
सचैलस्य पितु: स्नानं जाते पुत्रो विधीयते ।
जातकर्म यथा कुर्याच्छ्राद्धमभ्युदये च यत् ॥
2. This expression appears to be corrupt.
3. *विष्णुपुराण,* III.13.5 is quoted in *कृत्यकल्पतरु-श्राद्धकाण्ड,* p. 268 as —
कन्यापुत्रविवाहेषु प्रवेशे नववेश्मन: ।
नामकर्मणि बालानां चूडाकर्मादिके तथा ॥
4. *मत्स्यपुराण,* p. 31 reads उत्सवानन्दसंभारे for सर्वानन्दसन्ताने.

३४

सपिण्डीकरणम्

श्राद्धसागराधिकारे तद्विशिष्टं सपिण्डीकरणं निरूप्यते ।

शातातप:[1]—

> संवत्सरे तु विज्ञेयं सपिण्डीकरणास्त्विह[2]।
> सपिण्डीकरणान्ता तु ज्ञेया प्रेतक्रिया बुधैः ।।१।।

संवत्सर शब्दोऽत्र संवत्सरान्तदिनपरः ।

'संवत्सरान्ते प्रेताय' इति विष्णु (२१.१२) वचनात् ।

अत्र जिकन:—

अन्त्यमृताहेऽन्त्यमासिकं कृत्वा परदिने सपिण्डीकरणं कार्यम् । पूर्णे संवत्सरे इति गोभिलवचनात् । मासिकविधानानन्तरं ततः पूर्णे संवत्सरे इति कात्यायने तत इत्युपादानात् ।

अथ सपिण्डीकरणं संवत्सरं एकं पिण्डमुद्दिश्य समाप्ते संवत्सरे चत्वार्युदकपात्राणीत्यादि वा उपगृह्यदर्शनाच्च । एते नान्त्यमृताहस्य संवत्सरबहिर्भूतत्वात् मृताहात् प्रागेव संवत्सरसमाप्ते मृताहविहितं द्वादशमासिकश्राद्धं पुनराब्दिकं वदन्तीति निरस्तम् । संवत्सरमेकं पिण्डमनुद्दिश्य इत्यादिवचनैरजहत् स्वार्थलक्षणया संवत्सरपदस्य मृताहसहितसंवत्सरपरत्वावधारणात् । तन्न । संवत्सरे तु विज्ञेयम् ।

ततः संवत्सरे पूर्णे संवत्सर इति शातातप कात्यायन-गोभिलीयेन बैजपापगृह्यवचनेषु संवत्सरस्याधिकरणत्वेनाङ्गत्वावधारणात् । अनन्तरदिनस्य चाशब्दार्थत्वात् । तदनुपपत्तया संपूर्णसमाप्तशब्दयोः संपूर्णे तु ततो मासे पिण्डं समापयेत् ।

शूद्रस्य दशमः पिण्डो मासे हि दीयते । इति वदीषदसमाप्तपरत्वम् । एकदिवसो न संवत्सरव्यवच्छेदकत्वं च सम्यक् समाप्तपरत्वेऽन्त्यकलायाः श्राद्धाङ्गत्वाभावात् ।

अत एव 'संवत्सरान्ते प्रेताय' इति विष्णुपुराण[3]वचनमुपपद्यते । अनाशब्दस्य अवयवार्थत्वात् दशान्तरपर इतिवत् ।

---

1. The text of *शातातप* is quoted in *पृथ्वीचन्द्र-श्राद्धप्रकाश,* XXI.13, p. 491.
2. *Ibid.,* p. 491 reads ०करणं त्विह for ०करणस्त्विह.
3. Here the statement is not from *विष्णुपुराण,* but *विष्णुस्मृति,* XXI.12, p. 348.

यद्यपि दशाहान्ते पुनः क्रियेत्यत्र समीपार्थोत्यन्तशब्दो दृश्यते तथापि नानामुनिवचनेषु संवत्पदे लक्षणाप्रसंगात् अवयवार्थम् । एषान्तशब्दस्तस्मादनन्त्यमृताहशब्द एव सपिण्डनमिति स्थितम् ।

एतेन यत् पठन्ति —

पिण्डः पितृव्यप्राप्त्यर्थं पूर्णे संवत्सरे सति ।
मृताहात् परतः कुर्यात् सपिण्डीकरणं बुधैः ॥२॥

इति तदनाकरम् ।

अत्र च अर्वाक् संवत्सरावृद्धौ निमित्तभूतायां सपिण्डीकरणमनुवृद्धिनिमित्तं प्रागपि सपिण्डनमस्तीति ज्ञापयति । चतुरंगं जुहोतीति होमानुवाद इव होमविधिं तदा च वृद्धिनिमित्ते न सपिण्डनापकर्षे वचनाभावान्न मासिकायकर्ष इति जिकनप्रभृतीनां मतम् ।

अथ तदादितदन्तन्यायादपकर्षः । यथा दैक्षे पशौ तिष्ठन्तं पशुं प्रयजतीति वाक्यबलात् प्रयाजापकर्षे तदन्तकर्मकलापापकर्षः । न तत्र प्रकृतौ क्रमस्य क्लृप्तत्वात् क्लृप्तकर्मा करोघात् अमत्वपकर्षः । न च मासिकसपिण्डनयोरिह क्रमक्लृप्तिरस्ति । कल्प्यतामिति चेन्न । प्रयोगविध्यैके हि क्रमकल्पनेत्युक्तम् पञ्चमाध्याये । एतयोस्तु भिन्नफलत्वेन प्रयोगाविधिभेदात् । मासिकश्राद्धानां प्रेतत्वविमुक्तिमात्रं फलं सपिण्डनस्य प्रेतत्वविमुक्ति पूर्वपितृदेहप्राप्तिः । तत्र षोडशश्राद्धस्य प्रेतत्वविमुक्तिफलमिति प्रागेव यमवचनेन दर्शितम् । सपिण्डस्य पितृदेहप्राप्ति फलमित्याह विष्णुधर्मोत्तरे मार्कण्डेयः (२.११३.१६ब-१७अ)

कृते सपिण्डीकरणे नरः संवत्सरात् परम् ।
प्रेतदेहं परित्यज्य[1] भोगदेहं प्रपद्यते ॥३॥

भोगदेहः पितृदेहः ।

तथा विष्णुपुराणम्[2] (३.१३.३९अ)

प्रेते पितृत्वमापन्ने सपिण्डीकरणादा[3]न्विति सपिण्डीकरणानन्तरं हारीतः —

ततः प्रभृति वै प्रेतः पितृसामान्यमाप्नुयात् ।
विदन्ते पितृलोकस्ततः श्राद्धं प्रवर्तते ॥४॥

अतः फलभेदेन अधिकारिभेदात् । प्रयोगावधिभेदे कथं क्रमकल्पना? अतः सपिण्डनापकर्षे मासिकापकर्ष इत्याह सपिण्डीकरणान्तात्विति । सर्वैव प्रेतक्रिया सपिण्डीकरणान्तेति प्रतिपादनात् द्रव्योरेव साधिकारयोर्वाचनिकः क्रमः । दर्शपौर्णमासाविष्ट्वा सोमेन यजेतेतिवत् । ततः कृतमासिकस्य सपिण्डनाधिकाराद्वाचनिक क्रमानुरोधात् सपिण्डनापकर्षे मासिकाद्यपकर्षः । कल्पतरौ तु प्रेतक्रिया प्रेतशब्दोल्लेखेन क्रियासपिण्डनान्ता । अतोपकृष्य कृते सपिण्डनेऽम्बुघटश्राद्धं न प्रेतशब्देन कार्यम् ।

---

1. The *विष्णुधर्मोत्तरपुराण,* reads समुत्सृज्य for परित्यज्य.
2. The *विष्णुपुराण,* is quoted in *कृत्यकल्पतरु-श्राद्धकाण्ड,* p. 264.
3. *Ibid.,* p. 264 reads ००अनु for ००आनु.

किन्तु पितृशब्दो तं ह्युक्तं तन्न प्रेतसम्बन्धिनी क्रियाते[1]त्वक्रिया । न तु प्रेतशब्दोल्लेखेन क्रिया लक्षणाप्रसंगात् । शब्दस्य स्वरूपवाचकत्वाभावात् । तस्मादुक्तमेव व्याख्यानमुक्तम् । किं च सपिण्डनापकर्षे यदि सकलप्रेतश्राद्धापकर्षो न प्रामाणिकस्तदा सपिण्डनापकर्षेऽम्बुघटश्राद्धस्य स्वकाल एव प्राप्तत्वात् पुनर्विधानमनर्थकं स्यात् ।

याज्ञवल्क्यः (१.२५५)

अर्वाक् संवत्सराद्यस्य सपिण्डीकरणं भवेत् ।[2]
तस्याप्यन्नं सोदकुम्भं च[3] दद्यात् संवत्सरं द्विजे ॥५॥

किं च

अर्वाक् संवत्सरा[4] वृद्धौ पूर्णे संवत्सरेऽपि वा ।
ये सपिण्डीकृताः[5] प्रेताः न ते[6] यान्तु[7] पृथक् क्रिया ॥६॥

इति शातातपवचनमपकृष्य सपिण्डनेऽपि पृथक् क्रियामेकोद्दिष्टक्रियां प्रत्याब्दिकव्यतिरिक्तां निरस्यति ।

यतस्ततः प्रभृति संक्रान्त्यावुपरागादि पर्वसु ।
त्रिपिण्डमाचरेत् श्राद्धमेकोद्दिष्टं मृताहनि ॥७॥

इति मत्स्यपुराणवचनं सपिण्डनादूर्ध्वं मृताहनि प्रत्याब्दिक क्रियामेकोद्दिष्टं विधिना विदधाति ।

किं चापकृष्य सपिण्डने कृते प्रेतत्वविस्तारपूर्वं पितृलोकप्राप्तिरवगम्यते । प्रेतत्वविस्तारं च षोडशश्राद्ध इति कथं मासिकापकर्षः ।

यथा 'अर्वाक् संवत्सराद्वृद्धा'वित्यनेन सपिण्डनापकर्षमभिधाय शातातपः[8]—

न पृथक् पिण्डदानं[9] तु तस्मादूर्ध्वं विधीयते ।
प्रेतानामिह सर्वेषां यैः मन्त्रैश्च[10] नियोजिताः ॥८॥
त्वा[11] प्रेतत्वाच्चेह विस्तीर्णाः[12] प्राप्ताः पितृगणं तु ये ।९।

---

1. This expression appears to be corrupt.
2. *याज्ञवल्क्यस्मृति,* p. 90 reads 5a as —
   अर्वाक्सपिण्डीकरणं यस्य संवत्सराद्भवेत् ।
3. *Ibid.*, p. 90 drops च.
4. *कृत्यकल्पतरु-श्राद्धकाण्ड,* p. 261 and *पृथ्वीचन्द्र-श्राद्धप्रकाश,* XXI.20, p. 492 read संवत्सरात् for संवत्सरा.
5. *पृथ्वीचन्द्र-श्राद्धप्रकाश,* XXI.20, p. 492 reads ०असपिण्डीकृताः for ०सपिण्डीकृताः .
6. *Ibid.*, p. 492 and *कृत्यकल्पतरु-श्राद्धकाण्ड,* p. 261 read तेषां for ते.
7. *Ibid.*, p. 261 reads तु for यान्तु.
8. The text of *शातातप* is quoted in *कृत्यकल्पतरु-श्राद्धकाण्ड,* p. 261.
9. *Ibid.*, p. 261 reads पिण्डप्रदानं for पिण्डदानम्.
10. *Ibid.*, p. 261 reads मन्त्रैस्तु for मन्त्रैश्च.
11. *Ibid.*, p. 261 drops त्वा.
12. *Ibid.*, p. 261 reads निस्तीर्णाः for विस्तीर्णाः .

न तु सपिण्डीकरणे नरः संवत्सरात् परम् ।
प्रेतदेहं परित्यज्य भोगदेहं प्रपद्यते ॥१०॥

इति विष्णुधर्मोत्तर (२.११३.१६ब-१७अ)

वचनमपकृष्य सपिण्डने कृते संवत्सरान्तमेव पितृत्वप्राप्तिं बोधयति । अन्यथा संवत्सरात् परमिति व्यर्थं स्यात् ।

तथा आग्नेयपुराणम् (१६३.२८अ) ।

अर्वाक् संवत्सराद्यस्य सपिण्डीकरणं भवेत् ।[1]
प्रेतत्वमिह तस्यापि क्षेमं संवत्सरं नृपः ॥११॥

तन्न एतयोरेव मासिकापकर्षे प्रमाणत्वात् । अन्यथा प्रेतत्वपरिहारकारणाभावादेव प्रेतत्वसिद्धेरनर्थकत्वापत्तेः । तस्मादशक्त्या षोडशश्राद्धापकर्षविषयमिदं वचनद्वयं वृद्धिनिमित्तेत्वपकर्षान्तरमेव प्रेतत्वपरिहारः । तदर्थमेवापकर्षात् शातातपवचनाच्च ।

किं च मासिकापकर्षे तत् साध्यस्य प्रेतदाहपरिहारस्याजातत्वात् । तदभावे पितृदेहप्राप्तेरप्यजातत्वात् कथं नान्दीमुखे पितृपदप्रयोगः?

किं च

सपिण्डीकरणादूर्ध्वं न दद्यात् प्रतिमासिकम् ।
एकोद्दिष्टविधानेन दद्यादित्याह शौनकः ॥१२॥

इति छन्दोगपरिशिष्टविरोधः । अपकर्षपक्षे सपिण्डीकरणादूर्ध्वं प्रतिमासमेकोद्दिष्टविधानेन न दद्यात् । किन्तु पार्वणविधानेनेति वक्ष्यते । अतः सपिण्डीकरणापकर्षे मासिकापकर्ष इति सिद्धम् ।

यत्तु

यस्य संवत्सरादर्वाक् सपिण्डीकरणं भवेत् ।
मासिकं च उदकुम्भं च दद्यात् संवत्सरं द्विजः ॥१३॥

इति लौगाक्षिनाम्नावचनं लिखितं तदनुकरणम् । समूलत्वेप्यप्राप्तप्रेतत्वविषयं वेति वक्ष्यते ।

तथा पठन्ति—

श्राद्धानि षोडशान् दत्वा न तु कुर्यात् सपिण्डताम् ।
तद्धानौ च कृते प्रेतः पितृत्वं न प्रपद्यते ॥१४॥
श्राद्धानि षोडशाद्यादि विदधीत सपिण्डता ।

---

1. The stanza No. 11a is read in अग्निपुराण, as —
अर्वाक्सपिण्डीकरणं यस्य संवत्सराद्भवेत् । p. 329.

पितुः पित्रो विधान[1]ज्ञ इति पौराणिका विदुः ॥१५॥

गोभिलः —

पूर्णे संवत्सरे षण्मासे त्रिपक्षे यदहर्वा वृद्धिमापद्येत तदश्वत्वार्य्युदकपात्राणि सतिलपुष्पगन्धोदकानि पूरयित्वा त्रीणि पितॄणामेकं प्रेतस्य प्रेतमात्रं पितृपात्रेष्वासिञ्चति ।

ये समाना इति[2] द्वाभ्यामेतेन पिण्डो व्याख्यातः । पूर्णे संवत्सरे इति मुख्यः कल्पः । तदशक्तौ वत्सरान्ते विसर्जनं नवमास्यामिति कमलाकरभट्टः[3]। इति पैठीनसीवचनेनापि नवमो मासः । तदशक्तौ षष्ठो मासः । तत्राप्यशक्तौ त्रिपक्षः । तत्राप्यशक्तौ प्रथमे मास्यशौचापगमे द्वादशभिर्दिनैर्द्वादशश्राद्धानि निर्वर्त्य त्रयोदशाहः सपिण्डीकरणकालः । शूद्रस्य द्वादशाह एव । मासिकार्थवत् द्वादशाह श्राद्धं कृत्वा त्रयोदशे हि वा कुर्यात् ।

'मन्त्रवर्जं शूद्राणां द्वादशाहेऽहनि' इति वक्ष्यमाण विष्णुवचनात् प्रथममासविषयत्वं विष्णुवचनस्य निर्युक्तिकम् । षण्मासत्रिक्षविषयतैव कुतो न स्यादिति चेन्न । प्रथममास एव द्वाददशमासिकापकर्ष-सम्भवात् । तत्राप्यशक्तौ प्रथममासस्यैकाह एव द्वादशमासिकमाह तत् सपिण्डीकरणकालः ।

एकाहे द्वादशहवेति पूर्वोक्त मरीचिवचनात् । कल्पतरौ[4] तु उत्तरस्मिन्मासि वृद्धौ निश्चीयतामेते नवमषण्मासादयः । सपिण्डीकरणकाला इत्युक्तं तच्चिन्त्यम् । यदहर्वा वृद्धिरापद्येत वृद्धिरापन्ना सन्निहिता भवति सोऽपि सपिण्डीकरणकालः । एतेनेदं निरस्तम् । कथं वृद्धिसपिण्डनं वृद्धिश्राद्धस्य प्रातर्विधानात् सपिण्डनस्य पार्वणविधानातिदेशो नापराह्णप्राप्तेरिति । यतो वृद्धिदिने सपिण्डनं किन्तु वृद्धिसंनिहितदिन इति ।

इतिकर्तव्यतामाह —

उदकपात्राण्यर्घपात्राणि पितृणामेकप्रेतस्येतिपाठक्रमादनुष्ठानक्रमः कल्प्यः । मैत्रकं प्रेतस्येति अत्र प्रेतशब्दोऽचिरप्रमीतं जनकमाह । अत्र कश्चित् प्रकर्षेण इतागत इति व्युत्पत्या प्रेतपदं चिरप्रमीतवृद्धप्रपितामहपरतया व्याख्यातवान् । अतस्तस्यैव पिण्डपात्रजलयोः समर्पितत्वान्निवृत्तिः।

तथा शातातपः[5]—

अर्वाक् संवत्सराद्वृद्धौ पूर्णे संवत्सरेऽपि वा ।
ये सपिण्डीकृताः प्रेता न तेषां तु पृथक्क्रिया ॥१४॥
न[6] पृथक् पिण्डदानं तु तस्मादूर्ध्वं विधीयते ।
प्रेतानामिह सर्वेषां यै[7] मन्त्रैस्तु नियोजिताः ॥१५॥

---

1. This expression seems to be corrupt.
2. This refers to the text of बैजवाप quoted in *कृत्यकल्पतरु-श्राद्धकाण्ड*, p. 255.
3. For this view of कमलाकरभट्ट refer to *निर्णयसिंधु*, p. 605.
4. अयं च सपिण्डीकरणे नवमासविधिर्दशममासादौ वृद्धिश्राद्धनिमित्तसंभवे बोद्धव्यः । न ततोऽर्वाक् सपिण्डीकरणं कर्तव्यम् । *कृत्यकल्पतरु-श्राद्धकाण्ड*, p. 255.
5. The text of *शातातप* is quoted in *कृत्यकल्पतरु-श्राद्धकाण्ड*, p. 261 and *पृथ्वीचन्द्र-श्राद्धप्रकाश*, XXI.19, p. 432.
6. *Ibid.*, p. 261 drops न.
7. *Ibid.*, p. 261 and *पृथ्वीचन्द्र-श्राद्धप्रकाश*, p. 432 read ये for यै.

तथा[1] असपिण्डी[2]कृतं प्रेतं पृथक् पिण्डे नियोजयेत् ।
विधिघ्य[3]स्तेन भवति पितृहा चोपजायते ॥१६॥

सपिण्डीकृतस्य पार्वणे एकोद्दिष्टे पृथक् पिण्डनिषेधोऽवगम्यते । स च वृद्धप्रपितामहस्यैव घटते ।

तथा मत्स्यपुराणम् —(१८.१९ब-२२अ च २८अ-२९अ)

ये समाना इति द्वाभ्यामाद्यं[4]तु विभजेत् त्रिधा ।
चतुरस्य पुनः कार्यं न कदाचिद्यतो[5] भवेत् ॥१७॥
यतः[6] पितृत्वमापन्नः चतुर्थस्तदा पुमान्[7]।
अग्निष्वात्तादिमध्यं तु[8] प्राप्नोत्यमृतमुत्तमम् ॥१८॥
सपिण्डीकरणादूर्ध्वं तस्यै तस्मान्य[9]दीयते ।
पितृष्ट्वै[10]व तु दातव्यं तत् पिण्डो येषु संस्थितः ॥१९॥
त्रिभिः सपिण्डीकरणे वासैक त्रितयं[11] पिता ।
यदा प्राप्स्यति कालेन तदा मुच्येत बन्धनात् ॥२०॥
मुग्धोऽपि पतागित्वं[12] प्राप्नोति कुशमार्जनात् ॥२१॥

आद्यं आद्यपुप्ररुषसम्बन्धात् वृद्धप्रपितामहपिण्डमित्यर्थः । तथा चतुर्थस्य वृद्धप्रपितामहक्याग्निष्वात्तादिपदप्राप्त्या बन्धनविमोचनात् पिण्डदानकार्यं नास्ति । अतस्तत् पिण्डं त्रिधा विभज्य प्रपितामहादिपिण्डेषु समर्पयेत् । वृद्धप्रपितामहपिण्डो येषु समर्पितस्तस्य एव तदूर्ध्वं दद्यात् । वृद्धोऽस्तु मुक्तोऽपि लोपमात्रभागीति तदसङ्गतम् ।

ब्रह्मपुराणविरोधात् ।

यथा[13] प्रेतपक्षस्य हस्ते[14] चतुर्भागं जलं क्षिपेत् ।
ततः पितामहादिभ्यस्तन्मन्त्रैश्च पृथक् पृथक् ॥२२॥

---

1. *कृत्यकल्पतरु-श्राद्धकाण्ड,* p. 261 reads यः for तथा.
2. *Ibid.*, p. 261 reads सपिण्डी० for असपिण्डी०.
3. *Ibid.*, p. 261 reads विधिघ्नः० for विधिघ्यः०.
4. *मत्स्यपुराण,* p. 32 reads ०अन्त्यं for ०आद्यम्.
5. *Ibid.*, p. 32 reads ०अतो for ०यतो.
6. *Ibid.*, p. 32 reads ततः for यतः .
7. *Ibid.*, p. 32 reads सर्वतस्तुष्टिमागतः for चतुर्थस्तदा पुमान्.
8. *Ibid.*, p. 32 reads ००मध्यत्वं for ००मध्यं तु.
9. *Ibid.*, p. 32 reads तस्मान्न० for तस्मान्य०.
10. *Ibid.*, p. 32 reads पितृषु० for पितृष्टा० which is corrupt.
11. *Ibid.*, p. 32 reads अशेष त्रितये for वासैक त्रितयम्.
12. *Ibid.*, p. 32 reads लेपभागित्वं for पतागित्वम् which is corrupt.
13. *कृत्यकल्पतरु-श्राद्धकाण्ड,* p. 256 quotes these stanzas from *ब्रह्मपुराण* and drops यथा.
14. *Ibid.*, p. 256 reads तु for हस्ते.

ये समाना इति द्वाभ्यां तज्जलं[1] तु समर्पयेत् ।
अथ तेनैव विधिना दर्भमूलेऽवनेजनम् ॥२३॥
पितुर्दत्वा[2] पिण्डं तु दद्यात् भक्त स[3] तु पूर्ववत् ।
दत्वा पिण्डमथाष्टांगं ध्यात्वा तं च स्वमास्वरम्[4]॥२४॥
सुवर्णरूप्यदर्भैस्तु[5] तस्मिन् पिण्डान्[6]ततस्त्रिधा ।
कृत्वा पितामहादिभ्यः पितृभ्यः प्रेतमर्चयेत्[7]॥२५॥

अत्र पितामहादि जलपिण्डयोः पितृजलपिण्डसमर्पणमवगम्यते ।

मृते पितरि यस्याथ विद्यते व पितामहः ।
लेन देयास्त्रयः पिण्डाः प्रपितामहपूर्वकाः ॥२६॥
तेभ्यश्च पैतृकः पिण्डो नियोक्तव्यस्तु पूर्ववत् ।२७।

अत्रापि पितृपिण्डसमर्पणमवगम्यते ।

यथा विष्णुः[8]—(२१.१२)

संवत्सरान्ते प्रेताय तत् पित्रे च[9] तत्पितामहाय प्रपितामहाय[10] ब्राह्मणान्[11] देवपूर्वान् भोजयेत् ।

अत्र तत्शब्दात् प्रेतस्य पितृपितामहप्रपितामहानामवगम्यते । प्रेतशब्दादचिरप्रमीत एवावगम्यते । न च स पिता यस्येति बहुव्रीहिः । न घृतश्चेति व्रीहौ नित्यं कप्रत्ययविधानात् । तत् पितृकायेति स्यात् ।

आश्वलायनगृह्यपरिशिष्टम्[12]

चत्वार्युदकपात्राणि एकं प्रेतस्य[13] त्रीणीतरेषाम् ।

अत्र मृतशब्दादचिरप्रमीत एवावगम्यते । किं च गोभिलेनैकोद्दिष्टमभिधाय एतत् एतत् प्रेतश्राद्धमित्युक्त्वा सपिण्डविधानेकं प्रेतस्येत्युक्तम् । अत्र प्रेतशब्दात् पूर्वप्रेतशब्दोक्ताचिरप्रमीत एव प्रतीयते । तदविरुद्धबुद्धित्वात् । शातातपवचने तु प्रेतस्य सपिण्डानादूर्ध्वं पृथक् पिण्डदाननिषेधः । एकोद्दिष्टविषयो

1. *कृत्यकल्पत-श्राद्धकाण्ड,* p. 256 reads ०जले for ०जलम्.
2. *Ibid.*, p. 256 reads च after पितुर्दत्वा and before पिण्डम्.
3. *Ibid.*, p. 256 reads भक्त्या for भक्त स which is corrupt.
4. *Ibid.*, p. 256 reads सुभास्वरं for स्वमास्वरम् which is corrupt.
5. *Ibid.*, p. 256 reads सुवर्ण ०दभैग्नु for सुवर्ण ०दर्भैस्तु which is corrupt.
6. *Ibid.*, p. 256 reads पिण्डं०० for ००पिण्डान्००.
7. *Ibid.*, p. 256 reads ०अर्पयेत् for ०अर्चयेत् which is contextually wrong.
8. This refers to *विष्णुस्मृति,* XXI.12, p. 348.
9. *Ibid.*, p. 348 drops च.
10. *Ibid.*, p. 348 reads तत् before प्रपितामहाय.
11. *Ibid.*. p. 348 reads च before ब्राह्मणान् and after प्रपितामहाय.
12. The text of *आश्वलायनगृह्यपरिशिष्ट* is quoted in *कृत्यकल्पतरु-श्राद्धकाण्ड,* p. 253.
13. *Ibid.*, p. 253 reads मृतस्य for प्रेतस्य.

न पिण्डदानमात्रविषयः । पृथक् पदानर्थक्यापत्तेः । आद्यत्वं तु अधोगणनया पितुरुपपद्यत्ते ।

एवं मत्स्यपुराणेऽपि —

सपिण्डीकरणश्राद्धं देवपूर्वं नियोजयेत् ।[1]
पितॄनेवासयेत्तत्र पुनः प्रेतस्य निर्दिशेत् ॥२८॥

इत्यभिधाय

गन्धोदकतिल[2]युक्तं कुर्यात् पात्रचतुष्टयम्[3]।
अर्घ्यर्थं[4] पितृपात्रेषु प्रेतपात्रं प्रसेचयेत्[5]॥२९॥

इति । अत्रापि स एव प्रेतपदादवगम्यते ।

ननु कथं त्रिधाविभागः पितामहः प्रपितामहाभ्यामेव पार्वणेऽपृथक् दानात् पिण्डस्य । अतो द्विधैव विभागो युक्त इति । अत्रोक्तं चतुर्थस्य पुनः कार्यमिति तृतीय समर्पणे चतुर्थस्य विसर्जनं भवतीत्यर्थः । अत एव त्रीभिः सपिण्डीकरणे आसेचयेत् त्रितयं पित्रेति पितुरेवासेकत्रितयमवगम्यते ।

अथात्र संतोषस्तदाशाखिभेदव्यवस्थितोऽयं प्रकारः । प्रकृतमभिधीयते । एतेन पिण्डीभ्या[6]ख्यात इति पिण्डमिश्रीकरणे पात्रमिश्रीकरणपरिपाटी बोद्धव्या ।

विष्णुः (२१.१२)

संवत्सरान्ते प्रेताय तत् पित्रे तत् पितामहाय तत् प्रपितामहाय ब्राह्मणान्[7] देवपूर्वान् भोजयेत् ।

न दक्षिणेन वाचयेदक्षय्य स्थान इति शेषः । दैवपूर्वकमिति मातृश्राद्धे दैवपूर्वकश्राद्धोऽपि दर्शिता[8] लघुहारीतः ।

मातृश्राद्धं तु युग्मैः स्यात् सदैवं प्राङ्ःमुखैः पृथक ।३०।[9]
सदैवं मातृश्राद्धं पृथक् कर्तव्यमित्यर्थः ।

मार्कण्डेयपुराणे[10]—

वैश्वदेवविहीनं तु केचिदिच्छन्ति सत्तमाः[11]।३१।

---

1. The first line of stanza No. 28 is quoted in *श्राद्धकल्प*, p. 68.
2. *Ibid.*, p. 68 reads ००तिलैः० for ००तिल०.
3. *Ibid.*, p. 68 reads गोत्र० for पात्र०.
4. *Ibid.*, p. 68 reads अर्घार्थं for अर्घ्यर्थम्.
5. *Ibid.*, p. 68 reads प्रषेचयेत् for प्रसेचयेत्.
6. This expression appears to be corrupt.
7. *विष्णुस्मृति*, p. 348 reads च after ब्राह्मणान्.
8. This may be emended as दर्शितः for दर्शिता in view of context.
9. This line is quoted in *कृत्यकल्पतरु-श्राद्धकाण्ड*, p. 141 from the text of *शातातप* as —
   मातृश्राद्धं तु युग्मैः स्याददैवं प्राङ्मुखैः पृथक् ।
   निर्णयसिंधु, p. 499 also treats this as the text of *शातातप.*
10. The text of *मार्कण्डेयपुराण* is quoted in *निर्णयसिंधु*, p. 491.
11. *निर्णयसिंधु*, p. 491 reads मानवाः for सत्तमाः .

पृथग्वैश्वदेवविहीनमित्यर्थः । एतेन तन्त्रता दर्शिता । आवृत्तौ फलभूमाकल्पनीयः कमलाकरभट्ट[1]स्तु मातृश्राद्धं दैवरहितमेव कार्यम् ।

कात्यायनः[2]—

आभ्युदयिके प्रदक्षिणमुपचारः । पित्र्यवर्ज्यं[3] जपः[4]। ऋजवो दर्भा[5]। यवैस्तिलार्थः । संपन्नमिति । तृप्तिप्रश्नः । दधिवदारक्षतमिश्राः पिण्डाः[6]। नान्दीमुखान् पितॄनावाहयिष्ये[7] इति पृच्छति । नान्दीमुखाः[8] पितरः प्रीयन्तामित्यक्षय्यस्थाने नान्दीमुखान् पितॄन वाचयिष्ये पृच्छति । नान्दीमुखाः[9] पितरः पितामहाः प्रपितामहाः[10] प्रीयन्तां[11] न स्वधां प्रयुञ्जीत । युग्मान् अशेयेत्[12]।

न स्वधामिति स्वधापदप्रयोगो न कर्तव्य एव ।

आश्वलायनगृह्यम् —

आभ्युदयिके युग्मा ब्राह्मणाः समूलदर्भाः प्राङ्मुखेभ्यः उदङ्मुखो दद्यात् । उदङ्मुखेभ्यः प्राङ्मुखो वा द्वौ दर्भौ पवित्रे सोपयामानि पात्राणि चत्वारि शन्नोदेवीरित्यन्नमन्त्रिता स्वप्सु यवान् वपति । यवसि सोमेदेवायो गोसवो देवनिर्मितः पानमद्भिः पृक्त पृष्ठया नान्दीमुखान् पितॄन् प्रीणाहितः । स्वाहेति । नान्दीमुखाः पितरः प्रीयन्तामिति अपां प्रति ग्रहणं विसर्जनं चैवमुत्तरयोरपि पितामह प्रपितामहयोर्नित्यं चाग्नौकरणं स्वाहाकारेण होमश्चातो देवा अवन्तु न इत्यंगुष्ठ ग्रह इदं विष्णुर्विचक्रमे इत्यत्र पावमानी शास्वतां ऐन्द्रीव प्रतिरथं च श्रावयेत् । भक्तशेषेषु पिण्डदानमशियान गोमयेनोपलिप्य तेषु प्रातग्रान् कुशानस्तीर्थालंकृत्य पृषदाह्यमिश्रदन्तनो हरिः सर्वत्र तस्यार्द्धे नत्वे द्वे आहुतीर्जुहुयात् । नान्दीमुखाः पितरो जुहुयात् । नान्दीमुखा पितरः प्रीयन्तामिति विसृजेत् । प्रदक्षिणमुपचारः यवैस्तिलार्थः सर्वं द्विद्विरिति प्राङ्मुखेभ्यः उदङ्मुखो प्राङ्मुखोऽवेति छन्दोगविषयम् । प्राङ्मुखत्वस्य छन्दोगपरिशिष्टकृतोक्तत्वात् । यथा सर्वस्मादन्नमुद्धृत्य व्यञ्जनैरूपासिच्य संयोज्य यवकर्कन्दुदधिभिः प्राङ्मुखं सततः अवनेजवत् पिण्डान् दत्वा बिल्वप्रमाणकानिति वक्ष्यते ।

ब्रह्मपुराणे[13]—

> नान्दीमुखानां कर्तव्यं पितृकार्यार्थसिद्धये ।
> सयवैश्च तथार्जभिर्दर्भैः पूर्वमुखस्थितः ॥३२॥

---

1. कमलाकरभट्ट, in his निर्णयसिंधु, p. 491 states that यत्तु शातातपः 'मातृश्राद्धं तु युग्मैः स्यात् अदैवं प्राङ्मुखैः पृथक् । इति तद्भिन्नप्रयोगमातृश्राद्धपरम् ।
2. The text of *कात्यायन* is quoted in *कृत्यकल्पतरु-श्राद्धकाण्ड*, p. 270.
3. *Ibid.*, p. 270 reads पूर्वाह्ने before पित्र्यवर्ज्यम्.
4. *Ibid.*, p. 270 keeps the word जपः into the bracket.
5. *Ibid.*, p. 270 reads दर्भाः for दर्भा.
6. *Ibid.*, p. 270 reads सुसम्पन्नमितीतरे ब्रूयुः into bracket before this sentence.
7. Here the rule of सन्धि is not observed though this is observed in *Ibid.*, p. 270.
8. *Ibid.*, p. 270 reads आवाहयेत्यनुज्ञातो before नान्दीमुखाः .
9. *Ibid.*, p. 270 reads वाच्यतामित्यनुज्ञातो before नान्दीमुखाः .
10. *Ibid.*, p. 270 reads मातामहाः प्रमातामहाः वृद्धप्रमातामहाश्च after प्रपितामहाः
11. *Ibid.*, p. 270 reads इति after प्रीयन्तां and before न.
12. *Ibid.*, p. 270 reads ०आशयेत् for ०अशेयेत्.
13. This stanza cannot be traced in the extant *ब्रह्मपुराण*.

शातातपः

दद्यात्[1] प्राङ्मुखः पिण्डानेभ्यः[2] सव्येन[3] वाग्यतः ।
प्रागग्रेष्वदर्भेषु पिण्डान् दद्यात् यथाविधि[4]॥३३॥

अत्र कर्तुः प्राङ्मुखत्वे ब्राह्मणानामुदङ्मुखत्वं एकविधिनिर्देशात् ।

तथा —

दध्यक्षतैः सर्वदेवैः[5] प्राङ्मुखो उदङ्मुखोऽपि वा ।
देवतीर्थेन वै पिण्डं[6] दद्यात् कायेन वा नृप ॥३४॥

इति विष्णुपुराणोक्त (३.१३.३) तीर्थविकल्पः छन्दोगपरिशिष्टविषयः ।

नात्रापसव्यकरणं न पित्र्यं तीर्थमिष्यते ।
पात्राणां पूरणादीनि देवेनेव[7] हि कारयेत् ॥३५॥

इति छन्दोगपरिशिष्ट[8]कृतैककारेण तीर्थान्तरनिषेधात् । कार्यं प्राजापत्यमेवं च ।

नान्दीमुखानां कुर्वीत श्राद्धं:[9] पिण्डोदकक्रियाम् ।
प्राजापत्येन तीर्थेन वस्तु[10] किंचित् प्रजापतेः ॥२६॥

इति मार्कण्डेयपुराण (३२.१२) वचन शाखिभेदव्यवस्थितम् ।

द्वौ दर्भौ इति दर्भद्वयमात्रमत्रपवित्रमित्यर्थः । सोपयामानि कुशानि चत्वारि पात्राणीति देवसहितपुरुषत्रयविषयतया ज्ञेयम् । एकैकपुरुषपेक्षयेति हलायुधः । युक्ताशयेषु युक्तसमीप देशेष्वित्यर्थः । पृषदाज्यं सर्वं द्विद्विरिति सर्वमेव यवादि विकिरणं हविस्त्यागादि वाक्यं च द्विरावर्तनीयम् ।

छन्दोगपरिशिष्टं कात्यायनः[11]।

---

1. *कृत्यकल्पतरु-श्राद्धकाण्ड*, p. 271 reads प्रदद्यात् for दद्यात्.
2. *Ibid.*, p. 271 reads पिण्डान् for पिण्डानेभ्य.
3. *Ibid.*, p. 271 reads वृद्धौ after पिण्डानेभ्य of our text and before सव्येन.
4. The second line of the stanza No. 33 is quoted in *कृत्यकल्पतरु-श्राद्धकाण्ड*, p. 272 as —
   प्रागग्रेषु च दर्भेषु पिण्डान् दद्यात्तु वृद्धिषु ।
5. *विष्णुपुराण*, reads सबदरैः for सर्वदेवैः .
6. *Ibid.*, reads पिण्डान् for पिण्डम्.
7. *कृत्यकल्पतरु-श्राद्धकाण्ड*, p. 273 reads दैवेनैव for देवेनेव.
8. The stanza No. 35 is quoted in *Ibid.*, p. 273 from the text of *गोभिल* and not from *छन्दोगपरिशिष्ट*.
9. *मार्कण्डेयपुराण*, p. 167 reads प्राज्ञः for श्राद्धः which is contextually wrong.
10. *Ibid.*, p. 167 reads यत्० for वस्तु०.
11. This text is quoted in *कृत्यकल्पतरु-श्राद्धकाण्ड*, p. 272.

कर्मादिषु तु सर्वेषु मातरः सगणाधिपाः ।
पूजनीयं[1] प्रयत्नेन पूजिताः पूजयन्ति ताः ॥३७॥
प्रतिमासु च शुभासु[2] लिखिता[3] वा[4] पटादिषु ।
अपि वाऽक्षतपुञ्जेषु यवपुञ्जैर्विशेषतः[5]॥३८॥

इति । वाचस्पतिमिश्राः नैवेद्यश्च पृथग्विधैः ।

कुड्यलग्नात्[6] वसोर्धारां सप्तवारान्[7] घृतेन च[8]।
कारयेत् पञ्चवारान्[9] वा नातिनीचं[10] न चोन्द्रितान्[11]॥३९॥
आयुष्याणि च शान्त्यर्थं जप्त्वा तत्र समाहितः ।
षड्भ्यः पितृभ्यस्तदनु श्राद्धदानमुपक्रमेत् ॥४०॥
वसिष्ठोक्त विधिः कृत्स्नो द्रष्टव्योऽत्र निरामिषः ।
अतः परं प्रवक्ष्यामि विशेष इह यो भवेत् ॥४१॥
प्रातरामन्त्रितान् युग्मान् उभयतस्ततः[12]।
उपविश्य[13] कुशान् दद्यात् ऋजुनैव[14] हि पाणिना ॥४२॥
तथा[15] नियतो[16] हि[17] सव्यस्य जानुनोर्विद्यते[18] क्वचित् ।
सदा परिचरेद् भक्त्या पितॄनप्यत्र दैववत्[19]॥४३॥

---

1. *कृत्यकल्पतरु-श्राद्धकाण्ड,* p.272 reads पूजनीयाः for पूजनीयं which is grammatically wrong.
2. *Ibid.*, p. 272 reads शूद्रासु for शुभासु.
3. *Ibid.*, p. 272 reads लिखितासु for लिखिता.
4. *Ibid.*, p. 272 drops वा.
5. *Ibid.*, p. 272 reads नैवेद्यैश्च पृथग्विधैः . This reading seems to have been adopted by वाचस्पतिमिश्र as noted in the manuscript, *cf.* नैवेद्यैश्च पृथग्विधैः, p. 252.
6. *Ibid.*, p. 272 reads कुड्यलग्नां for कुड्यलग्नात्.
7. *Ibid.*, p. 272 reads ०धारां for ०वारान्.
8. *Ibid.*, p. 272 reads तु for च.
9. *Ibid.*, p. 272 reads ०धारां for ०वारान्.
10. *Ibid.*, p. 272 reads ०नीचां for ०नीचम्.
11. *Ibid.*, p. 272 reads च उच्छ्रिताम् for च उन्द्रितान् which is corrupt.
12. *Ibid.*, p. 273 reads तथा for ततः .
13. *Ibid.*, p. 272 reads उपवेश्य for उपविश्य.
14. *Ibid.*, p. 272 reads ०ऋजूनेव for ०ऋजुनैव.
15. *Ibid.*, p. 272 drops तथा.
16. *Ibid.*, p. 272 reads निपातो for नियतो.
17. *Ibid.*, p. 272 reads न before हि.
18. *Ibid.*, p. 272 reads जानुनो० for जानुनोः०.
19. *Ibid.*, p. 272 reads देववत् for दैववत्.

पितृभ्य इति दत्त्वेषु[1] उपविश्य[2] कुशेषु तान् ।
गोत्राणाम[3]भिरामन्त्र्य पितॄनर्घ्यं प्रदापयेत् ॥४४॥
नापसव्यकरणं न पित्र्य[5]तीर्थमिष्यते ।
पात्राणां पुरणादीनि दैवेनैव[6]तु कारयेत् ॥४५॥
जष्ठोत्तर[7] करान् युग्मान् कराग्राग्र पवित्रकान् ।
कृत्वार्घ्यं[8] संप्रदातव्यं नैकेकस्यात्र दीयते ॥४६॥
मधुमध्विति यस्तत्र त्रिर्जपोशि तु[9]मिच्छताम् ।
गायत्र्यनन्तरं गोत्र[10] मधुमन्तं[11] विवर्जितः ॥४७॥
नवाश्नवत्[12] सुजपेदत्र[13] कदाचित् पितृसंहिताम् ।
अन्यत्र वै[14] जपः कार्यः सोमसूर्यादिकः[15] शुभः ॥४८॥
यस्तत्र प्रकरोऽन्यस्य तिलवद्यवत[16]स्तथा ।
उच्छिष्टसंनिधौ सोऽत्र तुप्तेषु[17] विपरीतकः ॥४९॥
संपन्नमिति तृप्ताः स्थ प्रश्नस्थाने विधीयते ।
सुसम्पन्नमिति प्रोक्ते शेषमन्नं निवेदयेत् ॥५०॥
प्रागग्रेषु तु दर्भेषु आद्यमामन्त्र्य पूर्ववत् ।
अप[18]क्षिपेन् मूलदेशे अवनेनिक्षिपे[19]त्तिलाः[20]॥५१॥

1. *कृत्यकल्पतरु-श्राद्धकाण्ड*, p. 273 reads दत्तेषु for दत्त्वेषु.
2. *Ibid.*, p. 273 reads उपवेश्य for उपविश्य.
3. *Ibid.*, p. 273 reads गोत्रानाम्० for गोत्राणाम्०.
4. *Ibid.*, p. 273 reads ०अर्घं for ०अर्घ्यम.
5. *Ibid.*, p. 273 reads पित्र्यं for पित्र्य.
6. *Ibid.*, p. 273 reads हि for तु.
7. *Ibid.*, p. 273 reads ज्येष्ठोत्तर०० for जष्ठोत्तर००.
8. *Ibid.*, p. 273 reads ०अर्घं for ०अर्घ्यम्.
9. *Ibid.*, p. 273 reads ००अशितुं० for ००शितुं०.
10. *Ibid.*, p. 273 reads सोऽत्र for गोत्र.
11. *Ibid.*, p. 273 reads मधुमन्त्र० for मधुमन्तम्०.
12. *Ibid.*, p. 273 reads न चाश्नत्सु for नवाश्नवत्.
13. *Ibid.*, p. 273 reads जपेत् तु अत्र for सुजपेत् अत्र.
14. *Ibid.*, p. 273 reads अन्य एव for अन्यत्र वै.
15. *Ibid.*, p. 273 reads ०सामादिकः for ०सूर्यादिकः .
16. *Ibid.*, p. 273 reads ०यववत् for ०यवतः.
17. *Ibid.*, p. 273 reads तृप्तेषु for तुप्तेषु which is corrupt.
18. *Ibid.*, p. 274 reads अपः० for अप०.
19. *Ibid.*, p. 274 reads अवनेनिक्ष्व इति for अवनेनिक्षिपेत्.
20. *Ibid.*, p. 274 reads निस्तिलाः for तिलाः .

द्वितीयंश्च[1] तृतीयं च मध्यदेशाग्रदेशयो: ।
मातामहप्रभृतीस्तु[2] एतेषामेव[3] वामत:[4]।।५२।।
सर्वस्मादन्नमुद्धृत्य व्यञ्जनैरुपसिव्य[5] च ।
संयोज्य[6] दधिकर्कन्धुर्दधिभि: प्राङ्मुखस्तथा ।।५३।।
अवनेजनवत् पिण्डान् दत्वा बिल्वप्रमाणकान् ।
तत् पात्र क्षालनेनाथ पुनरप्यवने जयेत् ।।५४।।
उत्तरोत्तरदानेन[7] पिण्डानामुत्तरोत्तर:।
भवेदधश्चाचरणादूघोघ:[8] श्राद्धकर्मसु ।।५५।।
तस्मात्सर्वेषु श्राद्धेषु वृद्धिमति[9] सभवेषु च[10]।
मूलमध्याग्रदेशेषु कुशात्[11] सक्तां विनिर्वपेत् ।।४६।।
गन्धादीन्निक्षिपेत्तूष्णीन्तथा[12]ऽचामयेत्[13] द्विजान् ।
अन्यत्राप्येष स्यात् यवादिरहितो विधि: ।।५७।।
दक्षिणाप्रवेणे[14] देशे दक्षिणाभिमुखस्य तु[15]।
दक्षिणाग्रेषु दर्भेषु एषोऽन्यत्र विधि: स्मृत: ।।५८।।
अथाग्रभूमिमासिकं चेत्[16] वै[17] सुप्रोक्षितम[18]स्त्विति ।
शिवा आप: सन्त्विति च युग्मानेवोदकेन तु ।।५९।।
सौमनस्यमस्त्विति च पुष्पदानान्तरम्[19]।

---

1. *कृत्यकल्पतरु-श्राद्धकाण्ड*, p. 274 reads द्वितीयं च for द्वितीयंश्च which is grammatically wrong.
2. *Ibid.*, p. 274 reads ०प्रभृतींस्तु for ०प्रभृतीस्तु which is corrupt.
3. *Ibid.*, p. 274 reads तेषामेव for एतेषामेव.
4. *Ibid.*, p. 274 reads च after एतेषामेव and before वामत: .
5. *Ibid.*, p. 274 reads ०उपसिच्य for ०उपसिव्य.
6. *Ibid.*, p. 274 reads अक्षत after संयोज्य and before दधि. Here the word दधि seems to be redundant because of the expression दधिभि: which folows कर्कन्धु: .
7. *Ibid.*, p. 274 reads ००दानेऽपि for ००दानेन.
8. *Ibid.*, p. 274 reads ००अधराणामधर for ००अचरणादूघोष: which is corrupt.
9. *Ibid.*, p. 274 reads वृद्धिमत्सु for वृद्धिमति which is corrupt.
10. *Ibid.*, p. 274 reads इतरेषु० for सभवेषु च.
11. *Ibid.*, p. 274 reads ईषत् for कुशात् which is corrupt.
12. *Ibid.*, p. 274 reads तत: for तथा.
13. *Ibid.*, p. 274 reads आवाहयेत्० for आचामयेत्०.
14. *Ibid.*, p. 274 reads ०प्रवणे for ०प्रवेणे which is corrupt.
15. *Ibid.*, p. 274 reads च for तु.
16. *Ibid.*, p. 274 reads ०००आसिञ्चेत् for ०००मासिकं चेत् which is corrupt.
17. *Ibid.*, p. 274 drops वै.
18. *Ibid.*, p. 274 reads संप्रोक्षितं०० for सुप्रोक्षितं००.
19. *Ibid.*, p. 274 reads पुष्पदानमत: परं for पुष्पदानान्तरम्.

अक्षं[1] च अरिष्टं चास्त्विति[2] अक्षतानपि[3] दापयेत्[4]।।६०।।
अक्षय्योदकदानं च अर्घं दानवदिष्यते ।
षष्ठैव नित्यं कुर्यान्न[5] चतुर्थ्या कदाचन ।।६१।।
प्रार्थनासु प्रतिप्रोक्ते सर्वास्वेव द्विजोत्तमैः ।
पवित्रान्तर्हितान् पिण्डान् सिञ्चेदुत्तानपात्रकृत् ।।६२।।

युग्मानेव श्राद्धं षोडशं कर्तव्यम् । षोडशमिति विशेषणं जीवत्यपि पितरि पितामहमरणे षोडशबर्हिमत्त पार्वणाद्यन्वज्ञानार्थम् । तेनोभयथैव पौत्रस्य पार्वणाधिकारः । षोडशश्राद्धाधिकारे विशेष पितृमरणानन्तरं पितामहे मृते षोडशश्राद्धप्राप्तेः पुत्रवत्यप्राप्तत्वान्नैतत् पौत्रेणेति निषेधोऽनुपपन्नः । पर्युदासोऽप्यन्यत्र एव सद्यजीवत् पुत्रस्य पौत्रेण श्राद्धषोडश कर्तव्यमित्यवलक्षणः । स च प्राप्तत्वान्न विधेयः । उच्यते । पितृव्यसद्भावे पौत्रस्य षोडशश्राद्धानधिकारज्ञापनार्थं सर्वमुपपन्नम् ।

---

1. *कृत्यकल्पतरु-श्राद्धकाण्ड*, p. 274 reads अक्षतं for अक्षम्.
2. *Ibid.*, p. 274 reads ००च after ००इति.
3. *Ibid.*, p. 274 drops ०अपि.
4. *Ibid.*, p. 274 reads प्रतिपादयेत् for दापयेत्.
5. *Ibid.*, p. 274 reads तत् कुर्यात्० for कुर्यान्न. The second line is metrically defective.

अथ सपिण्डीकरणम्

[1]चत्वार्य्युदकपात्राण्येकं मृतस्य । त्रीणि इतरेषाम् । प्रथमं पात्रं पितृपात्रे[2] नियोजयेत् । समानीव आकृति[3]-रित्येवमेव प्रथमं पिण्डं त्रिषु पिण्डेषु नियोजयेत् समानीव[4]। मधुमतीभिः संगच्छध्वमिति द्वाभ्यामेवं चतुर्थे[5] अनुज्ञापितो भवति ।

न चात्र दैवं भोजयेत् । प्रागेव दैवेऽर्घमन्वादिकं[6] च दत्वा गन्धमाल्याद्यैः[7] पात्रमर्चयित्वा हुतशेषं पितृभ्यः पाणिषु दद्यात् ।

चतुर्थो वृद्धप्रपितामहोऽनुज्ञातो[8] विसर्जित इत्यर्थः ।

न चात्र दैवं भोजयेदिति प्रेतसम्बन्धितया न दैव याजयेदिति हलायुधः ।

पित्रादीनामासनदानादि पदार्थकाण्डे देवासनादि पदार्थसंकरं न कुर्यादिति कल्पतरुः[9]।

हारीतः —

समाप्तेऽब्दे[10] पशुश्राद्धं विधिवत् प्रतिपादयेत् ।
चतुरो निर्वपेत् पिण्डान् प्रथमन्तेषु[11] निर्वपेत् ॥१॥
वपां पशुं चरूश्चैव[12] ह्यवदानादि यानि च ।
हुत्वा पिण्डं तान् विधानेन[13] शेषान् पिण्डान् समापयेत् ॥२॥

---

1. This passage from *आश्वलायनपरिशिष्ट* is quoted in *कृत्यकल्पतरु-श्राद्धकाण्ड*, p. 253.
2. *Ibid*., p. 253 reads त्रिषुपात्रेषु for पितृपात्रे.
3. *Ibid*., p. 253 reads आकूतिः००० for आकृति०००.
4. The word समानीव appears twice in this sentence and is unnecessary and dropped in *ibid*., p. 253.
5. *Ibid*., p. 253 separates this sentence at संगच्छध्वमिति and reads चतुर्थो for चतुर्थे.
6. *Ibid*., p. 253 reads ००अन्नाद्यं for ००अन्वादिकं which is corrupt.
7. *कृत्यकल्पतरु-श्राद्धकाण्ड*, p. 253 reads गन्धमाल्यैः for गन्धमाल्याद्यैः .
8. Actually this may be emended as अनुज्ञापितो for अनुज्ञातो.
9. This view of कल्पतरु is found quoted verbatim from *कृत्यकल्पतरु-श्राद्धकाण्ड*, p. 254.
10. *कृत्यकल्पतरु-श्राद्धकाण्ड*, p. 256 quotes *हारीत* and reads समाप्ते तु for ०अब्दे.
11. *Ibid*., p. 256 reads प्रथमं तेषु for प्रथमन्तेषु.
12. *Ibid*., p. 256 reads पशूंश्चरूं चैव for पशुं चरुश्चैव.
13. *Ibid*., p. 256 reads नीतिविधानेन for पिण्डं तान् विधानेन. The second line of stanza no. 2 is metrically defective.

ततः प्रभृति वै पितृ[1] मासामन्ययाऽप्नुयात्[2]।
विन्दते पितृलोकं च ततः श्राद्धं प्रवर्तते ॥३॥

पशुश्राद्धं पशुमासेन श्राद्धं पशुं पशोखत्तं मांसान्तरामित्यर्थः । अवदानानि सूपशाकादीनि । सपिण्डनफलमाह । ततः प्रभृति पितृसामान्यं पितृसमानताम् । ततः श्राद्धं पार्वणमित्यर्थः ।

ब्रह्मपुराणे[3]—

चतुर्थश्चार्घ्यपात्रेभ्य एकं वामेन पाणिना ।
गृहीत्वा दक्षिणेनैव पाणिना च तिलोदकम् ॥४॥
संमार्जयित्वा[4] पृथिवीं ये समाना इति स्मरन् ।
प्रेतविप्रस्य हस्ते तु चतुर्भागं जलं क्षिपेत् ॥५॥
ततः पितामहादिभ्यस्तन्मन्त्रैश्च[5] पृथक् पृथक् ।
ये समाना इति द्वाभ्यां तज्जलन्तु[6] समर्पयेत् ॥६॥
अर्घन्तेनैव[7] विधिना प्रेतपात्राश्च[8] पूर्ववत्[9] ।
तेभ्यश्चार्घं निविद्यैव पश्चाच्च स्वयमाचरेत् ॥७॥
अद्य[10] तेनैव विधिना दर्भमूलऽवनेजनम्[11] ।
पितुर्दत्वा तु[12] पिण्डं तु दद्यात् भक्त्या च[13] पूर्ववत् ॥६॥
दत्वा पिण्डमुखाष्टांगं[14] ध्यात्वा च[15] स्वभास्वरम्[16]।
सुवर्णरूप्यदर्भैस्तु तस्मिन् पिण्डं ततस्त्रिधा ॥९॥
कृत्वा पितामहादिभ्यः पितृभ्यः प्रेतमर्चयेत्[17] ।
संसृजन्तु त्वा पृथिवी वायुरग्नि[18]प्रजापतिः ॥१०॥

---

1. *कृत्यकल्पतरु-श्राद्धकाण्ड,* p. 256 reads प्रेतः for पितृ.
2. *Ibid.*, p. 256 reads पितृसामान्यमाप्नुयात् for मासामन्ययाऽप्नुयात्.
3. The text of *ब्रह्मपुराण* is quoted in *कृत्यकल्पतरु-श्राद्धकाण्ड,* p. 256.
4. *Ibid.*, p. 256 reads संसृजतु त्वा for समार्जयित्वा.
5. *Ibid.*, p. 256 reads ०तत्तन्मन्त्रैः for ०तन्मन्त्रैश्च.
6. *Ibid.*, p. 256 reads तज्जले तु for तज्जलन्तु.
7. *Ibid.*, p. 256 reads अर्घस्तेनैव for अर्घन्तेनैव.
8. *Ibid.*, p. 256 reads पात्राच्च for प्रेतपात्राच्च.
9. *Ibid.*, p. 256 reads विधिपूर्वकं for पूर्ववत्.
10. *Ibid.*, p. 256 reads अथ for अद्य.
11. *Ibid.*, p. 256 reads ०अवनेजनम् for ०ऽवनेजनम्.
12. *Ibid.*, p. 256 reads च for तु.
13. *Ibid.*, p. 256 reads तु for च.
14. *Ibid.*, p. 256 reads पिण्डमथाष्टाङ्गं for पिण्डमुखाष्टांगम् which is corrupt.
15. *Ibid.*, p. 256 reads तं च for च.
16. *Ibid.*, p. 256 reads सुभास्वरं for स्वभास्वरम्.
17. *Ibid.*, p. 256 reads ०अर्पयेत for ०अर्चयेत्.
18. *Ibid.*, p. 256 reads ०अग्निः for ०अग्नि.

एतन्मन्त्रं जपेत् भक्त्या समानावन्तमेव च[1]।
ये समाना इति द्वाभ्यां पितृभ्यः प्रेतमर्चयेत् ॥११॥
सुवर्णतुलां[2] ततस्तान् त्रीन् पिण्डान् कृत्वा प्रपूजयेत् ।
अर्घपुष्पैस्तथा धूपै[3] दीपगन्धा[4]नुलेपनै ॥१२॥
मुख्यं तु पितरं कृत्वा पुनस्त्वन्यान् यथाक्रमम् ।
मृते पितरि यस्यार्थ[5] विधते[6] च पितामहः ॥१३ ॥
तेन देयास्त्रयः पिण्डाः प्रपितामहपूर्वकाः ।
तेभ्यश्च पैतृकः पिण्डो नियोक्तव्यस्तु पूर्ववत् ॥१४॥
मातर्यथ मृतायां तु विद्यते च पितामही ।
प्रपितामहीपूर्वस्तु कार्यस्तत्राप्ययं विधिः ॥१५॥

एकं प्रेतपवित्रवामेनान्तरं दक्षिणेन गृहीत्वेति सम्बन्धः । 'ये समाना' इति मन्त्रं पठन् प्रेतब्राह्मणहस्ते प्रेतपात्रस्थं जलं चतुर्भागं दद्यात् । तदनन्तरं पितामहाद्युत्सर्ग वाक्ये ये समाना इति द्वाभ्यां मन्त्राभ्यां प्रेतपात्रस्यभागत्रयं पितामहादित्रये मिश्रीकृत्य पितामहादिभ्यस्तिलोदकं दद्यात् । अर्घमपि पुष्पोदकं तेनैव विधिनेति । एतेन प्रेतब्राह्मणहस्ते उत्सृज्य दत्तस्यैवार्घजलस्य भागत्रयं पितामहाद्यर्घजलेषु मिश्रीकर्तव्यमिति प्रतीयते । अत एव दत्तस्यैव प्रेतपिण्डस्य मिश्रीभावं वक्ष्यति । व्यक्तमपरम् ।

छन्दोगपरिशिष्टे कात्यायायनः [7] —

पितुः सपिण्डतां कृत्वा कुर्यान्मासानुमासिकम् ।
असंस्कृतौ न संस्कार्यः[8] पुत्रपोचकैः[9] ॥१६॥

पापिष्ठमपि शुद्धेन शुद्धं पापं कृतापि[10] वा ।
पितामहेन पितरं कुर्यादिति[11] विनिश्चयः[12]॥१७॥

पितुः सपिण्डतां कृत्वैव प्रेतीभूतयोरपि पितामहप्रपितामहयोर्मासानुमासिकं प्रतिमासविहितं पार्वणं कर्तव्यम् । न तु तयोः सपिण्डीकरणप्रतीक्षा कार्या ।

---

1. *कृत्यकल्पतरु-श्राद्धकाण्ड,* p. 256 reads सममानीवन्तमेव च for समानावन्तमेव च.
2. *Ibid.*, p. 257 reads वर्तुलांस्तु for सुवर्णतुलाम्.
3. *Ibid.*, p. 257 reads धूपैः for धूपै.
4. *Ibid.*, p. 257 reads ०माल्य० for ०गन्ध०.
5. *Ibid.*, p. 257 reads ०अथ for ०अर्थ.
6. *Ibid.*, p. 257 reads विद्यते for विधते.
7. This text is quoted in *कृत्यकल्पतरु-श्राद्धकाण्ड,* p. 260.
8. *Ibid.*, p. 260 reads संस्कार्यौ for संस्कार्यः .
9. *Ibid.*, p. 260 reads पूर्वौ पौत्रप्रपौत्रकैः for पुत्रपोचकैः .
10. *Ibid.*, p. 260 reads पापकृतापि for पापं कृतापि.
11. *Ibid.*, p. 260 reads संस्कुर्यादिति for कुर्यादिति.
12. *Ibid.*, p. 260 reads निश्चयः for विनिश्चयः .

ननु सपिण्डनेनासंस्कृताभ्यां ताभ्यां सह पितुः कथं सपिण्डनाख्यः संस्कारः । तस्मात्तदर्थं सपिण्डीकरणमपकर्षणीयः । पितुरेव वा सपिण्डनमुकष्ट[1]व्यमित्यत आह । असंस्कृतौ न संस्कार्यविति पाठेऽप्यसङ्गशरीरकृतावमिश्रीकृतावसपिण्डीकृताविति प्रागुक्त एवार्थः ।

उत्कर्षाय कर्षौ न कार्यविरत्यनेन वचनेनोक्तम् । कथमसंस्कृतेन सह संस्कार इत्यत आह । पापिष्ठमपीति पापिष्ठमकृतसपिण्डनं पितरं शुद्धेन कृतसपिण्डीकरणेन पितामहेन पापकृता । अकृतसपिण्डीकरणेनापि शुद्धं कुर्यादिति श्राद्धे कृतनिश्चयः । अतो वचनबलाददोष इति तात्पर्यम् । संस्कुर्यादिति निश्चय इत्यपपाठः ।

अन्ये तु सत्पाठं कृत्वार्थं वर्णयन्ति । शुद्धमपि संस्कुर्यात् । यज्ञादिना अप्राप्तहेतुमपि सपिण्डयेदित्यर्थः ।

तथा विष्णुधर्मोत्तरप्रथमकाण्डम् —

> ये विष्णुं विविधैर्यज्ञैः पूजितो यैश्च केशवः ।
> प्रेतभावं न ते यान्ति तथा ये समरे हताः ॥१८॥

अप्रेतीभूतस्य प्रेतत्वविमुक्तिफलार्थं कथं सपिण्डनमिति चेत् । नित्यत्वादिति ब्रूमः । नित्यादपि फलसिद्धिरनुषंगिकी । पञ्चयज्ञादिवत् प्रत्यवायपरिहार पापक्षयादि ।

तथा च भविष्यपुराणम् —

> क्षयं केचिदुपात्तस्य दुरितस्य प्रचक्षते ।
> अनुत्पत्तिं तथा चान्ये प्रत्यवायस्य मन्यते ॥१९॥

नित्यक्रियां तथा चान्ये अनुषङ्गफलश्रुतिम् । तच्चिन्त्यम् । प्रेतगतसंस्काराभावे संस्कुर्यादिति अन्वयापत्तेः । सपिण्डनस्य नित्यत्वे प्रमाणाभावाच्च । किं च नित्यत्वेन काम्यस्य प्रसंगेऽनिर्मोक्षप्रसङ्गः । किं च नित्यकर्मणि कथं काम्यस्य प्रसङ्गः । कामिनः कर्तुरभावेन काम्यफलसामग्न्यभावात् ।

अत एव काम्यो नैमित्तिको वार्थो नित्यमर्थम् । विकृत्याभिनिविशते न नित्य इत्युक्तं द्वादशाध्याये[2]।

तस्माद् भविष्यपुराणे यन्नित्यस्यानुषंगफलत्वमुक्तं तत् कृत्यादि कीर्त्यादि दृष्टफलाभिप्रायेणेति । मातुः सपिण्डीकरणं कथं कर्तव्यमित्यत्राह ।

वृद्धशातातपः[3]

> मातुः सपिण्डीकरणं कथं कार्यं सुतैर्भवेत् ।
> पितामह्या सहैवास्याः सपिण्डीकरणं स्मृतम् ॥२०॥

एतच्च भर्तृसद्भावे तस्मिन् सर्वे सुताः कुर्युः । पितामह्या सहैवतु इति वक्ष्यमाण लघुहारीतवचनात् ।

---

1. This expression appears to be corrupt.
2. This has a reference to *जैमिनि कृत पूर्वमीमांसा,* XII.
3. This text is quoted in *कृत्यकल्पतरु-श्राद्धकाण्ड,* p. 258 and *पृथ्वीचन्द्र-श्राद्धप्रकाश,* XXI.54, p. 502.

तथा च पठन्ति—

पितामह्यादिभिः स्त्रीभिर्मातरं तु सपिण्डयेत्।
पितरि म्रियमाणे तु तेनैवोपरते सति ॥२१॥

छन्दोगपरिशिष्टं कात्यायनः[1] —

मातुः सपिण्डीकरणं पितामह्या सहोदितम्।
यथोक्तेनैव कल्पेन[2] पितृकाया[3] न चेत्सुतः ॥२२॥

पितामह्येति साधारणोऽयं निर्देशः। यथोक्तेन पूर्णे संवत्सरे षण्मासे त्रिपक्षे वा इत्यादि गोभिलोक्तेन एतच्च पुत्रिकापुत्रव्यतिरिक्तस्य पुत्रिकापुत्रस्यविशेषमाहोशना।

पितुः पितामहे यत्वत् पूर्णे संवत्सरे सुतैः।
मातुर्मातामहे तद्वदेया कार्या सपिण्डता ॥२३॥

पितामह इति पितामहादि त्रिकोपलक्षणं मातामह इत्यपि।

तथा बौधायनयज्ञपार्श्वौ[4]—

आदिशेत् प्रथमे पिण्डे मातरं पुत्रिका सुतः।
द्वितीये पितर[5]स्तस्या तृतीये च पितामहम् ॥२४॥

न च पार्वणमुखेन सपिण्डनाप्युक्तत्वात्। अन्यथैवंविध पार्वणानुपपत्तेः।

मृते पितरि मातृसपिण्डनमाह बृहस्पतिः[6]—

स्वेन भर्त्रा सह श्राद्धं माता भुङ्क्ते स्वधामयम्।
पितामही च स्वेनैव[7] प्रपितामही ॥२५॥
भर्तृगोत्रेण दातव्यं स्त्रीणां पिण्डोदकं सुतैः।
पितामहपितृभ्यश्च[8] स्वेन विधानतः ॥२६॥
पाणिग्रहणिका मन्त्राः पितृगोत्रापहारिकाः[9]।
भर्तृगोत्रेण नारीणां देयं पिण्डोदकं ततः ॥२७॥
चतुर्थी होममंत्रेण त्वङ्मांसहृदयेन्द्रियैः।
भर्त्रा संयुज्यते पत्नी तद्गोत्रा तेन सा भवेत् ॥२८॥

---

1. This text is quoted in *कृत्यकल्पतरु-श्राद्धकाण्ड*, p. 258 and *पृथ्वीचन्द्र-श्राद्धप्रकाश*, XXI.65, p. 504 quotes only the first line.
2. *कृत्यकल्पतरु-श्राद्धकाण्ड*, p. 258 reads कालेन for कल्पेन.
3. *Ibid.*, p. 258 reads पुत्रिकाया for पितृकाया which is corrupt. This is further evident from *कुल्लूक*'s gloss on the same.
4. This text is quoted in the *कृत्यकल्पतरु-श्राद्धकाण्ड*, p. 258.
5. *Ibid.*, p. 258 reads पितरं for पितरः.
6. The text of *बृहस्पति* is quoted in *कृत्यकल्पतरु-श्राद्धकाण्ड*, p. 259.
7. *Ibid.*, p. 259 reads तथैव after स्वेनैव and before प्रपितामही.
8. *Ibid.*, p. 259 reads ०पितृभ्यां च for ०पितृभ्यश्च.
9. *Ibid.*, p. 259 reads ००अपहारकाः for ००अपहारिकाः.

यद्यप्यत्र भर्त्रा सह साक्षात् सपिंण्डनं नावगम्यते तथापि पितृमातृपितामही प्रपितामहीनां स्वभर्तृपिण्डाभोक्त्री[1]त्वस्य तत् पिण्डैकफलत्वादवगम्यते ।

एतच्च भर्तृपिण्डांशभोक्तृत्वस्य सपिण्डनफलत्वं लघुहारीतवचने स्फुटी भविष्यति । तथा भर्तृगोत्रेण पिण्डोदकदानं भर्तृगोत्रभागित्वं च भर्तृशरीराभेदप्रतिपादकं च भर्त्रा सह सपिण्डनकारणतयोपन्यस्तम् ।

एतच्च स्फुटीकरोति लघुहारीत:[2]—

स्वेन भर्त्रा सहैवास्याः सपिण्डीकरणं स्त्रियाः ।
एकत्वं सा' गता यस्मात् चरुमन्त्राहुतिव्रतैः ॥२९॥
तस्मिन् सति सुताः कुर्युः पितामह्या सहैव तु ।
तस्यां चैव जीवन्त्यां तस्याः श्व श्वेतिनिश्चयः ॥३०॥
अप्रजायां[3] पिता कुर्यात् प्रजायां[4] तु पतिस्तथा ।
स्वेन स्वेनैव गोत्रेण संस्थितायां तिलोदकम् ॥३१॥
संस्थितायां[5] तु भार्यायां सपिण्डीकरणान्तिकम् ।
पैतृकं भजते गोत्रमूर्द्ध[6] तु पतिपैतृकम् ॥३२॥
[7]एकमूर्तित्वमायाति सपिण्डीकरणे कृते ।
पत्नी पति-पितॄणां तु तस्माद्[8] गोत्रभागिनी ॥३३॥
सपिण्डीकरणादूर्ध्वं यत् पितृभ्यः प्रदीयते ।
सर्वेस्वंशहरा[9] माता इति धर्मेषु निश्चयः ॥३४॥

तस्मिन् सति भर्तरि जीवति, अत्र भर्त्रा पितामह्या सहेति श्रवणं भर्त्रादि त्रिक पितामह्यादि त्रिकोपलक्षणार्थमिति हलायुधकल्पतरु[10]प्रभृतयः। मण्डनमिश्रास्तु भर्त्रा सहैव पितामह्या सहैवेत्येवकार श्रवणात् । पूर्वोक्त वृद्धशातातपवचने च एवकारश्रुतेः । पितामही च स्वेनैव स्वेनैवं प्रपितामहीति बृहस्पति[11]वचनाच्च । भर्तृपितामह्योरेव पिण्डे मातृपिण्ड मिश्रीकरणमिति वदन्ति । श्वश्र्वादिभिरिति

1. This expression appears to be corrupt.
2. The text of *लघुहारीत* is quoted in *श्राद्धतत्त्व*, p. 297.
3. *कृत्यकल्पतरु-श्राद्धकाण्ड*, p. 258 reads अप्रत्तायां for अप्रजायाम्.
4. *Ibid.*, p. 258 reads प्रत्तायां for प्रजायाम्.
5. The stanza No. 32 is quoted from the text of *शातातप* and *वृद्धशातातप* in *कृत्यकल्पतरु-श्राद्धकाण्ड*, p. 258.
6. *Ibid.*, p. 258 reads ०ऊर्ध्वं for ०ऊर्द्ध which is corrupt.
7. This stanza No. 33 is quoted from the text of *शातातप* in *मिताक्षरा on याज्ञवल्क्य*, I.254, p. 90.
8. *कृत्यकल्पतरु-श्राद्धकाण्ड*, p.258 reads तद् after तस्माद् and before गोत्रभागिनी; *मिताक्षरा*, I.254, p. 90 reads पत्नी पति पितॄणां च तस्मादंशेन भागिनी ।
9. *Ibid.*, p. 258 reads सर्वेषु० for सर्वेसु० which is corrupt.
10. This view of *कल्पतरु* cannot be traced in *कृत्यकल्पतरु-श्राद्धकाण्ड*.
11. The text of *बृहस्पति* is quoted in *कृत्यकल्पतरु-श्राद्धकाण्ड*, p. 259 and in stanza No. 25 above.

पैठीनसि[1] वचने चादिशब्दो जीवत्श्वश्रूविषयः । एतदेव स्फुटीकरोति—

तस्यां चैव जीवत्यां तस्याः श्वश्रोरिति निश्चयः ।३५।

अन्यथा जीवन्त्यामिति विशेषणानर्थक्यापत्तेः ।

अत एव पठन्ति —

पतिनैकेन[2] कर्तव्यं सपिण्डीकरणं स्त्रियाः ।
[3]सा मृतापि हितीवैध्यं[4] चरुमन्त्राहुतिव्रतैः ।।३६।।
मातुः सपिण्डीकरणं पत्या सार्द्धं विधीयते ।
तस्मात् पतिव्रतानां तु दैवसंगतिरिष्यते ।।३७।।

नन्वेवं पितामहप्रपितामहयोस्तथा प्रपितामही वृद्धप्रपितामहयोः सपिण्डश्राद्धान्तर्भावः । तन्न । यथोक्तेनैव कल्पेन इति छन्दोगपरिशिष्टकृता गोभिलोक्तस्य चत्वार्युदकपात्राणीत्यस्यातिदेशात् ।

एतत् सपिण्डीकरंणमेकोद्दिष्टं स्त्रिया अपि । इति याज्ञवल्क्य (१.२५४) वचनेन पूर्वोक्तपात्रत्रयमुक्तसपिण्डनस्यैकादशादि श्राद्धस्यातिदेशाच्च ।

किं च

मातर्यथ वृतायां तु विद्यते च पितामही ।
प्रपितामही[5] पूर्वस्तु ज्ञेय[6]स्तत्राप्ययं विधिः ।।३८।।

इति ब्रह्मपुराणवचने प्रपितामहीपूर्वपिण्ड त्रयदानावगमात् । तिलोदकमिति समस्तौ-र्द्धवदेहिकोपलक्षणम् । पितृगोत्रभोजन[7] श्वासुरादि[8] निन्दित विवाहोढा विषयमिति स्मृतिमञ्जरिकार[9] प्रभृतयः । उर्ध्वं तु पितृपैतृकमित्यत्र हेतुरेकपूर्तित्वमिति ।

एतेनासुरादि निन्दितविवाहोढायामेकमूर्तित्वमेकगोत्रत्वं च चतुर्थीहोमादिफलम् । किन्तु सपिण्डनफलमिति दर्शितम् । सकलस्त्री साधारणं सपिण्डनफलं भर्तृपिण्डांशहरत्वमित्यत्राह ।

---

1. The text of पैठीनसि is quoted in *मिताक्षरा on याज्ञवल्क्य,* I.254, p. 89 as —
   अपुत्रायां मृतायां तु पतिः कुर्यात् सपिण्डनम् ।
   श्वश्वादिभिः सहैवास्याः सपिण्डीकरणं भवेत् ।।
2. *मिताक्षरा on याज्ञवल्क्य,* I.254 reads पत्याचैकेन for पतिनैकेन.
3. A stanza similar to stanza No. 36 above is found quoted in eečeëtKe, p.86 as —
   भर्त्रा चैकेन कर्तव्यं सपिण्डीकरणं पुनः ।
   सा मृतापि हि तेनैक्यं गता मन्त्राहुतिव्रतैः ।।
4. This expression appears to be corrupt. Is it possible to emend हितीवैध्यं as हि तेनैक्यं on the strength of the authority of *श्राद्धमयूख,* p. 86, and *मिताक्षरा on याज्ञवल्क्य,* p. 89 ?
5. *कृत्यकल्पतरु-श्राद्धकाण्ड,* p. 257 reads प्रपितामहिपूर्वस्तु for प्रपितामहीपूर्वस्तु.
6. *Ibid.,* p. 257 reads कार्यः००० for ज्ञेयः०००.
7. *Ibid.,* p. 259 reads ००भाजनं for ००भाजन.
8. *Ibid.,* p. 259 reads चासुरादि० for श्वसुरादि० which is corrupt.
9. This view of *स्मृतिमञ्जरिकार* is quoted in *कृत्यकल्पतरु-श्राद्धकाण्ड,* p. 259.

सपिण्डीकरणादूर्ध्वमिति धर्मेषु धर्मशास्त्रेषु । नन्वेवं प्रथमं पितामह्या सहैवहीत्यनेन भार्त्रा सह सपिण्डनस्य स्थाने पितामह्या सह सपिण्डनविधानात् । तत्फलपितृलोकप्राप्तिर्भर्तृपिण्डांशहरत्व-साधनत्वावगते: । प्राजापत्यव्रतस्थानविहितधेनुदानस्यैव शरीरपावनात्मगत पापक्षयजनकत्वमदृष्टफलत्वे बाधकाभावात् ।

किं च पितामह्या सहेति लाघवात् साधनान्तर विधिरयं न कर्मान्तर विधि: । तदा च कथं फल-भेद: ।

अन्यथा जीवति पितामहे प्रपितामहादिना सपिण्डने कृते पश्चान्मृते पितामहे पार्वणे पितु: तत् पिण्डीभोक्तृत्वफलार्थं सपण्डिनावृत्ति: स्यात् । पूर्वसपिण्डनक्रिया विनष्टा । मृते भर्तरि कालान्तरे कथं भर्तृपिंडं भोक्तृत्वमिति चेद् दृष्टत्वात् वेति ब्रूम: । अत: कृते सपिण्डने पश्चान्मृते भर्तरि पुन: सपिण्डनं कार्यमिति स्थितम् ।

मृते भर्तरि प्रेतीभूतेऽकृतसपिंडने सति मातु: सपिंडनं प्रेतीभूतेनैव भर्त्रा सहेति पापिष्ठमपि शुद्धेन इत्यनेन तुल्यन्यायसिद्धम् ।

सपिण्डनफलमाह हारीत:[1]—

> तत: प्रभृति वै प्रेत: पितृसामान्यमाप्नुयात् ।
> विदन्ते पितृलोकं च तत: श्राद्धं प्रवर्तते ॥३९॥

सामान्यं समानता श्राद्धं प्रार्तते पार्वणादिकमित्यर्थ: ।

ननु

> [2]भ्राता वा भ्रातृपुत्रो वा सपिण्ड: शिष्य एव वा[3]।
> औरसवत् सुता ज्ञेया दत्तके च विशेषत: ॥४०॥

इति मनु[4]वचनादौ रसे देशान्तरस्थिते चेत् । सपिण्डदत्तकपुत्र: सपिण्डनाधिकारी विशेषणाग्रेप्युक्त: । अत्राप्युक्तं कस्यचित् भ्राम्यमूर्खस्य सन्देहनिरासार्थमेव ।

---

1. This text of *हारीत* is quoted in *कृत्यकल्पतरु-श्राद्धकाण्ड,* p. 256.
2. This line is quoted in *कृत्यकल्पतरु-श्राद्धकाण्ड,* p. 257 from the text of *वृद्धशातातप.*
3. *Ibid.*, p. 257 reads शिष्ट एव च for शिष्य एव वा.
4. This stanza, however, cannot be traced in the extant *मनुस्मृति.*

३६

अथ सपिण्डनोत्तर श्राद्धम्

शातातपः[1]

प्रदानं यत्र यत्रैषां सपिण्डीकरणात्परम् ।
तत्र पार्वण[2]श्राद्धं ज्ञेयमभ्युदयादृते ॥१॥
अर्वाक् संवत्सराद्वृद्धौ पूर्णे संवत्सरेऽपि वा ।
ये सपिण्डीकृता प्रेता न तेषां तु पृथक् पिण्डदानम्[3]॥२॥
[4] तस्मादूर्ध्वं विधीयते ।
प्रेतानामिह सर्वेषां ये मन्त्रैस्तु नियोजिताः ॥३॥
कृतार्थास्ते हि संवृत्ताः सपिण्डीकरणे कृते ।
प्रेतत्वाच्चेह विस्तीर्णाः[5] प्राप्ताः पितृगणं तु ये ॥४॥
यः सपिण्डीकृतं प्रेतं पृथक् पिण्डै[6]र्नियोजयेत् ।
विधिवद्य[7]स्तु न[8] भवति पितृहा चोपजायते ॥५॥

यत्र यत्रेति वीप्सा सपिण्डनोत्तर सकलश्राद्धव्याप्तर्था पार्वर्णवदमावास्याश्राद्धवदित्यर्थः । अनेन संपूर्ण त्रैपुरिषिक पार्वर्णश्राद्धमतिदिश्यते ।

तथा मत्स्यपुराणे — (१६.५१ब-५२अ)

एतदग्निमतः प्रोक्तमन्वाहार्यं तु पार्वणम् ।[9]
एथेन्दुक्षये तत्तवादन्यत्रापि निगद्यते ॥६॥

---

1. The text of *शातातप* is quoted in *कृत्यकल्पतरु-श्राद्धकाण्ड,* p. 261 and *पृथ्वीचन्द्र-श्राद्धप्रकाश,* XVIII.18, p. 432.
2. *Ibid.*, p. 261 reads पार्वणवत्० for पार्वण०.
3. *Ibid.*, p. 261 reads क्रिया for पिण्डदानं which is metrically defective.
4. *Ibid.*, p. 261 reads पृथक् पिण्डप्रदानं तु on the blank portion of our manuscript.
5. *Ibid.*, p. 261 reads निस्तीर्णाः for विस्तीर्णाः
6. *Ibid.*, p. 261 reads पिण्डे० for पिण्डैः०.
7. *Ibid.*, p. 261 reads विघ्निः for विधिवद्यः
8. *Ibid.*, p. 261 reads तेन for तु न.
9. The first line of stanza No. 6 above is read in the *मत्स्यपुराण,* p. 28 as — एतदस्त्विति तत्रोक्तमन्वाहार्यं तु पार्वणम् ।

अभ्युदयादृते इति अभ्युदयेन सम्पूर्णं पार्वणविधानमिति तात्पर्यम् । अपकृष्टसपिण्डनानन्तरमप्येकोद्दिष्टं न कार्यमित्याह । अर्वाक् संवत्सराद्वृद्धाविति । अत एव अपकृष्टमासिकश्राद्धं न स्वकाले कार्यमित्युक्तम् । पूर्णे संवत्सरे पतितमासिकश्राद्धं यथा पूर्वदिवो मध्याह्नप्राप्तौ अपि सपिण्डनानन्तरं कार्यम् । हेतुमाह । यस्मात् सपिण्डनेन कृतार्थभूताः प्रेतत्वनिस्तीर्णाः पितृलोकं च प्राप्तवन्तस्तस्मात्तेऽपृथक् कार्याः । करणे निन्दामाह । यः सपिण्डीकृतमिति लघुहारीतः —

सपिण्डीकरणे वृत्ते पृथक्त्वं नोपपद्यते ।
पृथक्त्वे तु कृते पश्चात् पुनः कार्या सपिण्डता ॥७॥

पुनः सपिण्डीकरणानिष्टदर्शनादियमेकोद्दिष्ट निन्दैव ।

जाबालः[1]—

पितृयज्ञं तु निर्वर्त्य मासिक[2]श्राद्ध[3] एव तु ।
श्राद्धं प्रातरुचौ चैव मातापित्रोर्मृताहनि[4]॥८॥
असपिण्डीकृतं प्रेतमेकोद्दिष्टेन तर्पयेत् ।[5]
सपिण्डीकरणादूर्ध्वं त्रिभिः सामान्यमिष्यते ॥९॥
औरसक्षेत्रजौ पुत्रौ विधिना पार्वणेन तु ।
प्रत्यब्दमितरे कुर्युरेकोद्दिष्टं सुता दश ॥१०॥
भ्राता वा भ्रातृपुत्रो वा सपिण्डः शिष्य एव[6] वा[7]।
औरसवत् सुता ज्ञेया दत्तके तु विशेषतः ॥११॥

पितृयज्ञं पितृतर्पणं निर्वर्त्य क्रियमाणे श्राद्धेऽहरहः क्रियमाण इत्यर्थः । तेनाम्बुघटश्राद्धे मृताहनि विहिते मासिके तथा विशिष्टद्रव्यतीर्थादिप्राप्तो प्रेतश्राद्धकरणेच्छायामसपिण्डीकृतमेकोद्दिष्टेन तर्पयेत् । त्रिभिः सामान्यमिति त्रयाणां पुरुषाणां सामान्यं वै त्रैपुरुषिकमित्यर्थः । विशेषमाह औरसक्षेत्रजाविति ।

मत्स्यपुराणे[8] (१८.२२ब-२३अ-२५)

ततः प्रभृति संक्रान्तादुपरागादि पर्वसु ।
त्रिपिण्डमाचरेत् श्राद्धमेकोद्दिष्टं मृताहनि[9]॥१२॥

---

1. The text of जाबाल is quoted in *कृत्यकल्पतरु-श्राद्धकाण्ड,* p. 261 and *पृथ्वीचन्द्र-श्राद्धप्रकाश,* XVIII.17, p. 432.
2. *कृत्यकल्पतरु-श्राद्धकाण्ड,* p. 261 reads मासिकं for मासिक.
3. *Ibid.*, p. 261 reads श्राद्धं० for श्राद्ध०.
4. *Ibid.*, p. 261 reads मृतेऽहनि for मृताहनि.
5. *Ibid.*, p. 257 quotes the first line of stanza and ascribes it to *वृद्धशातातप.*
6. *Ibid.*, p. 257 reads शिष्ट० for शिष्य एव.
7. *Ibid.*, p. 257 reads च for वा.
8. The text of *मत्स्यपुराण* is also quoted in *Ibid.*, p. 262.
9. *मत्स्यपुराण,* reads मृतेऽहनि for मृता०.

एकोद्दिष्टं परित्यज्य पार्वणं यः समाचरेत् ।
सदैव पितृहासस्यान्मातृभ्रातृविनाशकः ॥१३॥
मृताहे पार्वणं कुर्वन्ववोघ[1]यति[2] मानवः ।
संपृक्ते स्वांगली[3] भावः प्रेतेष्विह यतो[4] भवेत् ॥१४॥
यथा[5] यत्र प्रदातव्यं सपिण्डीकरणात् परम् ।
पार्वणेन विधानेन देयमग्निमता सदा ॥१५॥

अत्र महार्णवप्रकाशकारः[6]—

प्रत्यब्दं मृताहनि पार्वणैकोद्दिष्टयोस्तुल्यवद्विकल्पे प्राप्ते व्यवस्था । यथा औरसक्षेत्रजं च साग्निः प्रत्यब्दमेव पार्वणं कुर्यात् ।

औरसक्षेत्रजौ पुत्रौ विधिना पार्वणेन तु ।१६। इति ।
पार्वणविधानेन देयमग्निमता सदा ।१७।

इति जाबाल[7]मत्स्यपुराण[8]दर्शनात् ।

निरग्निकौरसक्षेत्रजावितरे दशपुत्राः साग्नयः निरग्नयश्च प्रत्यब्दं मृताहे एकोद्दिष्टं कुर्युरिति ।

किं च भ्राता सपिण्डो वा भ्रातृपुत्रो दत्तकः कृतश्चेत् को विचार? इत्यह आह । भ्राता इति मनुजाबालयोरेकविषये एकैवोक्तिः । कृतावा शब्देति भिन्नगोत्रस्य वा द्वितीया वा शब्दात् निश्चयार्थकं सपिण्डपदोपादानात् । तत् सन्तानस्य पुत्रकृतस्य श्रुतिस्मृतिप्रमाणात् चूडादिसंस्कारे द्वारयैव दर्शितः । तस्मिन् वयो न प्रामाणिकः । यतश्चूडादिक्रिया कार्या । तदभावे शिष्योऽपि दृष्टः । तेषां प्रमाणं सापिण्ड्यपुत्राधिकारे उक्तम् । औरसवत् सुता भवन्तीत्यर्थः । अत्र क्रियानुसारादुक्तम् ।

ननु औरसक्षेत्रजाविस्त्यस्याग्नमद्ववचनं[9] दर्शनाद्विशेषपरत्वं निर्वासनम् । सामान्यवचनस्य विशेषवचनदर्शनात् विशेषपरत्वं भवतीति चेन्न । अस्यापि निर्युक्तिकत्वात् वाक्यार्थभेदे श्रुतिभेदकल्पनावद् गौरवस्यादिति चेन्न । सामान्यश्रुतिमूलत्वसंभवे श्रुतिभेदकल्पनानुपपत्तेः । शास्त्रं शास्त्रान्तरमुपोद्बलयति । स्वर्गकामश्रुतेरिवाध्ययनलब्धविद्यत्रैवर्णिकपरत्वमिति चेन्न । स्वर्गकामश्रुतेस्त्रैवर्णिकपरत्वे कल्पनालाघवस्य कारणत्वात् सामान्यपरत्वे शूद्रस्य विद्यावियुक्तिकल्पनापत्तेः ।

न चात्र तथा विशेषणानर्थक्यपरिहारार्थं सामान्यस्य विशेषपरत्वमिति चेन्न । साग्निः सदा पार्वणं कुर्यात् । निरग्निरिच्छाया । न नित्यममित्येनावतापि विशेषणोपपत्तेः । किं च आग्निमतेत्यस्य

---

1. *मत्स्यपुराण* and *कृत्यकल्पतरु-श्राद्धकाण्ड*, p. 262 read ०अघोऽघो for ०ववोघ.
2. *Ibid.*, and *कृत्यकल्पतरु-श्राद्धकाण्ड*, p. 262 read याति for यति.
3. *कृत्यकल्पतरु-श्राद्धकाण्ड*, p. 262 reads संपृक्तेष्वाकुलीभावः for संपृक्तेस्वांगलीभावः
4. *Ibid.*, p. 262 reads ततो for यतो.
5. *Ibid.*, p. 262 reads यत्र for यथा.
6. The view of महार्णवप्रकाशकार is quoted in *कृत्यकल्पतरु-श्राद्धकाण्ड*, p. 262.
7. The text of *जाबाल* in stanza No. 16 above is quoted in *कृत्यकल्पतरु-श्राद्धकाण्ड*, p. 262.
8. *Ibid.*, p. 262 quotes the text of *मत्स्यपुराण*.
9. The expression अग्नमद्वचनं appears to be corrupt.

औरसक्षेत्रजपुत्रविशेषणकारणाभावात् । दशविधपुत्रविशेषत्वमेव न कृतः ।

किं च

अर्वाक् संवत्सरादित्येतस्य शातातप[1]वचनस्य यदि साग्निपरत्वं तदा पूर्णे संवत्सरेऽपि इत्येव संगतं स्यात् । साग्नेः पूर्णे संवत्सरे सपिण्डनाभावात् ।

अथ निरग्निपरत्वम्, तदा तस्यापि पार्वणसम्बन्धेऽग्निमतेति । विशेषणमनर्थकमेवापतितं निरग्निना चैकोद्दिष्टं कार्यमित्यस्य सम्बन्धमेव स्यात् ।

इदं पुनरुच्यते ।

> मृताहनिमित्त[2]कर्तव्यं[3] प्रतिमासं तु वत्सरम् ।
> प्रतिसंवत्सर[4]श्चैवमाद्यमेकादशेऽहनि ॥१८॥

इति याज्ञवल्क्य (१.२५६) वचनात् ।

> एकादशे चतुर्थे च मासि मासि च वत्सरम् ।
> प्रतिसंवत्सरश्चैवमाद्यमेकादशेऽ[5]हनि ॥१९॥

इति व्याघ्रवचनात् ।

> ततः प्रभृति संक्रान्त्यावुपरागादि पर्वसु ।
> त्रिपिण्डमाचरेत् श्राद्धमेकोदिष्टं मृताहनि ॥२०॥

इति मत्स्यपुराण[6]वचनाच्च ।

शातातप-लघुहारीत-जाबाल वचनानां सपिण्डनोत्तरकालं सर्वत्र पार्वणविधायकतया सामान्यविशेषन्यायात्तदितरपरत्वम् । एकोद्दिष्टं परित्यज्येति[7] विशेषनिन्दाश्रवणाच्च । एतदेव व्यक्तं वक्ष्यति शंखः —

> सपिण्डीकरणादूर्ध्वं यत्र यत्र प्रदीयते ।
> तत्र तत्र द्वयं कुर्याद्वर्जयित्वा मृताहनि ॥२१॥

मृताहशब्दोऽत्र निरूपदो मासांकित तिथिविशेषपरः । उपपदाच्च क्वचित्तिथिविशेषमात्रपरो यथा एवं

---

1. The text of *शातातप* is quoted in *पृथ्वीचन्द्र-श्राद्धप्रकाश,* XVIII.19, p. 432.
2. *याज्ञवल्क्यस्मृति,* p. 91 reads मृतेऽहनि for मृताहनिमित्त.
3. *Ibid.*, p. 91 reads प्रकर्तव्यं for कर्तव्यम्.
4. *Ibid.*, p. 91 reads प्रतिसंवत्सरं० for प्रतिसंवत्सरः० .
5. In the section on एकोद्दिष्टं, we have the another reading *एकोद्दिष्टं मृताहनि* p. 222 for आद्यमेकादशेऽहनि. This verse is not found in my critical edition of the *व्याघ्रस्मृति.*
6. The text of *मत्स्यपुराण* is quoted in *कृत्यकल्पतरु-श्राद्धकाण्ड,* p. 262.
7. The complete stanza 'एकोद्दिष्टं परित्यज्य' is quoted from *मत्स्यपुराण* in *कृत्यकल्पतरु-श्राद्धकाण्ड,* p. 262.

मृताहे प्रतिमासं कुर्यात् इत्यादौ । अतो न सामान्यविशेषयोस्तुल्यवद्विकल्पस्तेन प्रत्याब्दिकेतरपरत्वात् ।

अर्वाक् संवत्सरात् वृद्धाविति निरग्नेर्मासिकापकर्षविषयतयोपपन्नम् । पूर्णे संवत्सरेऽपिवेति पतितमासिक निषेधपरतयेति । एवं मृताहेतरे पार्वणनियमे कृते मृताह सर्वेषां पुत्राणामेकोद्दिष्ट शातातप-जाबाल वचनादौरसक्षेत्रजयोः पार्वणाधिकारः तौ च देयमग्निमता सदेति साग्निकाविति विशेषणीयम् । अन्यथा विशेषणानर्थक्यात् । न च साग्निकाभ्यामौरसक्षेत्रजाभ्यां नित्यमनग्निभ्यामिच्छया विकल्पेनेति वाच्यम् । नित्यानित्यसंयोगविधिवैषम्याद्वाक्यभेदापत्तेः ।

न च दशविधपुत्रविशेषकत्वमेवास्य न कृत इति वाच्यम् । तेषां पार्वणाधिकारप्रतिपादकवचनाभावात् । औरसक्षेत्रजाविति जाबलवचनैकवाक्यतया औरसक्षेत्रजोभयविशेषकत्वे प्रतीयते ।

किं च औरसक्षेत्रजयोः साग्निसाधारणः पार्वणाधिकारः । दशविधपुत्राणां साग्निकानां पार्वणं विधेयम् । अन्येषामेकोद्दिष्टमिति श्रुतित्रयकल्पनापत्तेः । मत्पक्षेषु साग्निकयोरौरसक्षेत्रजयोः पार्वणमन्येषामेकोद्दिष्टमिति श्रुतिद्वयं कल्पनीयम् ।

किं च एकोद्दिष्टप्रतिपादकानां वचनानां मुख्यपुत्रपरत्व न स्यात् । क्षेत्रजादीनां मुख्यत्वात् ।

तथा मनुः (९.१८०)

क्षेत्रजादीन् सुतानेतानेकादश यथोदितान् ।
पुत्रप्रतिनिधी[1]माहुः क्रियालोपान् मनीषिणः ॥२२॥

तस्मादौरसक्षत्रजयोः साग्न्योरेव मृताहे पार्वणाधिकारः । निरग्न्योरेकोद्दिष्टाधिकारः । औरसक्षेत्रजव्यतिरिक्तानां तु साग्निनिरग्निसाधारणमेकोद्दिष्टमिति सिद्धम् ।

अमावास्या कन्यागत कृष्णपक्षयोर्मृताहे निरग्निनापि पार्वणविधिना कर्तव्यं प्रत्याब्दिकम् । तदितर मृताहे एकोद्दिष्टमित्याह शंखः[2]—

सपिण्डीकरणादूर्ध्वं यत्र यत्र प्रदीयते ।
तत्र तत्र त्रयं कुर्यात् वर्जयित्वा मृताहनि ॥२३॥
अमावास्यां क्षयो[3] यस्य प्रेतपक्षे यथा[4] भवेत्[5]।
सपिण्डीकरणादूर्ध्वं तस्योक्तः पार्वणो विधिः ॥२४॥

प्रेतपक्षोऽत्र प्रौष्ठपदादूर्ध्वं कृष्णपक्षमात्रम् । अमावास्यापदवैयर्थ्यापत्तेः । एतच्च प्रत्याब्दिकमेव कार्यम्। न षाट्पौरुषिकम् ।

कर्षूसमन्वितमुक्ता तथाद्यं श्राद्धषोडशम् ।
प्रत्याब्दिकं च शेषेषु पिण्डाः स्युः षडिति स्थितिः ॥२५॥

1. *मनुस्मृति,* IX.180 reads ०प्रतिनिधीन्० for ०प्रतिनिधीम्०.
2. The text of *शंख* and particularly stanza No. 24 is quoted in *मिताक्षरा on याज्ञवल्क्य,* I.256, p. 93 and *अपरार्क on याज्ञवल्क्य,* p. 544 and *A.B.O.R.I.*, Vol. VIII, p. 101.
3. *अपरार्क* on *याज्ञवल्क्य,* p. 544 reads अमावास्याक्षयो for अमावास्यां क्षयो.
4. *Ibid.*, p. 544 reads अथवा for यथा.
5. *Ibid.*, p. 544 reads यदि for भवेत्.

इति छन्दोगपरिशिष्टवचनेन प्रत्याब्दिकव्यतिरेकेण षट्संख्यानियमात् । कर्षूसमन्वितमष्टकाश्राद्धं आद्यमेकादशाहादि श्राद्धम् । अथवा आद्यपार्वणस्यादिभूतं षोडशानां पूरणं सपिण्डनमित्यर्थः । अग्न्यादिनिमित्तेन प्रत्याब्दिकपार्वणं मातुरपीत्याह आपस्तम्बः[1]।

अपुत्रा ये मृता[2] केचित् स्त्रियो वा पुरुषाश्च ते ।
तेषामपि[3] देयं स्यात् एकोद्दिष्टं न पार्वणम् ॥२६॥
मित्रबन्धुसपिण्डेभ्यः स्त्रीकुमारिभ्य एव च ।
दद्याद्वै मासिकं श्राद्धं संवत्सरोनतोऽन्यथा ॥२७॥

अपुत्राह विशेषणं समुद्रायाः पार्वर्णाभ्यनुज्ञानार्थम् । एकोद्दिष्टमभिधाय न पार्वणमिति निषेधानुवादो अत्यन्तनिन्दार्थः । एतच्च मांत्रे पितामह्यौ प्रपितामह्यौ च ब्राह्मणान् भोजयित्वा इत्यनुष्टकादर्शनात् मातृत्रितयदैवतं कार्यम् । पितुरिव मातुरप्यमावास्यादौ श्राद्धं स्यादिति चेन्न । नरवाछनुन्नं[4] श्राद्धविधायकम् । किन्तु वचनान्तरप्राप्तं श्राद्धमनूद्य तस्य पार्वणत्वमेकोद्दिष्टत्वं विदधाति । अन्यथा विधिगौरवापत्तेः । न च मातुः श्राद्धं मृतावदमावास्यादौ प्राप्तम् ।

यत एतेषामेकोद्दिष्टं देयं दानार्हम् । अत एकोद्दिष्टं दद्यादित्याह । मित्रबन्धुसपिण्डेभ्य इति स्त्री परिणीता पुत्रशून्याकुमारी अनूढा । एषा मासिकश्राद्धं संवत्सरपर्यन्तं देयम् । अथ ऊर्ध्वमन्यथा न मासिकप्रकारेण न पार्वणविधिना । किन्तु सांवत्सरिकैकोद्दिष्टविधिना मृताहाज्ञाने कुत्र श्राद्धमित्याह प्रचेताः।

'अज्ञातमृतेऽमावास्यायां श्रवणदिवसे वा ।' मृतशब्दोऽत्र मृताहपरः । अनिश्चितमरणस्यौर्द्ध्वदेहिकममावास्यायां मासविशेषज्ञाने तिथिविशेषज्ञाने श्रवणदिवस इति व्यवस्था । तस्मादमावास्यावक्ष्यमाणतन्मासस्य कृष्णैकादशी ग्राह्या । मासविशेषाज्ञाने श्रवणदिवस इति व्यवस्था । मासज्ञाने श्रवणदिनविधौ मासान्तरे कर्मप्रसंगात् । तिथ्यज्ञानेति तिथ्यन्तरविधिर्युज्यते एव । एवं च संवत्सरविशेषाज्ञाने श्रवणदिनादारभ्य संवत्सरपर्यन्तं यथाक्रमं प्रेतकृत्यं समाप्य श्रवणदिने आब्दिकं प्रत्याब्दिकं च कर्तव्यम् । संवत्सर विशेषज्ञाने तु श्रवणदिनादारभ्य यावदशौचं पिण्डदानं समाप्याशौचान्ते आद्यं श्राद्धं कृत्वा कृष्णैकादश्यां प्रतितमासिकाद्धिकं प्रत्याब्दिकं श्रवणदिने प्राप्ते करणीयम् । मासीवशेषज्ञाने तन्मासस्यामावास्यायामेकादश्यां वा इति शास्त्रार्थः ।

यत्तु पठन्ति —

श्रुताहात् प्रेतकृत्यं तु आत्रिपक्षं समाचरेत् ।
दर्शे तु पतितं शेषं यथाकालं समाचरेत् ॥२८॥

तदनाकरम् । श्रवणदिनमवधारणदिनोपलक्षणम् ।

यथा पठन्ति —

गतस्य न भवेद्वार्ता यावद् द्वादशवार्षिकी ।
प्रेतावधारणं तस्य कर्तव्यं सुबान्धवैः ॥२९॥

---

1. The text of ***आपस्तम्ब*** is quoted by ***अपरार्क*** *on* ***याज्ञवल्क्य,*** p. 544.
2. *Ibid.*, p. 544 reads मृताः० for मृता०.
3. *Ibid.*, p. 544 reads च after तेषामपि and before देयम्.
4. This expression is corrupt.

लघुहारीत:[1]—

श्राद्धविघ्ने समुत्पन्ने मृताहविदिते तथा ।
एकादश्यां प्रकुर्वीत कृष्णपक्षे विशेषत: ॥३०॥

विघ्नोऽत्र द्रव्याद्यसम्पत्तिकृत: स चैकोद्दिष्टविषय: सपिण्डनविषयश्च । न पार्वणविषय: । मृताहसन्निधानात् । अत एव मृताहे पार्वणविधानाक्रियमाणस्यापि श्राद्धकरणमेकादश्यामविरुद्धम् । अशौचेन श्राद्धविघ्नेऽशौचान्ते कर्तव्यमाह ऋष्यशृंग:[2]।

देये पितॄणां श्राद्धे तु अशौचं जायते यदि[3]।
तदाशौचव्यतीते तु[4] तेषां श्राद्धं प्रदीयते ॥३१॥
शुचीभूतेन दातव्यं या तिथि: प्रतिपद्यते ।
सा तिथिस्तस्य कर्तव्या न त्वन्या वै कदाचन ॥३२॥

अत्र कमलाकरभट्टादयो[5] वचनार्थं वर्णयन्ति । एकोद्दिष्टविषयमिदम् । अशौचमध्येप्येकोद्दिष्टस्य विधि वा वयविहितत्वेन देयत्वात् । एकोद्दिष्टेतर श्राद्धानां शंखेन पर्युदस्तत्वात् ।

यथा शंख:[6]—

दानं प्रतिग्रहो होम: स्वाध्याय: पितृकर्म च ।
प्रेतपिण्डक्रियावर्जं सूतके विनिवर्तते ॥३२॥

सर्वेषामेव सामान्यशास्त्रप्राप्तशास्त्रीयनिषेधानां पर्युदासत्वं नञर्थविचारे दर्शितम् । प्रेतपिण्डक्रिया प्रेतैकोद्दिष्टं तद्धर्मग्राहित्वात् सांवत्सरिकमपि पिण्डदानमेव कुतो न भवतीति चेत् । तदैकोद्दिष्टस्यापि पर्युदस्तत्वेनादेयत्वाद्देये पितॄणां इति व्यर्थं स्यात् । अशौचमध्ये देयत्वे कुतोनानुष्ठानमिति चेन्न ।

तदाशौचव्यतीते तु तेषा[7] श्राद्धं प्रदीयते ।३३।

इति ऋष्यशृंगविरोधात् । विकल्प: कुतो न स्यादिति चेन्न । सामान्यविशेषयोरतुल्यबलत्वेन विकल्पायोगात् ।

अशौचेतरकालेऽप्यकोद्दिष्टविधिवाक्यानां चरितार्थत्वात् ।

---

1. The source of this verse cannot be traced.
2. The text of *ऋष्यशृंग* is quoted in *श्राद्धमयूख*, p. 16 and *पराशरमाधव*, Vol. I, p. 673. Also see *Studies in Dharma-Śāstra*, p. 69.
3. *Ibid*., p. 16 reads यदा for यदि.
4. *Ibid*., p. 16 reads अशौचे तु व्यतिक्रांते for तदाशौचव्यतीते तु.
5. This has a reference to *निर्णयसिंधु*, p. 339.
6. *A.B.O.R.I.*, Vol. VIII, p. 114 completely agrees with this text.
7. This line is quoted in *शुद्धिचन्द्रिका* on *षडाशीति*, p. 95 with तत्र for तेषां. Also see *Studies in Dharma-Śāstra*, p. 69.

अत एव गौतमः (१.६)

तुल्यबलविरोधे विकल्पः ।

अशौचे नित्यमननुष्ठानादशौचे देयत्वप्रतिपादकं शास्त्रप्रमाणं स्यादिति चेन्न । सामान्यज्ञानस्यैकदेशसत्वे प्रमाणाभावात् । क्लृप्तनित्यमनुष्ठानेहस्ते व्रीहिकार्यकरणवहन्यादिति शास्त्रस्येव । एवं सति सामान्यविशेषन्यायात् । यदाहवनीयवत् । सामान्यशास्त्रस्य तदितरैव स्यात् । न च पर्युदस्तस्य च द्वयोरेव विध्योस्तदितपरत्वे प्रेतपिण्डक्रिया वर्जमिति देये पितृणामित्यनर्थकं स्यात् । यदावहनीयादौ तु बाध्यबाधकाभावात् भवतु तदितरपरत्वम् । तस्मान्नैकोद्दिष्टविधिनामशौचेतरपरत्वं नाप्यशौचमध्ये विधानमृष्यशृंगविरोधादिति स्थितम् । अशौचे व्यतीते कस्यास्तिथौ क्रियतामित्याह शूचीभूतेति । शुचीभूतेन या तिथिः प्रतिपद्यते प्राप्यते तस्यां कर्तव्यं न तु मुख्यकाले पतितत्वात् । कृष्णैकादश्यादि वचनावकाश इत्याह । नत्वन्या वै कदाचनेति तदेतच्चिन्त्यम् ।

अमावास्यादि मृताहकर्तव्यस्य साग्निकर्तव्यस्य च प्रत्याब्दिकश्राद्धस्य पार्वणविधिना क्रियमाणस्याशौचे पतितस्य एकोद्दिष्टधर्मानतिदेशात् । अशौचापगमेनानुष्ठानं स्यात् । तदा च सकलशिष्टाचारविरोधः । वाक्यवर्णितं तनैव तच्चिन्त्यम् । अन्यसंकल्पवाक्यस्य मूलभूत श्रुतिभेदकल्पनापत्तेः । न च पृथग् वाक्यविधिनानुपपत्त्या श्रुतिभेदः कल्पनीयः । परिशिष्टकृता पार्वणादावत्र संकल्यवाक्यविधानात् । मनुष्येभ्य इति हन्तप्रयोगविधानाच्चतुर्थी अनुपपत्तिः । अतः पूर्वोक्तेन योजना कार्या । पार्वणानन्तरं नित्यश्राद्धविकल्पः ।

अतो मार्कण्डेयपुराणे[1]—

> नित्यक्रियां पितृणां तु[2] केचिदिच्छन्ति सत्तमाः ।
> न नृणाम[3]थैवो[4]न्ये शेषं पूर्ववदाचरेत् ॥३४॥

नित्यक्रियामिति पितृपकारार्थं विधानं न पितृणामित्यावश्यकत्वनिषेधपर इति व्यवस्था । पार्वणेनैव पितृपप्रीतेर्जातत्वात् प्रत्यवायपरिहारस्य जातत्वात् पूर्वार्द्धात् पितृणामिति प्राप्तो न पितृणामित्यत्र पुनः पितृणां ग्रहणं समकादीनामन्त्रोत्[5] सर्वाभ्यनुज्ञानार्थम् । सनकादि तप्ते पार्वणेनाजातत्वात् । न च देवश्राद्धादिवत् सनकादिश्राद्धमंगप्रमाणाभावात् । अत एव पितृकल्पे सप्तव्याधोपाख्याने सप्तानां भ्रातृणां श्राद्धसम्पादनमाहात्म्यकथनप्रस्तावे —

मत्स्यपुराणे —

> द्वौ दैवे भ्रातरौ कृत्वा पित्रे त्रीणित्वमुपक्रमात् ।
> तथैकमतिथिं कृत्वा श्राद्धदः स्वयमेव तु ॥३५॥

चकारमन्त्रवत् श्राद्धं स्मरन् पितृपरायणः । तथैकमतिथिं कृत्वेति सनकादि श्राद्धविषयम् । नातिथियज्ञपरं

---

1. The text of *मार्कण्डेयपुराण* is quoted in *कृत्यकल्पतरु-श्राद्धकाण्ड*, p. 226.
2. *Ibid.*, p. 226 reads च for तु.
3. *Ibid.*, p. 226 reads पितृणां for नृणाम्.
4. *Ibid.*, p. 226 reads ०तथा०० for ०अथ००.
5. This expression is corrupt.

श्राद्धप्रकरणात् श्राद्धफलोत्कर्षं कथनाय च । अन्ये तु साग्निना नित्यक्रिया न कर्तव्येति व्यवस्थामाहुः । तन्निर्युक्तिकम् । साग्नेरिव निरग्नेरपि पार्वणेन पितृतृप्तेर्जातत्वात् । तस्मात् पूर्वोक्तमेव व्यवस्था इति निर्गलितार्थः । कालौ द्विपितृकत्वाभावान्न लिखितम् । नास्माकं मतमेतत् । सदा क्षेत्रजस्य यद्विधानमुक्तं तदौरसमभिव्याहारात् तदपि केनापि न क्रियते । अत एव कैयटभट्टकमलाकरभट्टभाष्यास्मद् गुरुचरणादिभिर्यदुक्तं तदुक्तम् । नात्रदूषणम् । श्राद्धविधिपाठयोः फलश्रुतिमाह हारीतः[1]।

इमं श्राद्धविधिं पुण्यं कुर्याद्वापि पठेत्तु यः ।
सर्वान् लभते कामानन्ते मुक्तिश्च विन्दति[2] ॥३६॥

बृहस्पतिः[3]—

य एवं वेत्ति मतिमांस्तस्य श्राद्धफलं भवेत् ।
उपदेष्टानुमन्ता च लोके तुल्यफलौ स्मृतौ ॥३७॥

इति महामहोपाध्याय श्रीमत् कुल्लूकभट्टविरचितः सृतिसागरे श्राद्धसागरः समाप्तः ।

---

1. The text of *हारीत* is quoted in *कृत्यकल्पतरु-श्राद्धकाण्ड*, p. 233.
2. *Ibid.*, p. 233 reads second line of stanza No. 36 as —
   'स सर्वकामसंयुक्तो ह्यमृतत्वं च विन्दते।'
3. *Ibid.*, p. 234 quotes the text of *बृहस्पति.*

Appendix 'A'

Index of the *Smṛti* Works Quoted by Kullūkabhaṭṭa

Appendix 'B'

Index of the *Purāṇas* Quoted in the *Śrāddha-Sāgara*

Ādi Purāṇa — 216, 223

Agni Purāṇa — 243

Bhaviṣya Purāṇa — 79, 86, 110, 114, 197, 215, 225, 230, 257

Brahma Purāṇa — 80, 83, 85, 94, 99, 101, 104, 107, 109, 110, 115, 116, 117, 120, 121, 122, 124, 130, 131, 135, 136, 159, 165, 171, 172, 176, 182, 193, 196, 197, 220, 225, 226, 228, 233, 245, 248, 255, 260

Devī Purāṇa — 101, 109, 189, 201

Kūrma Purāṇa — 89, 217

Liṅga Purāṇa — 143

Mahābhārata — 108, 129, 134, 199

Mārkaṇḍeya Purāṇa — 135, 141, 147, 163, 247, 249, 269

Matsya Purāṇa — 78, 82, 90, 114, 122, 127, 131, 133, 149, 150, 152, 155, 158, 164, 165, 166, 187, 189, 191, 192, 193, 205, 207, 215, 217, 223, 226, 239, 242, 245, 247, 262, 263, 264, 265, 269

Narasiṁha Purāṇa — 76

Padma Purāṇa — 230

Varāha Purāṇa — 100, 211, 229

Vāyu Purāṇa — 94, 98, 99, 116, 118, 119, 122, 158, 159, 177, 179

Viṣṇu-Dharmottara Purāṇa — 98, 109, 110, 113, 120, 136, 144, 154, 166, 179, 241, 243, 257

Viṣṇu-Purāṇa — 78, 87, 124, 155, 173, 211, 238, 239, 240, 241, 249

Appendix 'C'

Index of the Commentators and Digest Works Quoted in the *Śrāddha-Sāgara*

Appendix 'D'

Index of the *Śruti* Passages and the *Sūtra* Works Quoted in the *Śrāddha-Sāgara*

Appendix 'E'

Index of Astronomical and Astrological Works Quoted in the *Śrāddha-Sāgara*

Appendix 'F'

Index of the Authorities Quoted in the Foot-Notes

Appendix 'G'

The *Mīmāṁsā* Doctrines Appealed to by Kullūkabhaṭṭa to Interpret *Dharma-Śāstra* Texts

Bibliography

Acāra Mayūkha of Nīlakaṇṭha, edited and published by Gujarati Printing Press, Bombay 1915, and by J.R. Gharpure, Bombay.

Agni Purāṇa, published by *Gurumandala Series,* No. XVII, 1957.

Angirasa Smṛti, edited by, A.N. Krishna Aiyangar, published by Adyar Library, Madras, 1953.

Āpastaṁba Dharma-Sūtra with the Commentary Ujjvalā of Haradatta edited by George Bühler, published by *Bombay Sanskrit and Prakrt Series*, Nos. XLIV and L. 1932.

Āśvalāyana Gṛhya-Sūtra with the commentary of Nārāyaṇa, published by *Anandashrama Sanskrit Series,* No. 105, Poona. 1936.

Bālaṁbhaṭṭa-Ācāra Hindu law text series, No. 5, edited by J.R. Gharpure, Bombay, 1914.

Baudhāyana Dharma-Sūtra, published by *Chowkhamba Sanskrit series* No. 104, 1972.

Brahmasūtras of Bādarāyaṇa with the commentary of Śaṅkarācārya and three commentaries of Bhāmati, Ratnaprabhā and Kalpataru, published by Nirnaya Sagar Press, Bombay,1934.

The commentary of Medhātithi on the Manu-Smṛti, edited and published by J.R. Gharpure in *Hindu Law Sanskrit Texts Series,* No. IX, 1920.

Dharma-Śāstra Saṁgraha i.e. collection of smṛtis, by Jivananda Vidyasagar, Calcutta, 1876.

Gautama Dharma Sūtra with the commentary of Haradatta, published by *Chowkhamba Sanskrit Series*, No. 172, 1966.

Gautama Dharma Sūtra with the commentary of Maskari, Published by Mysore University, 1917.

History of Dharma-Śāstra, Vols. I to V. by MM. Dr. P.V. Kane, B.O.R.I. Poona.

Jaimini's Pūrva-Mīmāṁsā Sūtras, edited with the commentary of Mādhavācārya, published by *Anandashrama Sanskrit Series*, No. 24, Poona 1892.

Jaimini's Pūrva-Mīmāṁsā Sūtras with the commentary of Śabara and Kumārila, published by *Anandashrama Sanskrit Series*, Poona, 1932, 1933, 1934, etc.

Journal of the Bharatiya Vidya, Vol. XXVIII Nos. 1-4 based on the article of 'The Position of Kullūkabhaṭṭa as a Mīmāṁsaka' by Dr. S.G. Moghe.

Kṛtyakalpataru-Śrāddhakāṇḍa of Lakṣmīdhara edited by K.V. Rangaswani Aiyangar, published by Oriental Institute, Baroda. 1950.

Mahābhārata (critical edition), published by Bhandarkar Oriental Research Institute, Poona.

Manu-Smṛti with nine commentaries. Published by J.H. Dave, *Bharatiya Vidya Series,* No. 33, 1975.

Manu-Smṛti with the commentary of Kulllūka, published by Nirnaya Sagara Press, Bombay, 1946.

Mārkaṇḍeya Purāṇa with Marathi Translation, by K.V. Lele, Wai.

Matsya Purāṇa, published by *Anandashrama Sanskrit Series,* Poona.

Mīmāṁsā Kośa, edited by Kevalānanda Sarasvatī, published by Prajna Pathasala Mandal, Wai, 1960.

Muhūrta Cintāmaṇi with the commentary pramitākṣarā, published by Venkateshvar Press, Bombay, 1928.

Nirṇayasindhu of Kamalākarabhaṭṭa, published by Nirnaya Sagara Press, Bombay, 1935 and 5th edition of 1949.

Parāśāra-Smṛti with the gloss or Mādhavācārya, published by Asiatic Society, Calcutta, 1974.

Reconstruction of the text of Sumantu, by Prof. T.R. Chintamani in *J.O.R.*, Vol. VIII.

Samaya Mayūkha of Nīlakaṇṭha published by Gujarati Printing Press, Bombay, 1918.

Saṁskāra Prakāśa of Mitramiśra, Published by *Chowkhamba Sanskrit Series*, Benares.

Smṛticandrikā of Devaṇṇabhaṭṭa, edited by J.R. Gharpure, *Hindu Law texts* No. 11, Bombay, 1918.

Smṛticandrikā of *Devaṇṇabhaṭṭa — Ānhika Kāṇḍa*, published by University of Mysore, 1914.

Smṛticandrikā of Devaṇṇabhaṭṭa — Śrāddha Kāṇḍa, published by University of Mysore, 1918.

Smṛtimuktāphalam — Śrāddha Kāṇḍa, by Vaidyanātha Dīkṣit, edited by J.R. Gharpure, *Collection of Hindu law texts*, No. 25 (4), 1940.

Smṛti-Saṁgraha, published by Manasukharai Mor, *Gurumandala Granthamala*, Vols. I to VI, 1955, 1952, 1953 etc.

Smṛti Samuccaya, Published by *Anandashrama Sanskrit Series*, No. 48, 1929.

Śrāddhacandrikā of Divākarabhaṭṭa, published by *Chowkhamba Sanskrit Series*, Nos. 423 and 424, 1934.

Śrāddh Kalpa of Śrī Dattopādhyāya, edited by Dr. Ashok Chatterji Shastri, published by Benares Sanskrit Vidyapitha, in the *Sarasvati Bhavan Studies*, No. 18, 1971.

Śrāddha Kalpalatā of Nandapandita, published by *Chowkhamba Sanskrit Series*, Benares.

Śrāddha-Kriyā Kaumudī and Dāna Kriyā Kaumudī, published by Asiatic Society, Bengal,1903.

Srāddha Mayūkha of Nīlakaṇṭha, published by J.R. Gharpure, No. XVIII, Bombay, 1927.

Śrāddha Prakāśa of Pṛthvīcandra — a Ph. D. thesis, by Miss J.H. Shroff, University of Bombay.

Śrāddha-Prakāśa of Mitraṃiśra, published by *Chowkhamba Sanskrit Series*, No. 413, 1933.

Srāddha-Tatva of Raghunandana included in the Smṛtitatvas, published by Jivananda Vidyasagara, Calcutta, 1895.

Śūrya-Siddhānta with the Sanskrit commentary, published by Venkateshvar Press, Bombay. Śaka, 1877.

Vāmana Purāṇa, edited by A.S. Gupta, published by Kashi Raj Trust, Varanasi.

Varāha Purāṇa, published under *Bibliotheca Indica Series*, Calcutta.

Vasiṣṭha Dharma-Sūtra, edited by A.A. Fuhrer, published by *Bombay Sanskrit and Prakrt Series,* No. XXIII, 1914.

Viṣṇu Dharmottara Purāṇa, published by Venkateshvar Press, Bombay.

Visṇu Purāṇa published by Venkateshvar Press, Bombay.

Viṣṇu-Smṛti with the commentary Keśava Vaijayantīu, edited by Pandit V. Krishnamacharaya and published by Adyar Library Madras 1964.

Vyāghra-Smṛti critically edited by Dr. S.G. Moghe on the basis oj two manuscripts from B.O.R.I, published by B.O.R.I, pune. 1985.

Yājñavalkya-Smṛti with the commentary of Aparārka, published by *Anandashrama Sanskrit Series,* No. 46, Part I, 1903.

Yājñavalkya-Smṛti with Mitākṣarā of Vijñāneśvara, published by Nirnaya Sagara Press, Bombay, 1949.

Yajñavalkya-Smṛti with the commentary of Mitramiśra, published by Chowkhamba Sanskrit Seires, Benares, 1930.

Yājñavlkya-Smṛti with the commentary of Viśvarūpa, published by *Trivendrum Sanskrit Series,* Nos. LXXX-LXXXI (1924) and LXXIV (1922).